Crisis of the
Black Intellectual

Crisis of the Black Intellectual

W. D. Wright

THIRD WORLD PRESS, CHICAGO

First Edition

Special thanks to the Lomax Companies for their generous underwriting of the production of this book

Printed in the United States of America

Library of Congress Cataloging-in-Publication Data

Wright, W. D. (William D.), 1936-
  Crisis of the Black intellectual / by W.D. Wright.-- 1st ed.
     p. cm.
  Includes bibliographical references and index.
  ISBN 0-88378-251-0 (pbk. : alk. paper)
  ISBN 0-88378-283-9 (cloth : alk paper)
  1. Black American intellectuals. 2. Black Americans--Intellectual life. I. Title.
  E185.86.W963 2007
  305.5'52'08997073--dc22
                                        2004024375

DEDICATION

For Wendy and Doug

ACKNOWLEDGEMENTS

I wish to thank my Editor, Gwendolyn Mitchell, for her steady and resourceful hand in guiding this book to publication, and the Copy-editor, Sheba White, who helped me keep the work tight and the arguments clear. I especially wish to thank Rhett Jones, whose critical comments and right-on suggestions have played an important role in the writing and publishing of my last three books. I finally wish to thank my friend and the first to lay a critical hand on my writing, Regine Bence.

CONTENTS

AUTHOR'S NOTES

Black people are an ethnic group and ethnic community of the black race in the United States. They are indigenous to the country, descendants of the African slaves and their progeny on American soil. There are numerous ethnic groups and ethnic communities of the black race in this country, such as Jamaicans, Barbadians, Nigerians, and others. These people, unless referred to by their ethnicity, are referred to simply as black in this work to distinguish them from Black people in America. Thus, a Black intellectual is not a black intellectual. This book is primarily about Black intellectuals, but it also touches on the subject of black intellectuals.

The word "white" in the lower case in this book is a reference to race. The capitalized words White and Whites are references to a large ethnic group in the United States, and to an even larger ethnic group of Western civilization.

White supremacy is a form of racism. Ebonicism is a form of racism. White racism is a reference to white supremacy/ebonicism, the two different forms of racism in tandem. This is how these terms are employed throughout the book.

Crisis of the
Black Intellectual

Chapter One

Introduction

Revisitation and Beyond

In 1967 Harold Cruse published *The Crisis of the Negro Intellectual.*[1] It appeared at a time when the Black Struggle for Liberation in America moved from its national citizenship and political and civil rights focus to a Black Power, Black community, and a Black aesthetic cultural development phase. Cruse had had an excursion in Marxist thought and had been a political activist and social critic before writing his book. The intellectual and political/social focus of his book was the Black ethnic group and the Black ethnic community and not the black race in America or a black racial community. What Cruse had recognized was that Blacks had evolved into an ethnic group and an ethnic community in this country, matching the white ethnic groups and communities in the land. His book was an appeal to Black intellectuals to help Black people recognize and know themselves as an ethnic group, and not simply as a racial group, in America, which he claimed they had failed to do. Black historian William Banks summarized Cruse's point on this:

> Black intellectuals who do not project an autonomous ethnic vision in their work are side-stepping an important responsibility, he says. The void they leave means that black aesthetic perspectives cannot be represented in the battle WASPs and other ethnic groups are waging for American cultural influence. Cruse criticizes twentieth century black intellectuals who, he claims, are content to let other ethnic group intellectuals, particularly Jewish intellectuals, frame the examination of Black life.[2]

Cruse, who regarded himself as a Black nationalist at the time of the writing of his controversial book that drew severe criticism from Black and white intellectuals, was engaging in what he thought of as cultural nationalist thought, which centered in ethnicity and not race. This was not typical of Black nationalists whose thought historically centered in race. Cruse was critical of Black intellectuals for being integrationists and not nationalists, which was one of the things that made them so susceptible as well as submissive to the thought of white intellectuals, especially Jewish intellectuals. Jews and other Whites feared Black collectivity, a strong Black ethnic group, a strong Black ethnic leadership (intellectual and political), and a strong Black ethnic community functioning in America with its own objectives that were determined considerably by Blacks themselves. Cruse wanted Black intellectuals to strike out for intellectual independence and build on it, which he felt could not be done, except on a Black nationalist and Black ethnic basis.

Cruse's book hit many white intellectuals in a painful, racist area in their minds, which they were not likely to acknowledge in their remonstrations with him, probably not even consciously aware of this area in their minds as the source of pain. There were many white intellectuals, especially in the 1960s and 1970s, who wanted Blacks in America to give up being Black. They did not mean racial blackness, which would have been a very difficult, and indeed, impossible thing for most Blacks to do. White intellectuals meant culture; they meant Blacks giving up their Black culture and cultural identity and just thinking of themselves as "Americans" or "individuals," most often the latter was the expressed preference.

These white intellectuals neither saw the racist character of this thinking, nor the racist objective sought. Nor did they see how similar these thoughts were to the thinking of vicious white racists. These racists could contemplate the physical removal or annihilation of Blacks to eliminate their presence from America. White intellectuals, and even the white liberals among them who were perhaps the most vocal of the white intellectuals desiring "American" or "individual" identities for Blacks, sought the cultural annihilation of the group. Blatant racists felt that Blacks could never be like white people in any way because they were too inferior for that. White liberal and other white intellectuals accepted the inferiority of Blacks to white people, but drew on the late nineteenth-century racist view of the great imitation capacity of Blacks–a view that still floated about in the racist inundated culture and social life of America–to argue that Blacks could imitate white people culturally and become culturally White. Indeed, this was the deep unconscious meaning of integration to them. Blacks integrating into what they frequently and consciously referred to as "white society" or "white America" (and not "White racist society" or "White racist America") became the pathway for Blacks to become "culturally White" in America. This was precisely the fear that Black intellectuals and other Blacks had about integration. They understood that many white intellectuals and other Whites viewed it as a cultural absorption or annihilation process for Blacks.

2

Before the advent of Cruse, James Baldwin reacted caustically to this situation when in 1963 he smoked the country and singed the frontal lobes of many white intellectuals and other white people with *The Fire Next Time*. He referred to the phrase "white society," a racist term to him, as a reference to a "burning house" and asked: who wanted to integrate into a burning house? He certainly could not see a reason for Blacks to want to. As to Blacks becoming culturally White, he ridiculed that idea when he said:

> White Americans find it difficult, as white people elsewhere do, to divest themselves of the notion that they are in possession of some intrinsic value that black people need or want. And this assumption-which, for example, makes the solution of the Negro problem depend on the speed with which Negroes accept and adopt white standards-is revealed in all kinds of striking ways, from Bobby Kennedy's assurance that a Negro can become President in forty years, to the unfortunate tone of warm congratulation with which so many liberals address their Negro equals. It is the Negro, of course, who is presumed to have become equal-an achievement that not only proves the comforting fact that perseverance has no color, but also overwhelmingly corroborates the white man's sense of his own value.[3]

James Baldwin was not a Black nationalist or a cultural nationalist. He wrote of Blacks as a racial, not as an ethnic group. This was also true of E. Franklin Frazier, the eminent Black sociologist, who in 1957 published *Black Bourgeoisie*[4] where he praised the southern Black folk culture that Blacks as a racial group had created and criticized Black middle-class people for abandoning this rich culture in the process of integrating into American society. Frazier felt that they were becoming "other-directed" people and White "cultural copy-cats." Two years later Frazier unloaded on Black intellectuals in an article entitled "Failure of the Negro Intellectual." He said that Black intellectuals had "failed to study the problems of Negro life in America in a manner which would place the fate of the Negro in the broad framework of man's experience in this world. They have engaged in petty defenses of the Negro's social failures."[5] Frazier further castigated Black intellectuals for the same behavior when he said, "the philosophy implicit in the folklore of the Negro folk is infinitely superior in wisdom and intellectual candor to the empty repetition of platitudes concerning brotherly love and human dignity of Negro intellectuals who are tyrants in the Negro world and never had a thought in their lives."[6]

3

In 1965 Black sociologist Nathan Hare published *Black Anglo Saxons*[7] which was influenced by Frazier's *Black Bourgeoisie* and was a severe criticism of Black middle-class people becoming culturally White. This was at the same time that Elijah Muhammad, Malcolm X, and the Black Muslims came onto the political scene, blasting white racists, Black middle-class people, and integration. Adam Clayton Powell, Jr. used the concept of Black Power in speeches in 1965, and Stokeley Carmichael made it a war cry the following year. Two years later, Cruse published *The Crisis*. Its publication signified that Cruse was following in a line of thinking by Black intellectuals and activists that made Black people and their existence in America the focus of their attention.

BLACKS AND WHITE LIBERALS

White liberals, intellectuals and others, were conceptually and emotionally excluded from these developments, which were invariably described as Black nationalist or cultural nationalist developments tied to race, not ethnicity, and considered outgrowths of racial thought and cultural behavior. White liberals were regarded as racists with "liberal skins" and were rejected as Black leaders or intellectual guides. They were eventually forced out of Black organizations or organizations that were more fully biracial when they did not voluntarily leave, resenting the rejection and ridicule and feeling that Blacks were showing great ingratitude.

Jewish intellectuals and other Jews who had been leaders (especially in bi-racial organizations), and who had been strong supporters of the Black struggle, exhibited an even stronger outrage about Black ingratitude. Jewish or other white liberals (intellectuals or otherwise) made efforts to remind Blacks of their financial and political support and of the other sacrifices that they had made, which had ended in the loss of life for some of them. These were valid remarks, and it is true that from the late 1960s on, Black intellectuals and other Blacks did not always give enough credit to the white allies of their struggle. But Jewish and other white liberals did not comprehend the great complexity that characterized the white liberal relationship to Black people, or their relationship to the Black struggle in America, and the deep resentment of or hostility Blacks harbored toward both subjects–especially with respect to the racism that many of these white liberals exhibited.

This was an old story that went back to the emergence of the white liberal as a political category and political element in America–when white people spoke out against slavery as despotism against Blacks and as a defilement of America. These were voices of humanism and risk. America was a racist society in the eighteenth century, first in its colonial manifestation and later in its early national development. It was also a society with Black chattel slavery. The racism inundated this institution throughout its existence in America. Blacks were considered innately inferior, especially cerebrally, innately inferior. It was believed that they were innately incapable of serious thinking and producing knowledge and that they had no rights that white people had to respect. These views facilitated the maintenance and perpetuation of Black chattel slavery.

It was very difficult for any Black voice to be heard, and certainly to be listened to, given this situation. Blacks did the best they could under the circumstances, but a White voice or voices were in great need. They emerged in sizable numbers between the 1830s and the war in the 1860s as anti-slavery or abolition voices. Very few of these white liberals, however, spoke out against racism. They did not speak out against white supremacy, the racism that alleged the innate superiority of white people. They did not speak out against what I call "ebonicism," the racism that alleged the innate inferiority of Black people (and any people of the black race wherever they existed). In America there was white supremacy/ebonicism, two racisms functioning in tandem. White liberals were reluctant to criticize these beliefs or political and social practices.

But white liberals did criticize slavery severely and took great risks in doing so. This was a reflection of their sense of morality and a sense of altruism. However, Black intellectuals and political leaders, mainly from the North, did not view these white liberals as they viewed themselves. They regarded their morality and altruism as attenuated, infected with white supremacy/ebonicism. Frederick Douglass noted this with respect to New England white liberals. He saw the racism of such people who sought to hide or deny it and recalled that:

> When I first went among the abolitionists of New England, and began to travel, I found this prejudice very strong and very annoying. The abolitionists themselves were not entirely free of it, and I could see that they were nobly struggling against it. In their eagerness, sometimes, to show their contempt for the feeling, they proved that they had not entirely recovered from it.[8]

Douglass was not the only Black intellectual or leader who noted the white supremacist/ebonicistic racism of Whites antagonistic to slavery. Black women abolitionists like Sojourner Truth, Harriet Tubman, and Sarah Parker Remond noted the racism of white female abolitionists and feminists. Their racism was white supremacy/ebonicism; it was a form of racism against Black women as such. They also, like white men, held sexist, racist beliefs about Black women that disparaged their gender, sexuality, and womanhood. There is still no general understanding among white female feminists, and essentially no understanding among Black female feminists and womanists, that sexism is a form of racism, a matter to be attended to later in this book.

What was a common thought among nonslave Blacks with respect to white liberals is that they regarded these individuals as necessary allies in the fight against slavery. However, they could not elicit much help from them in fighting against racism. A conscious strategy of Black leaders in the three decades before the American Civil War was to try to draw out northern and southern white liberals as allies. It was not easy to draw southern white liberals from their cultural-social moorings because it was very dangerous to be against slavery in the South. Most southern white liberals either fled the South or turned silent.

What Black intellectuals and other Blacks objected to with white liberals was their thinking of themselves as the "conscience" and the "moral voice" of the nation, when they clearly assigned those designations to themselves. They did concede the designation to some white liberals, such as Wendell Philips, but racists and slave holders, in the view of Black intellectuals and others, could not be the "conscience" or "moral voice" of America no matter how hard they tried, not given who they were and remained. This was not something that could be said to white liberals, especially desperately needed allies. So Black intellectuals kept silent on this matter and harbored it within, with all the anger and resentment it produced. It could not be shown, and certainly could not be shown toward having white people act as Black leaders. Some of the anger and resentment associated with white people acting as Black leaders did eventually surface, although not directly at white liberals, but rather indirectly through separate Black abolitionist organizations.

It was Booker T. Washington who first challenged the liberal idea that white people should be the natural leaders of Black people. He would not allow it and blocked every effort that was attempted in that direction. The Tuskegean developed, by the thousands, Black leaders for Black people as will be seen in Chapter Five. For twenty years Washington led Black people in America as what I call the Grand Black Leader. The millions of Black people he led were also led by other Black leaders; however, Washington and his many leaders did have white support. Another point to keep in mind is that The National Association for the Advancement of Colored People (NAACP) was led mainly by white people. Likewise, there were many Whites in the National Urban League that provided social services to southern Black migrants in the North and other northern Blacks.

Francis Oswald Villiard, then chairman of the NAACP, tried to maneuver that organization into a position to act as the leader of Black education in the South, but Washington prevented it with his own maneuvering. Washington was determined not to have the White national leadership of the NAACP (Du Bois was the only Black person on the national board) lead Black people in the North or South. He confided to his associates that they would attempt Black leadership through Du Bois, which was something they tried but could not succeed in doing, because Du Bois would not let them. Washington said the following in a letter to his private secretary, advisor, and frequent emissary, Emmett Jay Scott:

> There are a good many colored people who resent the idea of a white man assuming to lead and control the colored people. One point that Bishop [Alexander] Walters [and I] agreed upon was that we use our influence in all the colored publications to emphasize in every way possible the matter of Negro leadership for Negroes, that we welcome the assistance and advice of such disinterested men as Dr. Frissell, Mr. Ogden and others, but we are not ready to be taken charge of bag and baggage by any white man. The Bishop is heartily in agreement with this program.[9]

Timothy Thomas Fortune, a noted Black newspaper editor and firm ally of Washington prior to their break in 1905 (though an ally once again in 1914), also intensely disliked White leadership of Black people. Washington wrote the following to him, "[w]e are having the old game played over again of white people trying to lead colored people. I am not, however, alarmed, as I have passed through many sand storms in the past."[10] Washington looked upon white liberals as strictly helpers, which was precisely how he viewed the NAACP and the Urban League, although he was more favorable toward the latter as he had suggested its creation, had more influence with it, and it provided practical services to Blacks. Moreover, the Urban League enabled him to indirectly exercise a leadership over many of the Blacks who migrated from the South and directly exercise a leadership over those northern Whites who provided Blacks services.

During Washington's Grand Black leadership there were national, regional, state, and local Black women's organizations that rejected any kind of white female leadership–although there would not have been many white women seeking that role. Black women found it difficult to establish biracial organizations with white women, because of white women's racism and desire to seek women's right without Black women. White suffragists even excluded them from suffragist organizations, forcing Black women to establish their own suffrage groups.

Marcus Garvey provided the next major dent in the practice of Whites leading Blacks. He publicly condemned the practice and made some Black intellectuals and leaders hesitant to encourage it. Garvey's impact was abetted by the publicly belligerent attitude that so many Blacks had in the 1920s as a carry over from the war where Blacks had killed white people in combat. The attitude extended to the public demands that Blacks were making for rights and equality and the emergence of the Harlem Renaissance art movement, which emphasized racial blackness. But that renaissance of aesthetic culture, of poetry, literature, painting, and drama was considerably dependent on Whites for its financial support, for its encouragement, for its public promotion and approval. This kept the white liberal–Black relationship in tact and viable despite the Garvey drama and affect. Indeed, this relationship and alliance fought against Garvey and his movement. Eventually, Garvey hurt himself by trying to form a biracial coalition of his own with southern white racists thinking that this would lead to some financial aid and public support to help implement his program/movement aimed at getting black people to leave America.

The White leadership of Blacks was perpetuated through the NAACP's Black and White political alliance, which continued with the NAACP and the Urban League in the 1930s and through the Democratic Party to which Blacks shifted in this decade. The socialists and communists promoted this kind of leadership and political alliance. A. Philip Randolph, a Marxist socialist, before and during the 1920s (but a supporter of the New Deal and the social role of government during the 1930s and after) dented the practice of White leadership of Blacks, and a white liberal relationship to Blacks, when he led and strengthened the Brotherhood of Sleeping Car Porters. The union won legal status and rights against the racist Pullman Company.

In the 1950s and 1960s the Southern Christian Leadership Conference was led by Martin Luther King, Jr. and other Black leaders, although there were some white consultants and advisors. The organization engaged in a coalition with white liberals and worked with the biracial organizations they were in or led. Four of the prominent organizations in the Black Struggle for Liberation reflected this white liberal-Black alliance, and even some white leadership: the NAACP, the Urban League, the Congress of Racial Equality (CORE), and the Student

Non-Violent Coordinating Committee (SNCC). However, things changed when Elijah Mohammad and the Black Muslims exploded on the scene in the late 1950s, followed by the Black-led Black Panther Party that, once again, strongly rejected white leadership of Black people and white people acting as spokespeople of Blacks. The Black Power Movement of the late 1960s and the Black Arts Movement of the 1970s nailed the lid down firmly on that history.

DEVELOPING RACIAL CONSCIOUSNESS

Harold Cruse was fully in tune with the developing black racial consciousness of the 1960s and the increasing hostility Blacks were feeling towards white liberals. He gave vent to the latter in his book on Black intellectuals. Nevertheless, in a book of essays published the following year as *Black Rebellion or Revolution*[11] he was critical of Black Power advocates. He regarded them as being politically immature and unable to provide a consensus; and thus, they did not provide a generally workable view of the concept, let alone a general workable theory that could organize and galvanize a Black collective response. Cruse felt that the Black Power advocates refused to accept the origins of the notion of Black Power, which Cruse believed, began with Booker T. Washington. He invoked a Washingtonian origin through Bayard Rustin, the Black socialist who had recognized Washington's influence on the Black Power advocates. Cruse wrote:

> Bayard Rustin has put his finger on something very crucial about the Black Power slogan. Black Power is nothing but the economic and political philosophy of Booker T. Washington given a 1960's militant shot in the arm and brought up to date. The curious fact about it is that the very last people to admit that Black Power is militant Booker T-ism are the Black Power theorists themselves. A Roy Innis and a (Josef) Ben-Jochanan, for example, will characterize Booker T. Washington as a historical conservative (if not an Uncle Tom) and refuse to recognize him as part of their black nationalist tradition. Both of them will, of course, uphold Marcus Garvey with much nationalist fervor–completely over-looking the fact that Marcus Garvey was a disciple of Booker T. Washington.[12]

Garvey declared himself a Washington disciple in 1914 after reading *Up from Slavery* in London and then tearing back to Kingston, Jamaica to try to build a Tuskegee-type institution there.* Washington was not only anathema to what Cruse called Black nationalists, but all kinds of Black intellectuals, leaders, and many other Black people were against the Tuskegean; even white socialists and communists jumped on his case, trying to remove him as a historical figure of importance for Black intellectuals to study and for Black people to know.

What many Black people knew in the 1960s was that they wanted a different relationship between white people and themselves and any political or cultural struggle in which they were engaged in America. Whites were not to be leaders, just allies and supporters. This view was solidified for such people when white liberals turned against Martin Luther King, Jr. for publicly opposing American military involvement in Vietnam. The new view was applied to a number of Jewish liberals who were already backing away from Black and biracial organizations, and yet in various ways were also being supportive. They joined other white liberals who were doing the same, objecting to the militancy of a number of Black intellectuals and leaders, objecting to the Black Power theorizing, and objecting to the advocacy of Black collective political, social, and cultural action in America.

A chant of the Black Arts Movement of the 1970s was that Black literary and artistic elements were no longer going to follow "White" or "European" models or canons, and Black writers and artists were going to develop their own version of these things as both reflection and part of a "Black Aesthetic." Many white literary people excoriated this thinking and course of action. They resented the idea that their tutelage and the literary and artistic standards they had set were being abandoned by their Black counterparts. There were expressions of Black ingratitude, matched by the Jewish and other white intellectual or activist expressions of the same outrage, owing to Black criticism and rejection of these standards. And deep down, without a doubt, a resentment of and anger toward Black people for putting them, "white people," in "their place."

---

* Garvey visited Washington's grave when he came to the United States in 1916 to pay homage to him. The fiery leader even named one of the ships of his Black Star Line the *Booker T. Washington*.

The truth was that Black people had arrived on the American historical stage and social scene ready to do some independent thinking, to flex some political and perhaps cultural muscle as well, and also to demand the right to determine their destiny and to help determine the country's destiny. Many of the white liberal activists and white allies could not accept this. There was a discontinuity in American history, specifically with respect to White and Black relations in the country. For the first time in the history of America, Whites felt that they were "losing control" of Black people. Their psychological and social security was historically based on having that control and having an unrestrained ability to repress or punish Blacks as a means to keep them firmly in their "place." This feeling was aggravated by what they heard or read of black Africans rebelling against and throwing off White European colonial imperialism, at least in its old blatant form.

But in America the White aggravation and feelings of having lost control of Blacks had a specific, deeper source, which would have occurred whether or not black Africans had made efforts to free themselves from White domination. Whites had a strong sense that they owned Black people and had a right to control them. Whites felt that this was a moral obligation, but Blacks regarded it as an expression of blatant immorality. Two hundred and thirty years of Black chattel slavery had invested that idea deeply in American history, culture, and social life, and thus, in the minds, psychology, and being of most white people. The fifty years or so of a new form of Black servitude in the South, effected by horrendous violence, indebtedness sharecropping, peonage labor, convict-lease labor, fraudulent contracts, excessively low wage and income, among other things, between the 1880s and 1930s and 1940s, reinforced these views, particularly of southern Whites, who always held a strong sense of having a right to own Blacks.

The sense of White ownership of Blacks and its "moral" nature also came out of and was rooted in white supremacist/ebonicist racist beliefs. The sense of ownership from this source was not direct ownership, as in the case of owning slaves, but *having the right to own the consequences of direct ownership; that is, the right to do what an owner wished to do with what or who he or she owned.* This view and feeling was an expression of white supremacy/ebonicism and reinforced the racist belief that asserted that white people were innately superior and Black people were innately inferior. Particularly, Blacks were said to be cerebrally or intellectually, innately inferior. This, of course, was considered to be a permanent, natural condition, just as the alleged innate cerebral superiority of white people was considered to be real and permanent.

11

The racist belief that Black people were inherently incapable of serious or productive intellectual activity led to two other ebonicistic racist beliefs: that Black people could not produce any intellectuals, and owing to this, were incapable of producing knowledge, which is what intellectuals do. This meant that white people had to think for Black people, to speak on their behalf, and to represent them publicly before other white people. Thus, one can see that the emergence of Black intellectuals in America, which was not only not supposed to happen, but which was believed to be impossible, greatly perplexed and significantly frightened white people.

In any case, Black intellectuals could not be permitted to be independent in their thought. They had to be controlled. And that feeling that they had to be controlled grew strongly out of the racist/slave history and out of white supremacy/ebonicism alone. White people felt that they had a right to own Black people, in whatever form that emerged, or that they had a right to own the consequences of such ownership. White liberals had strong thoughts and feelings connected to the idea of owning the consequences of owning Black people. They felt they owned Black intellectuals this way. This was an additional reason for them—other than the racist environment—to not readily listen to Blacks and to endeavor to speak on behalf of them. It also meant that they felt they must represent Black intellectuals and other Blacks publicly. This kind of thinking and attitude led to the split between Frederick Douglass and William Lloyd Garrison, but it also led to the broad split between Black and white intellectuals in the three decades before the Civil War. It was a split that Black intellectuals had to keep mainly in their minds or sheltered in separate Black organizations, rather than acknowledge publicly.

In general, over the length of Black American history, there was a suppressant on the Black intellectual or Black activist response to white liberals or other white allies. At least there was until the 1950s and 1960s, when the Black Struggle for Liberation created the greatest opportunity ever for Blacks to put leadership and thoughts about their freedom (and the relationship of Whites to their struggle for freedom) fully in their own hands. This inaugurated the chasm between Black and Jewish intellectuals and between Black and white intellectuals in general.

ADDITIONAL COMMENTS ABOUT CRUSE

Cruse's *The Crisis of the Negro Intellectual, Black Rebellion or Revolution,* and his many public speaking engagements played a pivotal role in these developments. In looking back on the Cruse phenomenon several decades later, Black American Studies scholar Jerry Watts saw something less salutary with Cruse and his controversial book. He saw both as having a stultifying affect on Black intellectuals and their thought. The great encumbrance was the historian and social thinker's Black nationalist/cultural nationalist framework. Watts commented:

> In many respects Cruse's "crisis" was a sectarian ploy. He wanted to frame the issues of black intellectual life and politics along a rather simple minded axis between black nationalism and integration. Needless to say, he endorsed the former as the only authentic emancipatory outlook for creative black intellectuals. Instead of an on-going crisis in black intellectual life, Cruse was actually laying the intellectual groundwork for the emergence of a dominant black nationalist wing of intellectuals.[13]

The responsible Black intellectual in Cruse's view was a Black nationalist/cultural nationalist intellectual (to expand Cruse's viewpoint). Cruse believed that responsible behavior involved debunking integration and emphasizing the ethnic identity of Black people and their Black ethnic cultural and social existence in America, principally for the purpose of strengthening this ethnic group against white ethnic groups. He also argued that Blacks should seek to exercise some aesthetic cultural power and leadership in the country. Watts argued in his book, *Heroism and the Black Intellectual*, that Cruse seemed unaware of how committed Black people were to integration and how committed Black nationalist thinkers were to it. He noted:

> Simply put, Cruse had underestimated the degree to which the most vehement black nationalist intellectual was fundamentally committed to material acquisition and status attainment as anyone within the academy. That is, many of the black intellectuals who embrace black nationalism had little authentic commitment to black nationalism as an oppositional form of politics. Instead, they appropriated nationalism because they thought that it was rhetoric and ideology that could generate substantive benefits from the academy and/or the state. The willingness of many black intellectuals to join the black nationalist bandwagon often stemmed from their desire to legitimate themselves to the broader black activist community and to subsequently gain access to the mobility that the political system offered to black nationalist intellectuals in response to the maintenance of black quietude in urban areas.

Despite its militant-sounding rhetoric, black nationalism became an ideology of economic and status mobility for bourgeois intellectuals.[14]

My criticism of Harold Cruse, Jerry Watts, Black nationalists, cultural nationalists, and other Black intellectuals who accept either of these premises, is that Black nationalism—what is commonly understood by that term—is bogus political thought and promotes a bogus movement and politics; and which, consequently, makes cultural nationalism, as that term is usually understood and used, a fraudulent term.

Black nationalism is generally romantic thought. It continues not to be known or understood that this thought, even without formal conceptualization, had its intellectual development in the first half of the nineteenth century, when European romantic thought found its way into America and inspired the "Transcendentalists." It also helped to make a number of Black intellectuals and some other Blacks (particularly in the North) yearn for a Black country, that is, a Black country carved out of continental America. It also established the idea of Black people from the country migrating to an already existing black country somewhere in the Western Hemisphere, or to somewhere in Africa, to live and to help to build the country up and make it a strong independent country. One can see how cultural nationalism fits in with this kind of conception of Black nationalism. Black history shows that Black nationalism in its correct sense, in the sense of building a Black country within continental America or in the sense of Blacks going to a black country outside of America to live and to help strengthen, had always been very marginal intellectual and political activities until Marcus Garvey came along to expand the marginality of the second form of Black nationalism to the tune of several hundred thousand Black and black adherents. Black nationalism, as I will show in Chapter Three's discussion of the subject, is a term that is incorrect and often sloppily used by Black and black intellectuals(West Indian, African, or Hispanic).

Today there are many Black intellectuals who reject Black nationalism, although usually without having a good understanding of what it means. Like so many American intellectuals today, many Black intellectuals condemn or castigate writings or expressed thoughts without critical review. This is what so many do to Africancentricity, which is usually referred to as Afrocentricity or Africancentrism (terms I later explain in Chapter Three as inadequate). Those who condemn the Africancentrists most are the Black conservatives who have the public tag of being rightists. There are also some very prominent Black academic intellectuals who think of themselves as radicals or leftists and equally condemn Africancentrists. Some of these people are Marxists or socialists who often belong to formal socialist organizations. Those who are Marxists or socialists think they are more radical and leftist than others claiming this status. What I show in Chapter Four is that Black conservatives, Black liberals, and Black radicals are more alike in their attitudes and thinking than they know or would admit.

Looking back to when Cruse published his blockbuster books, one could see the same kind of division among Black intellectuals then: Black nationalists, cultural nationalists, religious intellectuals, liberals (further divided between radicals and moderates), and Marxists and socialists, even some communists. What was missing then were Black feminists and Black womanists (a term employed by Black womanist intellectuals to distinguish white feminists from Black feminists). There are Black feminists and womanists who think of themselves as Black nationalists. And, there are Black womanists who are trying to work out an intellectual and cultural relationship with what I call Africancentricity.

BLACK PUBLIC INTELLECTUALS

Black intellectuals were fragmented in the 1960s, and thus, so was Black thought. Harold Cruse was aware of this and one of his motivations for pressing the Black nationalist orientation was to try to draw more Black intellectuals together so that they could, as he said, do better by Black people, to help Black people to develop and emancipate themselves in America. Great intellectual fragmentation could not do this. But there was resistance to this kind of collaboration and consensus theory, policy, or programmatic construction.

The fragmentation of Black intellectuals and Black thought is wider than it has ever been in Black history. Perhaps this is because there are more Black intellectuals on the scene, more Black middle-class people than ever before, more Blacks with various reading or political or cultural interests, and more white people than ever before who are willing to read what Black intellectuals write and to hear what they have to say. All of these factors help to promote the fragmentation of intellectuals and intellectual thought.

There are many Black intellectuals who are pleased with this fragmentation, even proud of it. To them it shows white people that Black people are not a monolithic people, which is what different Black

15

intellectuals with different ideas show, what a diversity of Black social classes show, and what even an intellectual and cultural-social elite among Blacks show. It all stands as a refutation of the White racist view that Black people are all alike: look alike, think alike, talk alike, live alike, and promote the same kind of politics.

The frame of thought here is not Black people. It is certainly not representing them, speaking for them, or helping them. It is basically thought directed at white people in seeking their recognition and acceptance. It is also the acceptance of some as individuals among Blacks, as opposed to those who seek to promote a collective identity or Black agenda in America. Many white intellectuals understand this situation. They know that a number of Black intellectuals want in on America: to fit in, to achieve status as intellectuals, to be regarded as intellectual voices in the country, and to attain material rewards like their white counterparts. There are Black intellectuals who would separate themselves from Blacks, their problems and aspirations, to achieve these objectives.

Of course, not many Black intellectuals would admit writing to achieve White recognition, status, or largesse from them. This sounds too submissive and accommodating, too "Uncle Tomish." The images of Booker T. Washington as an "Uncle Tom," as an "accommodationist," as a "sychophant," or as a "betrayer" of Blacks, functions to protect these Black intellectuals from such charges. For instance, Black political scientist Adolph Reed, Jr. (like most Black academic intellectuals, liberals, radicals, and leftists known to loathe Washington), ties Booker T. Washington to those Black intellectuals who pursue White recognition, acceptance, approval, and the material rewards that come from that. What has come from that, deemed important to these Black intellectuals, is to be recognized as public intellectuals, in other words, Black intellectuals that Whites read and listen to.

Reed sees all of this connected to the ghost and legacy of Booker T. Washington. He has a chapter in his book, *Class Notes*, titled "What are the Drums Saying Booker?" He also writes about the Tuskegean in other chapters in the book, and it is mainly his loathing of and ignorance about Washington that glaringly manifest themselves, as when he states:

> This underscores the extent to which–beneath all the over-heated academic trendiness–the black public intellectual stance merely updates Booker T. Washington's role....

> As with Washington, the public intellectual's authenticity is conferred by white opinion makers. The typical trajectory of

stardom is instructive. First, one becomes recognized as a Black Voice in the intellectual apparatus of the left, which—out of a combination of good intentions and bad faith—stands ever ready to confer prominence on any reasonable, articulate black person willing to associate with it.[15]

It is incongruous for Reed to link Washington with Black intellectuals he describes as being on the left because this is not where Washington would be. Reed also said that Washington "became the first purely freelance race spokesman; his status depended on designation by white elites rather than any Black electorate or social movement."[16]

Washington was hardly a "freelance race spokesman." His leadership of Black people was rooted in the South, among southern Blacks. He built that leadership up over a fourteen-year period. Before he made his Atlanta Address in 1895, he was the most important Black leader in the South. Chapter Five in this book will show just how popular he was with Black people in both the South and the North, even among the Northern Black middle-class. And what may come as a great surprise to Reed and other Black and black intellectuals is that Washington led his own social movement among Blacks in the South, which was where most Black people lived in America at the time.

In addition, it is innocuous to talk about a Black electorate not electing the Grand Black Leader. Blacks did not have any institutions in America to do that. And the thought itself shows a lack of knowledge as to how a Black person became a powerful leader among Black people. They did so by possessing intelligence and leadership and rhetorical skills, which allowed them to build up and to organize and to galvanize a constituency, and by delivering the goods. That certainly was Washington.

Further, it has to be remembered that Washington gave the speech at the Atlanta Exposition in 1895 to an audience that included those who would later be his white benefactors. They did not tell him what to say on that occasion, but what he said became their ideas, their way of looking at the situation of Blacks in the South, and their way to help those Blacks. The general "Tuskegee Idea" became their general idea. On that September day in Atlanta, and for a period of twenty years afterwards, Washington inspired and mentored a lot of Black and white intellectuals who thought the way he did, the way he encouraged, persuaded, or pressured them into thinking. They helped him to be the Grand Black Leader for twenty years. Thus, Black public intellectuals today do not have a lineal descent from Washington, as Reed suggests.

If anything, today's Black public intellectuals should be associated with that historically racist tradition of white people thinking and feeling that they have the right to own Black people, including Black intellectuals, or to own the consequences of that ownership. Those Whites who have created the category of Black public intellectual are functioning out of that history, those thoughts, and those feelings. They really wish to control, as much as possible, Black intellectuals, what they write and publicly say. They do this by keeping Black intellectuals essentially confined to thinking, writing, and talking about Blacks. White intellectuals and other Whites, in various ways, discourage Black intellectuals from writing and talking about American history in a critical manner, as well as American society, American politics, domestic and foreign, or the racism of white people. They are specifically discouraged from writing about how racism has affected Whites or how Whites, acting as racists in American history, culture, social institutions, and social life, have affected these things. Only general criticisms that do not probe deeply and that do not require Whites to think harder or to take any action to correct matters are permitted.

Whites are not troubled by Black intellectuals talking about the "exploitative" or "oppressive" character of the American corporate economy, the "commodification" of the American people, the "corruption" of American life, the "corruption" of the American government, "moral" decline, or the "great violence" of the country. These are cliché categories of public criticism, available for all intellectuals in America to add their voice and commentary to. The discussions about these things are usually abstract discussions, mainly constructed for other intellectuals to ponder, and are not oriented to any serious practical efforts of trying to change American society or to eliminate the afflictions. When intellectuals primarily just chatter and separate themselves from practical activity (the Kantian notion of an intellectual) they, and what they write and talk about, are not seen as any threat by the powers that be.

When Black radical intellectuals talk about revolution in America, white intellectuals and other Whites understand this to be loud empty rhetoric, because they know that Blacks have no interest in engaging in societal revolution in the country. This kind of boisterous expression is always recognized for what it is. Frederick Douglass once said this type of empty rhetoric was a kind of "posturing" or "rattling [of] the air." It can also be said to be playing a game. But it is not a Black game.

Whites no longer speak on behalf of Blacks like they used to and felt they had a right to do. They no longer try to speak for or determine who Black people are, their identity, their value as a people, the things they should know and think about, aspire to be, or seek to accomplish. This kind of behavior would be seen as racist behavior and chastised today. Though it should be said that many Whites still harbor the historical white supremacy/ebonicism and often still express it, albeit in a more subtle manner. A manifestation of that subtlety is to find Black intellectuals who will speak on behalf of white people and say the things publicly that whites would like to say about Blacks. What white racists especially need today are surrogates, *Black surrogates*. They would be people who would project themselves as being Black, or at least speaking for Black people, and would seemingly represent their interests, when all the while they would be speaking for white people and representing their interests. These surrogates have been found, with some playing that role more intensely and regularly than others.

The Black intellectuals who stand out most doing this are Black conservatives. Strangely enough, some of these conservatives point to Booker T. Washington as a role model, which is guaranteed to keep his image in continuing murky depths with other kinds of Black intellectuals. Black conservatives identify Washington as a conservative, but this shows a lack of understanding the Tuskegean. He was conservative, moderate, and also radical. He was flexible in his thought and leadership to maximize their effectiveness among Blacks. The Alabamian was a holistic thinker, while Black conservatives today overwhelmingly are narrow, either-or, absolutist thinkers who have one-dimensional ideas and offer up one-dimensional programs or solutions. Invariably, these are the same programs or solutions that their White benefactors and/or supporters would offer.

On the other hand, more Black intellectuals than just Black conservatives think in narrow absolutist, either-or terms, especially those who call themselves radicals. Either-or thinking can also be found among Black feminists and womanists and among Black Africancentrists. Intellectuals in these three groups tend to fluctuate between engaging in either-or or holistic cognition. They recognize that Black people are, in general, a holistic-thinking people, an approach that has developed from their history, culture, and social life. But while it is easy for the mass of people to think in holistic terms, it is not so easy for Black intellectuals to do so. Black intellectuals are taught or tutored by white intellectuals, read white intellectuals's writings, seek White recognition and acceptance, find themselves drawn away from Black history and Black people, and are constantly pressured to limit the scope of their thinking, even with respect to Black people.

There is also the desire to be belligerent, to be radical, to carry on what is believed to be a radical tradition among Black intellectuals. For most that tradition dates back to the late nineteenth and early twentieth centuries, in the era of Booker T. Washington and his northern Black opposition, who at the time were called radicals. Some Black intellectuals see themselves as descendants of Washington's opposition. Their radicalism is also associated with presently debunking the Tuskegean, about whom most Black radicals, like most Black intellectuals, know little to nothing, and do not care to know much. But when Black intellectuals do not think in holistic terms and do not seek to help Blacks in that manner, they offer little assistance to them.

Black people are an ethnic group in America. Their cultural and social attributes are interrelated. They form a holistic group. They have to be spoken of and helped in a holistic manner. This idea has been a Black tradition most often carried out in a very strong manner by Black women. Seeking political and civil rights for themselves and Blacks in general, in no way shortened Black women's understanding of Blacks being a people, with cultural and social orientations. They were engaged in activities to promote both orientations.

Today there are many Black intellectuals who do not think of Black people as a people and have no wish to. They think of themselves as individuals and look upon Blacks that way as well. And this idea is espoused by more people than just the Black conservatives, although they have made a fetish of this kind of conception and Black social response in America. Black intellectuals are mainly from the Black middle-class. Historian and Africancentrist Maulana Karenga has correctly noted how the Black middle-class has lost–if it has not abandoned altogether–its historical mission, which was to help Black people as a people, as well as Black individuals, to advance and to be free in America. This had been the historical mission of Black intellectuals, yet so many Black intellectuals today are abandoning that mission. William Banks remarked on this broad development in *Black Intellectuals*:

> Ultimately, of course, the choices of intellectuals about what they do and how they do it are based on moral sensibilities of individuals. With the lowering of formal racial barriers, black intellectuals feel free to reject any identification with the black community at large, free to sidestep the troublesome questions posed by ongoing racial inequality. Both camps–intellectuals who advocate an organic relationship with the black community, and those who aspire to transcend ethnic considerations–are part of the unfolding saga of race and social thought in the United States. And members of both camps today are products of the same historical forces; they are intellectuals who have benefited from the victories of those who challenged racial barriers in earlier periods. Now, the individuals say, they are ready to move on, to take advantage of expanded

opportunities. In doing so, they are well received by the political cultural authorities who deny the lasting significance of race in American society. By emphasizing their own individual successes and accepting the thesis that being black is no longer a limiting factor, the individualists affirm the essential openness of the social order.[17]

While I can agree with Banks's assessment in a general way, I find it neither critical enough, nor trenchant enough; and it does not disclose enough reality about Black intellectuals functioning in America. These intellectuals en masse show that they do not know the difference between racism and race, which they invariably use interchangeably. To an individual, they say that it is the race of Blacks that has led to their victimization in America, not white people and their racist views of the black race or of Blacks as an ethnic group, or white people's mephitic behavior toward both groups. This is tantamount to Black intellectuals blaming the Black or black victims and exonerating white racists and essentially acting as surrogates for such people. Moreover, Black intellectuals, virtually to a person, do not know that there are many forms of racism, and that the latter is not necessarily related to race and does not have to be associated with it at all. I take up these various matters in the next chapter.

Black conservatives show that they do not understand, or do not wish to understand, the Black historical struggle in America, which was always about the development, advancement, and freedom of the Black collective, as well as Black individuals. The oppression and suppression of Black people automatically led to the same for individual Blacks. Individual Blacks made advances when masses of Blacks remained heavily encumbered and were prevented from advancing. But, when many Black individuals were able to advance it meant Blacks, as a group, were engaged in collective action to promote opportunities for Black individuals, as occurred in the 1950s and 1960s.

In regard to the role of the American creed of individualism with respect to Blacks, it can be explained simply by saying this was one among many American ideals, saturated with white supremacy/ebonicism to help oppress and suppress Blacks. Inundated with racism, this American creed of individualism took the form of the individual right to own Black people, the individual right to discriminate against them, the individual right to publicly humiliate them, and the individual right to physically abuse or even kill them. When Black conservatives praise the idea of individualism, which they often do, they cover up the racist reality and implementation of this idea and permit Whites to avoid dealing with this history or permit them to hide from it. And at the same time, they are permitting them to talk about individualism in a non–racist manner, as if they and other Whites have always thought of it and implemented it that way.

No Black intellectual has to identify with being Black, or even has to identify with being racially black. No Black intellectual has to identify with Black history, Black culture, or Black social life; in short, no Black intellectual has to identify with Black ethnicity and the Black ethnic community. No Black person is legally or in any other way required to associate with, date, or marry anyone Black or black. Those are individual choices. But any time Black intellectuals write or talk in a public manner about Black history, Black identity, Black life, and the means Blacks should seek to advance or be free in America, they forfeit their insulated individualist status. They dip back into Black life, even if not physically or socially, but nonetheless, by making remarks that could affect both Whites and Blacks. By these behaviors they have placed themselves and their remarks and motivations on the public docket, making them eligible for public scrutiny, which might well be severe.

Black Organic Intellectuals

There are Black intellectuals today who are being publicly taunted as "organic" intellectuals. Enough discussion has shown that this is a White designation of Black intellectual identity, which also shows that many Black intellectuals have accepted the designation with pride, vigor, and gratitude. The concept denotes those Black intellectuals who supposedly identify with Black people, Black history, and Black life, and who are dedicated to preserving and promoting both. But this is really a "cover up" definition that covers up the racist and/or the racist inundated individualist use of this concept developed by Whites who haven't the slightest interest in Black people as a people and who have meshed the "organic" concept with the traditional White racist concept of the "Black exception," meaning, that they are willing to see exceptional Black individuals make it and they are supportive of Black intellectuals who seek to aid that goal, too.

Black intellectuals who have accepted the designation and who regard themselves as organic intellectuals endeavor to show their affinities to Black people, usually by the method of talking about their individual Black experiences, their families, their personal histories, the lives of their families, or their personal or family dealings with White racism. These stories are authentic. But they in no way indicate an authentic organic relationship to Black people, or legitimize the right of those who produced them to speak on behalf of Black people, or project themselves as their public representatives. The whole thing is individualistically-oriented, a manifestation when read whole of an individual success story. Thus, it is a story that really shows how this Black individual has moved away from Black people and, at best, only associates with Black middle-class people, and probably just as often with white middle-class people. These associations are legitimate and ones that Black intellectuals have a right to engage in. But they also clearly emphasize the "in-organic" nature of these Black intellectuals.

It might seem that the authentic Black organic intellectuals would be Black female feminists, womanists, and the Black Africancentrists. The final chapter of this book is on the Black female intellectual. What one sees with Black female intellectuals, on the one hand, is an effort to develop an independent intellectual stance for Black female intellectuals, which is done more successfully by the Black womanists than by the Black feminists. On the other hand, one sees the great difficulty that Black female intellectuals have trying to be authentic organic intellectuals whose designation is determined by Black people and based on an actual relationship with Black people.

A number of Black female feminists are as individualistic and as "in-organic" as many, if not most, Black male intellectuals, especially those who are ivory–towered, cloistered, academic intellectuals. The identity that a number of Black female intellectuals seek is that of being "left" or "radical," which implies that they think in absolutist/either–or terms, not holistic terms, and it further shows how far removed they are from Black thinking. They are also far removed from being able to strongly relate to the Black collective identity and existence; and thus, to be "organic" Black women intellectuals.

The Black womanists do not automatically fall into the authentic organic intellectual status. The womanist concept was coined by Black writer Alice Walker. It was initially conceived to separate Black female feminists from white female feminists, and was also initially a concept conceived to effect a bonding of all Black people and to affirm and strengthen the Black community. Black womanists are growing in number and their thoughts are steadily expanding, with both developments offering a challenge to Black female feminists. This has sparked some hostility between the two groups of Black female intellectuals. There are Black womanists who are seeking to establish a bridge between their thoughts and that of the Black Africancentrists. At a quick glance, they both have the image of authenticity and seem to have achieved the status of authentic, organic Black intellectuals. But as seen, this is not an

23

automatic designation with Black womanists and the same goes for the Black Africancentrists.

Indeed, Africancentrists are much like Black conservatives in being "in-organic" Black intellectuals; however, they are so in a different and peculiar manner. The Africancentrists reject the Black identity of Black people, and they also reject Black history, Black culture, and Black social life. They regard all Black people to be black Africans, although they usually say just Africans, and Black history as African history, Black culture as African culture, and Black social life as African social life. The Africancentrists seek, as an ideal and as their goal, getting all Black people in the United States to accept themselves as Africans in a different place, living at a different time. This, of course, is romantic, a-historical, and either-or/absolutist thinking. It is contrary to the Africancentrists's knowledge of the general holistic thinking of black Africans and Black Americans.

On the other hand, I do not reject what I call Africancentricity. I feel that it is a necessary perspective for Blacks in America. There is undoubtedly an African connection to Black history and Black life, and Blacks should know what it is and be made privy to each advance of knowledge on this subject. But the Africancentrist perspective is an absolutist one. Implemented that way, with respect to Blacks in America, it would simply suppress Black ethnic identity, Black history, and Black life.

Black people and their identity, their history, and their lives have their own reality and authenticity, which I think I have captured under my own conception of *Blackcentricity*. Africancentricity helps Blacks in America understand their origins-things from a distant or immediate past, that are contributory to their existence and to which they are irrevocably linked (as a collective anyway). Thus, Africancentricity helps Black people understand themselves up to a point. Then it is the role of Blackcentricity to help them understand themselves beyond that point, to understand who they are based on the history they have made and lived in America.

Blackcentricity pronounces that Black people are an ethnic group of the black race that has its origins in Africa and that has since spread from there to the Western Hemisphere. Black people are descendants of black African slaves and their black progeny, with the latter, over time, evolving into a Black ethnic group, with that identity and status also being achieved by working African cultural remnants into them. These cultural remnants, Blackcentricity says, are now part of Black culture, not African culture. Blacks have made a history separate from Africa and black Africans and have defined a space within the folds of American history and culture;

more broadly, they have defined a space within Western history and civilization. Thus, they are making history and participating in a culture and a civilization along with white people. While Eurocentrism, which is a racist, inundated concept, does not apply to Black people, Eurocentric or a European orientation does-up to a point. Blackcentricity acknowledges, accepts, and utilizes this fact and reality, which Africancentrists reject. The Black ethnic group, being an ethnic group of the black race, has black racial features, but also exhibits gender groups, social classes, age groups, regional groups, and individuals with different sexual preferences. In my view, the authentic Black organic intellectual is the Blackcentric intellectual who uses the comprehensive character of the Black experience in America as the basis for viewing Black people, America, Europe, Africa, and the world.

The Black historical experience is one of the greatest and most complex experiences of human beings or humanity. The Africancentric perspective indicates that this was originally experienced by the black race that migrated from Africa, that is, *homo sapien sapien*. Later, this race populated the world and underwent numerous metamorphoses, producing numerous races in the world. The Black experience in America reflects some of the richest dimensions of the human experience and human existence and also some of its most oppressive and wretched realities. Black people are a people "up from slavery" who survived slavery, developed during slavery, and developed after slavery—all great historical achievements.

Throughout their history in America Blacks have battled against and have survived racist beliefs and practices; beliefs that said that they were "nonhumans" or "subhumans" or "Non-others," and they have survived cultural, political, economic, and other practices predicated on these beliefs that were implemented not only to demean and use them, but also to try to make them conform to the racist images concocted and imposed on them. This represented the racist psychological assault against Blacks, a continuous daily psychological assault that lasted for centuries, which most Blacks survived, even if this survival was in ways negatively impacted by the assault. This also shows the long-standing and substantive psychological, moral, and spiritual strength of Black people in general. These strengths were reflected in the way that Black people have been able to relate to white people-their former masters and their racist oppressors. These were people who acted toward them with impaired or no conscience, with little or no ability to think of them as human beings with human rights and dignity and a right to be treated as if they were human beings.

Blacks have been living an entire history with their country organized and functioning against them, oppressing and suppressing them. Nevertheless, they still exhibit a strong loyalty to it, in fact, exceeding the loyalty of any

25

other group of Americans. The historical record shows clearly that white people have been more loyal to white supremacist racism and *White racist America*, rather than America, i.e., the American ideal and what it is supposed to be about. Blacks have been very loyal to America's ideals, which have been a guide and a springboard for their behavior throughout the history of this country. The struggle of Black people in America has been precisely to make the ideals and the actual reality of America one and the same. In general, whites have historically sought not to do this and have sought to thwart and/or suppress the Black historical efforts.

Blackcentricity is not perceived or proposed as a monolithic intellectual viewpoint or method of analysis, but variation in either has to recognize and accept the minimal essentiality of the position. This perspective is "Black-centered" and not "black-centered" or "African-centered." Nor is it "class-centered" or "gender-centered." It is "Black ethnic centered," which takes in racial, gender, class, and other group features.

The great irony is that most Black intellectuals today are essentially running away from this great historical and human experience, or skimming the surface of it, instead of plunging into its depths to function as intellectuals, and to devise concepts, analytical categories, critiques and bodies of thought for Blacks to help themselves, and that helps Whites and other Americans understand Blacks. A result of the avoidance is the discernible inadequacy of much of Black intellectual thought and analysis, which is something addressed continually in this book. The Black experience in America is primordial. It is the primordial basis for critically evaluating the historical and social experience of white people in America and the country's history and social existence. Black intellectuals generally side step or skim these analyses, which reflects inadequacy of thought and analysis on their part. This continues to be unfortunate for Blacks and America.

In 1997, I published *Black Intellectuals, Black Cognition, and a Black Aesthetic*[18] in which I said that Black intellectuals were in a position not only to be important intellectuals in America, but to give the country some ideas and some understandings about itself that it desperately needs. I felt, and still do, that in abandoning a historical mission, Black intellectuals cannot hear the call. Harold Cruse heard the call and he got some Black intellectuals to respond to it as well. A hope of this book is that it will get even more Black intellectuals to hear the historical beckoning by Blacks and America, and to hear what might also be called "the beckoning of the times."

—❦ Chapter Two ❧—

Racism and Race: Lolling and Lumbering in an Intellectual Wasteland

One would naturally believe that Black intellectuals, if anyone in the United States, would be able to explain in a clear, understandable manner what racism and race were and how the two have always been different (although they have for centuries also been strongly interconnected). But Black intellectuals have not accomplished this task, and have, indeed, essentially failed at it. However, this is not a failure due to incompetence, for it can be shown that people all over the world have failed to have this success. A partial and accurate explanation for Black intellectuals's lack of achievement is that they have been too close to the subjects of race and racism to see and to understand them clearly enough. Both race and racism were harshly imposed on Black intellectuals and other Black people and were made such an integral part of their lives–as natural, necessary, and ubiquitous penetrations and realities–that it was difficult to distance themselves from the phenomena. They seemed to fit like gloves of Black life, so that critical Black thought was muffled or suppressed. It was always a question of intelligently and practically relating to such things.

Today, we have the concept of "critical race theory" and efforts to develop it philosophically, legally, and in other ways. But some of the people doing this, perhaps even most of them, are white intellectuals. However, they are not white people seeking to speak for or on behalf of Black people. They are white people who feel that they should know more about racism, and in particular feel that they should understand how, and to what extent, it still functions in American society. They wish to eradicate racism and wish to join Blacks and others in America in doing so. That effort presupposes learning more about it and its workings in American society.

DISTINGUISHING RACE FROM RACISM AND BOGUS RACE SCIENCE

Today, there are many Black intellectuals who are critical of the concept of race, but in ways different from critical race theorists. Their concern is to get "beyond" or to "transcend" race. They wish to focus on some other aspects of Black existence that are necessary and vital to Blacks and to examine critical factors that affect their lives. For example, Roy Brooks, a Black law professor at the University of Minnesota, opened the 1990s with a book entitled: *Rethinking the American Race Problem.* He was concerned with having social class given equal weight to race in evaluating Black life and Black political, economic, and social behavior in America.

This concern, and the call for adding social class as an intersected analytical methodology of race and class to the evaluative equation, had first been initiated by the Black sociologist William Julius Wilson, who called for rethinking along these lines with his 1970s book, *The Declining Significance of Race.*[2] Wilson gained some Black intellectual adherents, and he also got stiff resistance from many Black intellectuals who insisted that race was still the overwhelming determinative factor in Black life. These intellectuals noted that while social classes were forming among Blacks, they had not become full-blown and strongly structured, which, they predicted, would take some additional years.

Writing thirteen years later, Roy Brooks felt that social class stratification and crystallization had occurred among Black Americans and also noted that social class had finally and permanently come forth for conceptual analytical inclusion. He wrote that Wilson's *The Declining Significance of Race*:

> Asserts that one can no longer talk meaningfully about the problems of African Americans and the resolution of those problems without merging the question of race (which triggers civil rights laws and policies) with that of class structure–it is not an either-or proposition. The issue of race versus class, in other words, is a red herring, a non-issue, in today's African American society.[3]

Of course, in 1990 and throughout the decade, there were Black radicals: the socialists Angela Davis, Manning Marable, and Leith Mullings, for instance, who emphasized social class and essentially saw race as a red herring. There was also the Black radical feminist Joy James, who was less concerned about race or class as determinant factors in Black life. Instead, she regarded Black leadership to be the paramount factor, and regarded any leadership that was not radical as inept leadership. There were many Black feminists in the

1990s who argued that race and class were limited categories, determinant factors or tools of historical and social analysis. Strong arguments came from Black feminists like Johnetta Cole and Barbara Smith, who suggested that gender also had to be drawn into the new intersectional analysis.

Cornel West was aware of all these developments when in 1993 he published *Race Matters*.[4] It was a best seller. But it was not written to emphasize biological race as a factor in Black life (although he admitted its great prominence, in fact, regarding it as being too prominent to the point of being stultifying). West was explicitly condemnatory of what he called "racial reasoning" which, he argued, Blacks and Whites did in America. But he was particularly distraught with Blacks doing it, especially Black leaders. West believed "racial reasoning" prevented them from engaging in "moral reasoning." He noted, "the pitfalls of racial reasoning are too costly in mind, body, and soul—especially for a downtrodden and despised people like black Americans."[5]

Of course, it is wrong for West to use the phrase "downtrodden" in such a blanket manner with respect to Blacks. About one-third of the Black population is middle-class, or above, and live in very substantial dwellings in physically attractive neighborhoods. It is not clear that Whites today despise such people. This also necessitates a criticism of West's concept of "nihilism," which he uses in a blanket manner with respect to Black people. West defines nihilism as a negative psychological disposition: alienation, lack of self-esteem, lack of self-worth, self-hate, lovelessness, hopelessness, disconnection, despair and self-destruction. It would seem that the concept of nihilism is not applicable to at least one-third of the Black population. West is a Black intellectual of great intellectual gifts who has a wide-range of knowledge and is a prodigious writer. He obviously relishes being an intellectual. But when it comes to the subjects of racism and race, his thinking and writing are not distinguishable from that of other Black intellectuals in that it shows the same confusion other Black intellectuals have about racism and race and exhibits the same kind of inadequate racist analysis.

This is not a peculiarity of Black or black (West Indian, African, or Hispanic) intellectuals in America. White intellectuals in the country exhibit similar shortcomings. Racism is the most pervasive belief and practice found on this globe and has been for millennia. But racism as a phenomenon—in terms of what it is, how it functions, how it impacts, and how it perpetuates itself—is only slightly known and understood around the world.

My concern here is with Cornel West's understanding of racism and race. His confusion about these subjects is exhibited in the following quotation from *The House That Race Built*:

THIS volume rests upon three fundamental claims. First, white supremacy is constitutive, not additive, to the makings of the modern world. Second, anti-black racism is integral, not marginal, to the existence and sustenance of American society. The third, race remains the most explosive issue in the country today. In this sense, race matters in regard to how we conceive what it means to be modern, American and human in our contemporary world.[6]

In these remarks West made no distinction between racism and race, indicating that he did not and (as his recent writings suggest) still does not clearly know the difference. He equates the two. But, it should be made clear that White supremacy is a racist doctrine, not a racial doctrine. He was correct to distinguish white supremacy from "anti-black" racism, which I call *ebonicism*, but it is not clear that he saw white supremacy as a racist doctrine that pertained *only* to white people and that alleged their natural superiority. Ebonicism is distinct from white supremacy. It is the racist belief that Whites have concocted to allege the innate inferiority of Blacks (or black) people to rationalize acting toward them in a racist manner.

But this does not stop West from saying that race remains the most *"explosive"* issue in America. Why would he say this when he refers to two forms of racism that he regards as being more impactful in America and when White supremacy has an impact around the world? The answer to this posed question (which has to have a large answer based on West's own writings such as *Keeping the Faith*[7] and the book he co-authored with Henry Louis Gates, Jr., *The Future of the Race*[8]) is that West does not possess a clear or full understanding of the phenomena of racism. This also seems to be true with respect to his understanding of race. In *The Future of the Race*, and in other writings, Gates's thinking on these matters is just as blurred. But the two should not to be singled out, especially for this criticism. This type of thinking spreads easily across most Black intellectuals's analyses in America (and other American intellectuals as well).

Frederick Douglass knew the difference between racism and race. He made the argument that Black people did not suffer in America because of their race, but because of the racism of white people, which I refer to as white supremacy/ebonicism Because of their racism, Douglass said, white people were led to believe that Blacks were not human beings. Douglass referred to this as "race prejudice" (the common description in his day and for a century afterwards) and told how whites were led to believe that Blacks were not human beings and were not to try to act as such because it was forbidden and would be dealt with harshly. Douglass wrote:

Color is not the cause of our persecution; that is, it *is not our color* which makes our proximity to white men disagreeable....

If the feeling which persecutes us were prejudice against color, the colored servant would be just as obnoxious as the colored gentleman, for the color is the same in both cases; and being the *same* in both cases, it would produce the *same* result in both cases....[9]

The matter went beyond race, as Douglass saw it. It went to the extreme point of believing that Blacks were not human beings or that they were "subhumans" who were incapable of having human qualities and who should not dare seek to assert any. "The evil lies deeper than prejudice against color," he noted, "It is, as we have said, an intense hatred of the colored man when he is distinguished for any ennobling qualities of head and heart."[10]

White supremacy asserts that white people are "innately cerebrally superior" and their ebonicistic racist beliefs say that Blacks are "innately cerebrally inferior." White supremacy also claims that white people are "naturally morally superior," while ebonicism posits the idea that Blacks are "innately morally inferior." Douglass discerned and discussed these realities without the conceptualizations I am able to employ. There is no question that Douglass knew the difference between racism and race, even though he usually blurred this distinction by using the concept "race prejudice" to stand for two different sets of racist beliefs. It is the same mistake that Du Bois made when he used the concept of white supremacy to do double duty, and it is still widely done today by Black intellectuals. However, in their case, as opposed to Douglass and Du Bois, they do not know there is and that there has always been, a difference between racism and race, a difference that involves two different subjects and two different discussions.

Black philosopher Charles Mills referred to Douglass's article "Prejudice Against Color" in his book *Blackness Visible.*[11] He thought that the Black abolitionist had shown significant insight with his remarks, but he also entered a criticism against him for not developing this insight. One would think that Mills, a hundred and fifty years later and with more knowledge and understanding to work with, would have seized the opportunity to develop Douglass's insights further. But the black philosopher did not. In his book, which appeared five years after West's, he argued that race mattered and equated racism exclusively with race. Thus, like West, he did not perceive that it was racism that really mattered to Whites. However, Mills took the matter one step further. He argued that race did not exist, but that it still mattered. This projection is becoming a common and confusing way of thinking about racism and race by both Black and black intellectuals.

What I want to do here is to expand upon what I said in the previous chapter about Black intellectuals and the idea they often espouse that Blacks were oppressed and suppressed because of their race, and thus, also, to expand on Douglass's insights. So common is this colossal misunderstanding among Black intellectuals that it is imperative to bring some clarity to this matter.

In the late nineteenth and early twentieth centuries, white racist intellectuals, a number of them physical and social scientists, devised a term: *biological determinism*. But the definition was not about biology. The scientists among these racist intellectuals used science as a means to try to verify their white supremacist and ebonicistic racist beliefs, white supremacy/ebonicism. These beliefs are abstract, fanciful beliefs that create fanciful, non-existent "races" a white "race" and a black "race" with one "race" "innately" "superior" and the other "innately" "inferior." The white "race" has "superior" "inherent" "traits." The black "race" has "inferior" "inherent" "traits." The "superior" white "race" puts meaning to its "natural" "superior" "traits" by making the white race a "race" of "godly" or "god-like" "entities" and the black race, with its "inferior" "inherent" "traits" a "race" of "nonhumans" or "subhumans" who would also be described as "Non-Others"–something other than human beings. But the "race" of "godly" or "god-like" "entities" were "Non-Others" in the same sense. Race, something that is real, is *Other*, not "Non-Other."

What I have been describing here is racism, a belief system that can actually be many systems and is comprised of abstract fantasies that do not relate to any reality, to any embodied thing, or to any representational object. Neither of the "races" mentioned exist in this world. They only exist in the minds and abstract fantasies of white racists who can intellectually increase or diminish a "race's" "inherent" "traits." The white intellectuals who did this kind of racist thinking and construction and who used science as a means to try to verify and support them–to find "evidence" for them–have been called "scientific racists." They produced a field and understanding of "scientific racism." The bogus character of the whole operation was denoted by their abstract fanciful racist beliefs and by the fact that science could never corroborate or verify such beliefs, as they were wholly beyond science, wholly beyond any empirical reality or experience.

Yet racist scientists made use of these beliefs, which they used to construct a theory of "biological determinism," something that did not exist except as an abstract, fanciful concept. Still, racist scientists and other white racists in the decades past believed the fantasies to be actual biological embodiments or realities, reflecting these scientists's own racist afflictions: irrationality, pathology, abrogated conscience, compulsive thinking, and immorality. The racist scientists made use of these fanciful racist beliefs. In their own afflicted minds, they "invested" them in the black and white races. It went like this:

white supremacist racist beliefs created an abstract fanciful white "race" with "innate" and "superior" "traits": "intellectual," "psychological," "moral," and "social." In short, the white "race" and the white race were one and the same; they became a people whose thoughts, psychology, morality, social, and cultural behavior and the way they made history, were "determined" by "inner" "qualities." These "inner" "qualities" were then regarded as being the same as inner, racial qualities.

Similarly, ebonicistic racist beliefs created a black "race" with "innate," "inferior" "attributes": "intellectual," "psychological," "moral," and "social." These "natural" "traits" were synonymous with the actual black race (or Black people), making the black "race" and the black race (and Black people) one and the same. They became a people whose thoughts, psychology, morality, social, and cultural behavior, and the way the race made history, were determined by "innate" "qualities" believed to be the same as innate, racial qualities. The white racists of the late nineteenth and early twentieth centuries used race and science to promote racism. But they talked only in terms of race, as if it were really race that they were concerned about, that mattered to them, when all along it was racism that mattered! Race was clearly secondary–a medium through which to execute racist beliefs and practices.

BLAMING RACE RATHER THAN RACISTS

Most Black intellectuals do not have a clear understanding of the phenomenon of "scientific racism" because they do not know clearly what racism is. Their thoughts, writings, and talk are overwhelmingly about race. But they also have their own biological determinism argument, one that is implied in their discussion of race and that they are not aware of, and one that they constantly employ. It is made every time they say that Black people have been oppressed and suppressed in America because of their race, or their color, and not because of white people acting as racists towards them. This argument makes the racial biology of Black people the causative factor, something that provokes white people to act in a peculiar, compulsive, and deterministic manner, and that causes them to abuse Black people.

This argument intimates that Black people, through the presence and functioning of their biology and as a strange kind of masochism or perverse martyrdom, makes the racial biology of white people act in mephitic ways towards them. It is not something that white people want to do. They are forced to do it. Blacks *make* them. Whites, themselves, are guiltless, innocent, and non-responsible. Since Black intellectuals do not consciously make this absurd argument, and could not conceive of doing so, they are unable to perceive how they often make it in an implied way. And when they do they abet white supremacy/ebonicism.

The situation is similar to what occurs among Jews. Jews often say that they are mistreated or despised because they are Jews or because of their religious beliefs. But, in fact, this happens because there are people who have invested in them vile thoughts about Jews and their religion and then act on them. Likewise, women have said (and continue to say) that men oppress and exploit them because they are women, instead of saying that men invest themselves with some noxious ideas about women and their nature and then seek to execute them. It is similar to saying that a set of keys left in a car is the reason why the car was stolen. Or that a person was robbed because they had money in their pocket. In these instances (as with anti-Jewish or sexist thought and social behavior) it is necessary to investigate and analyze the perpetrator and their social environment.

The perverse self-blaming by Blacks for their mistreatment at the hands of white racists abets the latter's thinking that they are guiltless, innocent, and non-responsible people incapable of engaging in oppressive, despicable thoughts, and social behavior. Du Bois made a reference to this form of White racist thinking in the 1890s. In *The Suppression of the African Slave Trade to the United States of America* he wrote in reference to white Americans (without explicitly saying so), "We have the somewhat inchoate idea that we are not destined to be harassed with great social questions, and that even if we are and fail to answer them, the fault is with the question and not with us."[12]

What Black intellectuals almost never do, and certainly seldom do, is talk about the impact of white supremacist racist beliefs and practices on white people; that is, they never speak of the perpetrators. White people actually believe that they have not been affected or scarred intellectually, psychologically, morally, or spiritually after centuries of grossly abusing Black people. Yet, the Black Liberation Struggle of the 1950s and 1960s showed the depth and extent of this inner assault and maiming, especially among southern whites who thought of themselves as the most innocent, guiltless, and non-responsible of all white people in America, at times even the most Christian.

It would stand to reason that Black intellectuals would speak clearly and extensively to this matter. After all, they and other Black people have been victims of the internal maiming of white people, and a severe form of that maiming is a suppressed, or retarded, or obliterated conscience. Yet white people feel they are a people of great conscience and great morality. Every discussion of race by Black intellectuals, and not racism or the impact of racism on white people, feeds this fanciful and delusional thinking. Black historian Nathan Huggins once lamented: "Slavery has been seen as a pathological condition, studied as a disorder...racism and racial caste[s]... have been, in their turn, studied as the 'tangle of pathology' of blacks.... Very little thought has been given to the general health of the society that created and sustains them. Society and its historians have treated all these phenomena as aberrations, marginal to the main story."[13] Huggins was referring to white historians who did not want to write on the impact of white supremacist/ebonicistic racism on white people, and through writing about them, writing also about racism's impact on American history, society, and life. But he could have also extended this criticism to Black historians who have not done the same either and to Black social scientists, philosophers, literary and cultural critics, and others.

In the 1950s and the 1960s one used to hear Black intellectuals and Black leaders and activists chanting that white racists were "sick" and that American society was "sick." These claims were easy to see, available for study, extensive scrutiny, and explanation. But Black intellectuals did not seriously turn to this activity. Most Black intellectuals consciously or unconsciously avoided it. And they are doing the same thing today. One of the exceptions is the Black historian, Lerone Bennett Jr., whose recent book, *Forced Into Glory,*[14] employs a racist analysis, extensive documentation, and withering logical arguments, and discusses, at length, the white supremacist/ebonicistic racism of Abraham Lincoln and how it affected him and his presidency, and how the racism of white historians affects how they write on Lincoln and his years in the White House.

However, the Black conservative Shelby Steele, who is one of the darlings of the white conservatives, spent a whole book lashing the thought, character and social behavior of Black people. He makes references to the traditional White—meaning, White racist—view of the pathology of Blacks and Black life and by implication and direct commentary speaks highly of the thinking, morality, and social behavior of white people. This liaison with white conservatives began with his book *The Content of Our Character,*[15] which was written on the implied racist premise that white people had not been affected by their centuries of promoting racism in America. Steele even talked about this kind of racism still going on in the country; although, as he said, not so strongly as before, which is true enough. But however strong it is, if it is being implemented, it is impacting the perpetrators, internally inculcating authoritarian personality traits, self-righteousness, delusional thinking, and retardation of conscience when it comes to Blacks.

This was not Steele's view, and still isn't, as reflected in his more recent book *A Dream Deferred*[16] where he lamented the "loneliness of the Black conservative" and described his "loneliness" as a consequence of being rejected by so many Black people, and also described being outside the "authority" of his racial group. But it was the "authority" of the group more than the group itself said Steele that produced this "loneliness." He did not feel any estrangement from being separated from the Black group–just their authority. But why would this group extend its authority to him, when most of those in the group who read him or listened to him rejected him? The logic of the situation would be for Steele to enmesh himself with the Black ethnic group in America and seek to speak in a representational manner or stop speaking about it publicly with representational overtones.

Nevertheless, Steele keeps speaking publicly precisely because white conservatives are reading and listening to him. Steele is a model of the Black surrogate intellectual who does not feel "loneliness" among white conservatives or in his role as a surrogate. Indeed, he wrote in *The Content of Our Character*, "For every white I have met who is a racist, I have met twenty more who have seen me as an equal. And of those twenty, ten have wished me only the best as an individual. This . . . has been my actual reality.... None of this is to say that racism is totally dead and gone...."[17]

White racism may not be totally gone, but Steele gives the impression that there is not much left of it. His encounters with Whites are extraordinary and presumably take this form wherever he goes in America. But the reality is that Steele is a handsome, educated man. He is also a college professor, a man who could pass for white among most white people he encounters (not that he tries to do this) and a man who speaks frequently before white people who regard themselves, like Steele, to be conservatives. Steele, in speaking to Whites, appeals to their conscience and morality and even to their feelings of guilt and remorse. It is among these people that he meets his twenty (out of twenty-one) racist-free Whites. But if they are not racists and are not abusing Blacks, why does he speak of their guilt and remorse? It is not surprising that Steele is regarded well by Whites when he flatters their egos with his extensive praise of them, as does another Black conservative, Glenn Loury, who talks about White conscience, remorse, and guilt.[18]

An analysis of racism in America today shows that it is lodged strongly among the white people who regard themselves as conservatives, those who are against liberals, welfare, affirmative action, and bussing. These same conservatives are those who are in favor of "neighborhood schools," regard crime as an urban phenomenon, think or talk about the pathology of inner cities, consider drugs as primarily used and abused in inner cities, and object to anything labeled multiculturalism. These are all coded racist responses, the kind of subtle racism that Whites mainly promote in America and which is done persistently and extensively by white conservatives.

Steele, Loury, and other Black conservatives not only show that they do not wish to deal with White racism in America, but that they do not want to deal with the impact of racism on white people, on the perpetrators themselves. If White racism and white supremacy/ebonicism are still being practiced in America, as Black conservatives invariably say that they are, then there has to be recognition that the racism of the racists affects them. In fact, it should be a major discussion area. But Black conservatives avoid this understanding and discussion. Instead, they present blanket statements about White conscience, guilt, and remorse.

A racist analysis of those people who the Black conservatives say are still promoting racism would show that as racists they do not exhibit much conscience, guilt, or remorse toward their Black (or other) victims. Racists always feel innocent, guiltless, and non-responsible toward their victims. Ebonicistic racist beliefs toward Blacks infer that Blacks are an "innately" "inferior" people and that their low cultural or social status is related to that, to their alleged inherent incapabilities, rather than to the nefarious behavior of others.

The bottom line for racists, one of their many bottom lines, but the most fundamental of all, is that they regard themselves as being "godly" or "god-like," which means they can't think or do wrong, and also means that their victims are "nonhuman" or "subhuman," against whom wrong thinking or social behavior cannot be done. In this nexus is located the source of racist thoughts and feelings of innocence, guiltlessness, and non-responsibility, as well as elements of the psychological *racist reaction syndrome*. This syndrome stirs into action when racists are called on their racism. It includes psychological responses such as fear, anxiety, defensiveness, denial, self-righteousness, moral indignation, feelings of being put upon, an urge to flee the context, or an urge to retaliate–that is, to suppress the challenger.

If what I have just said makes sense to the reader, then he or she is learning something about racism, not race, which in itself has nothing to do with psychology, but with something physiological or biological. Racism is a belief system that leads to racist practices, and this produces psychological affects on those who adhere to and practice these beliefs. Racist beliefs are abstract, fanciful beliefs that have nothing to do with an extant reality, an extant embodiment, and thus, are irrational. Making references to "godly or "god-like" "entities" and "nonhuman" or "subhuman" "entities" reflects the range of racist afflictions already described. How extensive these psychological impairments are depends on how racist racists are. Racists vary in their racism and racist afflictions, and thus fit into various racist psychological types with shades of differences in between.

Black people have dealt historically with the generality and the specificity of White racist psychologies. Distinguishing differences among racists has always been a survival mechanism, a social tool, and a political device. For example, the blatant racist had to be understood and dealt with differently from the subtle racist. Different racist types could exist in the same family, which Blacks have had to relate to, also.

Black conservative intellectuals, like the ones mentioned earlier, or individuals such as the titular head of them, Thomas Sowell, or Black conservative scholars such as Walter Williams, John McWhorter, Clarence Walker, and Anne Wortham and journalists such as Armstrong Williams and Joseph Perkins, are not the only headline-grabbers for failing to understand racism in a significant manner or racism's impact on the White perpetrators, and who even refuse to undertake such an investigation or analysis. Most Black intellectuals share space on this odious marquee. A number share the latter in the peculiar manner of not wanting to talk about racism or race at all, rather they prefer to focus on social class or the topic of "underclass" or gender. But this is delusional thinking as well, because they will be talking about *Black* or *black* social classes, *Black* or *black* underclasses, or *Black* or *black* genders.

WHAT RACISM IS AND WHAT IT ISN'T

It can be immediately said that racism is a general phenomenon that can exhibit numerous specific forms. This is what Du Bois clearly discerned in the late nineteenth century. Upon comparing the treatment of Blacks in America and Jews in Germany, which he observed when he was a student there in the early 1890s, he saw similar thoughts, beliefs, and practices being implemented. He carried that understanding much further when he noted that Blacks, white men, white women, and those viewed as being in a lower social class, could be viewed and treated in racist terms. In a speech in 1912 before a white women's group, he reflected this understanding when he said, "if democracy tries to exclude women or Negroes or the poor or any class because of *innate characteristics* [italics mine] which do not interfere with intelligence then that democracy cripples itself and belies its name."[19]

Du Bois made public statements like these off and on throughout the twentieth century. They were based on his comparative observations, which showed him that racism was not the same as race, was not even necessarily related to it. But most of his writing on racism focused on its implementation through the vehicle of race, as it was defined by him as a way in which whites related to a race in a racist manner. His remarks in 1953 (after visiting the Warsaw ghetto) showed that he retained his understanding of what racism was: namely, a general and specific phenomenon with the specific forms capable of being numerous: "No, the race problem in which I was interested cut across lines of color and physique and belief and status and was a matter of cultural patterns, perverted teaching and human hate and prejudice, which reached all sorts of people and caused endless evil to all men."[20]

Du Bois did not have the concept of racism to work with over the many years that he wrote on the subject. He became aware of it in 1939, as revealed in his journal *Phylon*, but he did not make much use of it for the remainder of his life. He mainly used the concepts of race and racial prejudice, or race and racial caste, or white supremacy. He did not have–did not endeavor to devise–different names for the different forms of racism that he observed and even wrote about, such as maleism, racism that alleges the innate superiority of men, and sexism, or maleism/sexism, which he regarded as the earliest human racist belief. Neither did he have the concept of ebonicism, but he did write and speak on the concept of ebonicism under the concept of race prejudice and similar concepts. These were the same concepts he used to describe White racism towards the Chinese and Japanese, which I call *xanthicism*.

A retort could be made that I am using the concept of racism too elastically, taking the meaning out of it. I would respond that I am putting understanding and meaning into it. A reason that the reader may be unable to perceive this is because he or she believes that racism and race are the same or that racism is associated exclusively with race. Du Bois wrote on racism associated with race for eighty years, but he still knew that racism and race were not the same things and that racism could take many specific forms. This is because racism has its own ontology and ontological basis, its own metaphysical basis, that allows for multiple forms. Du Bois did not use this kind of terminology, but this was the kind of deep, original, and sophisticated writing he did on racism.

There have been others who have recognized that racism and race were not the same things, and that the former could have multiple faces. Jean-Paul Sartre alluded to White supremacy in his writings, which he used as a term to speak of the racist beliefs that white colonizers had for themselves in Africa, as well as the racist beliefs that they had towards black Africans. He also spoke of anti-Semitism, (which I refer to and regard as *anti-Jewism* because Arabs are Semites, and they are not anti-Semitic). The social psychologist Gordon Allport also recognized the multiple faces of racism. He subsumed racism under two different labels: "race prejudice" and "ethnocentrism,"[21] the latter an unfortunate choice of words, because ethnocentrism carries the meaning of loving one's own people, which can be done without any overtures to racism. Allport was incorrect to equate ethnocentricism with racism, as racism is about non-existent alleged "innate" "superior" and "inferior" "attributes" that are a-historical and are not bounded by time, culture or social life, as is ethnocentrism. The white feminist and psychologist Kate Millet also analyzed the general, specific, and thus, multiple character of racism in her book *Sexual Politics*, published in 1971. She wrote that Blacks and white women were associated with "inferior intelligence, and instinctual or sensual gratification, and [an] emotional nature both primitive and childlike." She also noted that they were described as people who were content "with their own lot which is...a proof of its appropriateness."[22] Five years later, white feminist Marlene Dixon made similar comments when she stated, "the very stereotypes that express the society's belief in the biological inferiority of women recall the images to justify the oppression of Blacks.... The fact that 'racism' has been practiced against many groups other than Blacks has been pushed into the background."[23] Dixon was not the only feminist to say such, the English feminist Floya Anthias wrote, "racism cannot be limited to the experience of black people but has taken different forms in relation to the Irish, the Jews, the gypsies...as well as other 'white minorities'."[24]

What Anthias, Dixon, Millett, Allport, Sartre, and Du Bois were saying is that racists can seek to treat any group of people or individuals in that group in a racist manner. All it takes is to pick out a group, devise a set of racist beliefs about it, and thus create an abstract, fanciful, non-existent "race" with the "inherent" "attributes" of a "superior" or "inferior" kind. Afterwards, one then arbitrarily invests this "race" and its "attributes" in a real group and regard them to be synonymous with the actual embodiments of that group or its individual members. These "attributes" then "determine" the groups thoughts and external behavior.

There are some Black intellectuals who are beginning to see the multiple character of racism, its metaphysical ontological basis that makes it possible to devise specific racist beliefs. Philosopher Naomi Zack is one of them. Zack has perceived similarities between racism and sexism and implies her belief in a metaphysical foundation to both concepts.[25] The way Black or black intellectuals usually indicate their understanding of a racist metaphysic, and the multiple racisms predicated on it, is by referring to two broad forms of racism: "biological racism" and "cultural racism." This, however, represents a misunderstanding of the phenomenon of racism and a racist metaphysic.

There is no such thing as biological racism. This is simply the late nineteenth and early twentieth century White racist "biological determinism" that was discussed previously. Racist beliefs, as a manifestation of the distinctiveness of the mephitic phenomenon, do not have to be based on any extant reality that could be used to devise a racist fantasy, such as the racist fantasy that white skin denotes intelligence, and black skin denotes criminality. Obviously, human skin does not have these kinds of determinant capabilities. But racists concoct racist fantasies at will. This is shown clearly by Hitler's anti-Jewish racist beliefs:

> Jews are small.... Their dress is un-clean, their appearance generally unheroic...they are inferior being[s], vampires, with poisonous fangs. The Jew is a garbage separator, splashing filth on the face of humanity. He is a scribbler-who poisons men's souls like germ carriers of the worst sort.... The...Jews are a race of dialectical liars; a people which live only for this earth; the great masters of the lie...a world hydra, a horde of rats...the Jew is a *parasite* in the body of other peoples...a sponger like a noxious bacillus keeps spreading as soon as a favorite medium invites him in.[26]

Whites in America have made similar remarks like these about Black people, as the content of their ebonicistic racist beliefs and many similar ebonicistic racist narratives show. What this kind of thinking and writing demonstrates is that race is not even a significant consideration. Hitler, and the Jews he oppressed and extinguished, were of the same white race. Further, most of the racist depictions or alleged traits attributed to Jews had nothing to do with any form of humanity: "poisonous fangs," "vampires," "world hydra," "a horde of rats" a "parasite" and "a noxious bacillus." Racists are about viewing themselves and other people as not being human beings and relating to these fantasies as if they were actual representations of actual human beings. To relate to themselves as if they were "godly" or "godlike" and their victims as if they were "nonhuman" or "subhuman," to be able to rationalize and justify their domination, control, and exploitation of them in a myriad of ways is the behavior of racists. Clearly, a racist could care less about a group's or individual's race. They are capable of treating any race (even their own), any ethnic group, any gender group, any social class, or any age group as if they were "nonhuman," or "subhuman" or "Non-other."

The concept of "cultural racism" has no extant representation, as it is without substance, just as "biological racism" is without substance. Black and black intellectuals will employ this concept even when they have not recognized the metaphysical basis of racism. William Julius Wilson made use of the phrase "cultural racism" in his 1973 book *Power, Racism*, and *Privilege.*[27] His point was to show that White racism had changed in America, from biological to cultural racism, which he said was not predicated on any biological attributes at all. Wilson remarked that his readers were not likely to think that he was talking about racism if it had no biological association.

Recently, the black English intellectual Paul Gilroy, who teaches at Yale University, and who for years has had some influence on some Black and black intellectuals in America, spoke to the matter of "cultural racism." He said that today's racism "frequently operates without any overt reference to either race itself or the biological notions of difference that still give the term its commonsense meaning. Before the rise of scientific racism in the nineteenth century, the term race did [double] duty for the term culture. No surprise then that in its postwar retreat from racism the term has once again acquired an explicitly cultural rather than biological...inflection."[28] Gilroy reiterated this view with additional arguments in his book *Against Race*[29] published a decade later.

My argument with Wilson and Gilroy is this: racism has not retreated in America in any of its forms; white supremacy/ebonicism, maleism/sexism, white supremacy/redicism (racism against Native Americans), bronzism (racism against the bronze people of Mexico and Central America) or other such forms. As seen earlier "scientific racism" was bogus science and a bogus field of study, but Gilroy refers to them as if they were both legitimate and knowledge-producing, as does the Black feminist Patricia Collins.[30] To say that people with "kinky hair" are criminals or that people with "white skin" are executive types, or that "thin lips" denote courage and that having a "broad nose" equals docility could hardly be called producing knowledge.

I wish to emphatically reiterate that racism has never had the form of biological racism. It is not the actual biological traits of human beings that determine thought, social behavior, or how one makes history, even though this is what racists believe and always tell themselves, which reflects the extent of their irrationality, pathology, immorality, and psychological compulsion. Racists "invest" abstract racist fantasies into actual biological attributes of a race, an ethnic group, a gender group or a social class, and it is these fanciful "investments" that are the alleged determinants of thought and social behavior.

Clearly, straight hair has nothing to do with being moral or brave. Black skin has nothing to do with a person or group with black skin being unproductive. Having a vagina does not make one incapable of being a politician or a scientist. Racists invest actual biological attributes with qualities and capabilities they do not have and could never have. Biological racism is just simply impossible, but "biological racism" can be a concept, an irrational, pathological, and immoral concept.

Since there is no biological racism it cannot be compared or contrasted to "cultural racism" (in the way that Wilson and Gilroy were using that term to speak of the shift in racist thinking in the United States and elsewhere). One of the ontological racist beliefs, as Du Bois discerned, was the alleged innate ability of the alleged superior people to produce sophisticated culture, or even civilization, and the alleged innate inability of the alleged inferior people to do so. This is the cultural argument related to racism that the thinkers alluded to did not apprehend. As said, and as discussed previously, racism is something that does not have to be associated with biology at all, anybody's biology, any kind of biology. But this is where the thinking is ingrained and stuck.

Book after book comes off the press repeating these old, inadequate understandings. There are Black and white scholars who feel they have advanced the study of racism by talking about race's relationship to urbanization, or race's relationship to nationalism, or race's relationship to globalization. There is no advancement if race is understood to be racism, and vice versa, and no advancement if racism is not understood for what it is, which is something that is rooted in a perverted metaphysic and ontology that can take numerous specific perverted forms.

But there is a legitimate way of associating culture with racism and using the concept of "cultural racism," although the latter would not be very helpful. All racist beliefs are cultural constructions and all racist practices are culturally laden, as well. But these understandings do not designate any specific form of racist belief or beliefs or any specific racist practice or practices. The shift in racism in America really amounts to a shift in the predominant method of racist expressions and racist practices towards subtlety, with respect to all specific forms of racism.

THE WHITE POSTMODERN ESCAPE FROM RACISM AND BLACK INTELLECTUAL ACQUIESCENCE

White postmodern thinkers have had an impact on the thinking of Black and black intellectuals about racism and race, which has continued to push both Black and black intellectuals away from understanding or even attempting to understand racism. I am speaking specifically about the impact of the phrase, "the social construction of race." This is a racist phrase, which Black and black intellectuals have yet to fathom. It is a device that white male postmodern thinkers devised to try to prove to others that they were not racists.

The shadow of Hitler and the Nazis still looms large in the Western world and there are many white men and white women, who do not want that shadow falling across them. They have come up with what they regard, consciously or unconsciously, as their shield and their means of proving that they are not racists, which really amounts to proving that they are. First they need a scapegoat: Hitler and the Nazis. They talk about the two as if Hitler and the Nazis invented anti-Jewism, racist oppression, and horrendous racist violence. To note, postmodern white intellectual, Elazar Barkin says, "The

Nazi regime has compelled us all to recognize the lethal potential of the concept of race and the horrendous consequences of its misuse. After World War II the painful recognition of what has been inflicted in the name of race led to the discrediting of racism in international politics and contributed to the decline and repudiation of scientific racism in intellectual discourse."[31]

The irrational, perverse, and immoral character of "scientific racism" was not enough to cast severe aspersions on it, or discredit it, when it was being employed to help promote White/Western colonial imperialism, or when it was abetting southern Whites in the United States to do vicious things to Black people, such as the 1899 burning of Sam Hose in Georgia. The killing was reported in the *New York Tribune*:

> In the presence of nearly 2,000 people, who sent aloft yells of defiance and shouts of joy, Sam Hose (a Negro who committed two of the basest acts known to crime) was burned at the stake in a public road, one and a half miles from here. Before the torch was applied to the pyre, the Negro was deprived of his ears, fingers and other portions of his body with surprising fortitude. Before the body was cool, it was cut to pieces, the bones were crushed into small bits and even the tree upon which the wretch met his fate was torn up and disposed of as souvenirs.
>
> The Negro's heart was cut in several pieces, as was also his liver. Those unable to obtain the ghastly relics directly, paid more fortunate possessors extravagant sums for them. Small pieces of bone went for 25 cents and a bit of liver, crisply cooked, for 10 cents.
>
> No indictments were ever found against any of the lynchers.[32]

In another incident, Walter White, Executive Director of the NAACP, witnessed and reported on the killing of Mary Turner for protesting her husband being lynched. He noted that:

> At the time she was lynched, Mary Turner was in her eighth month of pregnancy.... Her ankles were tied together and she was hung to the tree, head downward. Gasoline and oil from the automobiles were thrown on her clothing and while she writhed in agony and the mob howled in glee, a match was applied and her clothes burned from her person. When this had been done and while she was alive, a knife...used in splitting hogs, was taken and the woman's abdomen was cut open, the unborn babe falling from her womb to the ground. The infant, prematurely born, gave two feeble cries and then its head was crushed

by a member of the mob with his heel. Hundreds of bullets were then fired into the body of the woman, now mercifully dead, and the work was over.[33]

Could a case be made that racism, namely, white supremacy/ebonicism and its racist practices, both of which were implemented for centuries, had a serious impact on white people? Could a case be made that, in particular, it has had a serious impact on their internal make-up; how they thought, their ability to reason, to perceive, or to understand things, or their ability to empathize, sympathize, or to be humane? Any psychologist knows that persistent human behaviors like these produce incalculable psychological effects.

Elazar Barkin regarded the concept of race to be potentially lethal. Could that contention be proven by Black people in the United States who did not employ the concept of race to enslave, to segregate, to deny political and civil rights, nor to do violence to the white people who used it that way against them? Barkin clearly exaggerated the "painful recognition of what had been inflicted in the name of race," as black Africans and Asians, in their efforts to free themselves and their countries from White/Westerners, had to deal with it after the Jewish and Slavic holocausts and the Second World War. What's more, Black people spent two postwar decades fighting against a brutal racism in their struggle for liberation in America. Barkin's comments are self-serving and constitute an attempt to get away from and to cover up the Hitler-Nazi era, so that that shadow does not fall across white people. That shadow does not just fall across the Germans. It falls across white people and Western civilization, the producers of Hitler and the Nazis, whose antecedents go back to the late fifteenth century when Whites/Europeans inaugurated their pursuit of world domination and their ability to control and exploit people who were not white. That pursuit was marked by great violence and numerous instances of genocide.

The best way to keep the Hitler-Nazi shadow from falling, as many white male postmodern thinkers showed by their actions, was to deny that race existed, that it had any reality, that there could be anything called race. To deny the reality of race, they made use of language and with this language said that race was "socially constructed," meaning, that it did not exist. What existed was "race:" the idea, the notion, or the discourse or discourses about race, but not the reality itself. Thus with language, these white male intellectuals wiped out race and then took this irrational and illogical premise to its logical conclusion. If race did not exist, then there couldn't be racists. By extension, this meant that white people were not racists.

On the other hand, in a contradictory manner unknown to them, white male postmodern thinkers brought race back into reality. Postmodern thinkers object to criticism that says that they deny reality, that all that exists is language or language discourses. They do, in fact, say this and write this, but then sometimes contradict themselves and indicate that that reality does exist. This would mean that race would be an existent. However, postmodern thinkers, based on their philosophy that there is no reality other than language, are forced to deny any other manifestations of reality. They seek to meet the criticism against their position by the following, more elaborate argument. They say that all reality has to be defined, described, and discussed through language or discourse. The real issue for them, they say, is the discourse involved. The critical matter is to choose the appropriate discourse. But appropriate to what? It has to be the reality that the discourse presumably relates to, seeks to define, or elaborate. To focus attention only on the discourse is to focus attention only on language, and hence, is to deny a reality beyond language. But is not a discourse on a reality contingent upon such a reality? Is not a discourse on race contingent upon the reality of race? To say "no" is to say that discourses on race are just abstractions. But, this could be said about all postmodern discussions that follow the principle that it is the matter of choosing the appropriate discourse among discourses.

Reality exists beyond language or discourse, including a racial reality. Postmodernists cannot admit or accept this philosophically or logically. If they do admit it, then they are speaking or writing in a contradictory fashion. With regard to race, they don't want a contradiction, not with the Hitler-Nazi shadow looming so large. They rush to deny race. However, the real issue is not race. The Nazis did not develop racial theories; they developed racist theories. This is what most white male postmodern thinkers still don't know about Hitler and the Nazis, mainly because, like so many intellectuals in the Western world, they do not know the difference between race and racism. But they do know that racism is mephitic, that Hitler and the Nazis epitomized this vilest of human thought and social behavior. And they do not want to be associated in any way with these perpetrators. Thus, they deny race, say that it is "socially constructed," thereby finding a shield or an escape route from a racist-inundated history that produced them and Hitler and the Nazis before them. And they continue to make contributions to this continuing history, however extensive. Subtle contributions are still contributions, and they are contributions that keep blatant racists alive, functioning, and hopeful.

You would think that Black intellectuals would have taken white male postmodern intellectuals to task for denying race and confusing race with racism, for denying their own racism, for engaging in contradictory arguments, and for denying Black people their racial existence to be able to prevent any link that they and other white people might have to the great scourge of Western history and civilization. But most Black intellectuals did not pursue this line of thinking or criticism. Indeed, it was not anything that even crossed their minds to become a stimulus for thought or criticism. They looked upon white male postmodern thinkers as the new "wave of knowledge" or new "wave of light" in the Western world; apparently, or in actuality, thinking that their attack against "the dead old white men of Europe" and European-Enlightenment thinking, was a rejection of the white male intellectual, political, economic, and social ascendancy in the Western world and generally in the world itself. The thoughts and analyses of white male postmodern thinkers have made advances in various parts of the world and they have become what can be described as "the alive and young white men of Europe" writing the authoritative texts.

What so many Black intellectuals did, in an essentially unreflective manner, was to accept the white male postmodern idea that nothing existed beyond language and that all reality was "socially constructed." This meant accepting that reality existed only in the form of discourses or texts. They wholeheartedly accepted the postmodern argument that race was "socially constructed." For instance, the Black historian Barbara Fields denied that race was a biological reality and spoke, instead, of its "social construction" as a fabrication.[34] Philosopher Naomi Zack took the same stance.

Henry Louis Gates, Jr. regarded race as being "socially constructed" and warned Black and other American intellectuals about using the term: "our task is to utilize language more precisely, to rid ourselves of the dangers of careless usages of problematic terms which are drawn upon to limit and predetermine the lives and choices of human beings who are not 'white.'"[35] Gates's philosopher colleague, the black African Kwame Anthony Appiah,* who has had a significant impact on current Black and black intellectuals, categorically denied that race existed and regarded it as being "socially constructed." He even went so far as to come up with a very peculiar definition of a racist; that it is not a person who holds racist beliefs, but how he or she holds them. Appiah believes that a racist is a racist only if one "holds his or her prejudice in an ideological way, immunizing them from counter-argument."[36] Appiah sees racism as simply a set of beliefs, not beliefs that are abstract, fanciful, irrational, malignant, perverse, and that impair the mind and psychology of persons who utilize them over a lengthy period of time—at least to some degree.

The only "impairment" that Appiah can glean is when a racist becomes "stubborn" in his or her racist thinking and beliefs; that is, he or she is not able or is unwilling to recognize or listen to a "better" argument or presentation. Appiah is not seeing the perverted or deformed psychology helping to

*Appiah is currently at Princeton University.

produce this "stubbornness" and is talking about racism as if it were no different than talking about someone's beliefs about ice cream, or baseball versus football when racism is clearly about irrationality, pathology, perversion and immorality. It is heinous on the face of it.

Appiah is showing that he does not have much of a racist analysis and that he doesn't understand the phenomenon very well. He has slighted racist practices with his comments; indeed, he does not even mention racist practices, seeing the phenomenon only in ideational terms, minus its malodorous morphology. Thinking, believing, and acting as a racist over a lengthy period of time and in such a noxious manner over a lengthy period, i.e., years, even a lifetime, invests a racist with a racist psychology.

RACIST INTERIORITY

Racists can vary as psychological types but there is a common psychology that runs through all of them; a racist psychology that is part of the racist interior of the racist that affects their thinking methods, belief construction, beliefs adhered to, and social behavior. The racist psychology exhibits irrationality, compulsion, intolerance, a constricted conscience, a serious difficulty with introspection and a tendency to blame others. In addition, there are also feelings of guiltlessness, innocence, non-responsibility, and self-righteousness.

This psychological stance helps to engender, as well as perpetrate, compulsive denying and delusional thinking, rigid either-or or hierarchical thinking, fanciful thinking, and denigrating thinking. Racist psychology and the racist's way of thinking, both of which can vary among racists depending upon how racist they are, constitute the *racist interiority*. It is this interior reality that keeps him/her thinking, believing, and acting socially as a racist. Racists assure that history, a society, a region of a country, or a local community will be invested with a racist interiority that will seriously affect the way each area functions, and as a consequence, will become sources of investing a racist interiority in individuals born and raised in them as perpetual behavior.

Social conditions may change and a racist may find it difficult to act in a racist manner toward traditional victims, which has occurred with white racists in America, as well as maleist/sexist racists in the country. But the racist interiority is still there. It did not end just because laws or policies were written, or even enforced. Continued enforcement and changed conditions alters a racist psychology. That is why it is important to keep up the momentum against racism.

It is also important for another reason, an intact racist interiority is still functional and will seek expression. When unable to act against prior victims, racists will seek out other victims because the racist psychology or interiority requires that, compels it. The victims can be people normally not associated with racist treatment, such as the handicapped, the elderly, homosexuals, or certain religious groups. These groups and individuals in them will be treated in a racist manner, meaning, they will be treated as if they are "nonhuman" or "subhuman" or "Non-Other." This situation can be understood for the racism that it is when it is understood that racism is not necessarily about race. Racists are *anti-human being and anti-humanity*! Thus, *any group of people* or *any individual* can become a racist target and racist victim.

Years ago, a group of philosophers/social scientists, produced *The Authoritarian Personality*.[37] This book had its methodological flaws and received apt criticism, but also apt praise. The social psychologist Gordon Allport assimilated the concept and used it in his research on what he called "racial prejudice" and the "prejudiced personality," which he discussed in his book, *The Nature of Prejudice*. Other studies of the "authoritarian personality" were also produced at the time. Authoritarian psychological traits are: rigid hierarchical thinking, rigid either-or thinking, difficulty in thinking introspectively, stereotyped thinking, externalizing, or blaming others (and not one's self), scape-goating, projecting, strong self-righteousness, paranoia, and conspiratorial thinking. Authoritarian personality traits appear in racists and are part of the intellectual/psychological racist interiority of racists. These traits can be associated with any kind of significantly prejudiced, bigoted, or fanatical person. But prejudice, bigotry, and fanaticism are not necessarily associated with racism. One can be prejudiced against a certain sports team and prejudiced in favor of another. One can be a political or religious fanatic and a bigoted person might just be a person who is strongly opinionated and strongly intolerant of other thoughts or views. What distinguishes the racist from all of the above groups is that the racist is *anti-human being and anti-humanity*. He or she is someone who is compelled to deny and deprecate human status and humanity. This is a structured-in intellectual and psychological disposition. Authoritarian personality or psychological traits are associated with this disposition and the social behavior that comes from it. This means that racists are crippled intellectually and psychologically and engage in crippled, i.e., irrational, pathological, and immoral behavior.

Are they mentally ill? The Black psychiatrist, Dr. Alvin Pussaint, has argued that the "extreme racist" is mentally ill and should receive therapeutic help. He and other Black psychiatrists, for that matter, have been trying to get the white male dominated profession to do an intensive psychological investigation of white racists in America, but have had no success with their imploring. Dr. Pussaint is careful to talk about the "extreme racist" being mentally ill. Most racists are not extreme throughout their lifetime. But they, as all racists do, have within them the racist interiority to some functional degree, that is, a minimal amount of psychological impairment that cripples their thinking, their psychology, and social behavior. Racists do not always know when they are acting as racists, as this is characteristic behavior: just perpetrated and not reflected on. It usually takes the victim to point out to the racist when they are acting as racists and not realizing it. But racists sometimes know when they are acting as racists: when they consciously humiliate people, when they consciously discriminate against them, when they consciously avoid them, when they reject hearing anything positive about them, or when they do bodily harm to them.

The careless use of a "mental illness" label can be a serious liability, because it can function to feed and/or reinforce one of the strong delusional beliefs of racists: that they are innocent, guiltless, and not responsible and could work to support the strong delusional belief that they are "godly" or "god-like," incapable of thinking, believing, or acting in a wrong, evil, or unjust manner. However, if racists really believed this, would this make them mentally ill? Children engage in fanciful thinking for years, without always knowing the difference between their fantasies and the real world. But that does not make them mentally ill. People all across the globe believe in a supreme deity or in a life or world beyond the senses or death, but this does not make them mentally ill. Men are sent off to war to kill people, and when they do, this is not considered an expression of mental illness. These men know who they are, why they're killing, and what the consequences of all this can be. Racists, through rearing and the general socialization process, are invested with their intellectual/psychological racist interiority that exhibits a greater or lesser degree of intellectual and psychological impairment, i.e., deformity and pathology.

Those with the greater impairment/pathology might be diagnosed as psychopathic, aggressively antisocial, even violent and capable of hurting others. A psychopath is mentally impaired, not mentally ill. Psychopaths know when they are being aggressive towards people, when they are being socially abusive, when they are being violent toward them, when they hurt them, or kill them. This is also true of racist psychopaths. Indeed, such people often act in small groups, indicating the amount of thought, understanding, or even planning, involved in their executed behavior. Afterwards they reflect on it, applaud themselves, talk of the satisfaction they had derived from it, talk of how they "got away with it," and might even wax on about the consequences they would have suffered had they been caught. An individual psychopath, including an individual racist psychopath, could go through this kind of reflective process. This is not mental illness at work and certainly not insanity. It is an impaired mind and psychology at work. And as long as they exist, the behavior has a good chance of being repeated. In as much as there have been studies of "racial prejudice" "bigotry," "intolerance" or "ethnocentrism," it is almost unbelievable that anyone (Black, white, or other) writing or talking about racism, would not have at least the knowledge that there would be–as there would have to be–a certain psychology or psychodynamic associated with racism and racists.

REJECTING RACE AND ACCEPTING RACE AND PROMOTING CONFUSION

There are now Black and black intellectuals in America who strongly reject race, but who accept it in a strong manner as well. They do not accept it as a reality for themselves, but say other people accept this kind of reality for themselves. They believe that race exists and that they belong to a race. The Black and black intellectuals spoken of say that these are psychological and social realities that have to be taken into account when discussing the issue of race in America. Anthony Appiah spoke of this matter when he stated, "I have already declared myself very often on the question [of] whether I think there are races. I think there aren't. So it is important that I am clear that I also believe that understanding how people think about race remains important for these reasons, even though there aren't races."[38]

The black philosopher Charles Mills exhibits similar thinking, which amounts to rejecting race and accepting "race" not as a reality, but as an organizing and determinant belief that some people still have. He noted: "What needs to be shown–and what I try to show in this book [*Blackness Visible*]–is that room has to be made for race as both real and unreal: that race can be ontological without being biological, metaphysical without being physical, existential without being essential, shaping one's being without being in one's shape."[39] In effect, Mills is not referring to race at all in his book. Even when he uses the word race, he is not referring to that, but to "race," a make-believe thing. The purpose of his book, as strange as it sounds, was to try to make make-believe believable by devising a metaphilosophical basis for the make-believe, for "race."

Black sociologist Ron Taylor exhibits the same kind of thinking. In the journal *Race and Society*, which he edits, he wrote:

> In a thoroughly racialized society such as the United States, where race is deeply fused with power, cultural patterns, and social organizations, it is arguable whether dispensing with the concept (of race) will

significantly alter or disrupt well established perceptions of the "other" or attitudes and beliefs that sustain a racialized social order....

Moreover, despite its lack of scientific merit in the biological sense, race remains salient as a major source of personal and collective identity, a central category of recognition and self-representation.[40]

As said earlier, simultaneously denying and accepting the existence of race is beginning to be done by a number of Black and black intellectuals. But this thinking is *flight* thinking, *confused* thinking, and it is thinking that stems from White racist thinking. It is thinking that says that race does not exist, that it is "socially constructed," fabricated. White intellectuals no longer want to deal with racism. They are not only afraid of the Hitler-Nazi shadow, they are also afraid of their own racism being exposed. They do not want Black or black intellectuals investigating and disclosing the historical white male interest not to have their racism and that of other white people's racism exposed for other Americans to see, especially in its most vicious expressions in American history and life. Black intellectuals seemed to breathe a sigh of relief when witnessing white intellectuals not wanting the concept of race in their hands anymore, to abuse it with their racist beliefs. Of course, their game was to publicly try to deny that they were racists. This was not something they could do alone. They found help for their interests when William Julius Wilson came out with his book, *The Declining Significance of Race*.

In the typical way, Wilson used race and racism synonymously. In his book, he had said that White racism, i.e., white supremacy/ebonicism, had declined significantly in the American economy, but not elsewhere in American society. This was enough for white intellectuals and others seeking to escape being called racists. They publicly and widely claimed that he had said that racism had significantly declined in American society. Wilson was being used and he resented it and publicly said so.

But it did not have much impact on the people who had twisted his thoughts and had exploited him. Later, when they found they could not use Wilson easily, they found other Black intellectuals that they could. These became the Black conservatives, surrogate Black intellectuals, who took it as one of their major tasks to deny that racism was still a significant factor in American society and that it still had a determinant capability with respect to Blacks and their opportunities and successes in the country. To the surprise of these Whites, other Black intellectuals were of help to them, as well, helping them to hide their own racism, which they still practiced subtly. Their need to find Black surrogates to implement their plan was a reflection of their subtle racism.

Black conservatives denied that they were helping to foster subtle White racism in the country and the other Black intellectuals would not even give that idea a thought. They were against racism, said so publicly, and would even say that it continued as a strong force in the country. But they denied that they had anything to do with helping to keep it a strong reality that still negatively affected Black people. These Black intellectuals aided White racism when they did not point out that the concept "socially constructed" was being used in a racist manner. And that's probably because they simply were not that clear about it, or because they just did not want to deal with the concept of racism anymore. Of course, they never really dealt with the concept of racism anyway, although they thought they had with their concept of race.

The title of Wilson's book is *The Declining Significance of Race*, but race had not declined in America at all. The white race, black race, the yellow race, the bronze race (the lower Americas), and the red race all existed in the 1970s and still exist in America. What Wilson meant was that White racism had declined, but he hardly said anything about that phenomenon in his book. White people as racists and the impact of their racism on them, and through them, on American history and life, was a non-subject for Wilson. This could only be pleasing to white readers.

But Wilson, even as a sociologist, did not see his tragic, academic neglect. And that kind of neglect has been going on ever since, actually continuing the historical neglect of Black people not telling white people about how racism has affected them, and through them, the country. Black psychiatrist James Comer made the following comment about that in *Beyond Black and White*: "Blacks and whites have had a kind of secret pact over the years which has helped whites minimize their guilt and anxiety. Whites have said, 'Don't show me my white mind. Don't break down my defenses. Don't challenge the structure on which I base my identity. If you don't, I shall approve of you, I shall even open up a few token opportunities to you.'"[41] White men in America clearly still base their identity on a racist premise that interpenetrates white male gender, the white race, and social classes, and has them thinking that they are "godly" or "god-like," which their dominant position in American society reinforces for them. They want to hold on to the racist sense of who they are, which is more important to them than their racial identity, which does not carry any implication of any kind of "divinity" or "divine entitlement." White men generally do not distinguish their racist identity from their racial one, feeling them as being one in the same.

Black intellectuals could help them see that distinction and force them to deal with it. But they do not. They do not, for instance, ask why the concept of "social construction" is invariably used with respect to the black race and not the white race. The white males who developed and made the "social construction of race" a useable phrase wanted the focus to be on the black race (or other dark races). Not only did it deflect attention away from them (and also the fact that they were not using that concept in relationship to the white race), but it also preserved the historical practice of casting doubts on Black and black people, as to who they were, their authenticity, their integrity, their value, and even the nature and extent of their humanity.

The white postmodern thinkers have not cast doubts about the white race, and thus, about themselves and other white people. No white historian, a traditional or postmodern one, would ever cast doubts about George Washington, Thomas Jefferson, or Abraham Lincoln being white men, or any of the other American presidents. They would never say that there was not a white majority in the country (while there was still this reality). Nor would they say that the white race has not always stood in a hierarchical and dominating relationship to the black race and other races in the country. Indeed, this is what so-called "Whiteness Studies" are declaring these days; studies that purport to show how being white was critical to white people having status, power, rights, and opportunities in America. But what was really critical to these attainments was racism: the racism of the white people, their exercise of racist power, and their racist perversion and subversion of America's ideals and institutions. Whiteness Studies fail singularly in not dealing with the impact of racism on white people: negative intellectual, psychological, moral, and spiritual effects. They also fail to show how the racism of white people has affected the functioning of America. Whiteness Studies advocate Matthew Frye Jacobson recently wrote: "Racism no longer appears anomalous to the working of American democracy, but fundamental to it."[42]

Racism, which regards people to be "nonhumans" or "subhumans" or "Non-Others," which denies people human rights and political and civil rights, which socially segregates and excludes them, rather than integrating and including them, is undemocratic, or anti-democratic on the face of it. This is how white scholars in America readily describe countries that exhibit this kind of political behavior. But its exhibition here in America, especially against Black people, but other Americans as well, is called democratic political behavior and America is called a democracy. These same descriptions are found in Whiteness Studies.

White historians in the past, and such historians today, speak of the democracy of the "New South" of the late nineteenth and early twentieth centuries, when millions of Black people were returned to a new form of servitude, were disenfranchised, and subjected to horrendous public denigration and violence. Unbelievably, the South was called "democratic" during the 1950s and 1960s, when Blacks were engaged in a liberation struggle there and were attempting to bring democracy to the area, while Whites mobilized to thwart and suppress them.

While white men usually do not raise questions about the reality of the white race, they have not only succeeded in raising questions about the reality and existence of the black race and the nature of it, but have even gotten some Black and black intellectuals to deny that it even exists. In short, they have gotten them to act as surrogates, either willingly or inadvertently. And while Black or black intellectuals are preoccupied with this matter, they won't be too concerned about racism, what it is, or how the reality relates to and affects white people.

Because Black intellectuals will not deal with racism, as I have discussed it here, they are unable to tell when they have moved from a discussion of race to a discussion of racism. They do not see, in their writing and speaking, the transition that occurs. The black philosopher Lewis Gordon wrote the following in *Bad Faith and Antiblack Racism*: "By racism I mean the self-deceiving choice to believe...that one's own race is the only race qualified to be considered human." He also said, "How is it possible that human beings are able to regard some members of their species as fundamentally nonhuman?"[43] Talking about a race is one thing, talking about a "nonhuman" is another. Gordon did not perceive that he was dealing with two different matters.

Neither did the philosopher Charles Mills, when he stated:

> What is a (racial) "subperson...." What are its specific differentiae? A subperson is not an inanimate object, like a stone, which has... zero moral status. Nor is it simply a nonhuman animal.... Rather, the peculiar status of a sub-person is that it is an entity which, because of phenotype, seems human in some respects but not in others...who, though adult, is not fully a person.[44]

There is no such thing as a "subperson," or "nonhuman," or "subhuman," or "Non-Other." This is racist claptrap. But here is a black philosopher endeavoring to give reality or embodiment to this nonexistent thing, which is precisely what racists do, namely, they argue that the "nonhuman," or "subhuman" or "Non-Other" actually exists. Mills was, in fact, by trying to define and validate the "subperson," its status and characteristics, saying that the black race or Black people were "subpersons."

Mills does not regard what he calls "race" as being a "subperson" or "nonhuman" but he says it does not exist, except as an idea or notion in someone's mind and for him it is the mind of a black or Black person, by and large. Anthony Appiah and Ron Taylor also talk about "race" and also believe it does not exist, but accept its existence in someone's mind and again it is namely a black or Black person, or persons's minds. Mills calls "race" a metaphysical, ontological, and existential concept, meaning that "race" is real to people, meaningful to them, a motivation for their behavior and that it constitutes the necessary parameters of their social existence.

The Black philosopher Lucius Outlaw, Jr. argues differently. He insists that the black race is real and it is his interest to develop a Black philosophy based on this reality. This is in contrast to Charles Mills, who wishes to develop a philosophy based on the black "race" whose reality he does not accept. Outlaw rejects the concept of the "social construction" of race, and rejects trying to eliminate race by simply using language, or trying to substitute it with some other concept that seems palpable, but which would always be unstable because it would be astride the reality of race. Outlaw notes that:

> On the basis of a revised philosophical anthropology that draws on an enhanced social ontology mindful of social collectivities, then, perhaps those who philosophize would not mislead themselves in thinking that the elimination of antagonisms tied to invidious valorizations of raciality...can be facilitated by "lexical surgery" that removes "race" from usage and replaces it, instead, with references to, say, "communities of meaning," as offered by Kwame Anthony Appiah, since he claims there is no such thing as a race. It is as though something awkward or troublesome can be got rid of by the mere process of calling it by another name.[45]

A simpler argument to make, one which I believe is just as pertinent, is that those Black and black intellectuals who reject the reality of race and the reality of the black race continue to do so for faulty reasons that really condemn the behavior. The "social construction" argument is faulty. It is even phony in the way it is usually employed to make it appear that reality does not exist outside of a linguistic depiction or representation or a discourse about it existing. Is one really prepared to say that an elephant, a lion, and a rhinoceros do not exist, that they are just social constructions or linguistic depictions even as they walk on the Great Plains in Africa? Would one be prepared to say that a speeding car heading in one's direction was not really doing that, as if it were only some silly vision concocted with thought and words?

The truth about linguistic social construction is that it is something that human beings do naturally and all the time because they use language to classify, describe, define, to organize, and give meaning to objects or reality.

Things have existed in this world long before anyone gave a name, description, or meaning to them, such as lake, mountain, and sky. Language did not bring any of these things into existence. It just helped to clarify and to distinguish them from one another.

THE SCIENTIFIC VIEW OF RACE

Race existed long before it received a name. Thus, to reject race on the basis of the "social construction" argument is inappropriate, and even more so if one is doing this to help white men preserve racism. Most Black or black intellectuals who reject race and who say that it does not exist argue that a race has to be pure: that all the biological characteristics of a race have to be distributed in the same amount and intensity to all the members of the race. Otherwise the race is "impure" and an impure race cannot be accepted as a race by anyone.

This is Appiah's chief objection to race and the existence of the black race. He has had influence on some Black intellectuals. One of them is philosopher Naomi Zack who wrote, "Anthony Appiah has done seminal philosophical work in this area, and I found his work extremely helpful when I started. There is no set of... necessary and sufficient traits that all members of any race have in common." She also confidently remarked that biologists rejected the reality of race because, "biologists don't have such criteria. Race doesn't exist in biology."[46]

David Lionel Smith also rejected race in his essay in *The House that Race Built*. He said that no one has been able to come up with a definitive, even an adequate, definition of what it or blackness means. Smith wrote, "Black people can have white skin, blue eyes, and naturally straight hair; they can be half, three-quarters, seven-eighths, or more, white; they can even deny or not know that they are black. Claim what they will or look as they may, they are still by law and custom black."[47] Smith's argument is clearly an inappropriate reason for rejecting the concept and reality of race. He has employed extremes to obscure, and to invalidate, what is commonly understood. And clearly, law and custom are one thing; race is quite another.

Just as clearly, most Black people do not have white skin, blue eyes, and straight hair. This sounds like a caricatured description of white people, which is a strange description to use to describe the racial features of Black people. Most Black people have skin color that in no way could be regarded as being white. While most Black people are not literally black, some are. Most Blacks show a variation within the range of black: blackish-brown, light brown and yellowish-brown. One would find this range of black racial variation in Africa.

Black Africans who came here as slaves showed racial variation from black to light brown. While the word "black" cannot be used literally to describe most Black people in America (anymore than the word white can be used literally to describe white people, inasmuch as many are pinkish and brownish in skin color), it is a word that denotes a starting point, an origin, when the black race was itself black.

But as it evolved and spread across geographical areas, first in Africa, and then elsewhere, the blackness began to shade into variations on that color (just like whiteness, redness, and yellowness would ultimately undergo variation). So in a significant way the words black, white, red, and yellow, for instance, have historical reality and significance and also have a continuing biological presence that can be traced to an original biological source. For instance, one would not be able to trace yellow from a biological source of red or red from a biological source of white. Many things in reality cannot be described with precise, unambiguous language. What, for instance, is the precise definition of air, or intelligence, or talent? What is the precise definition of a tree, or a rock, or a dog, when we know that there are various definitions of each? But we are not likely to mistake a tree for a dog, or a cat for a cow, or a house for a car; this shows that something exists beyond language. There are enough discernable characteristics about each of these realities that identify each, despite variation within and marks each from other realities.

Race is like this. The first to say so are biologists, who, when not promoting some racist agenda or some postmodern linguistic/social construction agenda, say that a race is not a pure biological reality. They argue that pureness is not required for the designation of race. In the late nineteenth century the anthropologist Franz Boas said that races varied within but also exhibited racial characteristics that distinguished them from other races. Du Bois said the same in his book *The Negro* in 1915 when he stated, "today we realize that there are no hard and fast racial types among men. Race is a dynamic and not a static conception, and the typical races are continually changing and developing and amalgamating and differentiating. In this book then, we are studying the history of the darker part of the human family, which is separated from the rest of mankind by no absolute physical line,"[48] but by some distinguishable biological differences. Du Bois even discussed the racial variation among black Africans.

The Black biologist Richard Goldsby wrote the following in 1971: "Members of the same race have more of their hereditary components in common with each other than with members of different breeding populations. This does not mean that all members of the same race are alike. There is enormous variation within as well as between racial groups."[49] That same year biologist Richard Osborne wrote, "there has never been such a thing as a 'pure' race. Race formation and breakdown is a dynamic process subject to constant change."[50] And Zoologist L. C. Dunn wrote several years later:

> This then is the sense in which the word race may have a valid biological meaning. A race, in short, is a group of related inter-marrying individuals, a population, which differs from other populations in the relative commonness of certain hereditary traits. It is true that a definition like this leaves a good deal of latitude in deciding how big or how small a race may be, that is, how many people should be included in it, and also in deciding how many races we shall recognize. These last are matters of convenience rather than of primary importance. What is important is to recognize that races, biologically, differ in relative rather than in absolute ways.[51]

Biologist James King wrote in the early 1980s: "To a biologist the concept of race is an attempt to describe the manner in which individual variation within and between populations is related to hereditary, development, and environment."[52] The anthropologist Milford Wolpoff wrote a decade later: "Defined as a geographic form of human variation race is a useful concept. And there are, in fact, unique sets of physical features that set races apart."[53] Geneticist Michael J. Bamsha and science writer Steven E. Olsen recently wrote in *Scientific American* that "discreet" or pure races did not exist, but that "Polymorphisms" (i.e., tiny variations in DNA) that occur at different frequencies around the world can, however, be used to sort people roughly into groups.[54] Anthropologist Vincent Sarich and science writer Frank Miele presented a similar argument, based on genetic factors, in their recent book *Race: The Reality of Human Differences*.[55]

Three anthropologists, a zoologist, two biologists, two science writers, and a historian have confirmed the existence of race and human races. What more do Black or black intellectuals need? What is discerned about these intellectuals is that they even reject the scientific understanding of race! Ron Taylor was not just speaking for himself, but was speaking representationally when he wrote: "Moreover, despite its lack of scientific merit in the biological sense, race remains...." Charles Mills, Anthony Appiah, and Naomi Zack rejected the scientific understanding of race, as did Adolph Reed, Jr., who said:

> There is a long history of spurious claims about differences in racial biology. However, racial categories possess no real genetic legitimacy. This underscores their biological irrationality as a system of classifying people into groups. Geneticists recognize the range of variation within

a given "racial" population is usually greater than the range between any two populations. This seriously undermines the notion that racial groups are clearly separated, homogenous populations that they can be easily generalized about. Still researchers who work with racially defined sample populations tend to presume that what are merely political and sociological categories are also populations with biological integrity.[56]

The scholars and writers I have quoted confined themselves strictly to biology and gave that kind of explanation about race, although Du Bois carried the matter further, which I will speak to momentarily. Reed's conception of race, as easily discerned, is that it has to be something "pure" or has to be "clearly...homogeneous populations." White "scientific racists" talked like this, and so did absolutist metaphysical philosophers, all the way back to the eighteenth century when the concept of biological race took hold. But metaphysical philosophers were engaged in fanciful thinking about absolute or "pure" races and that fanciful thinking was their white supremacist/ebonicistic racist thinking, which was the ontological foundation of their metaphysical thinking, i.e., the metaphysical racist ontology, that interpenetrated their non-racial thinking and that led them to talk of the absolute or "pure" and "superior" white race and the absolute or "pure" and "inferior" black race.

Reed and other Black intellectuals reject the racist and the absolutist metaphysical philosopher's view of race, which were actually the same view because racism was determinant of the latter's conception of an absolute or pure race. An absolute or pure race is a fantasy. Reed and other Black intellectuals reject the concept of a "pure" race, less because it is a racist concept, but because they believe that they are being scientific in doing so. Scientists do, in fact, reject an absolute or pure race, but they still scientifically validate race. They see it as a biological reality, and thus, determined by biology. But they do not regard the behavior of races to be biologically determined, which racists argue. White postmodern thinkers and their Black or black adherents fail to see this distinction. They argue that if a race is biologically determined, its behavior has to be as well. Scientists reject this racist argument altogether and say that history, culture, and social life are the primary determinants of racial behavior. In addition to seeing race as a biological reality, they also see it as an internal, varied, biological reality and one that also varies, *vis-à-vis* other races. Scientists also see it as an in-marrying and in-breeding population, as having a geographical range that aids variation, as being large or small in size, and also as being capable of sub-dividing into ethnic groups that may well show racial and cultural variation.

The Inadequacy of "Critical Race Theory" and the "Racialization Concept"

The new so-called "critical race theorists" and "critical race theory" contribute confusion more than anything else to America's racist situation. These new theorists are mainly in the field of jurisprudence, but they have managed to attract adherents among scholars, educators, journalists, and others. The Black jurist and intellectual Derrick Bell is regarded as being the "father" of the new theory and argues that race (by which he means racism), would always exist in America. Most critical race theorists are not this pessimistic. In fact, more than their intellectual leader and others in society, they are interested in taking race beyond law and political and civil rights to focus on its implementation in a broad societal manner in the country. This is not as new a position as these people think, as Black people have always known, and have always complained about white people oppressing or restricting them in a societal manner. However, unlike the new theorists, they concentrated on political and civil rights, because they could be used as a battering ram against this behavior.

But the critical race theorists come to the table with the same limited view of what the real situation is in America: they say race, when they clearly mean racism. And they show the same lack of understanding that race and racism are not the same things and never can be. They do not understand that racism is a distinctive phenomenon that can take many forms, with respect to race, but with respect to other human groupings as well. Like others, critical race theorists do not deal well with race itself. Like others, they deny it or say that it is "socially constructed," with both views predicated on the false idea that a race has to be pure to be a race. But they also show great confusion about race, because they deny that it exists, while simultaneously arguing that it does exist. It is the same kind of confusion that other people show.

Richard Delgado, one of the leaders of critical race theory and Jean Stefancic, said the following in their book presented as an introduction to critical race theory:

> People with common origins share certain physical traits, of course, such as skin color, physique and hair texture. But these attributes are only an extremely small portion of their genetic endowment, are dwarfed by that which we have in common and have little or nothing to do with distinctly human, higher-order traits, such as personality, intelligence, and moral behavior. That society frequently chooses to ignore these scientific facts, creates races and endows them with pseudo-permanent characteristics, is of great interest to critical race theory.[57]

These comments exhibit great confusion and a great fear of racism itself. Prior to these remarks, the authors, joining with the postmodernists, said that race was "socially constructed," implying that it was not real and implicitly suggesting that a race had to be pure to be a race. But in the quoted remarks they accept the reality of race and even describe some of its features. Still later, they seek to deny the race they accepted by talking against racial features being permanent. Racial features can be determined by science, as they have been. But the authors do not attribute their reference to racial features to science. They, in effect, deny that science can depict such features because they deny that the racial features they described are scientific facts. What else could they be if they are described as actual biological features? And there was their efforts to discredit race by saying racial features were not permanent. Two things are involved here. The first is that the permanent-feature notion is predicated on the belief that a race has to be pure to be a race. As has been said by scientists, a race is varied within and without. Thus, the critical race theorists accept a racist view of race, while denying that they do or not knowing that they do, while rejecting a scientific view, which they employ at the same time.

But there is a comment to be made further about the "permanent feature" argument. The variation of racial features is an argument against the notion that an entire race has the same racial features that are permanent. But over a person's lifetime, racial features are permanent in individual members of a race. A black person with black skin and kinky hair will have these racial features their entire existence. A white person with white skin and straight hair will have these racial features throughout their lives. These features are not minor matters, certainly not to the people who have them, because they are, along with other racial features, defining attributes, i.e., their racial identity and membership in a racial group.

The critical race theorists are against a racial identity. They see it erroneously as a racist identity; that is, an identity that is imposed without by racists. But no racist gives a black person black skin or kinky hair. Black mothers and fathers and being born in the black racial species does this. What the racist does, and certainly has done, has been to criticize, demean, and reject these features. But the critical race theorists do the same. They are subtler about it, and for a number of the white critical race theorists, their position is an expression of subtle racism. It is specifically a subtle expression of racist *invisibilizing*. Postmodernists reject universalizing or universal characteristics and emphasize plurality, diversity, and the particular. Distinctive racial characteristics fall under these labels. Delgado and Stefancic refer to racial plurality or diversity as specific racial features, but then pour opprobrium on the idea by referring to these features by the word "dwarfed," as if they were not important and should not be considered as such. What was more important were the things that different races (their implicit argument) had in common.

Racial features are aspects of a person's humanity. Saying that they are not important or that they should not be regarded as such, is a deprecation of part of that person's humanity. This is what racists do; they invisibilize people. Many critical race theorists also do this, up to a point anyway, when they obscure or deprecate, play down or reject, aspects of a person's humanity. In the case of Black or black people, they are asking that they give up being Black or black and just be Americans or just *be* human beings. But the critical race theorists are not usually on record asking white people to give up being White or white. Indeed, critical race theory is not oriented to white people in a significant way. Meaning that when they say race is "socially constructed," they are not referring to white people. They do not talk about white racial features being "dwarfed" by common traits, mainly because the white racial characteristics are the common attributes that are subtly being referred to, not American cultural traits.

White critical race theorists are a new version of an old group in America: white liberals. Like other white liberals from America's history, they are primarily interested in protecting and promoting the power, status, and interests of white people. This is reflected in their inability or great difficulty in accepting a Black or black humanity. They feel, as white liberals have and continue to feel, that white people can relate better to Black or black people if they are more like white people, culturally and socially. They feel that white people would be more inclined to try to help Blacks or other black people if this were the case. Whether understood or not, this would be accepting White domination, White determination, and thus, White racism. It is clearly something that Black and black people have to reject in America. They are entitled by America's ideals to have rights, equality, opportunities, justice, and freedom, as Black and black people and also as Americans, just as white people are entitled to have them as white and White people and also as Americans.

There is one other significant confused way of looking at race in this country, and elsewhere, for that matter. This is the situation of those who use the words *racialized* or *racialization* (or racialised or racialisation) to relate to the subject of race. This is done more by European intellectuals and black West Indian or black African intellectuals, than by Black intellectuals and their white counterparts in America. The confusion centers in using the terms racialized or racialization to refer to race and to racism, usually the latter term. Instead of saying racism, intellectuals of various kinds say racialized. The racialized proponents regard race and racism to be the same thing, or think that racism is associated only with race; and thus, racialized or racialization are used and understood in this very narrow and erroneous manner, which prevents them from seeing that racism is not dependent upon or necessarily associated with race.

There are those who use the concept racialized and who also say that race is "socially constructed," adding further confusion and inaccuracy to their discourse. In particular, there are some Jewish scholars, and other kinds of Jewish intellectuals, who use the terms racialized and racialization to try to account for the racist treatment of Jews. They themselves think of Jews being white, but can document that they have been and continue to be treated as if they were the same as black or other dark racial peoples, or as if some how they were of the black, or some other dark, race. But when Jewish scholars and others use the terms racialized or racialization to describe the treatment of Jews, they are misusing terms. If the Jews are white, they are already *racialized*; that is, they are of the white race. And if they were of the black race or yellow race, or any other dark race, they would also be racialized.

If racialized is employed as a term to mean racism, this, too, is a misapplication that is inappropriate because it makes this understanding of racism synonymous with race, and suggests, by implication, that white people cannot be treated in a racist manner or that white people will not treat other white people in such a manner unless they invest them with black or "dark" racial features. Some white Germans, white Poles, white Romanians, white Lithuanians, and other white Eastern European people exterminated white Jews during the Second World War and they did it strongly guided by anti-Jewish racist beliefs. This phrase automatically covers Jews being treated in a racist manner, whether it is done by white people or people of different races. However, racism is not fundamentally about race. It's about people, racists, being anti-human being and anti-humanity, and seeking to treat people, any people they wish to target, by this noxious intellectual/psychological disposition.

BLACK INTELLECTUAL FEAR OF DEALING WITH RACISM

Many Black and black intellectuals in America today show a fear of racism and race as subjects to deal with, to explain to people, to help them understand them. This fear extends to even denying that race exists, to proclaiming that it is a "social construction" or to proclaiming that it is a fanciful fabrication. This fear exudes from individuals, whatever the exact nature of it, who are discernibly black racially or who clearly have black racialness in them, such as Ron Taylor, Charles Mills, Henry Louis Gates, Jr. Tommy Lott, Barbara Fields, Paul Gilroy, Hazel Carby, Lewis Gordon, Orlando Patterson, and Anthony Appiah. Black and black intellectuals deny that race exists, or accept that it does, and then these intellectuals beat up on each other about the matter. Not having a clear idea of what race is also sparks the arguments.

Anthony Appiah claimed that Du Bois provided a "historical-social" definition of race, not a biological one, which was a distortion, and also an "invention." Du Bois's prestige among Black intellectuals, he argued, has prevented them from seeing his misrepresentation and "social construction," but Appiah has drawn their attention to it in his book *In My Father's House*,[58] and in other writings. Black philosopher Tommy Lott did not object to Du Bois's historical-social definition in his book *The Invention of Race*, but he was off-base trying to explain what it meant and what the significance of it was. As noted previously, Du Bois had said: "In this little book, then, we are studying the history of the darker part of the human family, which is separated from the rest of mankind by no absolute physical line, but which nevertheless forms, as a mass, a social group distinct in history, appearance, and to some extent, in spiritual gift." Tommy Lott commented:

> Some of Du Bois's readers have rejected his socio-historical definition of race in favor of a definition based on physical differences. What Du Bois's detractors tend to overlook, however, is the fact that his definition does not deny the obvious physical differences that constitute race, nor does his discussion of race display any special commitment to the socio-historical view he sets forth. A close reading will reveal that he meant only to deny the viability of a strictly biological account of race.[59]

And further added: "If we consider Du Bois's socio-historical definition of race, along with his belief that African Americans have a special mission, his rejection of biological essentialism and his failure to make use of the idea of African cultural retentions, begin to appear quite troublesome. For as Appiah has keenly observed, his talk of Pan-Negroism requires that African Americans and Africans share something in common other than the oppression by whites."[58] Du Bois would be troublesome for anyone who looked upon race as something that had to be pure and who believed that races did not exist. Lott is indicted on both counts because he sees race as "invention."

Du Bois, indeed, saw race as biology, and on this basis, he saw definite connections between Black Americans, black West-Indians, and black Africans, particularly when he was promoting "Pan-Africanism" in the early twentieth century. But Du Bois saw race in another way, that Appiah, Lott, and many other Black and black intellectuals would not be able to see because they do not believe that actual races exist. Du Bois did believe that races exist and he believed a race was a group of people. As a people, they did what people did: they made history, constructed culture and a social life, and made efforts, as a people, to survive into the future. Du Bois's definition of race was biological-social-historical, or what I would call, for him, *racenicity*. Du Bois did not deal much with ethnicity, mainly because he thought of Black people in America as a racial group and never got around to regarding them as an ethnic group. That would have been viewing Black people far beyond how they viewed themselves and were viewed in America.

Only in very recent years has there been any significant talk of Blacks in America being an ethnic group, an ethnic group of the black race, which still pales before the view of Blacks as a racial group and racial community. Du Bois knew about the reality of ethnicity. He referred to it in his book, *The Negro*, in 1915, but he did not make much use of it. Nor did he later make much use of the concept of racism, although he knew about that too, and used it occasionally. He did not have a concept of racenicity, but that was the conceptualization, in fact, that he employed for decades writing about Black people in the United States: their history, culture, and social life. These things would come under my concept of Blackcentricity. Blackcentricity has the social focus of ethnicity–Black ethnicity–rather than race, or the black race.

Tommy Lott wrote: "When Du Bois defines race in terms of socio-historical, rather than biological, or physical, criteria, he seems to have blurred an important distinction between race and ethnicity, where the former is understood to refer to biological characteristics and the latter refers chiefly to cultural characeristics."[61] Du Bois argued that races *and* ethnic groups produced culture. It is clear that Lott did not closely read what Du Bois said in *The Negro*, where he talked about the black race being spread across the African continent and being subdivided into ethnic groups, actually using the word "ethnic," but mainly the word "tribe;" and discussed how these tribes, which today would be called ethnic groups, devised their own culture. Thus, Du Bois saw not only racial variation among black people spread over the entire continent in Africa, which he discussed on the page prior to his biological-social-historical definition of race, i.e., the black race making history and producing culture and social life, but he also saw ethnic variation in the race, with ethnic groups doing the same things.

Du Bois looked at the black race in a holistic manner, seeing multiple sides of it. He did not transfer this kind of understanding to America, most likely, because most black people in the country were Black people, descendants of the original black African slaves and their eventual Black progeny, and also because other black people, black Africans, and black West Indians, were regarded as Black people and were required to make Black history with them. Du Bois saw Blacks as a racial group that made history and that produced culture and a social life, which I call racenicity. But this concept could have been used to help bring understanding to why Du Bois talked of different races making history, having different physical appearances, and contributing something different or unique to history.

It is time for Black thought to go beyond a concentrated focus on race and concentrate on ethnicity, Black ethnicity. Race would still be a factor, as an ethnic group shows racial features. Light-skinned Blacks would still be Black ethnically, culturally, and socially. Black people are an ethnic group of the black race in America, which also exhibits other ethnic groups such as Jamaicans, Barbadians, Haitians, Trinidadians, Nigerians, Kenyans, South Africans and Cape Verdeans. Manning Marable has noted this reality, although not very clearly, when he stated:

> Since so many Americans view the world through the prism of permanent racial categories it is difficult to convey the idea that racially different ethnic groups have roughly the same "racial identity" imposed on them. For example although native-born African-Americans, Trinidadians, Haitians, Nigerians and Afro-Brazilians would all be termed "black" on the streets of New York City, they would have remarkably little in common in terms of language, culture, ethnic traditions, rituals and religious affiliations. Yet they are all "black" racially, in the sense that they will share many of the pitfalls and prejudices built into the institutional arrangements of the established social order for those defined as "black."[62]

Marable is an intense, ideological Marxist socialist who believes that social class is the only real social reality or social formation and who believes that a class analysis is the only methodology to provide a critical evaluation of the history and life of Blacks and America. He talks a lot about the White racist practices against Blacks, but says little and seems to know little, which is typical of Black intellectuals, about what racism itself is, and how it impacts Whites, and through them, America and Blacks. This means that he does not have a racist analysis or not a very strong racial analysis, and virtually no ethnic group analysis, although he seems to be developing a gender analysis-all of which are critically necessary to evaluating Blacks and America.

On top of this, Marable does not believe that race exists, not even the black race, as indicated by his choice to put the word black in quotes. He defines black, not by race at all, but by the suppressive conditions that groups of black people live under in America, and their specious identification as being "black." Thus, to him, race is symbolic. It seems incredible that Marable feels outraged by the fact that all the groups be identified have a "racial identity," which, indeed, he says was imposed on them. The groups he mentioned have the same racial identity, in a general way, because they are all from the same black race! While Marable saw different ethnic groups of black people in America, he did not really see, neither did he really argue, that the ethnic groups were of the black race and that they all had the same general racial component. This, he could not have done because he does not believe that race exists. This is like saying that the white race does not exist in America, which Marable would reject, because he writes about the white race in all of his books. Never once, that I have discerned, has he cast doubt on or rejected the existence of the white race in America. He talks about white people in Europe. He even talks about black people in Africa. But in thinking and talking about black people in America, he not only exhibits confusion, like other Black or black intellectuals, he engages in what often appears as just a pseudo discussion about race; sometimes even a non-discussion.

Marable's difficulties, as reflected in the example used to analyze his views on race and ethnicity and the thinking of Black and black intellectuals I have dealt with in this chapter, show that such intellectuals continue to "loll" and "lumber" in the racism/race intellectual wasteland. They bring little clarity to these subjects and little significant understanding. This is probably why, at a deep level, white people accept them as public intellectuals. They are conceded this status so as to be the ones to inform white people about Black people; not about themselves, as racists, specifically in terms of the affects of racist beliefs and practices on them, their minds, psychologies, and as human beings. But Black intellectuals, even when they play the role of informants for Whites and Blacks, do not take a discussion of racism or race very far. And this is not simply their fear of racism, their refusal to deal with it, or the largesse they obtain talking about the "racial matters" to which Whites are more amenable. It is also owing to the fact that they just do not know enough about the subject (and will never know until they develop the racist analysis or make full use of the analysis that is available, to augment it, or acquire the requisite knowledge and understanding). They would not lull themselves into thinking or let Whites get away with thinking (or saying) that ending racist practices necessarily eliminates racists.

All kinds of things can be brought to bear to end racist practices, such as actions by victims, governmental actions, court decisions, and other things. But the racists would still be there, owing to their racist interiority. This racist interiority continues to function and to seek outlets of expression. It is an inward compulsion that can be shifted to different targets or executed subtly toward traditional victims, both of which are presently occurring in America. Most Black and black intellectuals are presently, meagerly helpful to Blacks dealing with the subjects of race and racism. The Black intellectuals known as Black nationalists are generally just as meagerly helpful. But they have another feature that requires extensive and careful scrutiny, which will be done in the next chapter.

──❥ Chapter Three ❧──

Romancing the Black Nationalist Stone

There are some facts about Black history that must be emphasized and that cannot be ignored logically, safely, or morally. The first is that black Africans were brought here as slaves. This was done over a period of about two hundred and thirty years and equaled the length of time of Black chattel slavery in America, regarding slaves, and thus, Black people, as property.

Second, Black people are the descendants of the original black Africans and the black people they initially produced. In time, the black people continually produced would become the Black ethnic group of North America. This development was also aided by the cultural and social life they created. In addition, it was assisted by the "melting down" of the various black ethnic groups that came to North America over the years.

The slaves were reduced to a single black people that slowly, but steadily, evolved into a single Black people. Chattel slavery was involved in this process because it segregated and confined black Africans and black slaves, helping to "melt down" the black Africans and also facilitated black Africans and black slaves mating with each other. This ultimately produced Black slaves and the Black ethnic group. The ethnic status of Black people would not be discernible to people until sizable numbers of black people from other parts of the world (the West Indies, South America, and Africa) came into the country during the early twentieth century and onward. Clear and wide recognition and acceptance of this fact has yet to occur. Black nationalist thinking, at least in the way it was done by Black intellectuals, was a great impediment to that understanding and acceptance and continues to be.

The third unassailable and important fact that has to be acknowledged and emphasized is that most Black people who have ever lived in America were born here. They did not grow up in Africa. They did not know it or its people, nor did they have ties to or memories of its places. The black Africans who kept coming into the country by the early eighteenth century found themselves having to interact with Black people who were evolving in the country. These American Black people were constructing a life as slaves. Throughout this historical situation there was considerable initial friction, not only because of psychological and cultural differences, but because incoming black Africans had to be absorbed into the Black way of life, which they resented and resisted, sometimes as much as they resented or resisted being transformed into chattel slaves.

This brings us to the fourth salient fact to acknowledge and emphasize. Black people grew up, made history, and developed a culture and social life in a place far removed from Africa. The 350,000 to 400,000 black Africans that were brought to North America were their ancestral group; but, they also had another ancestral group that would be even more important to them, their Black ancestral group. It is clear that the African ancestral group is the subject of Africancentricity, while the Black ancestral group—based on the history they were making, the new culture and social life they were creating and maintaining, and the new ethnic group they were establishing—inaugurated what I call Blackcentricity.

NATIONALIST IDEOLOGY AND DISTORTED SCHOLARSHIP

However, Black nationalist historian Sterling Stuckey does not see it that way. He argues in his book, *Slave Culture*[1] that black Africans who became slaves in North America remained Africans-even "profoundly African," with an "African consciousness" that originated from African cultural retentions, or "Africanisms," and "African culture."

In the new environment, the slave environment, African cultural traits had to undergo change in order to stay viable. That was what they did and that was how some African cultural traits were retained. The full title of Stuckey's book is *Slave Culture: Nationalist Theory and the Foundations of Black America*. But, since the historian said that the chattel slaves of the English colonies, and then of the United States, remained African, his book should have been titled "Foundations of African America." Indeed, Stuckey usually refers to Black people in his book as African Americans. He talks of these Americans having an "African nationality," which he said was inaugurated by the initial African slaves and asserted this contention in the Preface of his book when he stated:

> The main argument, set forth in chapter 1, is drawn from a consideration of how slaves themselves responded to cultural challenges before them. That consideration led to the inescapable conclusion that the nationalism of the slave community was essentially African nationalism, consisting of values that bound slaves together and sustained them under brutal conditions of their oppression. Their very effort to bridge their ethnic differences and to form themselves into a

70

single people to meet the challenge of a common foe proceeded from an impulse that was Pan-African–that grew out of a concern for all Africans–as what was useful was appropriate from a multiplicity of African groups even as an effort was made to eliminate distinctions among them.[2]

I find it impossible to see what nationalism has to do with the black African and Black slaves of the United States and still less what "African nationalism" and "Pan-African[ism]" has to do with them.

Stuckey undermines, if not rends, his contention when he employs the term "African ethnicity" with regard to Black slaves. He goes on to say that "it is greatly ironic, therefore, that African ethnicity, an obstacle to African nationalism in the twentieth century, was in this way the principle avenue to black unity in antebellum America."[3] In making this assessment, and indeed, in arguing about slave nationalism and African nationalism, Stuckey shows the reader how strongly he was influenced by black African history of the 1960s and 1970s. These were decades of independence efforts, when the slogans "African Nationalism," "African Unity" and "African Independence" were prominent. Throughout his work, Stuckey demonstrated how strongly he was influenced by the Africancentrist perspective, despite its crushing blow to the Blackcentric perspective that I regard as appropriate when talking about Black slaves and Black ethnicity. Stuckey was showing a strong romancing of the Black nationalist stone.

One thing should be made clear before I proceed: Africa is a continent, not a country. Therefore, the identity involved would not be a national identity, but a continental identity. That means there could be no such thing as "African nationality," nor "African nationalism," as it would have to be a nationalism related to country, such as "Ghanaian nationalism" or "Kenyan nationalism." And clearly, "African ethnicity" is not the same as "African nationality." Indeed, both are erroneous, ideological, and romantic expressions. Stuckey's Africancentrist and Black nationalist orientation got in the way of studying Black slavery in America. It prevented him from deeply plunging into it. As he saw it, he was studying Africans in America–even though Black slaves saw how different they were from the black Africans that were continuously being brought on to plantations and slave farms.

An example of this awareness of difference has been recorded by the runaway slave, George Ball, who wrote in his autobiography or one of the slave autobiographical narratives: "the native Africans are revengeful, and unforgiving in their tempers, easily provoked, and cruel in their designs.... They feel indignant at the servitude that is imposed upon them and only want power to inflict the most cruel retribution upon their oppressors." Ball further

71

noted: "they are universally of the opinion, and this opinion is founded in their religion, that after death they shall return to their own country and rejoin their former companions and friends in some happy region."[4] Ball's comments invoke ideas of "we," "they," "us" and "them," "indigenous" and "foreigners," as well as Black people and black Africans-slashing the idea of "Pan-African Unity" that Stuckey said existed and was exhibited by Black slaves.

The following comment is from a former Black slave that also invokes the idea of separation between indigenous Black slaves and black Africans and that implies that the black Africans had to become acculturated to and integrated into the indigenous Black slave culture or Black culture. This brief description took place in the years before the Civil War, when Ball had been a slave. The former Black slave is quoted as saying: "Most of the time there was more'n three hundred slaves on the plantation. The oldest ones came right from Africa. My grandmother was one of them. A savage in Africa-a slave in America."[5]

The following three quotations, taken from former antebellum slaves, clearly show how the new Blacks saw themselves as being different from the black Africans and did not, and could not, envision any kind of unity between them as long as black Africans kept their original cultural and psychological dispositions. The first quotation is a reference to the Gullahs, whom Black nationalists and Africancentrists often point to when speaking of Blacks in America being African. The person remarked: "somebody give her de name o' Bettey, but t'weren't her right name. Folks couldn't understand a word she say. It was some sort o' gibberish dey called 'Gullah-talk' and it sounds dat funny."[6] Another ex-slave remarked: "Us all de time heard folkses talkin' about voodoo, but my grandma was powerful religious, and her Ma told us chilen voodoo was a no 'count doin' of de devil, and Christians was never to pay no attention. Us were to be happy in de Lord, and let voodoo and de devil alone."[7] And the third ex-slave stated: "We didn't have no...conjure folks at our 'wetney acres.' We all knowed about the Word and the unseen Son of God and we didn't put no stock in conjure. Course we had luck charms and good and bad signs, but everybody got them things, even nowadays."[8]

Both the Black nationalists and the Africancentrists seek to find the origins of Black nationalism among Black people in the black African slave trade and Black slavery. They endeavor to do this, not by providing historical evidence, because that cannot be done, as there is no such evidence, but by romantic, ideological, nostalgic, or wishful thinking. Stuckey wrote that African nationalism and Pan-Africanism, and what he called African ethnicity and African unity, occurred during the slave trade and then carried over into slavery. He wrote:

During the process of their becoming a single people, Yorubas, Akans, Ibos, Angolans, and others were present on slave ships to America and experienced a common horror—unearthly moans and piercing shrieks, the smell of filth and the stench of death, all during the violent rhythms and quiet coursings of ships at sea. As such, slave ships were the first real incubators of slave unity across cultural lines, cruelly revealing irreducible links from one ethnic group to the other fostering resistance thousands of miles before the shores of the new land appeared on the horizon—before there was mention of natural rights in North America.[9]

First, it should to be said that the black African ethnic groups that came to America as slaves already knew of the similarities of their separate ethnic cultures, coming from contiguous geographical areas, such as West and Central Africa. Given the horrendous cruelty of the "Middle Passage," which was usually a three-month trip that racked the mind, body, and the very being of its black passengers who were crowded like sardines in the holds, it is hardly likely that the slaves were thinking about a common identity, let alone a common African identity, African ethnic unity, African nationalism, or Pan-Africanism. What is more likely is that they were fighting off their disorientation and the threat of insanity. When their minds were lucid, they were probably filled with memories of being captured and taken from their families and villages, of dead people left behind in villages and warehouses, the foul smells and death on the slave ships, and a future that looked miasmic and foreboding. These had to be the things on their minds, rather than some abstract thoughts about political and cultural unity.

Stuckey claimed that African resistance and cultural resistance were taken into slavery, and thus, became the basis of a continuing kind of resistance in Black history and Black life. The Black culture of the slaves reflected something of group defiance and group resistance. However, the evidence overwhelmingly shows a group of people mainly focused on forging a new life for themselves. Slaves or not, this is what human beings do. They live by culture and social life. The Black slaves had the physical, social, and psychological space to do this kind of construction and they did.

The Black nationalist historian John Blassingame*, motivated by the theme of Black slave culture as a form and source of Black slave resistance, made the unsupportable assertion in *Slave Community*[10] that Black cultural construction and imbibement that occurred in slave quarters "away from the lash" were the most important experiences for Black slaves. He also argued

* Blassingame recently passed away.

that the work experience of slaves was not an important or meaningful one in their lives. There was no way for the work experience not to be important and meaningful to Black slaves. They worked sixteen to eighteen hours a day, from "can to can't," most days of the week, fifty-two weeks of the year, almost all the years they were slaves. There was also a direct connection between not working and punishment, which made slaves very conscious of the importance and meaning of work. This experience was also important and meaningful because work was often rewarded by off time or by some time for festivities. Much of Black slave culture, even Black religion, was created openly on the plantations and slave farms, with slave masters being acquiescent to it or not opposing it, even encouraging expressions of it. After all, Black slaves were a primary source of entertainment on slave plantations and farms.

John Blassingame's book appeared years before Stuckey's in 1972 and helped to launch vigorous writing on Black chattel slavery in America by both Black and white historians. Blassingame's study was well researched and argued in many respects. But, at the same time, it was a romantic and idyllic discussion of the subject, which is what has to be concluded when he plays down the oppression and brutality of the institution. Blassingame did not even give a sense of how Black slave culture was created as a response to slavery and oppression, as an adjustment to them, as a method of trying to cope and live with them, which was, for most slaves a life-long ordeal. If he had done that, he would have written about Black slavery in a holistic manner, which he did not do. Rather Blassingame wrote of Black slavery in an either-or manner, which made it possible for him to emphasize Black slave culture as a form and source of resistance. Blassingame neglected to write about Black integration into slavery and the slave experience, which included cooperation with the institution out of necessity.

During the 1960s and 1970s there were numerous Black nationalist historians who wrote about slavery and emphasized African cultural retentions or Black slave life, while omitting or playing down the oppressive character of that existence. In short, they presented essentially romanticized and idyllic views of Black slavery. Both Blassingame and Stuckey were of this group of historians. Stuckey's *Slave Culture* continued with this kind of historical writing, but his purpose in writing his book was more political and ideological. Stuckey was trying to establish the historical origins of what he called "African Unity," "African nationality," "African nationalism," "African ethnicity," and "Pan-Africanism" in the black African slave trade and Black chattel slavery in America. In reality, Black nationalist writing on slavery emphasized three themes, directly or indirectly: Black culture (based on African "retentions"), Black slave intellectual, and even psychological, independence, and Black slave resistance. The image that Black slaves were some kind of incipient Black "nation" growing up in and out of the slave experience, while simultaneously stuck in the bowels of an oppressive America, also came through some of the Black nationalist writings on Black slavery. Stuckey was influenced by these writings, as well as by white historians's writing on Black slavery, such as George Rawick's *Sundown to Sunup*[11] and Eugene Genovese's *Roll, Jordan, Roll*,[12] both of which were strongly romanticized and idealized. In Genovese's case, strong romanticization and idealization took place in discussing the white slaveholders more than the Black slaves. Other white historians projected positive, even benevolent images of white slaveholders. This was something John Blassingame did, as well, by default, when he neglected to significantly discuss slaveholders.*

Black nationalist historian, V. P. Franklin, seeing himself following in the ideological and historiographical footsteps of other Black nationalist historians, sought to convey the idea of Black people as a "nation" in America, "a nation within a nation," as Stuckey was later to say in his book. Franklin could well have been influenced by the Black Arts Movement of the 1970s and some of its writers, who were strongly nationalistic and had been strongly influenced by Harold Cruse's *The Crisis of the Negro Intellectual*. There was talk then of Blacks as an oppressed people in America, even a "colonized people" within the country. And there was talk that Black culture (what was generally called "black culture" then and not Afro-American or African American culture) was considered the key to Black liberation, as opposed to politics—even a politics informed and guided by Black culture.

---

* This issue is further discussed in a book I published in the late 1970s titled *Historians and Slavery*, in which I critiqued the racism of several white historian's writing on antebellum Black slavery and the romantic images they projected of slaveholders and Black slavery.

Black nationalist dramatist, cultural critic, and essayist, Larry Neal, who was a leading figure of the Black Arts Movement, wrote the following lines in his book *Visions of a Liberated Future*:

> The only way out of this trick-bag is to begin from the position that black people constitute a would-be nation apart from that of white America. Therefore there are two Americas—a black one and a white one; and black America very clearly must decide what its interests are, both in the national and international context. Consequently it is no longer a question of civil rights for Negroes; but rather it is a question of national liberation for black America. That means that we see ourselves as a "colonized" people instead of as disenfranchised American citizens. That means that our struggle is one with the struggles of oppressed people everywhere, and we alone must decide what our stance will be toward those nations struggling to liberate themselves from colonial or neocolonial domination.[14]

Here is the Black nationalist-produced fanciful, romantic image of Black people being "a country within a country," which is what being "colonized" (as captured, oppressed, and suppressed black African countries are in the English empire), means.

This was how Malcolm X talked the last couple years of his life, which doubtless had influence on Neal; as he had influence on many Black nationalists and non-nationalist Black thinkers. Malcolm X used to project an image of white people being a "minority" in the world and argued that it was "people of color" who were the majority. This took thought and imagery away from considering Blacks as a "colonized" people or "a nation within a nation." But, it also added to the idea of Black resistance to oppression. Blacks in America were not alone; they had history and population, great morality and justice on their side. They had something that could be called "cosmic justice" or "cosmic morality" on their side, and they had their liberation.

Dr. Frances Cress Welsing was also highly influential with Black nationalist thinkers. In particular, Black nationalist thinkers were impressed with her talk not only of the "white minority" on the planet, but she also addressed the rising White fear of a biologically and genetically stronger and larger population "of color." History, biology, and morality, all in cosmic portions, were on the side of Black people and their quest for liberation and freedom in America. This kind of thinking, of course, was romantic and seductive. It resonated with many Blacks and encouraged such Blacks in America to put themselves on the same political footing and reality as colonized people in the world: black Africans, black West Indians, and Asians. There are always similarities in the conditions of dominated and oppressed peoples, in terms of treatment and in their responses to these conditions or the outcomes sought. But colonized black Africans sought to regain the independence and integrity of their countries before they were turned into colonies. Colonized black West Indians sought to take control of the countries that they and their colonizers helped to build. With both the black Africans and black West Indians and also with colonized Asians, the object was to throw off and throw out the foreigner, or if not to throw them out, to seriously alter the way they functioned inside the liberated country. Thus for all of these groups racism, colonialism, and imperialism were all realities and realities that had to be defeated. This also meant, particularly with Africans and Asians, re-establishing national culture: literature, art, music, drama, and other forums. For black West Indians it was a matter of making culture produced during slavery and colonization the new dominant culture or the national culture in independence.

Today, we see black Africans and black West Indians in the Caribbean islands and in England (and even to some extent, in the United States) engaging in what they call a "post-colonial experience." The concept and practice of "cultural studies" in England and the West Indies could have some application to Blacks in America. There are things that Black intellectuals can learn from black African and black West Indian "post-colonial studies." And there would be similarities to explore between "post-colonial studies" and Black Studies, in terms of motivation for devising them, in content, and reasons for instructing in them, and even for similar political purposes. "Post-colonial studies" have a certain radical element or belligerency about them. This is also true of "cultural studies," which is part of their attraction to black intellectuals from Africa to the Western Hemisphere, as well as many Black intellectuals in America.

In general, Black nationalists like being belligerent and militant and like talking about resistance. One such Black nationalist was V. P. Franklin. He wrote in the Preface of his book *Black Self-Determination:* "SELF-DETERMINATION for politically and economically oppressed groups that define themselves as a people or 'nation,' but do not participate in a meaningful way in decisions affecting their lives and the lives of their children, has been one of the most volatile and explosive issues of the late twentieth century."[15] He then went on to equate Blacks in America with Palestinians, Namibia, countries in Southwest Africa, the Irish Republican Army, Grenada, and the Falkland Islands, which were all engaged in some kind of resistance that sought self-determination. But all of the groups that Franklin compared Blacks to were interested in liberation leading to the establishment of independent countries.

Against that, he wrote that some commentators interpreted the mass Black support for Jesse Jackson's presidential bid in 1984 as a recent example of the historical Black self-determination within the United States.[16] Franklin was fully in agreement with that assessment. But the general comparison itself was faulty, like comparing apples to oranges. The two realities had very little in common with each other. The proper basis of comparison would have been between Blacks and people in other countries in the same situation, for Blacks were not seeking to leave a country to establish a separate country, but seeking to be included in the country as equals to others and with a measure of autonomy within the folds of America's culture, national identity, and national unity.

Black nationalists usually do not frame the matter in this realistic and sensible manner. They take flights into fantasy and romance and talk about Black people in a way that historical evidence in no way suggests or corroborates. They ignore such evidence, even evidence of Black chattel slavery. Black history shows that there were two strands of Black nationalism and both were mainly talk. The first strand of nationalism supported the idea of Blacks in numbers, or altogether, leaving America and living in black countries and aiding their development. And the second strand of nationalism supported the idea of Blacks (with the assumption that they were a "nation" or "incipient nation") establishing a Black country within the confines of the United States or some other part of North America.

Marcus Garvey came to America with nationalist thinking that he called "African Redemption." It was commensurate with the first kind of Black nationalism found in America, and it attracted hundreds of thousands of adherents. But again, it was mainly just talk, motion, and some preparatory action. Franklin said that he was heavily influenced by his knowledge of Garvey and his movement and commented in his book that:

> Since Marcus Garvey did not arrive in the United States until 1916 and by 1922 had several hundred thousand followers, it was clear to me that he was appealing to a set of cultural values or "value system" that already existed among people of African descent in this country.... Garvey's program appealed to the interests and self-determinationist culturalist values that had developed among Afro-Americans from the eighteenth century.[17]

While Marcus Garvey had hundreds of thousands of followers, Booker T. Washington had millions of Black followers and just as many white supporters. How was that to be explained? A partial explanation of Washington's success with Blacks was that he appealed to the "value system" of Blacks, to the "interests and self-determinationist values" they had. Booker T. Washington was someone that Franklin did not want to discuss in his book. Certainly, he did not discuss how Washington had so many Black followers in America, both in the South and the North.

Washington was not a Black nationalist, and was against it. He was against Black political behavior that would later be subsumed under the label of Black nationalism, particularly the first strand of Black nationalism mentioned. This strand of Black nationalism was, in Washington's day, advocated by bishop Henry McNeil Turner who drew strong criticism from the Tuskegean. V. P. Franklin harbors great loathing for Booker T. Washington. In a recent book of biographies of important Black people in Black history and life, Franklin did not include the Tuskegean as one of his main portraitures.[18] This was the most prominent and dominant person at any time in Black history and Black life in America, yet Franklin continues the ritual of ignoring, excluding, and deprecating him.

In *Black Self-Determination*, he correctly rejected Washington as a Black nationalist, but not for the right reasons. Given what Washington did, and given what Franklin regarded as being Black nationalism, Washington was clearly a Black nationalist. On one occasion, Franklin wrote: "In drawing these distinctions between Afro-Americans and Slaves, Washington clearly revealed his particular understanding of Afro-American cultural values, as well as the political objectives of the black masses."[19] Franklin also said, "for those individuals who have aspired to leadership of the black community, the challenge of black self-determination has been to provide programs and strategies that were embedded in Afro-American values and cultural traditions and reflected mass (as opposed to elite) economic interests. Booker T. Washington appealed to some of these values—self-determination and education—but he did not understand the significance of the Afro-American religious tradition to black advancement."[20] The latter charge could never stick against Washington, who mobilized Black churches, lodges, and fraternal orders, which were money-generating and property-acquiring institutions and insisted that they help Blacks advance in the South. With respect to the Black church, Washington said something similar to the following on many occasions: "that kind of religion which will help him fill not only his heart, but his stomach, clothe and shelter his body and surround himself with some of the conveniences and comforts of life, is the kind that is best for the Negro."[21]

Franklin not only said that Washington was not a Black nationalist, he injected his own personal animosity toward him into his historical study when he made the political assessment (rather than an historical assessment) of Washington that he *should not* be considered the leader of Black people. This was obviously not a statement directed to Washington's contemporaries, but rather it was directed to Blacks, other historians, and people who read his book. Franklin was strongly influenced by his own "Uncle Tom" and "accommodationist" images of Booker T. Washington. These images stood in the way of Franklin's ability to view Washington in a holistic fashion or in a manner consistent with the evidence he did present. He said that Washington "appealed to these [cultural] values in his call for the support of black-controlled businesses, schools, and other social and economic institutions." Franklin expressed his admiration for all-Black towns because he saw them as manifestations of self-determination at work. But in his discussion, he failed to mention that Booker T. Washington fostered the establishments of all-Black towns and even helped to raise money for some of them, including the two towns Franklin mentioned in his book: *Mound Bayou, Mississippi and Boley, Oklahoma.*

Despite all this evidence that Franklin adduced and worked with, he still said Washington should not have been the leader of Blacks when history confirmed that he had been. He noted that:

> The dominant white group wanted Afro-Americans to accommodate to their demands for supremacy, and many white Americans felt reassured and comforted by the pronouncements of Booker T. Washington, the white-sanctioned black spokesperson. Fortunately [or unfortunately], Washington did not represent the values and interest of the black masses [after repeatedly saying he did] and therefore should not be considered their leader.[22]

More will be said about Booker T. Washington in the chapter on him and the refutation of a number of the erroneous images of him will also be taken up there.

It might be recalled that Harold Cruse criticized Black nationalists for rejecting Washington when he epitomized so much of what they stood for and their approach to Black history and Black life in America. But Washington was not a "militant," a "radical," or a "bellicose" public protester; he was not someone who flailed his words and fists in the faces of white people. Garvey also attempted to get southern White racist backing for his program for Blacks in America, but he is still deemed a Black nationalist and held in honor by Black nationalists.

MISUNDERSTANDING BLACK MARGINALITY

Black nationalists, historians, and others have not only distorted and buried the reality of Booker T. Washington (and continue to do so), but much of the reality of Black history itself. They do not like to show the impact of white people and the larger American society on Black history and life, beginning with Black chattel slavery. They do not use the Black experience, historical or social, (its history, culture, and social life) as the basis for evaluating America. They like to write about or describe Black people in isolation from these larger realities. Whether they know it or not, whether they accept it or not, this way of romanticizing Black culture *marginalizes* Black people in their own minds and in the minds of Whites, who need no help with that. Black people even think like a minority when they are in fact a majority or near majority population. They even think like this when they wield considerable political power in their areas through Black mayors, or councilpersons, or supervisors.

Toni Morrison's fiction, as she says, is predicated on the notion and the understanding that Black people are a marginal people in America. She wrote in *Inventing the Truth*: "My job [as a writer] becomes how to rip that veil drawn over 'proceedings too terrible to relate.' The exercise is also critical for any person who is black, or who belongs to any marginalized category, for historically, we were seldom invited to participate in the discourse even when we were its topic."[23] V. P. Franklin talked of Blacks being marginal, too, and in nearly the same way, not being participants in political councils and the like.

But these are not the only ways to participate in a society. One does not have to be in decision-making roles to do so. The contribution of Black people to America is extraordinary, which an image of Blacks as "marginal" people ignores, distorts, or suppresses. The literary critic and essayist, Albert Murray, once wrote that American culture was "mulatto." And the Black novelist Robert O'Meally was one of the two editors of a book who made the following joint statement, referring to Black cultural contributions to America:

> Coming from the bottom of the American social ladder-and for so long rendered untouchable and invisible by slavery and segregation-blacks ironically have been relatively freer from the rules enforced by the official culture monitors. As a group, they tended to care least about what, for instance, the black social dance called the Black Bottom, looked like to the proctors at the local ballet class (be they white or black). Thus it is no surprise that Blacks–who invented such definitely

81

American forms as the spiritual, jazz music and dance, as well as expressions associated with the cultures of rags, blues, bebop, and rap, have had such a potent impact on American cultural life and history. What would American culture be without their presence?[24]

Brenda Gottschild added to the history of Black contributions to American culture and, in her remarks, added some black African ones too when she stated: "American society is permeated by Africanist attitudes, forms, and phenomena, from African agrarian practices, which were basic to the success of plantation culture, to such African American specifics as potato chips, peanut butter, revival meetings, and the Charleston."[25] Gottschild talked of what she called the "Africanist" influences on the famous choreographer George Balachine: "Early on, he was introduced to the Africanist aesthetic through the world of other artists whom he admired. Among this group was the Russian constructivist Kazian Goleizovsky, 'whose cool, erotic-gymnastic etudes and interest in American jazz stimulated the Russian art world of the twenties.'"[26] Gottschild also talked of the "Africanist aesthetic" influence on Igor Stravinsky, White minstrelsy, and White popular musicians and singers. Gottschild did not write of Blacks being a marginalized people in contributing to American music, dance, or theater performance because she knew that in these areas they were major contributors.

She also put the notion of the racist invisibilization of Blacks in perspective, without consciously seeking to do so. As Ralph Ellison and James Baldwin made so clear the White racist invisibilization of Blacks was not to see Blacks for who they were, but to view them through their racist images of Blacks and to relate to them on the basis of these distorted and perverse images. Ellison's novel, *The Invisible Man*[27] and James Baldwin's essays *Nobody Knows My Name*[28] tell this fetid story. It is another way of saying that Black intellectuals have to be careful using words like minority, marginalization, racist invisibilization, and racist segregation when discussing Black history, Black social life, and Black social interaction with Whites. White racists of the nineteenth century held that Black people, while they could not think well, could *imitate* superbly. But Blacks had their own tale as to "who was imitating whom" in America. They knew full well how often white people imitated them in language, music, dance, singing, dress, gestures, and other things.

Black physical and cultural presence looms large in America, as it has since Blacks were slaves, when they were the legal, political, social, and indeed, the structural bottom of first the English colonies and then of American society. The bottom of a society is not marginal. It is *foundational*, and what is foundational always significantly impacts other parts of a structure. Black nationalist historians and other Black intellectuals today do not help Black people, or other Americans, understand that they keep isolating and marginalizing the Black experience, and thus, help to make Blacks invisible and diminish the Black presence and involvement in America. There are ways and times when Blacks can appropriately be analyzed and discussed as a functioning minority. But there are other ways and times when Blacks are much bigger than a minority group and should not be given a marginalized status, especially with respect to contributions made to given situations or their impact on them.

And then there is the other matter to consider. Blacks have always struggled to attain justice in America and are still doing so. When Whites think of Blacks as a minority or as a marginalized people their notion of justice towards Blacks falls very short. They do not believe that a minority has much, or can suffer that much loss, or that they are entitled to that much justice. This thinking is even more skewed when racism informs it, because then it is believed that Blacks as "nonhumans" or "subhumans" are not entitled to justice. For many white people, Black people are beyond justice, because they are guilty or evil by "nature" which cannot be touched by justice. And then there is the fact that white people, functioning as racists in America, have never developed much of a sense of social justice, certainly not toward Black people.

Thus, justice to Black people is a complicated thing in America. The injustice suffered by Blacks has been so great, it's difficult to know how or what kind of justice can balance it. And justice towards Blacks, on the basis of being a minority or marginalized group, would lead to inadequate justice in those places and times when the contributions or impact of Blacks greatly outstripped their numbers. It would call for a greater remuneration and that would be another kind of justice, altogether. This occurred when Black slaves and nonslave Blacks helped the North defeat the South, which resulted in the abolition of slavery, but it did not result in immediate political or civil rights for Blacks and, of course, there was no significant financial or economic help in the post-slave period.

THE NATIONALIST FAILURE TO UNDERSTAND SOCIETAL PROCESSES

Black nationalist historians, and other Black intellectuals, have not helped Blacks to understand certain cultural and social processes indispensable to their living, advancement, and struggle in America. E. Franklin Frazier made this criticism in 1962 in an article titled "The Failure of the Negro Intellectual." Frazier said that they had failed to help Blacks understand the concepts and processes of assimilation and integration. But Frazier had also

83

failed along these lines because of his own confusing way of looking at these matters. Black nationalist historians and other kinds of Black intellectuals show their confusion on the same subjects. In fairness to Frazier, and to the Black historians and other intellectuals (whether Black, white, or other), most show the same confusion and misrepresentation about common social and cultural processes in America that impact Black intellectual perceptions and understandings.

Black history—certainly as a Blackcentric perspective perceives and understands it—moves on a double, but interactive (meaning holistic) basis, namely, *separation* and *integration*. The Black nationalists convert separation into separatism, which is a false concept to apply to Black history, except where one is talking of the two Black nationalist strands of Black history. The Black nationalists add fuel to this misconception and misrepresentation by regarding Black people as a "nation" or a "nation within a nation," a country in America or at least one seeking materialization. They want this Black "nation" to separate from the rest of America. This is not only romantic fantasizing; it is nonsense that ignores the war of the mid-nineteenth century, where southern state secession was defeated.

No country likes to be dismembered and will take political or military action to prevent it, such as the prevention of Quebec's independence in Canada, the effort on the part of the Igbos in Nigeria to establish their own country, or the recent efforts of Chechnya to pull out of Russia. But this is how ideology, psychological needs, or a political agenda get in the way of dealing with facts and reality. A racial or an ethnic group could have separatist tendencies, particularly of two kinds. One is to separate, to establish a separate country and the other is to separate within a society by withdrawing from it, remaining in isolation from other population groups in the country, like the Amish and Indian tribes in America. Black nationalists like V. P. Franklin regarded the establishment of all-Black towns as separatism when it was not. The leaders of those towns were interested in integrating into the politics and economies of their states and region. And no matter what they felt, they would be forced to integrate anyway by paying federal and state taxes.

Blacks have participated in racial and ethnic separation in America going back to the days of chattel slavery. They not only lived as slaves; they were also segregated, geographically and physically. They were also socially confined to plantations and slave farms, with both white supremacist/ebonicistic racism and maleist/sexist racism involved in this confinement. These racist beliefs and attitudes were just as integral to segregation as they were to Black chattel slavery. Blacks were segregated as if they were "nonhumans" or "subhumans"—a perception and understanding in the minds of white slaveholders and other Whites that Black chattel slavery reinforced. Black people, as slaves, and within the confines of racist and slave segregation, developed a separate identity and life in America, an identity (in their minds) that separated them from the continuing influx of black Africans and a culture and social life that they regarded as their own. It was a life to which the incoming black Africans did not belong, but would eventually be integrated into. This separate Black life has been in America since the late seventeenth century. It always had a division in it because of the geographical division of Black people, those in the North and those in the South.

Most of the 4,500,000 Black people who lived in the country in the 1860s lived in the South. Northern Blacks were originally slaves. But in the late eighteenth century, the black African slave trade to the northern states was abolished. Black slavery in the region was put on a process of gradual abolition, which occurred by the early 1830s. The North was where most of the so-called "free" Blacks lived in the United States from the late eighteenth century to the 1860s, although they were not truly free and realistically could only be regarded as *nonslave* Blacks. It was important for these Blacks to describe themselves as "free," to have it publicly understood that they were "free," even though they truly weren't, because they did not want to be mistaken as slaves, be converted into slaves, or risk being kidnapped and sold into slavery.

Northern Blacks, even as slaves, were not as Black as the slaves of the South. The South was where the Black ethnic identity was being constructed as an outgrowth of a racial identity and the slave experience. The South was also where Black ethnic culture and social life were being constructed as an outgrowth of that identity and experience. Whether racial or ethnic, the identity reflected the synthesis of "Africanisms," the slave experience, and European-American identity and cultural attributes. This is clearly the Blackcentric view of the origins, creation, and development of the Black identity, Black ethnicity, and Black culture in the South and in America. Northern Blacks were not part of that construction and were not as culturally and socially Black as Black slaves, although there were some traces of their original slave life hanging on in their existence. But clearly, Northern Blacks had more White identity and cultural influences in their lives, which they did not necessarily interpret as being White. Whites were building America, and White and America, in many ways, were synonymous.

For instance, White people, that is, white men, could participate in government. This was also simultaneously American political behavior. White men could attend private schools and universities, but these were also American schools, and attending school and engaging in formal learning was American behavior. The way some white people practiced Christianity, or the way some established and operated mutual aid societies, or the way some Whites dressed, or mourned, or kept house were forms of White behavior that northern Blacks might copy and make part of their own cultural and social existence and behavior. This was northern Black separate life, with more visible forms of European-Americanisms and Whiteness in it. But it also had the manifestations of oppression, suppression and ostracism that were the same as, or that resembled, these features of Black slave life. Both groups of Black people had this common experience. It made the life of both groups similar in this way and similar in the way they responded to oppression, suppression, and ostracism or exclusion, as cultural modes of response.

Whatever group of Blacks we're talking about in American history and life, they had to integrate into their immediate cultural-social environment, village, town, city, and country. Even though this was much easier for northern nonslave Blacks to do, it was nevertheless a horrendous difficulty for them. Racist power, and cultural and social practices, which were also expressions of this power, stood in their way. The racist power did not prevent either groups of Blacks in America from living separately or from developing their separate cultural-social existence, although Whites often sought to interfere with that. What applications of racist power, racist/slaveholding power, racist segregation, or racist/slave segregation did was to block the cultural process of assimilation for Blacks and severely impeded their ability to integrate into their local area or region or country.

Invariably, Black nationalists are ideological and strongly against assimilation and integration. They also evidence that they really do not know what these terms mean. Both Black and black intellectuals view assimilation as a process of Black self-destruction. This is how Lorraine Hansberry referred to the term in her play *Raisin in the Sun*. This had also been the interpretation of integration that Harold Cruse held. He saw it as cultural annihilation or severe suppression in *The Crisis of the Negro Intellectual*. And this was how Malcolm X and the Black Muslims generally saw it, where it became one of their strongest criticisms of Martin Luther King, Jr. and other Black leaders at the time.

The black philosopher Bernard Boxill endeavored to show how Black or black intellectuals, such as Stokeley Carmichael and Charles Hamilton, have understood assimilation. Boxill showed, without being aware of it himself, that they had a confused view of it. His discussion of the subject showed his own confusion about assimilation, as well, when he wrote in *Blacks and Social Justice*:

To assimilate, or not to assimilate. To Black cultural nationalists, such as the poet Imamu Amiri Baraka (Leroi Jones), as the political theorists Stokeley Charmichael and Charles Hamilton, and most important, W. E. B. Du Bois, that has been the question in the race issue. Not, of course, that they imagined that blacks have had much of a choice about assimilation. Their question was and is about goals. Should the goal be to assimilate, or to become as much like the white majority as possible, to blend in? Or should it be to assimilate, to keep and even to accentuate the differences from the majority to stand out...? They maintain that to choose assimilation is to choose self-obliteration.... In their estimation...black people are not to cave in under the slings and arrows of the majority, they must affirm, maintain and even accentuate their distinctiveness. But their position has not gone unchallenged. There are black thinkers who have seen nothing crucial in the question of whether or not to assimilate, and no obligation to avoid assimilation. These so-called assimilationists, whose number included Henry Highland Garnet and Frederick Douglass in the 19th century and most of the leadership of the NAACP today, do not say that blacks must necessarily assimilate, though they usually believe that assimilation is inevitable. But they do not say that black people are not obliged not to assimilate.[29]

My first response to this statement is to point out that Boxill was wrong to group Du Bois with the intellectuals he grouped him with. For Du Bois, assimilation was not an either-or matter. He regarded Blacks as being Americans. Naturally, as he saw it, they would have to assimilate, which he understood to be, given the good sociologist he was, the cultural process of indigenous people imbibing the identity, the ideals, the beliefs, the values, and other aspects of a country's culture that makes them who they are in terms of identity, intellectual makeup, psychology, morality and, as Du Bois had it, spiritually, a part of that country. In *The Souls of Black Folk*, where he talked of the Black "double-consciousness," he remarked that what he wanted to see in America was Blacks being able to participate in the country as both Black people and Americans without penalization. As he said, "he simply wishes to make it possible for a man to be both a Negro and an American, without being cursed and spit upon by his fellows, without having the doors of Opportunity closed roughly in his face."[30] Du Bois regarded assimilation as being necessary and crucial to Blacks because it helped them to be and to understand, ideationally, culturally, and socially, what it meant to be American, which Black people were. Black American or Negro American, as Du Bois often phrased it, was their full identity.

Knowing what it meant to be an American and being an American in the sense of knowing it and feeling it, facilitated integration into American society. Integration means nothing more than participation. It means participating in the cultural and social life of a local habitat, society, or country. Thus, as Du Bois saw it, assimilation and integration worked together for Blacks when they were able to make them do so. But that was the rub, the problem. Whites neither wanted these processes working for Blacks, nor working effectively for them. They certainly did not want them working without their particular slant on them. In the case of assimilation, their particular slant was that Blacks should cease to be culturally Black and to become culturally White: not American, but White. But Black nationalists and other Black intellectuals do not make this kind of distinction about assimilation. They react to the White effort to implement it in a racist fashion towards Blacks, which would logically carry this process to the logical extreme of the cultural annihilation of Blacks.

But assimilation does not have to be carried that far. There is nothing logical, necessary, imperative, or inevitable that says it has to be. What is certainly logical, necessary, imperative, and inevitable is that people that live in a country, especially if they are indigenous people, assimilate. And also integrate. Black slaves integrated into America. They participated in the southern and American economy, some participated on the plantations as "house" slaves, meaning they integrated or participated in white families. They integrated or participated when some of them were part of the administration of slave plantations or farms, when they were overseers, clerks, or drivers. Black slaves attended White churches, served at White cultural and social functions, and some, in the cities, integrated as servants, or integrated some of the drinking establishments after hours.

The Black slaves assimilated. That was how they learned how to speak the English language. They took European-American cultural and social traits and made them their own. They used them to help construct a Black identity, culture, and social life. Black slaves could not legally marry, but they assimilated the White monogamous marriage and also the conjugal family, while still holding onto some African beliefs, feelings, and realities of the extended family. Black slaves assimilated the Christian religion, which they mixed with African religious "retentions" to produce a Black version of Christianity. And they assimilated some of the music of white people that they synthesized with African musical traits and the slave experience to produce the work songs, the plantation melodies, and later, the spirituals.

AFRICAN, NOT THE ORIGINAL NAME OF BLACK PEOPLE: A RETROSPECTIVE IDENTITY

Black nationalists, like other Black intellectuals do not plunge deeply into Black history to be intellectuals in America. They do not excavate or utilize Black historical material to construct ideas, critical evaluations, theories, or philosophies. They typically skim the surface, some even showing a fear or distaste for doing so, and showing a fear, or lack of desire, to deal with the Black slave experience at all.

There are Black male historians and other Black male intellectuals who do not want to deal with the history of Black women in America or the relationship between Black men and women over time in America. There are Black intellectuals, and this is particularly true of some called Africancentrists, who always want to jump over Black history or the general Black experience in America, to fix their gaze and writing on black Africa. If they do talk about Black history or the general Black experience, they come at it by way of Africa. They go to the extreme position of saying that Blacks in America are Africans, that Black history is African history and that Black culture and social life are African culture and social life. Black nationalists help to perpetuate this situation by equating Blacks with being a "nation" or "a nation within a nation." This keeps them equated with black African countries and abets the Africancentrist notion that Black people are Africans by identity, culture, and social life in America.

A truth that continues to elude Black people (and other people in the country, for that matter) is that the African identity was not the identity claimed or possessed by the black people brought here as slaves. Still less was it the identity of Black people who evolved during slavery. What Black nationalists, Africancentrists, other Black intellectuals and Black people in general have to know, is that the name African is not indigenous to that continent and the black people there. It is a name that came from an outside source in ancient times.

This means that the millennial black people who lived on that continent did not invent that name, did not call themselves Africans and that the black people who came to America as slaves did not call themselves African. This was not a name that most knew. Some heard it during the slave trade. But unless they spoke the language of their enslavers, they did not recognize it. Some would hear it in the United States, but not many. The word "African" appeared in the quotations I presented previously. George Ball learned of the word in the North after his escape. The other quotations were from ex-slaves who at the time were very old in age. These ex-slaves were interviewed by people from the Works Progress Administration in the 1930s who used the word "African" in the interviews.

The word "Africa" was an ancient Greek word, which the black Africancentrist and Kemetologist (instead of Egyptologist, using the original name of the country, Kemet, instead of the name the Greeks gave to it, Egypt) Joseph ben-Jochanan was not hesitant in revealing, saying that it "[c]omes from the Greek language, 'Afrik,' and it was the Greek 'ae' really and then you had 'ika,' so you had two Greek words that [were] compounded in one word to become 'Africa.'"[31]

Years before ben-Jochanan's disclosure, the black Kenyan political scientist, Ali Mazrui, said that black Africans learned that people in other parts of the world called their continental homeland Africa and the black people on it Africans, usually from missionaries in missionary schools.[32] Some of the Africans who were educated abroad (Europe or America) during the twentieth century, but before the post-Second World War period, would hear Africa and African for the first time.

In 1995, the Middle Eastern historian Bernard Lewis wrote in *Cultures in Conflict*, "the inhabitants of Asia and Africa...were as unaware of being Asians and Africans as the inhabitants of pre-Columbian America were unaware of being Americans. They first became aware of this classification when it was brought to them–and at some times and in some places imposed–by Europeans."[33]

Black nationalists and Africancentrists attach an African identity to the black people who came from the island continent to be slaves and to the Black slaves. All the former had were their national, ethnic, village, religious, and various familial identities when they came to North America or anywhere else in the Western Hemisphere, for that matter. Colin Palmer recently wrote, "until very recent times those people who resided on the African continent defined themselves solely in accordance with their ethnic name.... The appellation, 'African' was never employed."[34] Elliott Skinner has also recognized that the name African is foreign to the black people who reside on the continent. He wrote: "The Africans who were plucked away from their homeland and wished to return to a place they learned to call 'Africa,' thereby conflating their various homelands."[35]

There are black Africans now accepting these identities *in retrospect*. As a matter of convenience or for historical scholarship, but not of evidence or historical reality, the people who came to North America as slaves can be called African. But when this technical, convenient, and limited use of the term is turned into something that is believed to be evidentiary, an historical reality, and as something that is deeply embedded in black African history, passed onto millennial generations in Africa and from there to Black Americans, this is ideological and romanticism. In America, they became Black people. The people who came here as slaves knew they were of the black race, or were a black people, and had that description and name in their languages, such as tuntum in Fanti, *tuntumi* in Asante, *hibo* in Ewe, *ojii* in Igbo, and *dudo* in Yoruba (as my Nigerian colleague Samuel Andoh informs me).

Thus, when the Portuguese and the Spanish called their black slaves negroes, that name was initially just a reference to the color of the slaves, which in these languages meant black. This is something that Molefi Asante has ignored. Not seeing the varied or developmental use of the word, he equates Negro with slavery, which eventually became equivalent. He also objects to the word Negro because he believes it takes Black people and Black culture out of their African identities and functions to separate both from Africa as contiguous realities, as one black African reality from Africa to America (and the Western Hemisphere generally). He noted, "like the literary critics, the historians would dismiss the African elements that survived and developed on the American continents as purely temporal. They would usually call it 'Negro culture'.... The fact that the spatial referent is Africa is ignored and Negro becomes a crypto-term that is used to designate our degradation. In this way, the Eurocentric writer ties the African to Negro, a false concept and a false history, separate from any particular spatial reality."[36]

There are some comments to be made about Asante's thoughts. He talks of African cultural traits being retained in the Western Hemisphere during the centuries of slavery. But the fact is most of this culture and social life was destroyed during the centuries of the slave trade and slavery. This was especially true in North America. Traits that were retained often had to be transformed to survive and to be useable, clearly evident and true in North America. Asante also fails to recognize that Black people had their own way of interpreting and employing the identity of Negro. White people put negative connotations on it, but Black people did not. Negro was a name and identity that Black people invested with respect, value, and morality. The Negro identity in Black hands represented intellectual, psychological and moral independence and also resistance along these lines in North America. The identity also helped the black African slaves to transform themselves into Black people. And it helped them to be able to develop and nourish their ethnicity, to keep themselves clear in their own minds that they were a new people emerging, different from the white people around them and the black Africans they once were and that kept coming to the country. Negro history is Black history. Negro culture is Black culture. It includes more than just survived African cultural traits, most of which were destroyed in the slave trade and during 230 years of slavery. Those that have survived have long since been a part of Black culture, like certain elements of the European-American culture have long since been a part of Black culture: Black speech, Black music, Black religion, Black humor, and Black dance.

Brenda Gottschild talks of African and Black cultural traits, the latter she calls African American. But she is similar to Asante in not distinguishing the two and has a tendency to speak of both as simply "Africanist." She has said: "I use it here to signify African and African American resonances and presences, trends and phenomena. It indicates the African influence, past and present, and those forms and forces that arose as products of the African diaspora, including traditions and genres such as blues, jazz, rhythm and blues, and hip hop."[37] All of these cultural forms are Black, formed out of the Black historical, cultural, and social experience in America, even if some African cultural linkage can be discerned in forms. But one can trace European-American linkages in them as well.

Today many Black intellectuals, and mainly Black middle-class people, refer to themselves and Black people as African Americans. They do not know that this is not the original or even the most meaningful name of the people on that continent today. Africans mainly go by family, clan, tribal, religious, and national identities. Their African continental identity is decidedly last. But that is not unusual. Continental identities are the least used and appreciated identities of people, in general, unless the name of the country and the continent are the same, such as the American identity. But few people in America or Canada refer to themselves as North Americans.

While the black people on the island continent are coming around to accepting an African identity in retrospect (but still with great difficulty, because they cannot feel much affinity for it) there are Black and black people in America insisting that both groups be known as Africans. But most Black people regard themselves as being black or Black, as poll after poll among Black people has repeatedly shown.[38] Black intellectuals and other educated Black people, in short, some Black middle-class people, ignore them. They ignore history and what Black people say.

Many Black intellectuals (and others) continue to step outside of Black history, and Blackness and blackness, to jump over to Africa and grab an identity from there that is shaky at best. They seek to impose it on Black people and others in America. This kind of behavior leads to remarks like those of Asante and the kind of comment that Black historian Joseph Holloway made with respect to the Black identity in *Africanisms in American Culture* when he said, "thus this debate has come full circle, from *African* through *brown, colored, Afro-American, Negro*, and *black*, back to *African*, the term originally used by blacks in America to define themselves."[39]

It was not the term originally used, and it is still a term that most Black people do not associate with their identity in any form. In fact, polls show they emphatically reject this term to denote their identity to themselves. What makes matters worse is that people who insist that Black people are Africans or African Americans cannot seem to fix on either of these names. Indeed, they feel free to call Black people anything they wish. Marimba Ani called Black people Africans and Afrikans in her book *Yorugu*,[40] while Erriel Roberson referred to them as Afrikans in his book *Reality Revolution*.[41] But in America, Black intellectuals call Black people Africans, African Americans,

Afro-Americans, Afri-Americans, Afra-Americans, Blacks, blacks, black, Black, and even sometimes, still, Negroes.

This is abominable, a reflection of thoughtlessness and carelessness, even a caustic playing around with Black people's lives and their futures in America. All of these different names for Black people make it difficult to promote anything like a consensual identity, politics, strategy, or program to aid Blacks. It makes it difficult to produce anything consensual that potential white allies might be able to embrace. Many Black and black intellectuals and others seem to be proud of this situation, or amenable to it, because it demonstrates in their minds (and they hope in the minds of Whites) how Black thinkers and Black leaders are not all alike, that they differ individually, and that they differ in their objectives. It also says that these people are far removed from the Black people they claim they speak for, represent, or claim they wish to help. They keep the masses of Black people at a distance by names, as they maintain a social distance from them as well.

MISUNDERSTANDING AND MISUSING THE CONCEPT OF NATIONALISM

All of the above was something that Black nationalists and Black nationalist thinking could have prevented if Black nationalists had realized who they really were and what their Black nationalist thought really was. It would have prevented them from thinking of Black people as a "nation" or "a nation within a nation" in America. It would have prevented Black historian Deborah Gray White from including in her recent book, *Too Heavy a Load*, a chapter titled "The First Step in Nation-Making" and another titled "The Dilemmas of Nation-Making." Nowhere in her book did she discuss such things. Although, she did an excellent job discussing Black women's history and the role Black women have played in constructing Black life.

Black historian Wilson Jeremiah Moses, the foremost historian on the subject of Black nationalism, said in *The Golden Age of Black Nationalism*, that Frederick Douglass made remarks that Moses, himself, felt represented the "essence" of Black nationalism when Douglass said:

> In the Northern states, we are not slaves to individuals, not personal slaves, yet in many ways we are slaves of the community.... It is more than a figure of speech to say that we are a people chained together. We are one people-one in general complexion, one in common degradation, one in popular estimation. As one rises, all must rise, and as one falls all must fall. Having now, our feet on the rock of freedom, we must drag

93

our brethren from the slimy depths of slavery, ignorance, and ruin. Every one of us should be ashamed to consider himself free, while his brother is a slave.[42]

I do not see what any of this has to do with Black nationalism and still less with "Pan-Africanism," "African unity," or "African ethnicity."

And what is one to make of Wahneema Lubiano's definition of Black nationalism:

> For the moment I will define "nationalism" as the activation of a narrative of identity and interests. Whether or not concrete in the form of a state (or the idea of its possibility), this narrative is one that members of a social, political, cultural, ethnic, or "racial" group relate to themselves, and which is predicated on some understanding... of a shared past, an assessment of present circumstances, and a description of or prescription for a shared future.... My definition is Weberian in that it draws on his notions of a "community of memories" and a community of shared values, but it also draws on various nineteenth-century black intellectuals' descriptions of their groups' political imperatives (I have in mind Henry Highland Garnet, Maria Stewart, Martin Delaney, Frances E. W. Harper, and the early W. E. B. Du Bois). Black nationalism is a form of nationalism... easily forgotten if it is thought of only as a form of racial separation.[43]

One notices that Lubiano used the word race in two different ways, as "race" and as race. The first is the "race" of many Black intellectuals, the one that does not exist, except in the minds of most Blacks. Lubiano also used race, implying that it was something real that existed. Thus, she allows for an existent and non-existent race. She is equally imprecise in her view about whom or what group would be Black nationalists, interested in that ideology. She said a "social, political, cultural [or] ethnic" group. An ethnic group could be all of the other three classifications as well as itself. But can it be said with clarity what Lubiano regards Blacks to be? Does she think they are a racial group, an ethnic group, or both? Which one would be promoting Black nationalism? Instead of turning to Black people and Black history to gain or devise a concept of community, she turns to the German sociologist Max Weber to obtain one. Is the "community of memories" she refers to a racial group or an ethnic group? And Maria Stewart and Frances E. W. Harper were not advocates of Blacks leaving America for black countries or establishing a Black country in America, so they were not Black nationalists, but Garnet and

Delaney were (the latter for a time anyway). They were advocates of Blacks emigrating to help build a black country abroad.

What Black nationalist thought has to clear up, and be clear about, is whether it is racial thought, ethnic thought, or nationalist thought in the sense of thought and ideology pertaining to a nation-state. It has actually always combined two things (but not clearly) in the minds of the nationalists, or those who listen to or read them. Black nationalist thought is, and has always been, *racial* thought. Cruse was making an effort in the 1960s to make it ethnic thought. But Black nationalists have not moved in any significant numbers to a Black ethnic group focus of the thinking, as Wahneema Lubiano evidenced. Black nationalist thought has historically been thought in regards to how members of the black race in America could engage in constructing their own country. What has not been Black nationalist thought (but always thought to be by Black nationalists) is thought about the separate history and life of Black people in America, unrelated to thoughts, notions, or aspirations of Blacks seeking to leave the country or endeavoring to establish a country in North America. This is where cultural nationalism could legitimately be brought in, understood as the black race engaging in cultural thought or activities pertaining to nation-state construction. Simple talk about Black culture, produced by a racial or ethnic group in this isolated and unrelated fashion, is not cultural nationalist thought. Cruse considered himself a cultural nationalist, but he wasn't.

Cornel West also did not discern that Black nationalist thought was racial thought, as reflected in the following comment: "But these black nationalist responses may provide crucial psychological and existential insights into what it means, what it is like and what it takes to preserve black humanity in the modern West."[44] In *Race Matters*, West spent a chapter talking about Malcolm X's Black nationalist thought, which he depicted and analyzed to be nothing more than racial thought. West did not consciously or knowingly regard it as that. He thought the psychological dimension of this thought was Malcolm X at his best, which he noted when he said, "If we are to build on the best of Malcolm X, we must preserve and expand his notion of psychic conversion that cements networks and groups in which black community, humanity, love, care and concern can take root and grow (the work of bell hooks is the best example)."[45] At this point, I wish to recall what West also said in *Race Matters*: that "racial reasoning," and thus, racial thought, represented "pitfalls" in reasoning and thought that was detrimental to the "mind, body, and soul" of Black people and that lacked "any moral sense." West feels this way about Africancentric thought, or what he referred to simply as "Afrocentricity" and regarded as being no more than an expression of "escape" and "nostalgia." Such a blanket judgement put down, without any effort to investigate or

95

understand this phenomenon, to understand what the Africancentric methodology is and what it seeks to accomplish, implies that it is a worthless and immoral undertaking that is attempting to draw Blacks under its influence.

CHALLENGING AFRICANCENTRISM: THE FALLACY OF THE CLARENCE WALKER CRITIQUE

Henry Louis Gates, Jr. once referred to "Afrocentricity" as "Voodoo methodology." On another occasion, showing that he really did not know much about this methodology or its objectives, he wrote: "Of course, my vision of the academy centers on dialogue and mutual interrogation, not profound secessionism. And so I worry that the sort of cognitive relativism promoted by many Afrocentrists eventuates precisely in this sort of epistemic segregation, where disagreement betokens only a culpable failure to comprehend."[46] Houston Baker, another prominent Black literary critic, like Gates, rejected his colleague's chastising remarks when he stated:

> Now with Afrocentricity, I have always assumed that what scholars were talking about was a different orientation in the American academy toward African history, literature, culture, etc. To the extent that the study of such areas of world knowledge has been sharply limited in the American academy, Afrocentric scholars consider themselves redressing an imbalance. It has never seemed to me that they have called for any person of goodwill to stay away from the domain of study they have marked off for themselves.[47]

Black historian Rhett Jones also spoke to what he regarded as a White racist effort to suppress the new methodology, philosophical perspective, and the feared independence of Africancentrists when he stated: "Afrocentrist departments are stigmatized by American intellectuals, but only by the ill-informed. Unfortunately, these ignorant clods are supported by a "mainstream" media frightened silly by the black intellectual autonomy Afrocentrism represents."[48]

This was clearly Arthur Schlesinger, Jr.'s fear. In 1968 he had been critical of the independence of Black nationalist historians, accusing them of threatening the history methodology and the writing of history.[49] Thirty years later, he condemned what he and others commonly call Afrocentricity. He did so in his book *The Disuniting of America*,[50] saying that there was no significant value in teaching Black students about black Africa, its peoples, histories, cultures, and ways of life, much less about ancient Kemet (or Egypt). He said Black students were Americans and that that was the history and life they should know. He remarked callously: "If some Kleagle of the Ku Klux Klan wanted to devise an education curriculum for the specific purpose of handicapping and disabling black Americans, he would not likely come up with anything more diabolically effective than Afrocentrism." One can't help but see in these remarks the long-standing white male position in America. To them, Blacks don't have much capacity for intelligence and do not know what they are doing intellectually, as well as the desire, with respect to Blacks, of owning the consequences of ownership. One way to effect the latter is to deny people their history or seek to control what they learn of their history.

There are many reputable and good scholars in the group of Africancentrists. One of them is Jacob Carruthers who wrote in *Intellectual Warfare*, "in short, Mr. Schlesinger's examination of the position of African Americans on the African connection is bad history whether from purposeful distortion or mere ignorance." He also said:

> Teaching about the African origins of civilization and the historical role of African peoples is the exact opposite of the teachings of the segregationists and Hegelians (who argued that black people were nonhumans, and that history passed black Africa by). How could such diametrically opposite teachings achieve the same result? ...Whether African-centered education elevates the self-esteem of African American children is a proposition, which can be scientifically tested.... Does Schlesinger, Jr. really believe that teaching African Americans that Western civilization is superior to African culture will improve their self-esteem more than teaching them the truth?[51]

One clearly would not want Arthur Schlesinger, Jr. drawing up a curriculum for Black children. His own historical writing includes a number of books that either totally ignore Black people or just barely mentions them and leaves the overwhelming impression that Black people have always been an insignificant element in American history and have done nothing to help build and to perpetuate the country. When he recommended what he called a "Baker's Dozen" of books in an appendix to the second edition of The *Disuniting of America* that would help Americans understand their history and country, he did not recommend reading a single Black American thinker or writer.

For understanding the antebellum period, Schlesinger did not recommend reading the writings or the published papers of Frederick Douglass, but rather Harriet Beecher Stowe's *Uncle Tom's Cabin*![52] Anybody

Black, or black, who thinks of themselves that way, will not be in any doubt as to the kind of behavior that Schlesinger was exhibiting with the following comment: "Serious black scholars like Henry Louis Gates, Jr., and the group he has assembled in the department of Afro-American studies at Harvard, reject Afrocentricity."[53] In addition, this position reflects Schlesinger's desperate effort to find some *Black surrogates*.

One of the Harvard crowd was Anthony Appiah, whom Schlesinger included in his book because the latter made favorable comments about Mary Lefkowitz's *Not Out of Africa*,[54] where she had opined that "Afrocentricity" was pure "propaganda," especially when saying that ancient Greek intellectuals had gotten philosophy from ancient Kemetic intellectuals. Lefkowitz said, and thought she had proved her contention, not by comparing Greek and Kemetic philosophy, but by simply denying that the Kemets had a philosophy to compare. Anthony Appiah's remarks that Schlesinger referred to, which were on the back of the jacket of Lefkowitz's book, said of it, that it "is the best word so far in the debate about Egypt's influence on classical Greek philosophy. It goes far to settling the debate."[55] Appiah, who is part Ghanaian, demonstrated not only his ignorance of ancient Kemetic philosophy, but also his disinterest in becoming significantly informed about it.

This was also true of Black historian Clarence Walker who has come to the aid of white Western scholars desperate in their efforts to ridicule Africancentrists or destroy Africancentrism and keep Africancentrists from successfully, publicly conveying the knowledge that the ancient Kemets (Egyptians), or those who built the great civilization of the Nile Valley, were *black people*. He wildly, and without sense, accused them of being racist in making this claim. One wonders whether Walker would accuse white people of being racists if they claimed that white Western Europeans were the primary builders of Western civilization in Europe during the seventeenth through the nineteenth centuries. Or would this just simply be a fact?

In his recent book, *We Can't Go Home Again*, Walker tore into the Africancentrists and Africancentrism, focusing much of his attack on its most important figure, Molefi Asante. He said in his book that Mary Lefkowitz had been "courageous" in writing *Not Out of Africa*. Walker demonstrated that his interest was like those he was rushing to the support of, not in analyzing the Africancentric philosophy/methodology, but in simply trying to discredit it. It was obvious in his use of the methods others had used in endeavoring to do the same: he concentrated on the discernible weaknesses in the perspectives and ignored their strengths and importance. One could discredit any kind of philosophical/methodological posture and the scholarship that flowed from it on this basis, including what is referred to as Eurocentric thinking and scholarship.

Walker's book is full of specious assumptions and arguments that are the basis of his attacks against Asante and the Africancentrists. He makes no distinction between the ancient Egyptians who built the great civilization from those who came hundreds and even thousands of years later. Walker shows that he did not know the difference between racism and race, and in every instance misapplied the term racialized. He argued that the ancient Kemets could not have been black because they did not exhibit "race consciousness." Very few white people in America exhibit a "race consciousness," but they clearly understand that they are white and act accordingly. This reflects a deep "racial unconsciousness." More accurately, it reflects a deep racist unconsciousness, exercised through race and racial thought.

Walker said that the ancient Kemets could not have been black because race did not exist, that it was "socially constructed." He noted: "Since race is a social construct, not a biological datum as the Afrocentrists claim, we have to be skeptical of their reading of Egypt as a black civilization."[56] However, Walker showed his support of white Egyptologists and white classicists who argued that the ancient Kemets were of a "mixed race." This is saying that two or more races existed in ancient Kemet. But how could that be, how could races be mixed if there were no races?

He denied that the ancient Kemets were black because, as he said, they had Nubians and Semites in their societies who were ethnically and culturally different. This was mainly true long after the great civilization had been built. The Kemets eventually brought different peoples into their society or different peoples came in who conquered the civilization in its declining centuries. Clearly, being ethnically and culturally different does not mean that one is not talking about the same race. Races, after all, are made up of ethnic groups. And it should be said that all Semites of the ancient world were not white as Walker, Lefkowitz, and others have said and implied. There were black Semitic people known as Ethiopians and there were black Semitic people in ancient Mesopotamia. There are still black Semitic Ethiopians, black Semitic Sudanese, black Semitic Yemenites, and other black Semitic people in the Middle East and across the northern part of Africa. Walker even admitted that there was racial variation among the ancient Kemets when he wrote the following contradictory remarks, "Furthermore, the association of various combinations of other physical characteristics with the Ethiopian suggests that the Greeks and Romans were describing two types of people whom anthropologists today would classify as subtypes of the Negroid race."[57] This sounds clearly to me like racial variation.

Following his white cohort detractors, Walker said that the Africancentrists were seeking to impose a "modern" view of race on the ancient Kemets. Nothing could be further from the truth. That "modern" version was the one devised by the racist scientists in the late nineteenth and early twentieth centuries. It was the one that had all black people looking alike and looking very much unlike white people. Africancentrists utilize the scientific, as opposed to the pseudoscientific, view of race, to view the ancient Kemets: namely, that a race is not pure and varies racially within.

Where Walker shows equal ineptness in his book is in his effort to disassociate Kemetic thought and culture from ancient Greece. Again, he follows his white cohort detractors in doing this. Africancentrists argue that the ancient Kemetic civilization had a large impact on ancient Greece, ancient Judaism, ancient Rome, and the formation of Christianity. The denial by Walker and others of these realities flies into the face of very prominent white Egyptologists and classicists who have said the same thing. Walker and his group may not have known about this or simply chose to ignore or suppress this information in their analyses.

It should also be said that the white scholars who wrote in glowing terms about ancient Kemetic civilization did so on the racist premise that the builders of the great civilization were white. Egyptologist James Henry Breasted said the following in *The Dawn of Conscience*, originally published in 1934:

> We have seen the new capacities, which these new words [conscience and character] proclaimed, operating as social forces, and bringing about a new order, which the moral sages of Egypt also discerned and for which they had a term, "Maat," meaning "right, righteousness, justice, truth," and the moral order in which these things were the controlling forces. It is these terms, together with "conscience" and "character," all emerging historically in the written records of Egypt between 3000 and 2000 B.C., which are for us monuments of the transformation on our planet. In this epoch-making transformation, occurring for the first time on our globe, and so far as we know, for the first time in the universe, the Egyptians were the discoverers of character. It is fundamentally important that the modern world should realize how recent is that discovery. Civilization is built upon character.[58]

Egyptologist Joseph Kaster remarked in *The Wisdom of Ancient Egypt*:

> Already at the earliest period of the Old Kingdom, in the great pyramid-temple complex of King Zoser, we find the tall, graceful, fluted columns and the clean, soaring lines strikingly similar in style and feeling to those

of the Greek temples of almost two and a half millennia later. Columns and their capitals and the technical methods of architectural construction based upon sound engineering principles, aesthetic canons and artistic techniques in sculpture, relief painting (and particularly portraiture in these media), styles and techniques in metalworking, cabinetry, and the art of the lapidary, can all be traced back in a direct line of development from the achievements of classical Greece to their origins in ancient Egypt.[59]

One of the great authorities of Kemetic art, Jean Capart, remarked: "Our final conclusion may be that Egypt reveals to us the knowledge of one of the sources—perhaps the source—from which the great river of beauty has flowed continuously through the world."[60] Egyptologist P. E. Peet argued that Greek as well as Hebrew literature was significantly impacted by Kemetic literature: "At the same time, Greek literature cannot have sprung full-blown like Venus from the Waves, any more than did Greek art, and though we may never learn the manner in which Egyptian influence made its way into Hebrew and Greek literature, it may reasonably be doubted whether either the one or the other would have been what it is had it not been for Egypt."[61]

Mary Lefkowitz made the categorical remark that the ancient Kemets did not have a philosophy that the Greeks could borrow, let alone "steal." But it is the view of the Swiss Egyptologist Erik Hornung that philosophy originated with the Kemets, which he noted in his recent book *Idea into Image* when he said: "It is appropriate to characterize Egyptian thought as the beginning of philosophy. As far back as the third millennium BC, the Egyptians were concerned with questions that return in European philosophy... questions about being and nonbeing, about the meaning of death, about the nature of the cosmos and man, about the essence of time, about the basis of human society and the legitimization of power."[62]

Philosopher Jay Lampert wrote the following comments about Kemetic philosophy:

> Egyptian speculative writing has a very long history, beginning with the texts written directly onto the walls of the tombs inside the pyramids (ca. 2600 BCE—the early dates are disputed). The texts of philosophical interest that we possess today would fill perhaps ten volumes, covering such issues as creation and world-order, eternal life and divisions of the soul, the gods and their combinatory relations, justice, language, and intellect. Drawing from 2500 years of Egyptian speculation, of course, we find texts offering a wide variety of systems, syntheses, and genres.[63]

And finally, philosopher Dan Flory penned the following comments on the subject:

> Erik Iversen's *Egyptian and Hermetic Doctrine* closely compares Ancient Egyptian inscriptions to the Corpus Hermeticum as we have them and finds that many of their supposed Greek philosophical notions may well stem from Egyptian thought as old as the Fifth Dynasty (ca. 2300 BC)...the work of Jean-Pierre Mahe since the mid-seventies has shown the much more deeply Egyptian character of the philosophical Hermetic writings and by implication possible other texts we have traditionally thought of as Western philosophy.[64]

So where does that leave the argument regarding the Africancentrists and their claims about the cultural and civilizational achievements of the ancient Kemets and their impact on others: Hebrews, Greeks, Romans, Christians, and other ancient peoples? Even if the Africancentrists cannot make the case that ancient Kemet was the "mother" of Western civilization, they certainly can make the very strong case that the ancient black Kemets had a large impact on that civilization through such cultural transmission belts as the Hebrews, Greeks, Romans, and Christians. Clarence Walker finished his book stating: "Afrocentrism, with its emphasis on a usable past... is risible."[65] What is really risible was the effort that Walker consciously made to ridicule this philosophical and methodological viewpoint.

It is not really a laughing matter. It is a tragic situation of a Black historian feeling the need to trash other Black and black scholars on behalf of white ones, as their surrogate trasher. Walker apparently never stopped to raise a question about the Eurocentrism position he was upholding by criticizing Africancentrists. Namely, the question that if ancient Greeks lived in south-eastern Europe and built their civilization there, how can ancient Greece be the beginning of Western civilization? And why is it that Blacks "Can't Go Home" to ancient Kemet, but "Can Go Home" to ancient Mesopotamia, Greece, and Rome? It's a strange argument, indeed, a racist one, and Walker endorses it.

I identify with the point that Jacob Carruthers was making with respect to Arthur Schlesinger, Jr. and what he and other Africancentrists would say to their white detractors: *it is not up to white people*, today, or at any other time, to tell Black or black people how to relate to black Africa. Nor is it their prerogative to decide for such people who the appropriate or worthy scholars are for them to read and study. These are things that Blacks will decide for themselves. And they will make decisions about Black or black scholars that do not have formal or much formal academic background on the subject, but who have labored hard and long and productively in the vineyard, such as Joel A. Rogers, John Jackson, John Henrik Clarke, Ivan van Sertima, Runoko Rashidi, Anthony Browder, M. D. Charles Finch III, Asa G. Hilliard III, and Legrand H. Clegg II.

OPTING FOR BLACKCENTRICITY AND AFRICANCENTRICITY

While I accept and utilize Africancentricity, I am also a Blackcentric. I see these philosophical/methodological orientations as being different from each other, but necessarily related. In terms of methodology, a Blackcentric perspective focuses directly on Black people: their history, culture, and social life in America. From there, Blackcentricity reaches out to other areas of knowledge, other areas of America, other peoples and places in the world. Black nationalist thinkers were always Blackcentric, even when they dealt with the two strands of Black nationalism. Certainly they were always Blackcentric when they spoke of Black people and their history and life in the country; whether this was done in racial terms, or as I hope it will be done in the future, in ethnic terms. Blackcentricity accepts the African (in retrospect) origins of Black people and the retention of some African traits in Black life. It accepts a connection with black Africa and the possibility of more of these "retentions" being discovered when comparing Black life with black African life.

Whatever is found in the way of "Africanisms" in Black life, they will more than likely show how they had long since been transformed by the Black experience to become an integral part of it. They will show how Black ethnicity enhanced them and will show how there are some European-American influences in the synthesis. These Africanisms will not be regarded as African, any more than Black people regard their religion, the blues, jazz, their dancing, "signifying," or "playing the dozens" as being African. Blackcentricity rejects the idea that Black people in America are Africans, just Black and black people of black African descent. But Blacks in America can be, in many cases, also part white in racial descent, with considerable European-American cultural descent. Blackcentricity rejects the concept of Africancentrism as an idea to work with, and such concepts as Afrocentricity or Africentricity, or Afrikancentricity or Afracentrism. Black Africans are Africans and they should not be referred to as anything else: no "Afros," "Afras," or "Afris," or any similar prefix, nor should these prefixes appear before forms of African thought or other forms of culture. It is time for Black and black intellectuals to stop playing around with the names of black people, in Africa or elsewhere.

I reject the term Africancentrism because it is an extreme term. This is absolutist either-or thinking going on. But a number of Africancentrists think this way, including their leading light, Molefi Asante. His has been a remarkable story. He has gone further than anyone to develop Africancentrism as a philosophy and methodology, which are both integral parts of a Ph.D. program in this subject that he, along with others, was able to establish at Temple University. Both the man and the program have inspired and are inspiring duplication at other major colleges and universities. Asante is a much more profound and elaborate thinker than his critics seem to know. One achievement his prolific and full work signifies is the establishment of an independent intellectual and analytical position for Black and black scholars. Asante is clearly one of the significant Black intellectuals in America.

However, my objection to Asante and those who follow him, other than their view that Black people are black Africans, is the absolutist character of their thinking and analysis, the sexist thoughts sometimes evident in their commentary, and their romanticism. For instance, they claim that Eurocentrism is absolutist. That it is just a particularistic perspective, but Whites/Europeans keep trying to make it a universal one, applicable as an intellectual and analytical perspective on all human history, human society, and human behavior. Asante roils at this view, stating:

> Without severe criticism, the preponderant Eurocentric myths of universalism, objectivity, and classical traditions retain a provincial European cast....Applied to the African world, such conceptualization becomes limiting, restricting, and parochial....Furthermore, there is neither recognition of African classical thought nor of the African classical past in the Eurocentric formulations.... The Afrocentric analysis reestablishes the centrality of the ancient Kemetic (Egyptian) civilization and the Nile Valley cultural complex as points of reference for an African perspective in much the same way as Greece and Rome serve as reference points for the European world. Thus, the Afrocentrist expands human history by creating a new path for interpretation.[66]

These remarks refute Henry Louis Gates, Jr.'s remarks (and anyone who argues like him) that Asante wants his methodology and philosophy to function in some kind of "secessionist" manner in colleges and universities. He does not advocate elimination of the Eurocentric perspective, as critics have erroneously said in attempting to discredit Asante, his work and ideas. He sees it as one perspective that has its place in the academy; but, he also feels that Africancentrism should have a place, as well.

These thoughts do not reflect absolutist either-or thinking, but his concept of the "African world" does. He says Africancentrism refers to "African themes in the Americas and the West Indies, as well as the African continent." And he posits this absolutist position: "The Afrocentrist will not question the idea of the centrality of African ideals and values but will argue over what constitutes those ideals and values."[67] These are comments that meet with criticism by a conscious Blackcentric like myself. I reject the idea that Black people in America are Africans and that Black culture is African culture. And I reject the view that Black people are making African history in America. I further argue that Black people are considerably historically, culturally, socially, and psychologically different from black Africans.

In short, Blackcentricity does not romanticize black Africa or black Africans and does not accept a romantic version of Africancentricity. Further, it does not accept the theme of alienation that is promoted directly or indirectly by Africancentrists in their verbal or written efforts. The argument is that Black people are "alienated" from their African identity and African culture. But the notion of alienation is more complicated than that. Africancentrists also believe that Blacks should seek to be alienated from their Black identity and their Black culture, to free themselves up and to claim their African identities and affinities. For Blacks to give up their Black and black identities that are grounded in Black history, culture, and social life, for identities that are rhetorical, ideological, and expressions of wishful, romantic thinking, would be foolhardy, in my view.

Blackcentricity accepts two of the philosophical/analytical categories of Africancentrism, namely "place" and "location." However, they are accepted in a somewhat different manner than Africancentrism. Asante argues that Africancentrists have to think of "place" and "location" to engage in research, analysis, and expressions of thought. "Place" and "location," though, are not historicist or relative concepts for Asante. They are absolutist terms. Asante and other Africancentrists do not accept the concept of black African descent. They recognize only black Africans. They recognize only black African culture. So, wherever black people are on this globe, they are, to Asante and to Africancentrists, black Africans and their culture is black African culture. Asante speaks of "cultural differentiation" among black African people, but for him, the culture is always black African culture, however varied. He refuses to recognize how the cultures of black peoples inside and outside of Africa have been impacted by outside cultures, such as Western culture itself. He would reject the view expressed by Paul Gilroy in *Black Atlantic*[68] that the cultures of black people in the Western Hemisphere have been greatly affected, indeed, synthesized, by the interpenetration of Western culture.

Africa, for Asante and the Africancentrists, is not simply the African continent. It is wherever there are what they describe as black African people, which would apply to the aborigines of Australia, the black people of the Fiji Islands, New Guinea, and Hawaii and it would apply to the black people in India, the Middle East, Africa, and any place in the Western Hemisphere. Thus, for Asante and other Africancentrists "place," "location," "context," "African centrality" or "African cultural centrality"–terms of the philosophy/methodology–have no boundaries, except what is called the "African world," which is global. This is absolutist thinking, the same kind of thinking that Asante and other Africancentrists ascribe to Eurocentrism, and which they criticize.

Joyce Ann Joyce, as an Africancentrist, is critical of Eurocentrism. However, as an Africancentrist she is no less absolutist in her thinking and analysis and also considerably romantic, which leads to faulty thinking and analysis. She accepts Chancellor Williams's argument expressed in *Rebirth of African Civilization* that there is a unity in black African culture, despite different tribes and languages. She says, "too many students of Africa have stressed the differences in culture, language, religion, and even race as insurmountable barriers to overall unity of purpose, thought and action. One of the unexpected developments... is an underlying sense of unity among Africans throughout the continent."[69] Williams's position makes matters fuzzy, which Joyce did not perceive. It's one thing to talk about an "underlying sense" of cultural unity and another to talk about the political unity of black African peoples and countries across the continent, which does not exist. The Europeans have shown that they can transform their underlying civilizational unity into political unity. They have also shown that this is an awesome thing to try to accomplish. Black African efforts, thus far, have yielded inconsequential results. Something that Joyce recognized, but ignored at the same time, was the fact that Chancellor Williams was talking about black Africans and the African continent. As an Africancentrist she proceeded to move black Africans, black African culture, and black Africa itself to the Western Hemisphere. But this was a specious move because she ideologically and romantically imposed black African culture on all black people in the Western Hemisphere. She did this by implying that that culture could be found among all people and all places.

By this kind of thinking, the history of all black people in the Western Hemisphere is wiped out. Their cultural deletions, transformations, and cultural additions, which involved synthesizing Western cultural traits, are wiped out. This includes their national and ethnic identities. This is establishing, in an ideological, romantic, and even fanciful manner, "Pan-Africanism" or "Pan-African Unity." Joyce described the history of all the black people in Africa and the Western Hemisphere as "Black history." One could make the case for black racial history from Africa to the Western Hemisphere. But when one says that this is also African history, then things get very fuzzy. There are white people on the African continent who are Africans. It is a continental identity, and they are just as entitled to that identity as any black person is. Thus, black African history would be a more appropriate term. But then the question would be (which Joyce simply ignored) whether the history of black people in the Western Hemisphere was part of black African history. Because black Africans and black West Indians are different people and black Africans are clearly different from Black Americans or Black and Black Canadians* with historical or cultural similarities. But Africancentrists, illogically and incredibly, will not make any distinctions between any black people or play such distinctions way down. Africancentrism (or as some also say "Afrocentrism") is an absolutist term, fostering essentialism, either-or thinking, singular thought, singular analyses, and errant views. I prefer the concept of Africancentricity because it is not absolute and does accept boundaries. It accepts "black African centeredness" when the people involved are "black Africans." But it gives way to concepts that can show where the original black African people had become a different kind of people, best described as people of "black African descent."

This is what the concept of Blackcentricity does. It stands in criticism of Africancentrism because of that position's refusal to accept transformation, difference, and uniqueness. Blackcentricity also rejects the term because, with its all-embracing quality, it suppresses or distorts the history, culture, and social life of black people, that is, black people of black African descent who have since undergone transformation and who have become a different kind of black people, making a different kind of history, and making a different kind of life for themselves.

* Thousands of Black people migrated to Canada in the 19th century and still have a presence in the country, along with black people from other parts of the world.

It should be recalled what Du Bois once said, in *The Souls of Black Folk,* that Black people should not seek to "Africanize America, for America has too much to teach the world and Africa." This was also Du Bois's way of saying that Black people should not seek to become Africans, which would be the way they would seek to Africanize this country. Du Bois was fully aware of and wrote about the cultural (among other) impact of Black people on America, which he did not regard as an African impact. Du Bois was a Blackcentric, as his many writings and commentary make very clear. However, he regarded Blacks as a racial group, rather than an ethnic group. Blackcentricity, as I am casting it, asserts that Black people are an ethnic group, evolving into an ethnic group from the original black race that was transplanted here. Blackcentricity accepts that they are still holding on to that racial status as well.

Blackcentricity rejects Black nationalist thought, while recognizing its manifestation in Black history as separatist, emigrationist, and romantic thought about Blacks building a Black or black countries. It also accepts the fact that Black nationalist thought, as it has usually been employed in Black history, has been employed in an erroneous manner as "nation-building" thought, when it was simply racial thought. It was thought about the black race, the black racial community, and things like black racial pride, black racial unity, and black racial power. This was important thought in Black history, as Black nationalist thought, in this racial form. It helped Blacks to think differently and positively about themselves, their race, and their humanity. It helped them to resist, as well as to confront, White racism and White racist oppression, and helped to inspire and galvanize them to pursue and achieve full freedom in America. However, Africancentrism interferes with understanding and writing fully and truthfully on these matters. This is why Africancentrism has to be viewed with limitations, with boundaries. In short, it needs to be put in its proper "place" and "location." In these designations, it will be more helpful to Black people, Blackcentricity, and to itself.

And this is especially important to do for some other considerations. There is considerable pressure being placed on Black scholars, Black intellectuals, and black intellectuals to look globally at black people. While there is this pressure from the increasingly global thinking and writing of the Western world, it is also true that Black and black intellectuals, as Robin Kelley has pointed out, have been in a global orientation for a number of decades. They have used terms like "Black Diaspora" or "African Diaspora" or "Pan-African"[70] that have also been translated into academic studies areas. In recent years, there have been new names and study areas added that have also contributed to the globalization pressure on Black and black intellectuals.

These new areas are called "Black Atlantic Studies," "Africana Studies," "Transnational Studies," "Postmodern Transcultural Studies" and "Black Cultural Studies." All of these concepts, including the first ones mentioned, are primarily references to black people, from Africa to the Western Hemisphere. Although, black people in England, black Africans, black West Indians, black people in Germany, and thus, England itself, are drawn into this presence.

FROM AFRICAN DIASPORA TO AFRICAN EXTENTSIA

What occurs with the re-naming of these areas, and what for me is a point of criticism, is a plethora of names to identify what is generally the same subject in the same general geographical area. It's the old story of Black and black scholars being loose with names and indifferent to the way they describe black people. The phrase "African Diaspora" would cover all of this if it were understood that it was a reference to black Africans, and thus, black Africa and black people of black African descent, including the black Africans and people of black African descent on the European continent. Theoretically, the concept could extend to black Africans and people of black African descent all over the globe. But this is not how this concept is usually used. It is usually employed in reference to black people from Africa, through England and throughout the Western Hemisphere. Even when the concept is employed in this limited sense, it is usually done without a millennial orientation or assumption and usually without making clear-cut distinctions between the different kinds of black people who fall under the general description or who have different identities (ethnic or national identities), or different cultures (ethnic or national). It is the same problem as when all the black people in the Western Hemisphere are referred to as "African Americans." It neither denotes nor allows for any distinctions among the peoples under this identity. In America, Black and black intellectuals use the phrase "African American" for all the black people here. But who is this really a reference to? Laura Chrisman, Jasmine Griffin, and Tukufu Zuberi recently wrote, "the creation of a truly Africana Studies, a study of Africa and the African diaspora whose starting point is the commonality of experience but honestly recognizing our differences is imperative at this historical moment."[71]

While I can agree with this sentiment, I have reservations about the way it has been stated here, because as stated it is considerably confusing. What is meant by "commonality of experience"? Do they mean common historical experience, common cultural experience, and common experiences of domination, control, and exploitation? What exactly? And what is the reference to differences? The difference may be more important to and at least equal to what is regarded as "common." Thus, an "Africana Studies" program or intellectual orientation has to eliminate the hierarchy of thinking or ordering and look at the intellectual matter in individualistic and equal terms, preferably in a holistic interactive manner.

I am also not clear what the writers meant by "African diaspora." Is this a reference, similar to the reference of the Africancentrists, to what they regard as black African people in the world and the variation of black African people and black African cultures? Or does the concept also include a reference to people who are no longer African, but are of black African descent, and such people with altered or transformed cultures and lives? Or does it refer to each black African ethnic group that has left Africa and which lives beyond it, as an "African diaspora" all by itself, as some Black and black scholars have referred to as "overlapping diasporas?" This makes the African diaspora concept meaningless, and any discussion of individual or overlapping diasporas, along with a general African diaspora, extremely confusing. It's one thing to talk about a black African ethnic group or community, or a group or community of black African descendents in an African diaspora, but it is quite another to put "African diaspora" next to each grouping. A Cape Verdean diaspora is *not* the same as an African diaspora!

Phrases like "Transnational" or "Transcultural" are also very problematic. The phrase Transnational is logically a reference to nation-state or country. Transcultural is rather nebulous. It could be a reference to nation-state or country, but also to an ethnic group, even to both at the same time, such as Liberia and the Liberians living in America as an ethnic group, or Nigeria and the Nigerians living in America as an ethnic group. So is the African diaspora to be a study area of black countries or black ethnic groups, or both? Or is it to be a study of one massive "transnational culture" that embraces all black groups, those that are Africans and those of black African descent, which is how one sees the concepts of African diaspora and "Black Atlantic," as well as the concept of "Black diaspora" sometimes presented. This, of course, is absolutist, romantic, and ahistorical.

This whole matter resembles what I described in chapter two as the "Lolling and Lumbering" in the wasteland of race and racism: a discourse area of inadequacy and confusion. For myself, I have cut through this confusion with my own concepts and with my Africancentric philosophy/methodology, that relates to, and that straightens out the difficulties in looking at black people in a global manner. One of my concepts is the concept of *African Extensia*, which subdivides into four other concepts: *Southern African Extensia* (Africa itself), *Eastern African Extensia* (Middle East, Asian sub-continent,

and Far East), *Northern African Extensia* (all of Europe), and the *Weste.*
African Extensia (the Western Hemisphere). The argument here is that Afric.
is the origin of human beings and the first human beings were black people.

The human race was originally the black race. These first humans were
referred to as *homo sapien sapien*. They migrated from Africa to other parts of
the world creating the various Extensias. This was the original human
dispersal, or diaspora, a true black African diaspora. This diaspora preceded all
other human diasporas by millennia. Each of the Extensia is to be viewed as
existing over millennia up to the present day. Each acknowledges continuity,
change, development, and also transformation. The Extensia concepts make it
possible to view Africancentricity as something that has global reach, but
which is also a concept of limitation, because each of the three specific
geographical extensia from Africa accepts the end of black Africans, unless
they are in fact present, who would come under the geographical extensia
concept. Extensia is a concept that might speak specifically to black countries
and black ethnic groups, or countries or ethnic groups of black African
descent, even a general culture produced by black people with discernible
variations. "African Extensia Studies" would be the title of my global study of
black people in the world. The African diaspora concept and "African
Diaspora Studies" could work here if both were visualized with the millennial
assumption, and reality, and global continuity and breakage that my African
Extensia and African Extensia Studies do. However, inasmuch as the diasporic
concept is used so haphazardly and is so contentious among Black and black
scholars/intellectuals, I don't see it being put to this kind of intellectual or
academic use.

To end confusion, in my view, any Black Studies program or department
in America's colleges and universities should be composed of a comprehensive
study of the history, culture, social life, psychology, thought, and so on of
Black people in the country. If only an Africana Studies program or
department existed, then, in my view, the study of Black people should be the
basic focus. At the same time, the program could reach out with courses or
cultural programs to other black people in America and elsewhere. This goal
should also be obtained with something called an African Diaspora program
or department. As a Blackcentric, I am against Black people in the United
States, who number in the tens of millions, playing second fiddle to other
black ethnic groups that are numerically much smaller and have made smaller
contributions to this country's history, culture, and social life in academic
programs at colleges and universities. And the study of black African people
or any black people in the world cannot be made at the expense of Blacks in
America when it comes to academic programs either.

Africancentrists would slight Black people this way, not only in terms of the emphasis on black Africans and black African culture, but also by denying the existence of *Black* people and *Black* culture. Black people simply cannot learn much about themselves, as Blacks, by studying the Igbos of Nigeria, the Massai of Kenya, or the Asante of Ghana. Studying such people would give them only partial knowledge, even as important as it might be. That is the grist of Africancentricity and that is also where Blackcentricity comes in to fill out the story. As said earlier, it takes Africancentricity and Blackcentricity working together in a holistic manner to understand Black people in the United States.

These two philosophical/methodological perspectives would not be accepted by Black conservatives, who indeed feel it is an unnecessary "fuss" for Black or black intellectuals to be concerned about the identity of Black people in America. While they are usually not postmodernists, they are usually extreme individualists, and think that being an individual is enough of an identity for any black person in America. An individual, in their minds, is also "cosmopolitan" in the way that the term is used in Webster's dictionary: "At home throughout the world or in any spheres of interest."

But there are two "spheres of interest" that most Black conservative intellectuals, and others who have influence with and over Black conservatives, do not feel "at home" with and that is blackness and Blackness. Black conservative intellectuals, for the most part, come out of Black life, but not out of Black history to be intellectuals. By immersion, they come out of White, and even White racist history. Black Marxists and Black Socialists come out of Black life, but their thinking and political approaches come out of White history, even while rejecting its racism and racist social expressions. Black liberals exhibit confusion about what it means to be a liberal in the United States. However, they are not the only ones to demonstrate that confusion. Black conservatives and Black radicals do so as well. Indeed, most American intellectuals and most Americans, in general, exhibit this confusion- all of which will be discussed in the next chapter.

Chapter Four
Three of a Kind: Black Conservatives, Black Liberals, and Black Radicals

The Black intellectual Kelly Miller wrote the following comments in a chapter of his 1908 book *Race Adjustment* (the book was re-issued in the late 1960s as *Radicals and Conservatives in Negro America*):[1]

> When a distinguished Russian was informed that some American Negroes are radical and some conservative, he could not restrain his laughter. The idea of conservative Negroes was more than the Cossack's risibilities could endure. "What on earth," he exclaimed in astonishment, "have they to conserve."
>
> According to a strict use of terms, a "conservative" is one who is satisfied with existing conditions and advocates their continuance; while a "radical" clamors for amelioration of conditions through change. No thoughtful Negro is satisfied with the present status of his race, whether viewed in its political, its civil or general aspect. He labors under an unfriendly public opinion, one which is being rapidly crystallized into a rigid caste system and enacted into righteous law.[1]

To Miller, as to many other Black intellectuals at the time, the Black "conservatives" were Booker T. Washington and his followers. The "radicals" were individuals like W. E. B. Du Bois, Monroe Trotter, E. H. Morris, Ida B. Wells-Barnett and Clement Morgan. Mary Church Terrell, however, was sliding between Washington and the "radicals." Thus, she was considered a moderate at the time, as was Miller, himself, although Terrell broke with Du Bois in 1911, following Ida B. Wells-Barnett's earlier separation from him. William Ferris, author of the two-volume *The African Abroad*, had been a Black "radical" and also fiercely anti-Booker T. Washington. However, he turned against the "radicals" and towards Washington in 1907, saying in a letter to the Tuskegean: "while I do not always agree with everything you say, I believe that the greatness of your work and the grandeur of your achievement and your grasp of the industrial condition in the South entitles you to rank with the great constructive geniuses of the century."[2] Ferris would eventually become a Garveyite and an editor of one of the movement's newspapers, *The Negro World*.

Kelly Miller observed that conservatives and radicals agreed on the ends for Blacks, but disagreed about the methods to achieve them. This disagreement not only divided Black intellectuals and Black leaders, but also abetted the very racism that they were all against and attempting to defeat. Miller said, "And so, colored men who are alike zealous for the betterment of their race lose half their strength in internal strife, because of variant methods of attack upon the citadel of prejudice."[3] Nearly a hundred years later, one would think there would be something new to add to Miller's comments. There is, but it is not propitious. There is a much larger number of Black intellectuals today who are more divided than they were during Washington's ascendancy. The Tuskegean actually had most Black intellectuals in the North and the South on his side.

This contention might seem preposterous, but historian August Meier cleared up this point in the early 1960s. In his prodigiously researched book, *Negro Thought in America*, he wrote: "In reviewing the data we have presented on the thinking of an illustrative sampling of Negro intellectuals, it is evident that most of them-even those with a college education—were at one time or another(if not all the time) either enthusiastic or luke-warm supporters of Booker T. Washington, and that doctrines of racial pride, economics, solidarity, and self-help loomed larger in their thinking, though of course, their goal was full citizenship rights."[4]

Today there is no over-arching Black leader like Booker T. Washington. Most Black intellectuals are happy about that and would likely decry such a leader. They feel that that type of leader is no longer necessary. They chide Jesse Jackson for trying to be one. They nip at the Reverend Al Sharpton as he keeps edging in the direction of a larger leadership role that would enable him to lead Blacks far away from New York—on an individual issue basis. Most Black intellectuals and leaders regard Louis Farrakhan as nothing more than an "enclave leader" among Blacks, as leader of the Nation of Islam or his Black and black Muslim followers. As a group, Black intellectuals seem to think that they can fill the gap left by the lack of an over-arching leader. The over-arching leader is an activist. He might also be an intellectual, as Booker T. Washington was. Washington was a prolific writer and speechmaker; and when he was not writing his own books or articles, he had people write them over his name.

For thirty-five years altogether, and for twenty as the Grand Black Leader, Washington bombarded Blacks and Whites in America with the "Tuskegee Idea." The Tuskegee Idea was a theory of race pride, race unity, race solidarity, and race modernization and development. Are there Blacks today who need to undergo modernization and development? What about the people that most seem to talk about: the Black "underclass"? Especially when considering that it is estimated that 30 to 40 percent of the Black population is below o_____ hovering at the poverty level.

The black conservative Orlando Patterson claimed in *The Ordeal of Integration* that by his calculations "at least 35 percent of Afro-American adult male workers are solidly middle-class. The percentage is roughly the same for adult female workers who, while they earn less than their male counterparts, are in white-collar occupations to a much greater extent."[5] But these figures, as Patterson has to know, say that roughly sixty-five percent of Black male and female workers are not middle-class. He said that "if we use a median family income of $35,000 as the cut-off point for the middle-class, then 36 percent of Afro-American families may be considered middle-class, which would also mean that sixty-four percent were not. Patterson was clearly impressed by the fact that the top five percent of Black families in America "averaged $122,558 in household income (1995) compared with $82,397 in 1967 (in 1995 dollars)." These people, he said rather gleefully, earned "elite incomes."[6]

In the television documentary "The Two Nations of Black America," Henry Louis Gates, Jr. interviewed Black Harvard sociologist William Julius Wilson who said that the income level between the top Black social class and the Black lower class was steadily widening. He also remarked that the top five percent (the Black upper class), and some members of the Black middle class, possessed almost half of the total Black wealth. In America, generally, one-percent of the population possesses nearly forty-six percent of the country's financial wealth, while ninety-nine percent share the other fifty-four percent[7].

Black conservatives tend to emphasize the economic progress of Blacks without talking about or minimizing the large income and opportunity gap between those who have made progress and the larger number of those who have not. Black radicals and liberals talk of the progress and the gaps, but disagree in many ways about how to close the disparities; the big difference is that the Marxist-oriented radicals propose that America become a socialist country. In their minds this would resolve problems between Blacks and Whites and most other problems of the country. But these two groups are particularly reticent to talk about what kind of Black leadership is going to help Black people catch up to other Blacks and Whites in America. Black intellectuals feel that they can provide this leadership, an idea that is dubious and raises the question of what a "public intellectual" is. Presumably, it will be the Black "public intellectual" who will lead the mass, about two-thirds of the Black population, to the "Promise Land" of a middle-class status in America. Although, it is still not clear whether this is the goal of today's Black intellectuals for the mass of Black people not living in the middle-class. Black intellectuals have achieved middle-class status, but there has not been a strong r concerted public advocacy for this status for the mass of remaining Blacks, those whom Jesse Jackson is still inclined to describe as, "the boat's still stuck on the bottom."

DEFINING THE BLACK PUBLIC INTELLECTUAL

Black American Studies scholar Johnnella Butler has provided this definition of the public intellectual: "Whether associated with higher education or not, the public intellectual traditionally speaks from an informed position on serious moral, social, cultural, or political issues, bringing the issues to the public with clarity, foresight, and honesty. In the broadest and most useful sense, the public intellectual is a scholar-activist."[8] Butler's description and dimension is problematic, because it carries the image of formal and extensive collegiate education and training, along with membership in professional scholarly associations.

There are Black intellectuals (as well as other intellectuals, for that matter), who function outside the academy. Du Bois did it the last thirty years of his life; Ida B. Wells-Barnett and Ella Baker did it; A. Philip Randolph, Martin Luther King, Jr., and Malcolm X did it as well. Indeed, many Black intellectuals, those who have been and many today who are potentially useful for Blacks and America, would not make the status of public intellectual as defined by Butler. Although, it can be said that they may strongly fit the category of Black "organic intellectual," such as the Black conservative Robert Woodson (a rarity among this crowd) or Lerone Bennett, Jr. A number of Black male and female journalists would also be regarded as public intellectuals. For instance, the journalist Carl Rowan had attained this status and Earl Ofari Hutchinson, Julianne Malveaux, and Paula Giddings would also be considered public intellectuals today.

The description and dimension of "activist" raises some concerns. It is understood that Butler is providing an idealized concept of a public intellectual, the way she would like to see them be, based on what she has observed about such people. However, not many intellectuals–public or otherwise–are activists or want to be; indeed, they operate from an academic/professional code that they should not be. They believe that they should be detached, objective intellectuals, not taking any side or public political stance on an issue. They are scholars and experts, which they feel entitles them to research matters and to present public accounts of them. But after that, their job is finished. They would argue that it is up to others to take matters from there: politicians, educators, journalists–others. This is the

Kantian notion of the intellectual that had been taken over by the positivistic philosophers and social scientists in the late nineteenth and early twentieth centuries. Kant espoused a paradigm of science: detachment, objectivity, and letting retrieved knowledge speak for itself. Du Bois tried this approach as a Black intellectual and tried to help Black people with his scientific studies of Blacks. But he discovered that the information he and his associates painfully adduced and presented to the public did not have much of an impact. So he became a public advocate and activist.

With this in mind, is the definition of the public intellectual one who devises ideas, strategies, policies, or programs and then publicly advocates them and seeks practical ways in which to implement them, such as participating in public organizations or associations to do so (as Du Bois did when he participated in the Niagara Movement and the NAACP)? This concept of a public intellectual would eliminate most intellectuals in America–Black, white, or other. It would also eliminate virtually all Black conservatives and virtually all Black academic intellectuals. It would, however, include many of the Black liberal intellectuals, a number of whom are already intellectuals, advocates, and activists at the same time–people such as Jesse Jackson, Hugh Price of the Urban League,** Kwesi Mfume of the NAACP, Marian Wright Edelman of the Children's Defense Fund, and the Reverend Willie Barrow* of Operation PUSH. Does that qualify her, or others like her in Black communities (or other communities), as public intellectuals?

Certainly, much of what goes on in ethnic communities does not fall under privacy. A number of the Africancentrist scholars are also advocates and activists who conform to this definition of a public intellectual. These are people such as Ivan van Sertima, Molefi Asante, Marimba Ani, Charshee McIntyre, Jacob Carruthers, Maulana Karenga, Asa Hilliard, and Leonard Jeffries, of which Du Bois, Kelly Miller, Anna Cooper, Nannie Helen Burroughs, Fannie Barrier Williams, Monroe Trotter, and Alain Locke were early models. There are admitted difficulties in defining the public intellectual, but I can readily accept such people being thinkers, advocates, and activists, especially those people who devise strategies and plans with the entire community in mind.

** Marc Morial is the present head of the Urban League.
* Reverend Willie Barrow is a community intellectual, activist and, organizer in Chicago.

A narrowing of the definition could certainly sift out a lot of public intellectual wanna-bes. The definition could include a lot of Black academic intellectuals who teach and write books and speak before academic audiences, but do not publicly advocate or engage in public action with respect to any public issue, policy, program, strategy, or problem. Academic individuals who provide public information on any of these matters and do no more than that, I would prefer to call academic public intellectuals, because they operate on a Kantian/positivistic orientation which prevents them putting their feet, or any other part of their body, in troubled waters.

AMERICA'S POLITICAL CONFUSION AND POLITICAL FANTASIES

Defining what a public intellectual is can be vexing, but it pales in the face of the much more acute social problem, which has significance, of having an accurate description of American society in which all intellectuals of any kind function and everyone else as well. White intellectuals, and other Whites, without thought, automatically call America a democratic society. They say that America is democratic, that it is a democracy. And they say this without using either of these words with the word society. One would think that white intellectuals, who could admit that America had Black chattel slavery for 230 years, exterminated and reservationized Native Americans, functioned throughout its entirety as a racist inundated society, denied masses of people human, political, and civil rights, and did not extend the vote to the majority of the population until the 26th Amendment in 1971, would be able to see that referring to America as a democratic society is sheer fantasy and wishful thinking. These indisputable facts, including the great disparities of wealth, do not add up to democracy of any kind.

America has been a federal republic since its national formation. It operates by a federal constitution and under a federal system of government. It is a society where public officials are elected to office by voters and can be removed from office by voters. A republic does not occlude political appointments, as there can be many. Election of government officials is the main political principle. But a federal system of government, an elective form of government, is not necessarily a democratic government; it does not necessarily denote a democratic republic or society. Moreover, an elective, representative government, federal or otherwise, is not necessarily a democratic government. The Soviet Union under the communists was a federal republic with an elected federal representative government, but neither the republic, nor the government, was democratic. Indeed, the elected federal representative government, and all the republican features of the Soviet Union were all structured into the totalitarian framework of Soviety society, i.e., a very dictatorial, societal framework where political power was exercised in a very dictatorial manner.

In America, white politicians, scholars, journalists, and other kinds of intellectuals are quick to call any country that has an elected representative government a democratic government. Who or what it represents seems to be of little concern. Nor does the reality that the majority of the voting-age population, or a gender group, or a given social class, or a regional area of the country might be excluded from the franchise seem to be of concern to them. In America, there are lobbying groups powerful enough to impair the functioning of the national or state legislatures or to suppress what might be the expressed majority view on a national or state issue or political practice, such as a majority view on gun control, or national health insurance. Nevertheless, America is called a democratic society with a democratic government and has been since the early nineteenth century when there was Black chattel slavery, the extermination and reservationizing of Native Americans, the disenfranchisement of Blacks and white women, and strong censorship in the South. A democratic society functions on the basis of a constitutionally elected strong central government, majority rule, the sovereignty of the people and equality; with respect to the latter, it promotes equal rights, equal opportunities, equal access, equal distribution of power and wealth, and other manifestations of equality.

Political scientist Paul Goldstene says that Americans are not democrats. He argues that they have always been liberals in their political and social thinking by believing in constitutional, limited representative government. They have always believed in individual rights (as opposed to equal rights–a democratic principle), individual distribution of power and wealth, individual access, individual opportunities, and other individual features. These individualistic ideals are often summed up by the single, absolutist phrase "individualism." In *The Collapse of Liberal Empire* Goldstene wrote:

> By assumption, attitude, and ideological reflex, Americans are liberals. They are liberals in opposition to democracy, as they are liberals in opposition to conservatism. This is historically true of Americans; however, the politically shrewd, and politically ignorant, employment of "conservative," "liberal," and "democratic" vaporizes these terms beyond recognition and content...confusing liberalism with democracy... Americans fail to come to grips with a reality they cannot and, indeed, refuse to understand.[9]

Goldstene erroneously juxtaposes liberalism to conservatism because over its entire national history American liberalism and conservatism have meant the same thing. What it meant to be conservative was that one held on to American liberal beliefs, ideals, and values. However, years before Goldstene, political scientist M. Morton Auerbach said that Conservatism in America was an "illusion." In a book titled, *The Conservative Illusion*,[10] Auerbach explained that there was a political philosophy of Conservatism, spelled with a capital "C" that originated from the philosophies of Plato, Edmund Burke, Joseph de Maistre, or the Russian Constantine Pobiedonostsev. But in America, this kind of Conservatism did not exist, even as an ideal, although there were some southern white slaveholders who tinkered a bit with this kind of thinking.

In America in the eighteenth and nineteenth centuries the main non-racist political ideal for white American males during these centuries was liberalism, which was not only associated with individual rights, but capitalism in the form of individual or private ownership of the means of production, and the individual distribution of wealth based on private property ownership. However, white American males rejected equal access to property, equal right to enterprise ownership, and the equal distribution of wealth to Blacks, Native Americans, and even to white women. In other words, the practitioners of liberalism rejected democracy.

On the basis of liberalism alone, Whites rejected democracy. But their white supremacist/ebonicistic form of racism, and other forms of racism, functioned similarly and even stronger at times. It was always easier for white men to promote liberal ideas rather than democratic ones and to promote liberal political and social practices, rather than democratic ones, the latter of which they hardly ever promoted. In the early nineteenth century, they learned to emphatically mouth democratic ideas and phrases in public. They did this to placate, as well as manipulate, the lower classes of white men coming into political power in America, facilitated by the dropping of property qualifications for voting.

EMERGENCE OF THE WELFARE SOCIETY

In the late nineteenth century, the corporate economy began to appear, and by the early twentieth century it was the dominant part of the American economy. These corporations were not acknowledged in the national constitution, and thus, fell under no constitutional conception, principles, or regulations, although they did come under some national and state laws. Congress approved an income tax amendment to the Constitution in 1909 that was ratified by the states in 1913. A graduated income tax was passed the following year, inheritance tax two years later. The economic corporations and America's governments (which all grew in size to remain competitive with the powerful economic organizations and to be able to serve them and the new corporate economy) expanded the size of the country's middle-class by adding a large number of administrators, public relations personnel, clerical and technical staff, analysts, accountants, lawyers, engineers, scientists, market experts, and researchers.

The growth of colleges and universities added to the further growth of government, corporate economic, and other institutional administrators, and also greatly increased the number of other professional people, such as doctors, dentists, engineers, social workers, teachers, scholars, and other professional people who were all added to the new and large "white collar" ranks of the American middle-class. The middle-class became the *managerial class*, providing managerial specialists for the political, economic, religious, and other social institutions found nationally, regionally, and locally in the country.

The middle-class was called upon to manage the relationship between the upper-class and the lower-class in America, which now consisted of farmers, factory workers, domestic employees, and employees in hotels, restaurants, hospitals, mental institutions, and department stores. Middle-class managers were especially called upon to distribute the national wealth between the upper-class, the middle class, and the lower-class. It could only slightly do this through its members in economic corporations. It was concluded it could only play this role effectively if it had political power and greater access to politicians and political institutions. This helped to launch the "Progressive Movement," and what was called "progressive" or "reform politics" in America.

As it participated more effectively in political parties and governmental institutions, the middle-class concluded that bringing the economic corporations and the corporate economy under greater public control would enhance its ability to help distribute wealth. They had to fight the corporate owners and their powerful national and state political allies on this. But the middle-class learned that it could use lower-class elements to increase its political and social clout against these opponents and force more respect and cooperation from them.

Meanwhile, the lower-class saw the middle-class's dependency upon them and concluded that it could use the middle-class's historical, national, and social strides as openings and opportunities to increase demands for political, economic, and educational concessions. What the upper and middle-class in America feared the most was the lower-class demanding that America become a democratic society. This was a demand being made by many lower-class white men. Yet their idea of democracy did not include Black people. This was especially true of southern lower-class white men who were also not anxious to have white women in politics and government or striving for economic and social equality with them.

Upper-class white men in the South adamantly opposed the development of democracy in the region. This was clearly reflected in the "Jim Crow" laws, the disfranchisement of most eligible Black male voters, and the millions of Blacks returned to a new form of servitude that centered in the Black-Belt states. Lower-class white men had made a half-hearted attempt to form a political alliance between themselves and some Blacks, but their racism made a strong alliance impossible, which served to weaken them and Blacks against Upper-class white men. But the demand for democracy that came from the South and failed (but, which could rise up again), scared northern upper-class and middle-class white males. Lower-class white men in the North were sending up shouts for democracy, particularly factory, mining, and dock workers, but also some middle-class white men with less political power, income, and opportunities.

And then there was the American Socialist Party that was formed in 1901. It advocated a combination of socialism and democracy, aptly called social democracy. This was an attempted transfer of European political culture to America. Social democratic parties were numerous and strong in Europe where they threatened powerful economic corporate elites and their institutions, but also powerful European aristocratic landowners and their agrarian interests. The social democrats wanted the national government to take over the means of production, to distribute the wealth and opportunities of the society, and to implement strong regulation of economic and social institutions, even culture and social life. The social democratic state was to assume the constitutional, political, and legal power to produce and maintain the good life for all the citizens of the social democratic society. This was considered the practical and moral thing to do.

White upper-class and middle-class men who dominated their social classes did not want social democracy coming to the United States. But it was also clear that liberalism was no longer going to carry the day on its own. There was the joint fear of democracy. So upper-class and middle-class white men worked out a compromise. It involved combining liberalism and what was called state socialism (not social democracy) to produce an ideology that is best described as *welfarism* that was used as a rationale and justification for creating the *welfare* society.

The welfare society in America was created in the late nineteenth and early twentieth centuries and was consolidated in the 1930s and 1940s with

Roosevelt's New Deal programs, with war production, and with postwar social programs. The programs of socialists and communists were co-opted to continue to expand and consolidate the new welfare society. This political move stole the thunder of these groups and isolated them from mainstream politics. An ideological fast one was also pulled off at the same time. The welfare ideology, involving liberalism and state socialism, was called a "new progressivism," or the "new liberalism" or "modern liberalism" to cover up its plethora of socialist attributes. A number of white male journalists and academics helped to affect this cover-up and helped to promote these new political labels, including Walter Lippman, John Dewey, John Kenneth Galbraith, and Arthur Schlesinger, Jr.

Senator William Howard Taft, then a powerful figure in the United States Senate, did not like this "new liberalism" or "modern liberalism" because of the strong economic and social role prescribed for government. People in and out of government disliked the promotion of socialism in this country, specifically such things as social security, aid to dependents, collective bargaining for unions, the progressive income tax, the Railroad Act, the National Labor Relations Bill, and the National Labor Relations Board. Although, there was the acceptance of the socialist regulation of banks and the stock market, the Securities and Exchange Commission, the municipal control of certain public utilities, the minimum wage, workers's compensation, agricultural subsidies, and the acceptance of socialist institutions, such as the Tennessee Valley Authority and the Hoover Dam. Seldom were these programs referred to as socialistic programs. This would also prove true of the later promulgation of the socialist G.I. Bill and the "Great Society" programs of the 1960s.

Senator Barry Goldwater felt an even stronger dislike for the American welfare society. He denounced it in two books titled, *The Conscience of a Conservative*[11] and *Conscience of a Majority*.[12] In countless speeches as Senator and Republican Party Presidential Candidate in 1964, Goldwater emphasized liberalism and individual rights, but not under the liberal banner. He called it conservatism, but it was the liberalism of the eighteenth and nineteenth centuries that I earlier referred to and that eventually became known only as conservatism. The Republican Party became the standard-bearer of conservatism. The public came to understand liberalism to be "modern liberalism," which was actually the welfare doctrine–a combination of liberalism and state socialism. Even the Democratic Party, which became the champion of "modern liberalism," kept the public unaware of this socialism. The Republican Party became roughly the party of the right and the Democratic Party became roughly the party of the left. All of this only helped to obscure from view the reality of America's welfare ideology and America's welfare society.

123

Figure 4:1 A Schematic View of America's Welfare Society

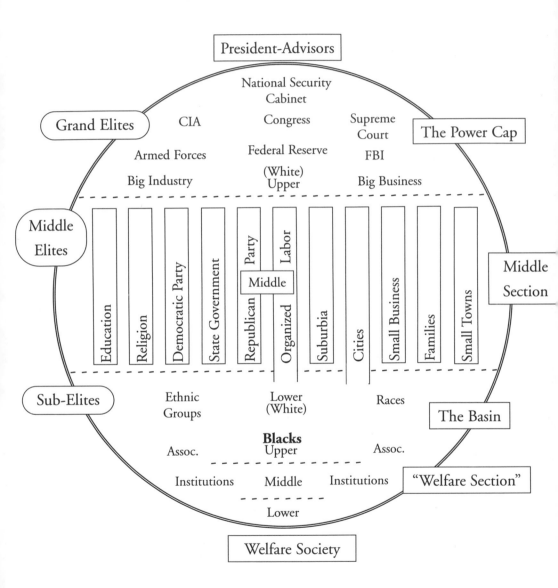

RACISM AND THE FUNCTIONING OF THE AMERICAN WELFARE SOCIETY

America's welfare society has a Power Cap on top of it. (See figure 4.1) This Power Cap houses the Grand Elites and is composed of national, political institutions, the largest and wealthiest economic corporations, and the upper-class, of which some members are the primary owners and/or managers of these economic institutions. Here is where one finds the one percent that owns so much financial wealth. This is also the social location of others in the upper-class who own 46.7% of the financial wealth. This means that 20% of the population owns, as Edward N. Wolff said in *Top Heavy*, 92.2% of the national financial wealth, while the remaining 80% of the population own 7.8%.[13]

The Power Cap reflects an enormous amount of power sitting on top of American society. Sociologist C. Wright Mills had talked about the "Power Elite," and his protégé, sociologist G. William Domhoff, and those who became his cohorts, continue to talk about them. But, as can be seen, the situation is about more than just political, economic, or social elites, or even about powerful institutions. In reality, the situation has more to do with massive power concentrated at the top of American society, contrary to any kind of notion about a democratic organization of society and a democratic distribution of power. Thus, it all leads back to the idea that an elected representative government is not necessarily the same as, nor necessarily interchangeable with, a democratic government.

Below the Power Cap there is the Middle Section of America's welfare society. It is the largest section and contains Middle Elites, a very large middle class, and middle-class institutions. In the third and bottom section of the society, the Basin, is found Sub-Elites, the lower-class, and—at the very structural bottom of this society—Black people and their culture, social classes, and institutions. There are other races and ethnic groups in the Basin, with each of the latter possessing its culture, social classes, and social institutions. The Basin is also labeled the "welfare" section of the society, because most white people believe that Blacks and other "racial minorities" (sometimes referring to them as "ethnic minorities" or "minorities of color") are on "welfare," i.e., an undeserved "hand-out" or "dole," while white people are not.

The truth is that in America's welfare society (as in the same kind of societies in Europe) *everyone* is on welfare or public assistance, that is, government assistance, that can take a multiplicity of forms. Individuals, groups of people, social classes, institutions, regions, and local areas of the country receive welfare or public assistance. They do so through *welfare politics*. Welfare politics are the politics of social recognition and government, (i.e., public) distribution of political power, cultural and social opportunities, goods and services, wealth, and consumer spending capability. These politics also involve working the hierarchical structure of society for benefit.

It is also necessary to look closer at the welfare society diagram and the welfare society, to focus on its interior, which I did not fully etch out in the diagram. The top structures of the society, the Power Cap and Middle Section, are comprised mainly of white people. The social classes of these sections of the society are the national upper-class and middle-class, but white people have essentially usurped these classes for themselves. White men dominate both social classes, and thus, the top two parts of the society, which means that these white men exercise a *white male gender* domination of the society itself. White men constitute the overwhelming number of Grand Elites, the elites who make the major national and foreign policy decisions, the decisions that can get America into war. They also constitute the largest, by a considerable margin, number of Middle Elites, who make the major state and local political, economic, and other impactful decisions.

Some middle-class people get an opportunity to function as Grand Elites, those individuals elected to the United States Congress as Representatives and Senators, or those who are appointed as officials in the national or central part of America's federal system of government, or who function as powerful economic corporate executives. However, ordinarily, middle-class people function as Middle Elites in America's welfare society and in the hierarchically structured and centralized institutions in the Middle Section of the society that relate to individuals, groups, or institutions in the state and local areas on this basis.

The Basin has its Sub-Elites. They function among lower-class Whites and also among the Black and other ethnic groups in the section. People from the Basin can be elected to the national government and become Grand Elites, which a number of Black people have achieved and do continue to achieve. Some Blacks have even become Grand Elites as a consequence of their position in economic corporations. There are Sub-Elites who become Middle Elites, through political elections, political appointments, or via positions in Middle Section institutions. And there are Sub-Elites who can function with the capacity of Grand Elites without being part of the Power Cap structure. These are individuals who function from a powerful social constituency in The Basin that enables them to exercise a powerful voice within the realm of the Power Cap, and impact it and the Grand Elites there and that can also impact America's domestic and international politics and agendas. A. Philip Randolph, Martin Luther King, Jr. and Jesse Jackson have been such Sub-Elites. One could argue that Jackson still functions in this capacity.

The elites of a welfare society are plural, as social analysis invariably discloses. For many analysts this disclosure proves to them that America is a democratic society aided in being a democracy and functioning as one by its elites, leading to the concept of "democratic elitism." Analysts usually do not get into the contradictory nature and false claims of this term. But what their analyses do not show is that America's elites are stratified on a hierarchical basis with differentiations of status and decision-making contexts. This stratification represents an anti-democratic structuring in America's welfare society. The hierarchical stratification of America's elites rends the Marxist concept of the "ruling class." Many intellectuals in America still subscribe to this concept, including a number of Black and black intellectuals. But, the hierarchical structuring of elites in America's welfare society shows that rule cuts across social classes, races, ethnic groups, and genders, and even across sections of society.

When looking at Figure 4:1, it would be appropriate to talk about a "ruling structure" in this society. One that straddles the society in a hierarchical manner, exhibits a wide range of people, and functions as a "ruling system" when the various parts of the structure interact with each other on a hierarchical basis, or when any segment of the structure functions within its area.

Sociologist C. Wright Mills referred to this as the "circulation of elites." But Mills had a limited concept of American elites, seeing only three kinds of them: political, industrial, and military. He saw them moving between these three institutional areas; that is, "circulating among them": functioning as a political elite on one occasion, as an industrial elite on another, or as a military elite at another time. These were what Mills called his "Power Elites." But the sociologist did not fathom the extent of America's societal elites, or how they functioned in segments of American society, or how varied they were, and all functioning, with power. Nor did he glean how elites in America "circulated" in both a hierarchical and lateral manner in American society.

An even closer look at the America's welfare society shows that white men are the dominant ruling group in the country. They use their positions in the Power Cap and Middle Section of society and their resources to stay the dominant ruling group. They also use their position and power to maintain their social elevation, i.e., their gender group elevation in the top social classes of American society (subordinating the white female gender in these classes) and they almost always have the first and best opportunity to have access to and to benefit from America's opportunities and largesse. This is the *white male genderization* of American society. It is a racist-inundated genderization, because white men function as racists through their gender status and class status in America. From these positions they dominate America, politically, economically, and socially, and contribute greatly to American society's racist interiority. They pass their status, power, and wealth, as well as their capacity to promote the racist interiority, onto their sons, who pass these attributes onto their sons...ad infinitum. This constitutes *white male racist affirmative action* in the American welfare society.

White male racist affirmative action is old, traditional behavior in America. White men have dominated America since the seventeenth century. They have used the country to *affirm* themselves, as reflected in the phrase "a white man's country," or "a white man's society," or in Abraham Lincoln's proclamation that the Declaration of Independence "is the white man's charter of liberty." It can be heard in the phrase used by Lincoln and Stephen Douglas in their debates, when they noted that the American government is "a white man's government." Affirming was not only ideological; it was practical. White men used numerous forms of racist power to bar Black men, Black women, white women, and lower-class white men from access to America's national, regional, or local institutions. If they allowed their presence at all, it was always a subordinate presence, specifically severe for Blacks. They eliminated all of these people from any serious competition with them for America's power, opportunities, and largesse. They used national, regional, local, political, economic, religious, educational, familial, and other institutions in these geographical categories to invest themselves with *public recognition, great power, privilege, status, entitlements,* and *preferential treatment* in America, which all produced and maintained a large *quota* of white men with political and financial support, with education, training, skills, and experience to take advantage of a myriad of choice political, economic, and cultural opportunities that *guaranteed* their desired outcomes. They believed this to be their due as white men.

But this is not entirely accurate. They were not just white men; they were white men who viewed themselves in white supremacist and maleist terms, which meant that in their own eyes they were individuals with innate or natural superior qualities. This further conveyed to them a sense of their alleged divinity, omnipotence, omniscience, infallibility, and their believed "inherent" deserving of all they attained. White male historians of the past, and of today as well, speak of how unlike Europe America is in that it did not have an aristocracy and did not have a society of inheritance predicated on birth. But this is just these historians's racism blinding them to a racist American reality that promoted power, inheritance, status, and opportunity predicated on birthright.

The racist orientation, i.e., the racist interiority of white men, also induced them to believe that they had a natural and inherent right to decide who else in America was deserving of affirmation, of access, of opportunities, and of largess, to decide when, where, how much, and how soon. The American welfare society produces great wealth and great opportunities, especially for upper-class and middle-class white men, with each class of men having first access to power, opportunity, distribution of goods and services, and wealth on a generational basis. The 1% of the population that owns 45.5 percent of all financial wealth are mainly white men; and, the next nineteen percent that owns 46.7% of such wealth are mainly white men. Thus, twenty percent of the population, mostly white men, own 92.2% of the financial wealth of the country. The rest of the population, collectively, owns a meager portion.

The large number of white men prepared and available to take advantage of opportunities and to acquire great bounty is often described (especially by other white men) as *objective* facts or *objective* realities. Such people do not like to refer to these facts and realities as *consequences*, certainly not as *racist consequences* which include: subjective racist thoughts and subjective racist social behavior, including the application of great racist power and racist practices that produced objective social consequences, or realities, or objective social facts. Racist defenders naturally do not like to focus on the racist links to the consequences or facts and invariably deny that there are any links.

In engaging in this racist denial, white men convince themselves that objective non-racist facts and an objective non-racist social reality explain why white men are in the positions they are in, and why they possess the power and wealth that they do. But, not only were the facts and realities produced by racist power and racist social behavior, the racism continues to live on in these consequences, realities, or facts, as indicated by the continued white male hegemony in America and their continued monopoly of access, opportunities, and largesse. It lives on in the condition of so-called non-racist tests, criteria, or procedures that subtly promote racism and white male opportunities and hegemony.

White men do not talk about white male racist affirmative action. Yet it is the oldest, longest-continuing, and most lucrative affirmative action there has ever been in the country. White men still promote it with great determination and success for themselves and their male progeny. Indeed, they shield themselves behind the other affirmative action program that most people in America understand as that subject and talk about. In the popular White imagination, affirmative action is the program that establishes a special Black recognition, and that creates Black *quotas*, that produces Black *privileges* and Black *entitlements*, that gives Blacks *preferential* treatment, and that *guarantees* Blacks access, opportunities, and benefits in society.

The affirmative action program that most Americans regard as "the Black affirmative action" program has existed since the 1960s. It was a concession that powerful white men, promoters of the white male racist affirmative action program, had to concede to Black liberation demands. There was great resentment at having to make this concession. White men were used to monopolies (or near monopolies) and made up to 95 percent of the top-level managers in the biggest and richest and most powerful economic corporations in America. They attacked the program they established as a concession to Blacks, saying that it gave them "special recognition," "special privilege," "entitlements," and "preferential treatment," and that it established Black "quotas," and offered Blacks "guaranteed" outcomes. These were the very attributes of white male racist affirmative action, projected onto others in a typical racist manner and attacked in a racist manner. There were even some Jews who joined this attack. They argued against "entitlements," "preferential treatment" and especially against "quotas," saying how the latter had been particularly damaging to them over their history in America. These Jews felt that quotas had kept Jews from advancing in the societies where they lived. But this was a partially specious argument, because it was precisely through quotas that some Jews were able to advance and to keep that door, as limited as it was, open to other Jews.

Now powerful white men have others to publicly attack what is understood to be affirmative action. This attack provides them with a cover for the way they use the welfare society to continue promoting their racist affirmative action program. The cooperating individuals are Black conservatives who function as surrogates, *Black surrogates*, on behalf of powerful white men. But they are not the only Black intellectuals and/or leaders who function as surrogates. Black intellectuals or leaders who do not talk about white male racist affirmative action and instead *only* talk about the affirmative action that alleges privileging and benefiting Blacks, function as *inadvertent surrogates* and as a shield for the promoters of white male racist affirmative action. Most important, they serve as inadvertent partners in promoting white supremacist/ebonicistic racism, Black denial, and Black deprivation.

These Black individuals usually do not mention, let alone discuss, how white women benefit from what is called affirmative action more than Black people do. But white women have always been recipients of affirmative action. Historical white male racist affirmative action benefited them as wives, daughters, and female relatives. It is similar to the way in which European countries not engaged in direct colonial imperialism benefited from the countries that did. White female feminists know the extent to which white women benefit from what is called the Black affirmative action program in today's welfare society, but rarely make public references about it and usually do not criticize white people who bash Black people for benefiting from affirmative action. By their usual silence about white female affirmative action, Black intellectuals, Black leaders, and other Blacks, abet this racism.

WHITE RACISTS SPEAKING THROUGH BLACK VOICES: THE JOHN MCWHORTER SURROGACY

Black conservative and academic John H. McWhorter has recently come on the scene to play the role of *Black surrogate* with a hubbub similar to that of Shelby Steele. And with the same kind of success among the Whites he speaks before and on behalf of. His book, *Losing the Race*, is being talked about with as much excitement as was extended to Steele's *The Content of our Character*, published years before. Affirmative action is a target of McWhorter's book. However, he feels that affirmative action is one or many things "sabotaging" Black life. Indeed, the subtitle of his book is "Self-Sabotage in Black America." The popularity of this book and its considerable specious presentation necessitates extended comments.

Losing the Race is a strange title to give to a book about Black people. It conveys the impression that Black people were ahead of white people in a race for social and cultural advance or were even with them in that race, presumably owing to the passage of political and civil rights laws in the mid 1960s and thereafter. But Black people are now "losing the race," intimates McWhorter. These are ridiculous projections. Black people have never been in a race with white people and they have always been behind white people politically, economically, socially, and in many ways culturally. They were the slaves in America, after all. As such, they were subjected to brutal treatment and deprivation. And as nonslaves, Blacks were subjected to racism and racist segregation and suppression. They were denied political and civil rights and social and culture opportunities for centuries. But McWhorter prefers to account for the "losing" situation differently. He attributes it to three things: Black "Victimology" (his wording), Black "Separatism," and Black "Anti-Intellectualism." McWhorter then talks of a "Cult of Victimology" in his book. He says it "has become a keystone of cultural blackness to treat victimhood not as a problem to be solved but as an identity to be nurtured."[14] He also blames white people for helping to encourage the "Cult of Victimology" among Blacks; and in doing so, McWhorter shows how much his thinking has been influenced by Shelby Steele, which is made clear when he says:

One of the most important things about these three currents is that whites in America do nothing less than encourage them. This is partly, as Shelby Steele argues, out of a sense of moral obligation that leads most whites to regard Victimology, Separatism, and Anti-Intellectualism as "understandable" responses to the horrors of the past....

Whites also unwittingly encourage all of these currents via well-intentioned social policies like open-ended welfare and permanent affirmative action, which are intended to help blacks overcome, but in practice only roil the waters under all three currents. Whites are now implicated in nurturing black self-sabotage not because of racist malevolence, but because of the same historical accidents that have encouraged blacks to embrace these thought patterns.[15]

What "historical accidents" could McWhorter be referring to? Is he speaking of the centuries of Black chattel slavery and the additional fifty years plus of servitude that embraced millions of Blacks in the South and that did not end until the 1930s and 1940s? Is he speaking about the centuries of racism, racist repression, and racist psychological assault, or the centuries of public humiliation, intimidation, and racist violence? Or is McWhorter referring to the centuries of assaulting the Black family? One could go on. Were all of these things *just* historical accidents or historical "inconveniences" as McWhorter's cavalier attitude would suggest? Or were they *generational patterns* of White thought and social behavior? Could it be said that they were patterns of *perverse* thought and social behavior? McWhorter did not say that they were. Instead, he resorted to a form of the White racist "Blameology," that Blacks have always experienced in America: "When a race is disparaged and disenfranchised for centuries and then abruptly given freedom, a ravaged racial self-image makes Victimology and Separatism natural developments."[16]

Blacks were not "abruptly given freedom" in America. Slavery ended by an amendment to the constitution (certainly not by Lincoln's proclamation). White supremacy/ebonicism was in full form and expression at the time. Thus, former Black slaves had to face the racist beliefs and practices of old. They were a hindrance to their freedom in the country, as was the fact that they were not initially extended political or civil rights and were not given the economic wherewithal to commence a nonslave life. On top of all of this, they had to face unchecked White violence.

But Blacks did not exhibit a "Cult of Victimology" then. That was precisely what perplexed and angered so many Whites, especially southern Whites. Blacks showed an aggressiveness, a resourcefulness, and a determination that caught southern Whites off-guard. To their way of thinking—given what Blacks had been through for centuries and what Whites had put them through for centuries–they were supposed to be enfeebled or vitiated, docile, and directionless; in other words, dependent. Instead, they clamored to participate in southern politics, asked for and even demanded land, and made a startling determination to be educated.

Whites met this situation with violence and other forms of suppression. The Supreme Court decisions in the early 1880s took away the national citizenship and national political and civil rights that Black people finally gained by amendments. Southern states proceeded to disenfranchise Blacks and to pass "Jim Crow" laws to exclude and segregate them. Southern Whites, with northern Whites acquiescing, and in ways supporting them, produced a vicious public racism to assault the mind and psychology of Blacks and engaged in physical and social assaults against their bodies.

In 1896, the Supreme Court made the segregation and the suppression of Blacks in all major areas of American life constitutionally, thus legally, the normal existence of Blacks, insuring White domination, control, and exploitation of Blacks. This constitutional (legal) sanctioning became the norm for White-Black social relations. This strong racist situation, with some Black servitude in the bargain, went on for decades. Black people unleashed a strong and sustained assault against the oppressive situation in the 1950s and 1960s. They were able to do that considerably owing to the strength and nourishment of their separate life in the country that had begun in slavery, which was where the cultural, social, and psychological insulation against slavery and racism and their ravages occurred. It was a psychological insulation that was meant to deflect or mitigate these ravages, to keep the Black mind and psychology from being emaciated by White racism and Black chattel slavery.

McWhorter seemed not to have a clue about the insulation barriers and the intellectual and psychological strengths it produced among Blacks, initially as slaves, but since has been part of Black life. Black life in America is steeped in histories of great oppression and suppression. What McWhorter was unable to see about Black intellectual and psychological strength, psychiatrist Alexander Thomas and psychologist Samuel Sillen saw: "The powerful thrust of the black liberation movement dramatically testified to the courage, determination, and resourcefulness of masses of blacks–qualities that could arise only from psychological health, not pathology."[17]

A series of pertinent questions have to be put to McWhorter, Shelby Steele, Glenn Loury and other Black conservative intellectuals when they start talking about White conscience, White guilt, White remorse, and White morality. The first would ask: When, in a centuries-long history of regarding masses of people as being "nonhuman" or "subhuman," of exterminating and reservationizing people, of enslaving and grossly exploiting people, of segregating, and denying people rights, opportunities, and anything resembling fairness or justice, did White people develop the sublime human traits that they assign to themselves and that Black conservative intellectuals assign them? These were not traits that Whites in large numbers could have developed prior to the 1950s and 1960s, making that kind of history and engaging in that kind of social behavior. In most white people this history and social activity produced a deep and extensive racist interiority that repulsed a strong conscience, a strong sense of morality, or a strong sense of social justice. That racist interiority was in full evidence in the 1950s and 1960s. It functioned in masses of Whites in the South and the North, making them resistant to Blacks trying to achieve rights, equality, justice, and freedom in America. So the development of the sublime traits would have had to occur among large masses of white people some time during the 1970s and to this day—about three decades!

How much progress could actually be made along these lines? The White racist "backlash" began to set in in America in the late 1960s and functioned in cycles in the decades since, especially in the thoughts and the political and social behavior of people calling themselves "conservatives." These people played a large role in electing three "white man's" presidents: Ronald Reagan, George Herbert Walker Bush, and George Walker Bush and will be doing their best to elect others. Given the multiple expressions of this lingering "backlash:" the attacks against affirmative action, the interest to destroy or diminish "welfare" programs (understood in a racist manner as something associated with Black people or other "racial minorities"), the urge to "crack down" on crime and drugs (also believed to be Black activities), and to keep education away from any "diversification" in terms of students and curricula, Whites will continue to not find the intellectual, psychological, or moral space to be the kind of thoughtful and humane people they believe themselves to be and that Black conservatives say they are.

McWhorter's book shows that he does not have the slightest understanding of welfare politics or America' welfare society. Nowhere in his book does he talk about white male racist affirmative action. Nowhere does he talk about the effects of White racist thought and social behavior on white people. McWhorter has no knowledge or appreciation of what I call a racist interiority. Specifically, he has no knowledge of the White racist interiority and its investment in America's welfare society, how that interiority stretches across the regions and communities in America, greatly affecting how they function.

McWhorter talked at length about Black "Separatism." But he did not say a word about White "Separatism" which, of necessity, would have to be linked to Black "Separatism." When Whites segregated Blacks for centuries in

America (and still do in various ways, like confining Black intellectuals like McWhorter to thoughts and writings on Black people) they simultaneously promoted White "Separatism" to keep from having Blacks in their lives, in their neighborhoods, or from having anything to do with Black people. White "Separatism" and the White segregation of Blacks work to keep white supremacy/ebonicism in the White geographical-social space, in the culture and social institutions and social life of the White social world; and thus, in the mind and psychology of white people, i.e. the racist interiority of white people.

This interiority is passed onto the children in child-rearing practices and in various forms of socialization, something that completely escaped McWhorter, who insisted that white children brought up in a White "Separatist" social world were devoid of racism. He claimed that "as such, to the younger white person who never knew segregated America, watching middle-class black people depicting themselves as partners with Kosovar Albanians in victimhood because they are occasionally by-passed by a taxi in Manhattan or trailed by a sales clerk looks like paranoia. Separatism starts as a healthy reclamation of identity and is then distorted to Victimology into what is felt to be a necessary battle posture, but to modern white eyes, Separatism is parochial."[18] But not their own "Separatism." Do most young Whites live among Whites? Do most young Whites attend private, public, or parochial schools with others like themselves? Do most young Whites date young Whites? Do most young Whites marry young Whites? White college and university students or faculty and administrators will talk about how Black students sitting together in the cafeteria as a practice of separatism, while ignoring how they're sitting in all-white groups observing this.

It is quite possible to pass on unconscious thoughts and behavior, as it is quite possible to pass on conscious ones. Subtle White racism is considerably unconscious racism. It is behavior that appears to be devoid of racism, that is apparently non-racist, but which functions from silent or hidden racist beliefs, assumptions, and understandings. White children and youth are invested with unconscious racism just as such groups have always been invested with it. Subtle White racism is not new in America. It is just presently the predominant form. In some respects it is a more insidious form of racism than blatant racism. It intensifies the racist feeling of being guiltless, innocent, and non-responsible. It fosters greater delusional thinking about being more honest, more moral, or more thoughtful and understanding. How moral, thoughtful, or understanding is the white youth who remarks: "why don't you just think of yourself as an American, rather than as a black person? Why do you always have to bring race into it, to identify with race?" How racist is the white youth who believes that God is white? How racist is the white youth who does not like studying about Black people in school, or who feels very uncomfortable doing so? And how racist is that youth when he or she sees nothing offensive to Blacks (or to other ethnic groups, for that matter), when they argue that there is nothing wrong, unfair, or racist about having just white people as Presidents?

John McWhorter wrote: "Separatism spawns... a strong tendency toward Anti-Intellectualism at all levels of the black community. Founded in the roots of the culture of poverty and disenfranchisement, this tendency has not become a culture-internal infection nurtured by a distrust of the former oppressor."[19] There is nothing in the history of white people in America, in the history of their relationship with Black people, in the history of how they have used American society against Black people, or their continuing racist way of relating to Blacks—albeit more subtly—that would induce Black people to look upon white people as paragons of conscience, morality, virtue, truth, integrity, or as being trustworthy.

As to poverty as the root of a Black "Anti-Intellectualism," McWhorter should look again to history. Black people lived in great poverty for 230 or so years as chattel slaves. During this time, they were legally prevented from being educated. When slavery ended, Blacks made a massive effort all over the South to go to school, to be educated. At that time, the South had no public school system, so one was established in southern states by former Black slaves and their northern and southern white allies in that brief period after the Civil War when former slaves participated for a time in southern state governments and attained some political and civil rights. Black interest in education continued. Northern Whites helped to fan their interest by going south to teach Blacks, by establishing schools, or by helping Blacks to do so. And of course, there was Booker T. Washington. The Tuskegean made education synonymous with Black modernization and development. The seeds for many Black colleges and universities were planted in this period that grew over the decades and that ultimately, in the twentieth century, produced many genuine colleges and universities.

So "Anti-Intellectualism" among Blacks has to be explained some other kind of way. The general anti-intellectual orientation of the American people would be an important explanation. Historian Richard Hofstadter won the Pulitzer Prize writing on that subject in his book: *Anti-Intellectualism in American Life.*[20] White historians and other kinds of white scholars have detailed this same phenomenon. There is also a great disparity in the amount of money spent on the education of white and Black children in this country. McWhorter acknowledges this, regards it as an explanation, but makes it a minimal one, as if the money disparity was not that important. Both of these explanations go against McWhorter's primary argument of the "Cult of

Victimology." To emphasize this, he prefers to talk of how certain Black cultural traits (a la Thomas Sowell) primarily promote this "Anti-Intellectualism." He gives examples like the lack of a "high priority" on education in Black homes, or Black folklore about "mother wit" or "street smarts." He regards the most decisive thing as the Black view that intelligence, academics, or "making good grades" are "white things." This, in his mind, is a reflection of the "sabotaging" effects of Black "Separatism."

College or university instructors across this country and from every ethnic background could talk at length about so many of their students from different racial, ethnic, gender, or class backgrounds who are anti-intellectual. They will not read. They will not study. They are afraid to discuss. They have no concept of critical thinking. They use libraries for social activities and less for research and study. Indeed, they are afraid to think. This is the typical kind of discussion on college and university campuses in this country. Black students fall into these anti-intellectual slots as well. Maybe more so than other students, because they are so often academically less prepared than other students. Prepared enough to get into a college or university, but lacking that stronger preparation that acts as a continuous springboard over the education years. There is no doubt that Black students, like other students on college and university campuses, are affected by the anti-intellectual milieu of the student subculture–a source that McWhorter missed. Something that would not have crossed his mind is that Black college or university students might not see the strong association of young Whites with intelligence, academics, and making good grades. They see many white students at colleges and universities who are very much like themselves in these three categories: less than sparkling and trying to hold on and get through.

McWhorter failed to understand something that would have been clear to him had he had a racist analysis and had he used it to analyze the racist behavior of white people. Racism is by definition anti-intellectual. This—along with centuries of Black chattel slavery predicated on white supremacy/ebonicism and White efforts to keep Blacks from making progress or to prevent society from changing in ways to make that possible—is what is at the deep root of anti-intellectualism in American history and life. White people made a fetish, a racist fetish, of lauding their own intellectual capabilities. This was not done on the basis of how their minds shone, but on the basis of how they deluded themselves into thinking that they did. White people then implemented these racist beliefs by making it illegal for Blacks to be educated, by barring them from schools, by poorly financing their education, or by making sure they went to poor schools–all as efforts to try to make Blacks conform to their racist image of them as being "innately" "incapable" of intellectual activity or anything beyond mediocrity. And also, and rather desperately, to keep them from becoming competitors with Whites.

What we have in America is white people identifying a close relationship between white people and intelligence, projecting it as a racist cultural ideal, and then imposing it strongly and maintaining it strongly in the Black social world, so that Blacks would come to believe it. There were those who did, over the history of Blacks in America. But too many Blacks knew how Whites thought: the irrational, pathological, and immoral character of so much of their thought. They saw how difficult it was for Whites to think about them, except in racist terms. They saw how difficult it was for Whites to think of America in the way its ideals said it should be. Black people saw that many anti-intellectualism white people, in racist compulsive fashion, reinforced the imposition by suppressing or restricting Blacks in educating themselves. This, of course, produced anger, fear, and frustration among Blacks. The phrase Black "Anti-Whiteism" would work better than the phrase Black "Anti-Intellectualism" to explain some of the Black responses to education, Whites, and what appears to be anti-intellectualism among Blacks.

Former Black slaves learned that it could be dangerous attempting to be educated in the South. This is something that Blacks would have to contend with even in the twentieth century. Whites, generally speaking, really do not know how to relate to an intelligent, educated, or cultured Black person. They used to look for "white blood" to account for these attributes. They were prepared to ridicule, beat, or kill an intelligent or educated, Black person. They tried to understand and relate to the person on the basis of their notion of the "black exception." A Black person who does not conform to their racist image makes many white people anxious; it confuses them; it makes them want to avoid such Blacks or keep conversations short. What are we to make of the fact that today (according to Black philosophers) there are white philosophers, especially white male philosophers, who do not think that Black people are capable of being philosophers. Whose anti-intellectualism is this?

And there is this for McWhorter to consider (which obviously did not cross his mind): these are times when Blacks are focusing more attention on their history, culture, and social life, when they are publicly emphasizing Black humanity, Black dignity, and Black self-respect, when they are putting demands on Whites to publicly acknowledge and accord these interests and emphases. None of these things can be promoted among Blacks by a White-oriented education. As Black children and Black youth absorb this Black orientation and deeply make it their own, they will resent being educated exclusively or strongly about white people, who are invariably the human subjects referred to in public school, college, and university instruction; or being educated as if they were white.

This can lead Blacks to equating intelligence, academics, and good grades with white people, not out of anti-intellectualism ideas, but out of anger and resentment. And it can clearly affect their academic performance. The phenomenon of anti-intellectualism is not as extensive among Blacks as John McWhorter says it is. Nor is it as simple as he believes it to be. The complicated character of it is only ascertainable if one employs a racist analysis in an extensive manner and completes the picture of White racist behavior to help explain it. McWhorter did not have or employ a racist analysis. White involvement, as he saw it, was simply Whites being "unwitting" contributors, owing to their stressed consciences and deep-seated senses of guilt and remorse. In short, owing to their *innocence*, the traditional racist-afflicted thinking and feeling, with a Black intellectual fanning it.

Clearly, McWhorter's book was primarily written for white people—his contention to the contrary notwithstanding. It shows that Black people need, and are entitled to have, Black intellectuals who claim to represent them, or seek to help them, who know something substantial about America's White racist history and about the kind of society America is and how it functions. These intellectuals need to be able to tell Black people how America's welfare society accommodates individual and group recognition and how it distributes power, opportunities, wealth, and consumption. They need to know, in short, how welfare politics work and how it intersects with the possession and implementation of power.

Blacks need and are also entitled to have Black intellectuals who know what racism and race are and who are not in doubt, who are not confused, and who do not confuse Whites or encourage them to engage in this confusion. Black intellectuals, even some Black conservatives, insist that white supremacy/ebonicism significantly functions in American culture, institutions, and in American society, but they do not exhibit a knowledge of how because they really do not have a significant understanding of what racism is and how it works. They do not have a *racist analysis* as Du Bois and some other Black intellectuals have had.

WHAT DO WE HEAR FROM HARVARD?

In his 1998 documentary titled: "The Two Nations of Black America," Henry Louis Gates, Jr. said that in America, "the real issue was class." He also said "No one should think that the Black middle-class has escaped racism." Clearly, the Black middle-class has a racial orientation, otherwise, why call it that? Here Gates shows a distinction between racism and race, but he also said in this piece, "the country is embarking on a national conversation on race, but that may be the wrong conversation." Gates was back to race—once again he regarded it as interchangeable with racism. The panel at the Du Bois Institute's Conference on Race at Harvard, which included Gates, Cornel West, Christopher Edley, Patricia Williams, Orlando Patterson, Randall Kennedy, and Kathleen Cleaver, did their best to talk about the real problem of social class, but always found themselves coming back to what Gates said was not the real issue in America, race.

Harvard law professor Christopher Edley then responded that, "it seems to me that the difficulty is that the measures that one would want to take to address the issues of class and income in America require that we cap a well of compassion within the American public, a compassion that depends upon our ability to connect with each other. And the fact is, that our ability to connect with one another is today still too often handicapped, disabled, by color."

Gates said race. Edley said color. Edley could not have meant that, because if he had, then he would have had to say that the white race was handicapping and disabling the connection between Blacks and Whites. Blacks have always been trying to establish that connection throughout their history in America, while white people, generally, have always sought to avoid it. The public spotlight was on the Black intellectuals at Harvard, especially those associated with the Du Bois African American Studies Department. This group was expected to provide illumination on what were deemed "racial matters" in America, not "racist matters." To deal with the latter, they would have to focus their scholarship and discussions directly on white people. They would have to explain how their own racism has affected them; and how they, in turn, have related to the country and Blacks when they have been afflicted by their own racism.

Black people also need and are entitled to have Black intellectuals who can help them make advances in this society, from the communities in which they live and at the stage of development they are in. They need them to do what E. Franklin Frazier said they should do in his 1962 article on "The Failure of the Negro Intellectual," help Black people, as a people and as a community, relate to the larger American society with benefit. This failure continues with Black intellectuals.

Cornel West* has the spotlight when it comes to this issue. It is always something that he writes and talks about publicly and for which he receives accolades from Black and white intellectuals alike. But the fact is that this is one of West's demonstrably weak areas. In fact, West continues to show great confusion of thought in this area. He has described himself as a "prophetic pragmatist" who combines "the best of liberalism, populism and democratic

* Who is now at Princeton University.

socialism that takes race, class and gender seriously."[21] Yet, there is no mention in West's list of racism. Maybe that is implied in his category of race? But that cannot be taken with assurance and, in any case, something serious cannot be something just implied. It has to be stated and dealt with directly and clearly.

By his own description, West clearly put himself on the left side of the political continuum, the assumption being that Black conservatives appear on the right side. West's ideological orientation is eclectic; he also calls it "synthetic." That implies that it is holistic. But when West thinks of himself as being politically left, with the implication that there is a right, he is thinking in absolute/either-or terms. Historically, and presently, Black people are generally a holistic thinking people. This has been recognized and said by many folks, including Lerone Bennett, Jr. who once wrote, "We black people are one people, and we are going to rise or fall together. For us, there can be no such thing as individual salvation. We're going to be saved together, or we are not going to be saved at all."[22] The Black psychologist Joseph White, Jr. wrote: "We should also recognize that black people have a great tolerance for ambiguity and uncertainty, for living with seemingly contradictory alternatives. As practitioners, then, we must eliminate the tendency to think in either-or terms, with respect to the black experience."[23] And Toni Morrison reflected her understanding of Black holistic thinking when she said, "Black women seem able to combine the nest and the adventure.... They are both safe harbor and ship; they are both inn and trail. We, black women, do both. We don't find these places, these roles, mutually exclusive."[24] Africancentrist Maulana Karenga demonstrated his own holistic thinking, and employed it with respect to how Blacks should relate to America, and even beyond, in remarks made in Gate's documentary, when he said, "So the question is: how do we sustain community? And then [how do we] engage in a mutually beneficial relationship with the rest of the world. And how do we sustain community so that we can sustain the power, the capacity, to define, defend, and develop our interests and to seek to speak our own special cultural truth to the world." One does not see comments like these coming from any of the Black intellectuals at Harvard and at a number of other colleges and universities in this country.

Cornel West attempts to do this, but in an inadequate and confused manner. It is as if he rejects Black racial or Black ethnic power or Black Power. He seeks to speak to the Black collectivity, which he does, mainly in a religious or cultural manner. Those eclectic, synthesized political ideals show just how much his political thinking is not drawn from Black history or Black life and how the ideas themselves would not be of much use to Blacks. Ultimately, it is not clear which liberalism West is referring to.

Previously, I described two types of liberalism, genuine liberalism and so-called "modern liberalism," which is actually the combination of liberalism and state socialism or the welfare ideology. Black conservatives espouse liberalism, but they do not seem to know it. Still, they know they are against the second kind of liberalism, which they regard as being antithetical to conservatism when, in fact, it partly embraces their kind of liberalism. So what does West mean when he says "the best of liberalism?" He frequently refers to America as a "capitalist society," suggesting that it is not a welfare society and has no socialism, when it is a welfare society and has a great deal of socialism. As a democratic socialist, he would be against a welfare society. But why, when it has so much state socialism in it? West says he likes the best of "populism," but the latter is anti-liberal, as it is collective and egalitarian. West already has that with democratic socialism.

And then there is the matter that further confounds West's position. Recently, he has seemed to be trying to cast off the public socialist label in favor of referring to himself publicly as a reformer or progressive or "radical democrat," thoughts and actions that are discernibly socialistic; and thus, West finds himself doing what many socialists have always done in America: obscuring, hiding, or denying their socialist orientation with reform, progressive, or democratic labels; even their talk about "reforming" capitalism, or trying to make it more moralistic, democratic, or humane. They attempt to put a "human face" on capitalism, similar to the way that socialists used to talk about putting a "human face" on socialism to counter the communist effort to build socialism in Eastern Europe and the Soviet Union by crass dictatorial and bureaucratic means.

West is similarly confused when he speaks to Black people, as a people. He makes no distinction between race and ethnicity with Blacks. Indeed, West talks about the black race producing culture in the forms of the "black preacher" and "black musical tradition," which he believes are the sources of the Black intellectual tradition. He does not mention Black thinkers as a source of that tradition. West says he is against "racial thinking," but he does it a lot, as reflected in "The Dilemma of the Black Intellectual" where he talks about Black intellectuals that are creating their own "cultural truths" or "regime of truth." These ideas reflect what he calls the "black intellectual predicament," a concept that he believes:

> Remains relatively unexplored and will remain so until black intellectuals articulate a new "regime of truth" linked to, yet not defined by, indigenous institutional practices permeated by the kenetic orality and emotional physicality, the rhythmic syncopation, the protean

improvisation, and the religious, rhetorical, and antiphonal repetition of African American life. Such articulation depends in part upon elaborate black infrastructures which put a premium on creative and cultivated black thought; it also entails intimate knowledge of prevailing Euro-American "regimes of truth" which must be demystified, deconstructed and decomposed in ways which enhance and enrich future black intellectual life.[25]

What one does not find in these comments is how the Black community will play a role in the construction of the "cultural truth," to which Karenga referred. West knows, but seems to forget, how it was the Black slave and the Black community (made up overwhelmingly by the Black lower-class) that produced and sustained Black culture. It is from the mass of Blacks that the preaching and musical traditions come.

In the above discussion, West dichotomized the Black cultural situation to the extreme of removing the creators and perpetrators of Black culture. West seemed to be turning over the cultural reigns to the Black middle-class people who will not be able to do what he wants them to do, divorced from the Black community and from Black life, as many are. Many think in individualistic terms and draw heavily on European-American intellectual and cultural traits. Despite this, West contradictorily says that what will be utilized will be what has been "demystified, deconstructed and decomposed." Something decomposed is weak, unworthy, and useless.

The musical tradition of Black people is in serious jeopardy because of the movement away from the deep roots of Black music. Jazz took an experimental turn that took it from its swing and blues beat and even its listening audience. There is "pop gospel" today that reaches Whites, but it vitiates the roots of Black gospel music. A Europeanized Black gospel choir is Black "soul-destroying." There is today *talk-sic*, not music, which reflects neither understanding, nor appreciation of music. There are those who wish to be musical who have produced a strange form of acapella with music with a repetitious, monotonous, droning, and boring beat presented in a tasteless, slovenly manner. There are Black musicians no longer interested in musical instruments. There are Black singers and musicians no longer interested in the blues, and it is white singers and musicians who are plunging into it. Blacks need to be less concerned about popular trends and European borrowings at this point than they do about returning to and refurbishing their musical roots and reflecting on what gave Black music, musicians, and singers their special qualities and even genius. Crossing-over can mean crossing out.

West calls and thinks of himself as a radical, an eclectic radical. But in the comments quoted above he does not appear radical at all. Maulana Karenga appeared as a radical. As a radical, West would have to explain why he would be joining others of the Harvard Du Bois African American Studies Department to work out a "subtle defense" of affirmative action, as commonly understood, and as understood by this group. The fact that West is a radical, Gates is a moderate, William Julius Wilson is a liberal, and Orlando Patterson is a conservative might explain this "subtlety."

WHAT CONSERVATIVES SAY AND DON'T SAY

In a Spring 2000 speech at Yale University, Gates said his group was working on a "subtle defense." This followed his blast against Chief Justice Clarence Thomas, who had used affirmative action to advance his career and then turned against it. But given how America is organized, as a welfare society, with white men dominating it in powerful, centralized national, state, and local institutions, and using welfare politics and these institutions to promote white male racist affirmative action, what is the value of a "subtle defense" of affirmative action? Does this mean that white racists and other white people might accept it better-especially when it's got some big "household names" in support of it and because it is not asking for much?

The Black conservatives are hand and foot against affirmative action for Blacks. Shelby Steele said "Affirmative action... is 'justified;' you can't support it by principle. It is a violation of principle."[26] Thomas Sowell has been ragging against affirmative action with a messianic thrust, since his 1984 book *Civil Rights: Rhetoric and Reality.*[27] His biggest salvo is that the program did more for Black middle-class people, than Black lower-class people. Did he actually believe that a program that white men established as a concession to Black power and demands would be established for Black lower-class people? People that established powerful white men haven't the slightest interest in? People who exist way down in the welfare societal Basin area? The affirmative action program, at best, was for the Black middle-class or for Black people on their way to becoming that. Sowell and other Black conservatives should have seen all of this and then taken a public stand that the program was for Black middle-class people and those able to move into that class with help. They should have realized that another kind or kinds of programs had to be created for the mass of Blacks, like Whitney Young's "Marshall Plan" for urban areas, or even William Julius Wilson's idea of government programs that are not "race-specific" and that would help all needy or all "truly disadvantaged" in America.

What Sowell, Steele, and other Black conservatives were showing, ironically and irrationally, was a lack of interest or desire in building up the

Black middle-class. This is the leadership class of Black people. One would presume that the larger, the wealthier—and the more powerful the class, the more effective it would be. The leadership not only has to lead Black people, it has to engage in welfare politics to reach beyond Blacks and across the structural parts of America's welfare society. It also has the task of trying to lead, guide, or influence Whites to help the mass of Blacks with necessary and needed programs. So what will a "subtle defense" of affirmative action do for the Black middle-class or the Black lower-class? Here we see conservative, moderate, and liberal Black intellectuals, doing what, as public intellectuals? Not much to help those Black people in great need.

Black liberals, conservatives, and Black radicals who reject affirmative action for Blacks alarmingly seem not to know anything at all of another form of affirmative action that has existed historically in America. This shows how Black intellectuals do not deeply root their efforts to be intellectuals in Black history and life. This is the *Black affirmative action program*. This is not "identity politics," as someone who interprets such politics as similar to a simple and static "politics of recognition" might think. Black affirmative action goes much deeper and is more meaningful and dynamic than that. Blacks have lived their entire existence in a country that has been acutely racist, and which has denied the very humanity of Black people. Black people have had to affirm their own humanity, which they did with their racial thought and which was helped along by Black nationalists. By constructing, continually altering, and advancing their culture, and by their practical efforts of cooperation and struggle in the country, Black people have developed a reality of racial thought.

The Black Struggle for Liberation in the 1950s and 1960s, for instance, was a powerful Black affirmative action movement. It affirmed that Black people had not been enfeebled by racism and racism/slavery or by continuous public psychological assault, suppression, denial, and the inordinate amount of violence perpetrated against them. Blacks had, in fact, demonstrated their ordinary and heroic character, a heroic character so large in dimension that it permitted Black affirmative action to *affirm* the United States. They affirmed a country that has been historically abusive and unjust towards them in order that they could affirm the best of what America was and could be, but that White racist behavior always retarded.

This affirmative action was also powerful and large enough to open up America and to open up opportunities for many Black individuals. Many of these same individuals now call themselves conservatives, liberals, and radicals, forgetting what the Black lower-class people did for them. Now so many in these groups, including intellectuals in each of them, seek to get away from or to offer just the meagerest of help to Black lower-class people. The

Africancentrists have shown no recognition of historical and continuing Black affirmative action for Blacks when affirmative thinking and action helped to open doors for them, too. The Africancentrists also leave the mass of Black people in the lurch. They do not advocate ideas or programs that will help Blacks relate to the American welfare society or that will help them get aid from it, so that they can build and strengthen Black communities. Their interest is to take Blacks out of their Black consciousness and to invest them with an African consciousness, so that they would be looking away from their own history and experience.

Africancentrists want Blacks to enroll in some other people's history and experience, even if it is done by romantic, mystical, and fanciful thinking. Maulana Karenga is an exception here, as his focus is on Black people in America. In this respect, Karenga, in my mind, is really a Blackcentric. He wants Blacks to reach out to Africa and elsewhere from this historical-cultural-social base and he has been critical of Black middle-class people for not helping Blacks do this.

Africancentrists aside, no group of Black intellectuals has abandoned Black people like Black conservatives. Most of these individuals do not even consider themselves Black or black; they are individuals, or as Dick Gregory would say, a kind of "clear people." How do "clear people" relate to Black people? Many, if not most, Black conservatives come out of a Black life and a Black community. But as intellectuals they function out of America's White racist history. This, they cannot see. They emerged in America as individuals, and then as a growing group, when the White racists were trying very hard to slow or put a stop to Black progress. White racists's goal at the time was to take back as much as they could of what Blacks had gained. They were especially interested in taking away national and state government aid from Blacks or to pare it down in a serious manner.

Throughout the history of America, white men had used government to affirm, support, and advance themselves on a continuous, generational basis. They did not object to the bigness of government, as much as they did its regulatory powers and activities. But they never thought that government political, economic, legal or educational help in any way impaired their intellectual abilities, damaged their "moral fiber," or caused them to become disgraceful and despicable dependents. They never saw government aid as founding a group of people who lost the will or interest to be productive citizens. Yet, according to them, government aid to Blacks supposedly does precisely these things to them. A positive, supportive government for Whites, but not a positive, supportive government for Blacks.

Here is how the Black conservative Brian Jones adheres to this prevailing racist view: "The prevailing African-American leadership inherits from the civil rights generation a profound belief in the pervasiveness and 'institutionalization' of white racism in America. Accordingly, its lodestar is a paternalistic stateism that serves ostensibly to 'protect' its clients from unfair treatment."[28] This "paternalistic statism" fundamentally protects white men in America, particularly upper-class white men, and has been doing so since the seventeenth century. For centuries it has provided them with great public assistance, which, of course, is not in Jones's interest or vision. But neither is his interest in the American welfare society, to which he is oblivious, preferring to dwell on the great "stateism" that is so visible.

Economists, politicians, journalists, and others talk endlessly about the "free market," but the heads of every major economic corporation in America know that the "free market" is a myth. In fact, such people are against a "free market" and have been since the late nineteenth and early twentieth centuries when they saw that government regulation was a benefit to them, their corporations, and the corporate economy. Today "a free market" could spell ruin for many of the Fortune 500 corporations in America. These companies are oligopolies in structure that function and rely extensively on government subsidies, legal protection, local police protection, military protection abroad, and the ability to control prices for production and consumption.

Economic corporations in America especially desire state help against their white collar and blue-collar workers, with respect to the demands that they can make against them, the remunerations they would have to dish out, and the institutions that could be organized. The big corporations turn to local governments to get the kind of regulation they want on the domestic market and to the national government and so-called international institutions to get regulations for the international or global market that best suits them, their structuring, their ability to domestically and globally move financial and production capital, their profits, and their ability to prevent threatening domestic or international entry competition. The state or "stateism," in short, helps to prevent or seriously constricts a "free market," domestically and internationally. This is the "lodestar." This is a type of "stateism" that Black conservatives seem to know nothing about or that they do not want to talk about.

Stateism is clearly an integral part of America's welfare society and welfare politics. This is what Black liberals know. They know this without seeming to know that America is structurally a welfare society or that there is the reality of welfare politics. The things they clearly know is that the American government is the government of all the people of the society and that no group of people have a right to monopolize it for their own use or have a moral right to use it to oppress and suppress American citizens (both can be done without being blatant about it). They also believe that the powerful economic corporations, those that reside in the Power Cap, do not have the right to dominate, abuse, and grossly exploit people either. And they further know that these economic institutions and the corporate economy that dominates the general American economy have a strong alliance-not just relationship-with the national and state governments that enables the economic corporations to function the way they do at home, and as much as possible, the same way abroad. So it is necessary to focus on government, politics, economic corporations, the economy, or *welfare political economy.*

But Black conservatives invariably do not do this. Thomas Sowell–book after book, article after article, speech after speech–invariably ignores the white male racist-gender domination and white male racist affirmative action in America. He demonstrates no understanding of America's welfare politics or welfare economy. Nor does he seem to know that America is a welfare society. Indeed, he talks of America right out of the White racist mythology, when he says such things as:

> But what was different about Western civilization was the way it attempted to cope with the sins that have plagued mankind. It is only the fact that the peoples of Western European nations share all the shortcomings and evils of other peoples that makes their experience relevant to the rest of humanity and their example an encouragement to others. This is especially true of the United States, which has very few indigenous people and is populated by the peoples of other lands. It is the American traditions and American institutions that keep us free, not our individual virtues or our individual wisdom.[29]

This could be considered a new version of the "Gettysburg Address." "Four score and seven years ago, our forefathers brought forth a country conceived in liberty...." These words were uttered at a time when Blacks were still enslaved, Native Americans were being exterminated, and white women could not vote. White Americans especially like to talk about America in terms of its ideals, and compare these ideals to the actual conditions of other countries, which is a faulty methodology. Sowell apparently forgot about Hitler and the Nazis of Western civilization. He also forgot about the communists and totalitarianism, both of which had their origins in the West. And Sowell does not mention that one of the reasons why the Western experience is like the experiences of other countries and peoples in the world is because Whites/Westerners effectively dominated the planet between the nineteenth and the first half of the twentieth centuries. They imposed their way of life and their problems on the people they dominated, and exacerbated problems that people already had, without taking any or much responsibility for anything. In the quest for domination and global exploitation, whites believed they were "guiltless," "innocent," and "non-responsible."

The American welfare society is duplicated across Western civilization, but it is most evident in America, Canada, and Western Europe. In fact, it is evident, to some extent, in all parts of the Western Hemisphere and is presently undergoing construction in Eastern Europe, and somewhat in Russia. Sowell and other Black conservatives ignore this. They grasp American ideals and particularly the ideal of individualism. Most not only espouse individualism, but regard it as a social panacea for Blacks, for Blacks's lingering ills and the lingering ills of race, meaning racism.

However, it would seem that they confuse the American ideal of individualism with that of the individual presence in the market economy. *Individualism and the market economy!* Black conservative Telly Lovelace has declared: "Historically the black community has prospered most when it has embraced free markets and entrepreneurship. Black Americans have advanced by embracing these institutions despite slavery, segregation, Jim Crow laws, and various forms of well-meaning but addled government assistance."[30] Lovelace, and anyone else, would be hard pressed to prove that southern white slaveholders allowed their slaves to be Black capitalist entrepreneurs. And what conservatives do not know is that Blacks *used* racist segregation to promote capitalist entrepreneurship and capitalism among themselves. *Black capitalism*, as it has been called, would be capitalism found in the Basin of America's welfare society; although, some Black capitalists are presently lifting their enterprises out of the Basin and into the upper sections of American society.

Telly Lovelace, like so many Black conservatives before him, has hidden within his commentary the notion of White patronage and White benevolence. Nevertheless, this commentary is discernible and it resonates with the thinking of White racists in America. It is the voice that continually notes *how much* white people *have done* for Black people, and intimates the question: where would they be today without that long-standing self-less, even altruistic help? It suggests that white people have "bent over backwards" to help Black people. The truth is quite the opposite; namely, what Whites have *done* to Black people historically. And there is the other side of that truth; namely, *how much* Blacks *have done* for Whites and this country and without commensurate compensation.

There is also the White racist belief that so many Black conservatives subscribe to, and in so doing join subtle white racists, and that is that Blacks's advances in America will relate directly to, as it has for Whites and them, espousing and living by American ideals, beliefs, and values. When Black conservatives take this public position, it shows how they come out of White racist history and social life to be intellectuals in this country. One thing that Black history demonstrates, without a doubt (and this is also true of the historical interaction between Whites and Blacks in this country), is that white people, as a people, have over the history of this country, defiled and perverted America's ideals, beliefs, and values. They have shown enormous difficulty trying to live up to them and by them. American history records the continuous scenes of Whites throwing America's ideals, beliefs, and values to the ground and trampling over them. It has also shown Black people picking them up, cleansing them of their perversions, and handing them back to Whites to give them another go at trying to live up to them and by them.

Black conservatives and white conservatives, many of whom are subtle white racists, talk endlessly about "family values." But Black people have always known that racist values were not only a part of White "family values," but that they interpenetrated all the other family values that made white individuals and families relate to Blacks in racist ways. Today, subtle racist values are a strong part of White "family values." Black conservatives like Shelby Steele, Glenn Loury, John McWhorter, and the Reverend Jesse Lee Petersen obscure this with their public commentary.

Reverend Jesse Lee Petersen did with his recent book *Rage to Responsibility*,[31] where he admonished Blacks to adhere to and follow "traditional" Black family values, arguing that they were "transformative." Blacks have always understood the efficacy of American ideals, beliefs, and values. These have always been a part of their core "family values." No group in American history has valued such ideals more. But that did not prevent two historical periods of bondage, racist segregation, and racist suppression. Nor did it prevent the denial of rights, equality, opportunities, and social justice. Thus, it has always taken more than subscribing to and trying to live up to, or trying to implement, America's ideals. It has always taken more than employing culture for Blacks to advance in this country.

THE "CULTURE MATTERS" FALLACY

Indeed, the efficacy of culture is the new subtle racist argument that is most often used by white male American social scientists and that some Black conservatives (with Thomas Sowell leading the way) have bought into and have helped to advance in public discourse. The culture argument shows the influence of postmodern thinking and the influence of American sociologists's development of cultural sociology. The argument is that "culture matters,"[32] certain ideals, values, skills, and beliefs matter. The argument is designed to be able to avoid dealing with how "racism matters." The new argument is that "cultural factors" explain modernization and development, and, it is also argued that they explain the establishment and development of what are called democratic or free societies.

In some ways, the cultural argument is an extension of William Julius Wilson's argument initially made in the late 1970s. Wilson argued that race (meaning racism) was in decline in America, According to Wilson, racism was no longer a significant factor in the American economy, although it was still a significant factor in other areas of American life. However, White racist intellectuals distorted Wilson's argument. Indeed, they falsified it so that it read that there was significant decline of White racism in American society. So if racism was no longer an important factor related to Black existence in America, then their continued development behind Whites had to be explained by other factors; namely, cultural factors. The cultural sociologists promoted this subtle racism in America, and also in England, where cultural factors were to explain why black West Indians or black Africans had not made great advances in the country. Now the subtle racist cultural factor argument is used to explain why black Africans have not modernized and developed as other people have done in Canada, America, Europe, or Asia.

According to the "culture matters" advocates, cultural factors shape world modernization and development. The United States has played a large role in helping to shape the present world, in Asia, Africa, and elsewhere. It did so, not relying on cultural values, but national power: political, economic, technological, and military. A country does not become a "super power" by having the correct values. It attains the status by a ruthless capability and by exercising great power. The West has not become a broad "super power" in the world because of its cultural values, but because of its long history of being a vast colonial imperialistic power, exercising economic, political, and cultural domination and exploitation of the world's countries and peoples. Some it dominated, controlled, and exploited more, or worse, than others. This is specifically true of the United States. But when America and the West "shaped" the present world, they did it to the disadvantage of many countries and peoples on this planet, forcing them to try to modernize, develop, or play "catch-up," with fewer capabilities to do so. Within that context, if America or the West saw modernization or developmental efforts as a threat, then they would move against them in a manner that would suppress or control them. They would deny, however, that they were doing so. In fact, they would invariably say that people were not advancing, or were not advancing much because of their own indigenous or internal problems–things that they were completely responsible for and had to overcome themselves.

For a number of years in America, white racists used to talk about Blacks being "culturally deprived." They projected this argument as the reason for Blacks' lack of advancement in America. It was not attributed to racism. Rather, it was argued that White racism had "declined" to the point where it was no longer a significant factor affecting Blacks. White people, as racists, have played a large role in helping to "shape" Blacks or Black capabilities and responses in America. This was mainly done to the disadvantage–politically, economically, educationally, socially, and culturally–of Blacks and to the advantage of Whites in all these areas. But, as the racism of Whites had it, Black "social problems" were to be attributed to Black cultural and social deficiencies of their own making.

America and other Western countries argue that White racism, Western colonialism, and Western imperialism are not responsible for the lack of substantial modernization and development in Africa or other areas of the world. This may be true of the past, pre-colonial days, but not anymore. Now it's the lack of requisite values on the part of people which, somehow, is not related to the centuries of racism, colonialism, imperialism, and the current Western behavior of interfering with efforts on the part of formerly dominated, controlled and exploited people, to advance economically, politically, educationally, or technologically. This is another way of saying that the adoption of Western values does not necessarily help non-Western people to develop because Whites/Westerners still continue to pervert or subvert Western values with forms of racism and racist psychological attributes. And they continue to suppress efforts on the part of formerly dominated and exploited people to employ them. How many times have white people in America suppressed the efforts of Blacks to be and to act like Americans in this country: economic suppression, political suppression, and educational, cultural, and social suppression?

Whites in America have always regarded Black progress with fear and suspicion. There has always been a reluctance, owing to their racism, for Whites to try seriously to help it along. And one understands why. It threatens their individual and collective racism, their individual and collective sense of who they are and how important they are, and threatens Whites with competition. It generally threatens Whites's deep-seated idea that America belongs to white people, that it is a "White" or "white country." White people of the West, but also generally white people of Europe, still feel that the world belongs to them, or that they should have a large share of it. This is one of the objectives of the present American/Western/European economic global expansion. Domination and control of the entire world had been the previous objective, and this had achieved great success. Through numerous surrogate dictators, the United States established a considerable hegemonic position on the planet after the Second World War and called its part of it the "free world." Yet, it was a "free world" based on dictatorship and suppression, as America had been a "free society" or "free country" based on racism and slavery.

Black people have made their most political, economic, educational, and general social progress in America when white people have fallen out with each other, as in America in the mid-nineteenth century, and when white Europeans fell out with each other, resulting in two world wars that placed a demand on Black labor and fighting capacities and that resulted in gains. It also happened when Blacks, in one way or another, were able to pressure or persuade White cooperation in order to make gains, as Booker T. Washington and his leadership had done. And it happened a third way when Blacks engaged in a direct confrontation with Whites and extracted concessions and a share of America's opportunities and rewards from them. America's "cultural values" played a role in these successes, mainly on the side of Blacks who employed them as weapons of confrontation, cooperation, or struggle, while Whites mainly averted or perverted them by investing them with racism, and using them in this way as sources of resistance to demands, change, and progress. White altruism had little to no presence in any of these situations. Black conservatives and subtle White racists ignore all of this history and reality and seek to get Blacks to ignore them, too.

The newest incarnation of this argument is the subtly racist "cultural factor" argument, which helps to perpetuate this form of racism and works against Black people in the end. What advocates of the "cultural factor" won't acknowledge is that so much of White/Western or White/European power, modernization, development and prosperity was derived from ignoring, averting, and even perverting Western cultural values. And, it was further achieved by using inordinate political and economic power, and war, to achieve these objectives.

There are subtle white racists who are against affirmative action and diversity in higher education or they are, at the very least, for its considerable prevention. These subtle white racists take the racist stance of saying that admission to colleges and universities should be on the basis of socioeconomic need. They claim that this is a moral principle and one of social justice. Many sociologists, psychologists, and educators know that there is a very strong correlation between socioeconomic and education status and achievement on academic tests. This was something that the nefarious *Bell Curve*[33] conceded. Now, among Blacks of low socioeconomic and educational status, there would be those individuals who would show the ability to succeed in higher education. But they would also be exceptions. Thus, white racists would be able to hold on to their racist "exception" belief with this kind of argument and position. They would also be able to do more than that. They would be able to exclude masses of Black people from higher education.

A socioeconomic and educational criteria works against most Blacks who register low on the scale. But if the tactic proves successful, then this would work against Blacks of a higher socioeconomic and educational status, because these Blacks could publicly be opposed by anti-affirmative action and anti-diversity talk, or even more desperately, anti-quota talk, or talk against "preferential" treatment for Blacks. But would not making socioeconomic and educational status the criterion for higher education be showing "preference?" Would it be thought of as "preference" for Blacks? This contradiction is not what white racists would see. The kind of "preference" involved would be the kind that they could appreciate, because it would not send many Blacks off to colleges and universities. What so many Whites still seek are ways to continue acting in a racist manner toward Blacks. Particularly, they are looking for ways to get Blacks to help them do so.

CHANGE A-COMING WITH CONSERVATIVES?

What Black conservatives themselves tend to do is to separate some of America's ideals (what they call "conservatism"): merit, individualism, virtue, social class, family values, cultural values and the market, from their racist interpenetration or their racist interiority. They write and talk about them and enthusiastically direct Blacks to them, as if all of these things do not function through the racist context of America's welfare society. They divorce the American national, state, and local governments from the American economy to talk or write in abstract terms about the "market economy" or the "free market."

But this was not true of Gary Franks. Franks is a Republican and someone who is regarded as a conservative, but he speaks more like a Black liberal or, at best, a moderate Black thinker and politician. In this passage, Franks describes the Black conservative goals:

> Black conservatives have to get involved and argue that a new approach is due, including support of private business and its efforts to improve the quality of schools. Government has been left behind in many respects....Government must encourage more companies to participate, particularly in the inner urban areas, large and small....
>
> Small businesses are the backbone of our economy, and quite frankly, it will work to have government take a more constructive

approach to improving the economic climate for medium to small companies. Small businesses can benefit from a successful empowerment program. If we strengthen the ability of business to find qualified candidates, then efficiency, new products, and expansion will result.[34]

Franks sounds like he had been talking to Robert Woodson, another Black conservative, on whom that label does not fit well, because Woodson favors judicial government aid to Blacks and (other people in need) and also wants American businesses to get involved with Blacks's lives and to work with them for mutual benefit. In *The Triumphs of Joseph* he wrote:

> Now as never before, community leaders who have promoted healing and development in low-income areas have much of value to offer business owners and corporate executives. In the past, business was often depicted as the enemy of the "little people"–the low-income entry-level workers....The vast majority of problems confronted by business today are related to human resources. Many employers cannot obtain the quality of people they need in order to operate successfully. A base of loyal, honest, enthusiastic workers is what businesses desperately need because these qualities directly affect the quality of their services and products.[35]

Even Glenn Loury now accepts some government intervention to help what he regards as Blacks with the most need, frowning upon any government aid that goes to Blacks who have already made significant economic, educational, and social advances in America. He regards this help as an obligation on the part of the government, imposed by America's racist history that suppressed the development of so many Blacks and the lingering affects of that suppressive history. Loury looks at the mass of Blacks with needs as individuals and wants aid on an individual basis. However, he shows little to no interest in Black institutions receiving government assistance, although they were suppressed, damaged, or thwarted by this country's racist history as well.

Black Conservative Stanley Crouch is critical of what he regards as the reckless, hedonistic, and violent nature of so many young Blacks. He sees it as detrimental to Black communities in the country and talks values, self-knowledge, and self-help. But he also favors some government aid to strengthen and even transform Black communities.[36]

From these examples, it seems that the ranks of the Black conservatives are not as ideologically rigid and constituted as some Black conservatives like to suggest and that many of their white supporters, who view them as surrogates, like to emphasize even more. There are some Black conservatives (not many) who might be marking a new path among them. They seem to realize that there are some human efforts, activities, and concrete efforts towards making progress that require government and economic help. People, especially those deep in the Basin, are up against huge, suppressing obstacles. Alone, and without help, they can do nothing. They couldn't help themselves even if they wanted to. They are fighting structural changes in the economy, activities and problems in the global economy, programmatic economic slow-downs to combat inflation that in turn reduce employment, and changes in formal education in the country that are so distant from their lives. Some Black conservatives are learning that they cannot talk out of both sides of their mouths. They cannot separate themselves from the masses of Blacks, offer them no leadership, no practical help, and then condemn government aid to them as well.

THE RACIST VIEW OF WELFARE AND THE INADEQUATE BLACK RESPONSE

The Black liberal law professor Roy Brooks has written the following (and in the process criticized two prominent Black conservatives):

> Some—Thomas Sowell for example—actually discount civil rights laws and policies, instead citing an alleged deficiency of human capital among African Americans as a primary cause of socioeconomic inequality. This theory, however, fails to explain the rise of a genuine African American middle class since the 1960s and, moreover, is too dismissive of the role that factors external to the market—mainly government—have played in the establishment, protection, and even loss of position and wealth. Other commentators, such as Glenn Loury, who argue that African Americans must look beyond civil rights fail to understand that many socioeconomic problems, from unemployment to housing discrimination, require government intervention because of their scope or nature.[37]

Derrick Bell, black liberal and former Harvard law professor, resigned from his position because the law school did not have a Black female instructor, as he said in *And We Are Not Saved.*[38] In his book, Bell argued that despite the struggle of the 1950s and 1960s, and the civil rights laws of the 1960s and the follow-up and expanding legislation of the 1970s and 1980s,

Blacks still were not fully free in America. Many Blacks were still left behind with a bleak future for material progress. Bell even spoke to the White racists who were trying to take back as much of the Black gains in political and civil rights, and in material progress, as they could. He understood that it meant that they were attempting to weaken the Black middle-class, because a Black middle-class has always been a fear of white racists.

This white racist tactic is the same tactic used by the American Colonization Society in the first half of the nineteenth century. The American Colonization Society tried to get and aid northern nonslave Blacks to leave the country and go to Liberia, an established American colony. It was an attempt to get potential middle-class Blacks away from America so that they could not be voices against Black chattel slavery. However, they could not get many nonslave Blacks to leave. They then tried to weaken and severely impair the nonslave Blacks, who were constructing a middle-class existence in America, by criminalizing them, which had been initiated in the late eighteenth century when a number of nonslave Blacks appeared in the region and began emulating white middle-class people in developing their cultural and social existence. This early criminalization of the early Black middle-class was discussed by Africancentrist and historian Charshee McIntyre in *Criminalizing a Race.*[39]

This is how many white people, functioning as racists in America, view Black people on what they call "welfare:" as engaging in essentially criminal behavior. They see welfare as something that Black people receive that others in America don't (others, meaning white people). They believe that Black people receive this "handout" as a "dole" and because they're too "lazy," "shiftless," or "dumb" to work and earn their way. These white people do not refer to government aid as public assistance. If they did it might point them to the public assistance that they themselves receive from the American welfare state and society, such as a state subsidy for college and university education, Medicare, pharmaceutical subsidies, rent control, community grants, farm aid, government research subsidies, aid to dependents, disability aid, and other kinds of public assistance.

The upper-class rich like the public assistance of tax cuts and tax shelters. They like the government assistance of upward distribution of wealth, charity laws that protect or expand their wealth or their charitable institutions, economic corporate subsidies, and tax write-offs of various kinds. They like the government assistance of "bail-outs," national or state subsidies, government money to buy out (take-over) or merge companies and corporations, and government assistance in exporting capital and jobs. They don't flinch a bit when people of the Basin, have their "welfare" or public assistance taken from them by cutting away programs and shifting the money up to the Power Cap. Neither do they seem to care when public spending is reduced on these programs. Shifting money from the neediest in America to the upper-class rich and the economic corporations that they own and/or manage is also a form of public assistance. This situation is what the Reverend Jesse Jackson has frequently called "reverse Robin Hood," taking money from the poor and giving it to the rich. Richard Nixon, Ronald Reagan, Bill Clinton, and two Bush Presidents did this with great ease of mind.

Black liberals have especially harpooned this kind of racist behavior. The Black conservatives usually just complain about Blacks being on "welfare." They agree with Whites that Blacks shouldn't be. But this is common fare in America. Most Black conservatives, liberals, and radicals think and talk of what they regard as the reality of "welfare," all the while knowing who is actually on it. Most Whites think it is mainly Black people or other "racial minorities," but the truth is, as many people know, it is mainly white people who are on "welfare." To be precise, it is mainly white women, white children, and white indigents who are on "welfare."

Yet the misunderstanding is produced and maintained by racist thinking and racist practices that constitute the racist interiority (namely white supremacy/ebonicism) of the American welfare society. It operates like the skeleton in the human body. The entire welfare society is interpenetrated with this racist skeletal reality to which all societal parts adhere, and that functions through them daily, albeit, mainly in subtle ways.

Black liberals fight with Black conservatives about "welfare," as they fight with them on the issue of "affirmative action." This divides Black political thinking and Black politics, and it occurs mainly because both groups will not reject the concept of "welfare." At times, some Black liberals like Jesse Jackson, the Reverend Al Sharpton, or Kwesi Mfume (former head of the NAACP) will talk of American upper-class elements and economic corporations receiving welfare. Some Black radicals do the same: Julian Bond, for instance, who is a member of the Democratic Socialists in America. The Black radical Adolph Reed, Jr. has also criticized welfare for big corporations and the rich, as evidenced in *Class Notes*, and extended his criticism to University departments and research programs that he describes as new "poverty pimps," fraudulently taking monies from foundations and governmental institutions.[40]

But this kind of discussion of welfare by Black intellectuals and Black leaders are passing shots. They mainly talk of "welfare" and beat themselves up about it, as they also do when talking about "affirmative action." Nothing is more disheartening, if not disgraceful, than to watch Black leaders and Black intellectuals in public forums debating whether Blacks should receive "welfare," and not talking about America as a welfare society–how everyone is on some form of public assistance, and how it is, and has historically been, unfairly distributed in America. The same could be said for when they debate whether Blacks should or should not receive affirmative action and whether it is or is not beneficial to them, while not having any discussion about white male racist affirmative action and white female affirmative action, either, of which exceeds what Blacks receive.

The Black liberals, by focusing on "welfare" like the Black conservatives do, allow Black conservatives to talk publicly about how welfare policies have, and continue to, hurt Black people. When they talk like this they do not put "welfare" in quotes and often just refer to welfare as "public policies" or "governmental policies." These are policies, programs, and monies that go to the people in the Basin, to mainly poor people, Blacks, Hispanics, and lower-class Whites. Black conservatives show just how much they talk out of White racist history, and function as Black surrogates for white racists, when they attack these policies, programs, and monies the way they do.

Indeed, they show that same orientation when they complain about Black liberal intellectuals and leaders not talking more often about the "pathology" of Black community and life: the break-down of Black institutions and family life, single-parent families, out of wedlock children, and lack of educational success. Black conservatives obscure the fact that they do what they claim Black liberal intellectuals and Black liberal leaders do: they exploit "Black victimization" or, as John McWhorter said, "Black Victimology." They do not do this on behalf of Black people, as they say the Black liberals do. Instead, they employ these perceptions, phrases, and realities for their own individual benefit. If there were no Black victims, that is, Blacks still showing the effects of an oppressive history and social life, there would not be a phalanx of castigating Black conservatives.

There would certainly not be that many Black conservatives, beyond a handful, in which white conservatives would be interested. If Black conservatives just espoused what is considered conservative thought in America, making no references to Black people or the situation of Blacks in America, like so many white conservatives do (although in their case, racist premises are usually discernible), they would not have such a white audience. They have this audience because they mix their conservative talk and writing with a negative presentation of millions of Blacks. They tell white people that Blacks have pathologies, something that white conservatives believe about Blacks and need to hear some Blacks tell them to justify their racist orientations and to feel good about themselves.

Black conservatives do not talk much about Black successes, but then neither do white conservatives. They simply do not wish to hear about them. But it is curious that when white conservatives do refer to Black successes, they seem to work some kind of praise for white people into the situation. For example, a common conversation will introduce the idea that Blacks experience success because they followed "White values." But Black poverty, or Black crime, or Black violence, or other Black "pathologies" are always divorced from White association. Black conservatives invariably make this divorcement, which means they "blame" Black victims, which white racists/conservatives appreciate, as it legitimizes in their minds their "blaming" Black victims. Where would Black conservatives be if they did not blame Black victims, that is, if they did not have Black victims to blame? Where would they be if there were no Black victims in America? They need Black victims to be who they are. They need Black victims to be able to lambaste them, to be able to ingratiate themselves with white conservatives, to be able to obtain praise and largess from such people. Is this exploiting Black people?

Let Black conservatives talk about white male racist affirmative action, or about the subtle expressions of white racist thought and social behavior in America, or about some of the social problems of white people in America: violence, crime, drug addiction, drunk driving, out-of-wedlock births, suicides, runaways, mental illnesses, alcoholism, and a host of other things, and then see how white conservatives would relate to them. How much praise and recompense would they have for them then? Would Black conservatives be able to talk about a "White Victimology," be able to "blame" white victims, and have white conservatives demanding more such talk and writing? Who do white people blame their own social problems on? They usually don't blame anybody because they usually don't talk about them and they would not like it if Black conservatives did, especially to the extent that they talk about Black social problems.

The primary way that Whites have thought and written and spoken of Black people for hundreds of years has been in very negative terms, often reaching heinous depictions. The only "good" Black person was a slave, and the only "good" nonslave Black was the one who knew his or her "place." There were vile racist epithets as well, references to Blacks as beasts, vermin, feces, parasites, savages, depraved, debased, villainous, fiendish, demonic, and the like. Black life has publicly and privately been portrayed as being pathological, backward, licentious, criminal, and immoral. These are still the prevailing images of Black people and Black life in America, which television news still projects as staples.

This continuing disparagement is done primarily out of a White racist need, that is, as an outgrowth and reflection of the damage that the racism of white people has done to them, to their psychology, to their morality, and to their spirituality. This damage is something that Whites do not like to think about or talk about, and even less, like to reflect on. One way to keep from this kind of serious or deep introspection is to keep the vile images of Black people before their gaze. They batter themselves and others with these images. Another way for whites to keep from this kind of serious introspection is through racist practices of myriad kinds that force Blacks to live in a way that makes them conform in some way to the vile images. This is always a conscious and unconscious purpose of racist segregation and exclusion.

These racist-produced realities of Black life present great problems for Black leaders. They have to deal with and lead Black people who reflect their oppression and suppression. They have to be realistic about that and have to make certain that Blacks stay realistic, too, and not think they are riding chariots, when they are driving mule-pulled wagons. But Black leaders cannot just continually talk about the negative things about Black life and then attempt to motivate, galvanize, or organize the people they are trying to lead or raise up. Too much negativism would just help them dig holes of deeper deprivations.

Of necessity, Black leaders have had to learn how to be optimistic, to make optimism work for them as a motivating tool. That is why they tend to stress and over-stress cultural or social successes, which then function as magnets to draw Blacks into progressive or developmental activities. Blacks on the far bottom had to see a lot of Blacks making it to believe that they had a chance to do so. This was the kind of thinking and leading of southern Blacks that Booker T. Washington did for thirty-five years.

Some northern Blacks (the so-called "Talented Tenth") frequently criticized the Tuskegean because he did not talk enough about Black wretchedness. His most important and recent biographer, Louis Harlan, accused Washington—one of the many things he lampooned him for—of being too optimistic and always looking for a "silver lining." But Washington was a modernization leader of people just "up from slavery," who had to be stimulated, motivated, and galvanized in certain ways. Washington did this in an environment of daily public disparagement, great violence, and great inhumaneness, while Harlan and Black intellectuals were just that—intellectuals—and comfortably decades removed from the horrendous reality of it.

In reality, Black liberal intellectuals and leaders have talked about the debit side of Black life. When they have not talked about it, they have just dealt with it the way they saw it. They have drawn on available community resources and have tried to get aid from government agencies or aid from local economic institutions to help the very ailing. But things like powerful Black youth gangs were not easy to deal with. Drugs weren't either. And neither was it easy to deal with the availability of guns from outside the Black community or the criminalized police who worked in Black neighborhoods. And the movement of Black middle-class people, not necessarily from Black neighborhoods, but from involvement with Blacks from the lower-class, was another serious aggravation of the situation.

But Black conservatives usually ignore these realities, just like their white counterparts do. They insist on Black leaders disparaging millions of Black people for the same reasons as their white counterparts; they wish to justify to themselves why they do not have to share their bounty with them or seek to aid them. And they wish to rationalize to themselves why they are not in any way responsible for this reality. At the same time, they want to be able to lean back and throw some American ideals at the situation, as "corrective" tonics. They throw out phrases, such as "be an individual," engage in "individual effort" or "acquire the right values," "work hard," "pull yourself up by your bootstraps," and "face the direction of the market economy." At the same time, they blast Black liberals and their allies for throwing money and programs at the situation.

What is understood as "welfare" is not only a racist program, but a racist program of *social maintenance* and a program designed for the Basin. It is a program that maintains the millions of people of the Basin who can be described as poor, near poor, and living just above the poverty line. (Affirmative action, on the other hand, is a program for individual advancement, not maintenance). The social maintenance of people at the bottom of American society began with the maintenance of Black chattel slaves to keep them physically and psychologically able to work, but no more than that. This is a recurring paradigm. In the latter nineteenth century, the American Indian Bureau was established within the Department of the Interior and Indian tribes across the country received national government public assistance, but in the shape of "welfare," which Bureau officials and their political or economic allies fleeced at will. Many tribes, at times, did not receive the assistance allotted to them.

I did not put the Freedman's Bureau in the category of "welfare" because as underfunded and as ineffective as it was it was conceived as an agency with programs to advance the former slaves economically and educationally. The Bureau had some beneficial consequences for Blacks, but in the late nineteenth and early twentieth centuries, when the American welfare society was being constructed, millions of Blacks were returned to servitude in the South and were kept away from the new public assistance. Indeed, Blacks did not become significant beneficiaries of welfare public assistance until they forced their way into it in the early 1960s as part of their Struggle for Liberation in the country. Their struggle put a fire under then President Lyndon Baines Johnson, Adam Clayton Powell, Jr. (then Chairman of the House Education and Labor Committee) and then Speaker of the House,

Sam Rayburn. Together, supported and aided by the in-put of organized labor, they developed and got the Congress to pass "Great Society" social programs, such as affirmative action, of which Blacks were beneficiaries.

But the beneficiaries were mainly Black middle-class people, or those on their way up to that class. Poor Blacks in northern and southern rural and urban areas were not aided much–until the "War on Poverty." The legislation to enact the guidelines, appropriations, and programs of that war allowed poor people to have a big hand in implementing what was now public assistance for them. But southern white racist national and state politicians found this intolerable. They fought against it and finally won the battle. They did not like Black or poor white people in the South receiving large sums of government money and using it at their discretion. They did not like seeing poor Blacks and poor Whites getting out from under their control and exploitation. Just as important, they wanted the money that went into the South to be used as they and their allies in the region wanted to use it: in the traditional racist ways. Poor people were put on "welfare," with the lowest payment transfers to the South. "Welfare" payments were always kept low to force people to work at low-paying jobs to supplement meager "welfare" benefits. And "welfare" recipients always had to deal with some form of intimidation. This is when a number of Blacks and Whites migrated from the South to the North, to places where "welfare" payments were higher and programs of aid were better. They believed they could live better.

As far as the direct recipients were concerned, wherever "welfare" was distributed it was distributed for maintenance. But there were hidden parts to "welfare." One is that a large part of the national and state budget went to the upper-class rich, which they received by providing industrial and business services for "welfare" programs. Another is that the middle-class was also a large beneficiary of national and state "welfare" spending. Their salaries as administrators, consultants, staff, investigators, and others came from it. Also "welfare" agencies's equipment and maintenance came out of national and state, and also county, city, and municipal "welfare" budgets. Thus, "welfare" spending and programs augmented American middle-class affluence. And the third hidden part of the operation was that "welfare" helped to expand the Black middle-class whose members functioned as administrators, staff, investigators, and so on, in national, state, county, city, and municipal "welfare" offices and programs.

Most Black conservatives have remained woefully or willfully ignorant of "welfare." They do not know what it is, how it functions, and who its beneficiaries are. This is reflected in their persistent comment that "public policies," "public spending," and "public programs" do not work for Blacks and make them dependent, inert, unproductive, and prone to pathological behavior. But they really do not blame the "welfare" spending and "welfare" programs, because their argument is that if Blacks had "character," "acquired the right values," and "pulled themselves up by their bootstraps," they could emerge from misery and advance. This is how white racists talk and most Black conservatives mimic and express this racism.

Robert Woodson is one who does not. One of his greatest complaints about "welfare" is that it benefits the rich and affluent. In Woodson's view, seventy-five percent of the "welfare" monies intended for the poor goes to the "welfare" bureaucratic apparatus.[41] There are some other Black conservatives who see this too. Like Woodson, they want the Black poor to get off "welfare." But off "welfare" without education, technical training, or jobs will increase the burden of the poor. And a cut in "welfare" would also specifically hurt the Black middle-class, with whom the Black lower-class spends money for goods and services.

It's a dilemma for Black intellectuals and Black leadership, a dilemma the racist-inundated American welfare society produces. The "welfare" reform passed by Congress and President Clinton a few years back was primarily a money-cutting operation that sent "welfare" payments to the lowliest in the Basin. The reform took the cut money and shifted it upwards in the welfare society. But, there were also cuts that hurt some of the upper-class and middle-class, specifically middle-class professionals and small businesses.

It is not to be thought, for one second, that Whites will not hurt Whites in America. The history of poor Whites in the South disputes that racist notion, as does the millions of poor white people in the country today. Racists do not care what race a person is from. At the same time that white male "scientific racists" were using science to promote their racism against Blacks, they were also using the same pseudo-science against white women and the white eastern and southern Europeans flocking to the country. They especially engaged in a specific racist castigation of Jews from Eastern Europe and Russia.

And then there is the maleist/sexist racism discernibly involved in this pattern of thinking. Most people on "welfare" are women and children, people who have no humanity or rights and that so many men still feel they don't have to respect. This is a reference primarily to white men who devise, administer, and control the public "welfare." These are the same men who have succeeded in making Black women the goat of the situation, concocting an image of a Black "Welfare Queen," a symbol of how aggressive Black women and their presumed flocks of out-of-wedlock, un-mothered, and unruly children are the ones who really fleece the public and take from other worthy Americans. While Black liberals do not like "welfare," they regard it as immoral not to have Black lower-class people (or other lower-class people) at least maintained. One sinks morally very low not accepting that.

ENTER REVEREND JESSE L. JACKSON

For years Jesse Jackson has been the main public advocate for the poor in America, specifically the Black poor. For nearly two decades, he has been telling American political parties and the American people that the poor work hard every day. They just do not make much money. On top of that, they do not have medical and health benefits, because they cannot afford it given what they typically make. In addition, education cannot be top priority for them because sheer survival and maintenance take first place. Jackson presented this message to the political parties and the American public over two presidential nomination campaigns. He also said some other things that the country needed to hear, but that the political parties did not specially want him to say or hear. Black liberal scholar, poet and activist, June Jordan* pointed out Jackson's achievements when she wrote that he was:

> The first presidential candidate in 1988 repeatedly to plead the plight of 650,000 American farmers who had lost their farms within the eight years of Reagan's reign the first to identify drugs as the number one menace to domestic security...the first and only candidate... to demand that South Africa be designated a terrorist state and treated accordingly... the first and only candidate to call for self-determination and statehood for Palestine... the first and only candidate, Republican or Democratic, to propose an international minimum wage.[42]

Black intellectual Stanley Crouch, who considers himself a "hanging judge," also had high praise for Jackson's presidential nomination efforts and his leadership abilities, although he thought Jackson could be devious and had a propensity to employ harsh methods against his opponents. However, he generally regarded Jackson as a strong politician. Crouch noted that Jackson affected change "by challenging Negro Americans to do better, and by making possible an atmosphere of multiracial coalition unrivaled since the most inspiring moments of the Civil Rights Movement, Jackson has changed the positions of his listeners from often disgruntled spectators to potential participants."[43]

*Jordan passed away in 2002.

Jackson's Black critics invariably chastised him for not "following through" on his chosen projects, even as they saw him carry off two presidential nomination campaigns to their conclusions with meager funds, and even though Jackson is still affecting change. Jackson's continuing project is to increase the number of Black registered voters. And he has been leader of (or in the thick of negotiating contracts from) major American corporations that benefited Black businesses, such as the Coca-Cola Company, Burger King, Anheuser-Busch, Southland Corporation, Kentucky Fried Chicken, the Seven-Up Corporation and the recent ten year $7.8 billion dollar deal with Toyota Motor Sales, USA, Inc. These are clearly examples of his tough-mindedness, leadership abilities, negotiating skills, and his ability to exercise power. It also shows his determination and his capacity to follow-through.

After many years of strong leadership, Jackson finally put his liberal philosophical and political thinking in book form through the help of edited speeches. Titled *Straight from the Heart*, Jackson remarked in the Preface that:

> In my preaching, teaching, and activism over the past quarter of a century–and hopefully in this book–I have tried to illustrate that the issues of life flow primarily from the heart, not from the head, and that at the center of every political, economic, legal, and social issue is the spiritual, moral, and ethical dimension.
>
> Thus, those who would build this national house, these United States, and make a difference in the world, must build on the solid foundations of truth, justice, mercy, peace, equality, and freedom. They must fight for humane priorities at home and human rights abroad measured everywhere by one yardstick....
>
> It is this human struggle to have good religion and good politics that I hope you will sense through this collection of speeches.... As we struggle with the public issues confronting the men and women of our day, none of us has achieved perfection and none is beyond redemption. We must constantly rebuild relationships, revive broken spirits, forgive, and move on to the next challenge.[44]

Jackson is the epitome of the public intellectual, and thus, of the Black public intellectual as I would ideally define such a person. He is an intellectual, advocate, and activist. Jackson is the arch Black liberal, as he has been for years. However, he is not the arch Black leader, which Martin Luther King, Jr. and Booker T. Washington had been. It is not even clear if Jackson wants that status. It is clear, however, that Black intellectuals and other Black leaders would fight against him achieving it. But Jackson is the kind of leader who does not need that status. He likes being able to go where the action and the need is, whether it is a Black need, a White need, or a Hispanic need–hence, his "Rainbow Coalition" that he has tried to pull together in order to make a strong political force in America.

The "Rainbow Coalition" represents Jackson's efforts to organize people from the different races and ethnic groups in the Basin. At a minimum, this is a horrendous task, and something very difficult to achieve and sustain. But Jackson has had his successes. He has tremendous political savvy and skills that are not exceeded by any politician or anyone else in America today. He is on par with every politician and often surpasses most people in being able to identify important public issues and articulating them. He also excels in negotiating with people or mobilizing people to get concrete action out of them. There is always a harshness of method involved in this. It's inevitable. The stakes are high; the opposition is strong. One has to be tough, a fighter, determined.

Strangely enough, it is the Black radicals (either the radical liberals, or the Black Marxists, or the socialists) who are some of Jackson's main critics. Adolph Reed, Jr. finds nothing noteworthy about Jackson or what he did in his historical presidential nomination campaigns. He does not see anything significant about Jackson's leadership efforts among Blacks and other Americans. He views Jackson as a "showboat," a "hustler," and an "opportunist." Sadly, what has to be said about Reed, is that he seems not to like anyone! He has considerable intellectual ability, can be incisive and insightful, but the only thing he seems to like is what he himself says. Also, one cannot say what he does in relation to the things that he says should be done in and for America. His arrogance, intolerance, and cynicism undermine him as a Black intellectual, which he does not seem to see. However, Reed has a rival in his rejection of Jackson, and that is Manning Marable. Possibly the most important Black radical in the country, Marable's problem with Jackson stems from the way Jackson lopped off some of the Rainbow coalition leaders who Marable thought were some of his best local leaders and workers.

Black, white, and Hispanic radicals, politically speaking, have no place to go in America. The American democratic socialists (of which Marable, West, Bond, Reed, Hutchinson, and others are members) are an inept group and have been for years. This reflects the inability of socialists to build a strong and wide constituency in the country and transform the political landscape. Thus, radical or activist elements, like those mentioned above, moved to the Rainbow Coalition to find a home. But, at most, their interest was to take over the Coalition, and at minimum, it was to invest it with their own ideals or ideology and actions. In the end, Jackson saw this element as a threat not only to his leadership, but also to the Coalition. In the larger picture, he saw this as a threat to his influence and the Coalition's influence with the

Democratic Party and to their protest capability against the Republican Party. It could have also proved to be an impediment to get more middle-class people in the Coalition. Marable excoriated him for sacking radicals in *Beyond Black and White* when he said: "Back in 1988, Jackson had briefly had the people, resources and organizational capacity to launch a major independent campaign to challenge both capitalist parties.... Jackson's refusal to launch an independent group which could contest elections with both parties created the political space which permitted the DLC [Democratic Leadership Council] and Clinton to seize the offence."[45]

But there is something that Marable just refuses to see: Jackson is not a socialist, not a social democrat or a democratic socialist (a name change that the American socialists thought would help them in the country). Jackson is a liberal, which means he accepts capitalism and socialism in interaction. In short, Jackson accepts the welfare state and welfare society and sees his leadership task as one to try to extend the welfare society's benefits especially to people in the Basin of the society. He sees the Democratic Party as the best hope for that, but there may be something else in the future.

My strong suspicion is that the Black conservative movement is going to come to an end, or be reduced considerably in membership. There are conservatives, and more will emerge, who will see that government aid is simply indispensable, not only to help Blacks, but to help others in the country. This is going to turn some conservatives toward liberalism, and thus, towards a moderate political stance. They will be moderates in the Republican Party, which already has such moderates. But the new moderates have to be of a different order. Moderates in the Republican and Democratic parties are "middle-of-the-roaders," or "fence-straddlers." The new moderates would be *active moderates*, those who regard themselves as the axle or the spoke of the parties that make them go round. They would be moderates who supply the ideas and the strategies and seek to form the alliances or coalitions within the parties and without. They take control of parties and direct them; they keep them from going to extremes; and they keep the "middle" from being soft or mushy, with the end goal of making the party dynamic and directional. Black moderates of this sort in the Republican and Democratic parties could form an alliance, even a joint Black political leadership that could be joined by Black leaders of major Black organizations and that worked through the two major parties.

If nothing else, Black people have got to get away from putting all their eggs in one political basket. Right now that basket is the Democratic Party. Blacks should learn to use the two major parties more effectively. This is opposite to the advice some Black conservatives have been giving for years: they tell Black people to split their votes between the Republican and

Democratic Party. Victims, minorities, and those on the short-end do not voluntarily split themselves to be conquered, dominated, or manipulated. This is something that Black intellectuals certainly have to learn. Blacks should be flexible in relating to the two national parties. There may be a time when a Republican Presidential or gubernatorial candidate, or a Senator, or Representative, or a state Republican might be perceived as serving the interests of Blacks and others in America better. Thus, Blacks could vote for a Republican President, while voting for Democratic and Republican Senators and Representatives. Or they could vote for a Democratic President and Republican and Democratic Senators and Representatives. This kind of voting could be done in state houses and city and town governments. This kind of voting could also be led by a united Black activist leadership, which would put a unified and varied national Black leadership back into Black ethnic and political life.

BLACK RADICALS OR WHITE POLITICS

This is the kind of thing that Black radicals, or even people calling themselves Black activists, would likely be against. This would not be *leftist* enough for them. Nor would it be *radical* enough for them. Black radicals and activists make a fetish of being seen as leftist, as if it carried some kind of inherent political or moral superiority. What these and other Black intellectuals, leaders, and activists have yet to realize, is that left and right political thinking is White male racist thinking. This kind of political thinking emerged in Europe in the latter eighteenth century and took clear form in the early nineteenth century. The Conservatives were called the right, and the left was comprised of liberals, emerging democrats, and socialists. But in each of these cases mainly white men were involved, not white women.

The political struggles in the early nineteenth century were *inter*-male and *intra*-male gender struggles, not class struggles. Women from the different classes, which the men were also from, were excluded from these struggles except, perhaps, in some auxiliary fashion, such as cooking for occasions, making signs or insignia, or appearing at parades or rallies. This was the maleist/sexist racism at work that became the racist foundation of the non-racist, left-right political thinking and politics. This type of maleist/sexist racism suffused and guided both forms of thinking and political action. When left or radical European men talked of being "progressive," or talked about rights and equality, or talked about individual and equal opportunities, or even when they spoke of universal rights and opportunities, they meant men only.

This racist-inundated, left-right political thinking and politics effectively came to America in the late nineteenth and early twentieth centuries when welfare politics and the welfare society were being constructed. At the time, the Republican Party was considered the conservative party and the Democratic Party was also considered conservative. But the Democratic Party got an infusion of socialist thinking from so-called "progressives" who sought to build strength in the Party and orient it towards a synthesis of state socialism and liberalism. The Democratic Party took on an aura of being left, but not a full leftist sense, which in the eyes of intellectuals and politicians, was *pure* left.

Later, the communist party appeared and it *was* pure left. But the Democrats stole the ideas and social programs of the communist and socialist parties and became known as the left party, while the Republican Party became known as the right party. This, however, did not fully happen until the mid-1960s, when Barry Goldwater and his constituency allied western Republicans with southern Democrats and southern Republicans. The communist and socialist parties functioned haphazardly, but were leftist parties nonetheless. They, like the major parties then, were racist as well. Communists and socialists were just better able to hide their racism at a time when other political parties did not particularly seek to hide theirs. So both left and right parties in America were always suffused with white supremacy/ebonicism.

In *Speaking Truth to Power*, Manning Marable provided a discussion of racism in the American Socialist Party and the socialist movement. He said that racism was a major reason why Blacks stayed away from it.[46] In this same book, he called for a revitalization and reorientation of American socialists when he stated:

> The struggle to define the Left and to build movements for radical democracy will fail, though unless progressives squarely confront the issue of race....
>
> Historically, racism has been the most decisive weapon in the arsenal of America's ruling elites to divide democratic resistance movements, turning fearful and frustrated whites against nonwhite working people. Today, we live in a nation in which nearly 30 percent of our population is Latino, American Indian, Arab-American, Asian/Pacific American, and African-American. By the middle of the twenty-first century, the majority of the working class will consist of people of non-European descent....

Part of the Left's problem is the rupture of the theory and practice of social change. A good number of white socialists have the luxury to contemplate "class struggle" in the abstract. People of color and working people don't.[47]

Nearly a hundred years ago, in 1913 to be precise, Du Bois made a similar statement after he left the American Socialist Party. He remarked:

The general attitude of thinking members of the party has been this: we must not turn aside from the great objects of socialism to take up this issue of the American Negro; let the question wait; when the objects of socialism are achieved, this problem will be settled along with other problems....

Can the problem of any group of ten million be properly considered as "aside" from any program of socialism? ...If socialism is going to settle the American problem of race prejudice without direct attack along these lines by socialists, why is it necessary for socialists to fight along other lines?[48]

Nearly a hundred years later Manning Marable is still asking essentially the same questions. He and other Black socialists, radicals, or activists are dealing with the same White racism, but whose greater complexity has now to be dealt with. Multiple forms of White racism have now to be countered: white supremacy/ebonicism, white supremacy/bronzism, white supremacy/xanthicism and maleism/sexism. Marable, like other Black Marxists or socialists, thinks of racism in singular, not multiple, terms. Thus they are circumscribed in their thinking and analyses.

They also show the same kind of romantic thinking that Marxists and socialists have shown since the nineteenth century, that the "working class" will act as the radical or socialist Messiah and redeemer. For instance, Robin Kelley, a historian and Democratic socialist, endeavored to write a history of what he calls "black working-class resistance." His book *Race Rebels*, he says, "begins to recover and explore aspects of black working-class life and politics that have been relegated to the margins."[49] Marable, as seen, puts hope in Black workers and others of the "working class" in America. The Black Marxist Cedric Robinson sees some radical or socialist revolutionary possibilities in some of the alienated Black youth of the "inner cities." Indeed, he is sanguine about them being part of a Black phalanx of socialists to function in a socialist movement in America and notes: "Without them the inevitable urban uprisings are empty, episodic expressions of rage. With them,

171

it is always possible that the next Black social movement will obtain that distant land, perhaps even transporting America with it."[50]

Two of the telltale weaknesses of Marxists, socialists, and communists are the penchant for romantic thinking and airy ideology. Many readily substitute ideology for facts, evidence, or reality, and then act as if the ideological construction is real. They have this in common with racists who act on the basis of fantasies and then act as if the fantasies were actual representations of concrete realities. The simple truth, which has always been a truth, is that there is no such thing as a "working-class" *because all social classes work*! There is no such thing as "workers," as these elements understand the concept, because "workers" would have to include anyone who labors and that's more than just factory workers.

Another myth to explode is the existence of an "underclass." Adolph Reed, Jr. rejected the concept and reality of an American "underclass." He saw it as a "put-up" job by white, Black, and other research scientists, to get money for research and for "welfare" agents to acquire a clientele and money to work with. Whites, Blacks, and others who emphasize the concept of "individualism" contrast and flatter themselves by comparing their success to the lack of success of the "underclass." Reed saw clearly how the concept was a racist concept because the "underclass," to no one's surprise, was composed mainly of poor Blacks and Hispanics. He wrote in *Stirrings in the Jug* that many of the behaviors ascribed to the "underclass," such as use of drugs, out-of-wedlock children, divorce, and educational underachievement could be found "no less in upper-status suburbs than in inner-city Bantustans. The difference does not lie in the behavior but in the social position of those exhibiting it." He also added:[51]

> Characterizing those phenomena as behavior reveals a zeal for validating the underclass concept, but doing so may also betray a fundamental inclination to seek the sources of poverty in the deficiencies of individuals. All versions of the underclass notion center on the behavior of its categorical members, even though liberals typically hedge that move with genuflections toward the ultimate weight of historical or structural forces. (The differences on that score, however, are not that great. Today's conservatives also frequently genuflect toward structural pressures and past oppression before enunciating one or another brand of tough-love remedy).[52]

Looking for the "underclass" in the American welfare society is like looking for the racist "nonhuman" or "subhuman." None of these things exist or have ever existed. The "underclass" was an ideological construction, like the "working class," and then "evidence" was sought to prove its "existence." This is the same scenario that happened when white "scientific racists" obtained "evidence" to prove that "nonhumans" and "subhumans" existed.

Putting theory or ideology aside, in any society where there is a hierarchy of social classes, all classes below the top one are "underclasses"! The Black middle-class and the Black lower-class are "underclasses" in the Black social class structure. Black upper-class people can say that they are members of the American upper-class on the basis of income, wealth, housing, and other indices, but they would also have to admit that they do not live in the neighborhoods of white people with comparable exhibited indices, nor do they usually attend the same functions, belong to the same churches, the same clubs, travel together, or inter-marry. The Black upper-class functions within itself as a sort of Black "high society." But the Black middle-class functions within itself, too, as does the Black lower-class. They all function in a circumscribed Black geographical area, even when Black upper-class and middle-class people move to suburbia. What one usually sees is a contiguous geographical area stretching in a straight line from the Black area in the city to the Black area in the suburbs.

One may wish to say that racism has nothing to do with this and that social class plays a determinant role in the decisions made by Black upper-class and Black middle-class people. The fact that Whites live in many parts of a suburb and that Blacks (purported to be making decisions based on objective criteria) invariably live in a single and essentially confined area, especially when they are financially capable of living in the other sections, shows the ugly head of white supremacy/ebonicism involved. White supremacy/ebonicism is reflected in the situation in another way, in that the decision by Blacks not to live among Whites in suburbia shows their attempts to avoid their racism. Another reflection of the racism involved in this situation is that Black areas appear in suburbs mostly because Whites move out when they see Blacks moving in.

The great weakness and impairment of Black intellectual analyses of Blacks (other than the failure to understand what racism really is, owing to a lack of an adequate racist analysis) is that they detach Blacks from the very society in which they live and function in order to analyze them. When liberals, radicals, and conservatives talk about a Black "underclass" they do this. And when they say that race and class are the primary categories for social analysis–as if racism does not exist–they do this. White supremacy/ebonicism runs deep in America's welfare society. Everything in America is attached to that skeletal racist interiority. White male racist affirmative action is certainly attached to it, and so is American white feminist activity, trades in the American economy, and, of course, "Black jobs."

When William Julius Wilson talked about the decline of White racism in the economy, liberal scholar Sharon Collins came back with her discussion of "Black jobs." She noted that "Black jobs" are ones in which one sees concentrations of Black employment in the criminal justice system, in "welfare" agencies, and in community relations departments in economic corporations.[53] In the big corporations, Blacks usually find a ceiling on their clients and on their promotions, and thus, a ceiling on their incomes. Sometimes those incomes can be very high, as among Black entertainers and Blacks in sports. But haven't these two areas historically been areas for "Black participation," "Black jobs," "Black remuneration," and "Black incomes?"

White intellectuals, virtually all of whom do not want to deal with racism (especially those who support Black conservatives) are completely unaware that racism is connected directly to Black economic and social advance in a considerable manner. In their own racism and their inability to deal with it (or that of other Whites), they argue Black economic and social progress equals the absence of racism. The white editors of *Black and Right*, for instance, are gung-ho supporters of Black conservatives and Black conservatism. Beginning in chattel slavery, Blacks learned that you have to use the system of oppression to try to advance. An example of this is the Black slaves who were able to hire out their labor as slaves, with the master's consent. They earned money that way and found that they might end up being able to buy themselves or their family members out of slavery.

Northern nonslave Blacks got their own churches and schools with the aid of White financial support. They did this by agreeing not to try to attend white schools and churches. Lest we forget, it was the White racist segregation of Blacks that forced Blacks to develop their own economy and schools and professionals. Was it not using racism when Blacks filled the jobs that white workers gave up or lost striking, jobs that they knew would pay them less than what white workers had been getting for their performance? And don't Blacks use the racism of Whites to buy homes and to expand their living area, knowing that Whites will usually not want them as neighbors. And don't Blacks use white racism when it comes to political allegiances? For instance, aware of its racist image, some Republican Party leaders thought it would be wise for the Party to bring in some Black people and even offer them substantial opportunities in the Party or in Republican dominated governments and agencies as racist "token" Blacks. Those who became "tokens" used this racism to their advantage.

These discussions could go on. White racism and Black progress has always gone side by side and hand-in-hand, even though the progress of Blacks moves to diminish racism. What we have both Black and white intellectuals doing (especially Black conservatives) is engaging in what I call *consequence social analysis.* This involves analyzing Blacks, races, and genders as categories and verities, not only detached from the society in which they exist and function, and that affects them, but taking these realities and consequences and analyzing them on an independent, isolated basis. They become social realities independent of contexts and structures.

Historically, what White racists have always done has been to use the consequences of their racist thinking and social practices against Blacks. These consequences have equaled lowly Black "social conditions," which were then, in turn, used to criticize or condemn Blacks, thereby severing the racism from these conditions. Whites used these conditions to justify keeping Blacks segregated and isolated. But that was not where it stopped. They also used the same conditions to be able to publicly state how they were protecting the public order, or American society, or American ideals. Today, white racists, Black conservatives, and others take the consequences of racist behavior, such as Black "successes," to prove that racism no longer exists. In many instances, this can only be done if one disconnects White racism from Black "successes."

THE WALTZ OF THE CONSERVATIVES, LIBERALS, AND RADICALS

Black conservatives and Black liberals frequently say that if there were no racism tomorrow masses of Blacks would still be in the socioeconomic hole without a significant future ahead because their "condition" ties them to this bleak situation. But the "condition" is related directly to racism, which is what the intellectuals admit when pressed. However, these same intellectuals then do the peculiar thing of saying that racism is in the past, is over. But it is not over, as it lives on in the "conditions" of the masses of Blacks. A manifestation of these "conditions" are the Black conservatives who relate to Black people like subtle white racists, often speaking on the latter's behalf either directly or indirectly. They invariably deny this and on occasion will make some criticism of Whites acting as racists. But the criticism is usually so bland and is more like an aside comment, not one that digs into their racism and exposes the extent and perniciousness of the racist behavior.

To say that there is still some discrimination against Blacks, without tightening in on that subject, is the same as helping to promote racism, and it also promotes the delusional belief that white racists have that they are guiltless, innocent, and non-responsible. Discrimination might mean the inability to get a job or the loss of a job or income, the inability to buy a house (or the greater difficulty in doing so), or the greater difficulty of sending a son or daughter to college, or putting adequate food on the table. Discrimination costs the victim. It is not behavior to be minimized at anytime, and indeed, it is behavior that should always be condemned. Political scientist Martin Kilson has been critical of Black conservative superficial criticism of White racism, saying that it amounts to "a veneer-level inference, not part of a rigorous causal explanation of how, from Emancipation through all of the twentieth century, the racist American political economy has tormented, harassed, oppressed, and constrained modern social development among African Americans."[54]

There is a new way and method of comparing Black middle-class people and white middle-class people that is done by Black and White conservatives, and that is by comparing similar indices and arriving at similar conclusions about them. Once this is done they argue that race was not a factor, just social class. Or they try to emphasize the class factor. But this is clearly a matter of extracting these groups from American society, because race was not the critical factor to begin with, racism was. And that racism might well be connected to Black middle-class people who are in a position to be compared to white middle-class people—if one understood how racism functioned and lived on.

But there is even more to this matter of sociologically analyzing Black people. Who is being analyzed? Black people, as American Black history shows, are the descendants of black African slaves and their Black progeny. This is the Black ethnic group in America, which is obscured by focusing on the black race. Black people are a black ethnic group, but there are several black ethnic groups in the United States and each has its middle-class. These various black ethnic middle-class groups, however, are not members of the Black middle-class. But are they included in the analyses, discussions, and measurements of Black middle-class progress in America? They seem to be, which means that this is inaccurate, and even faulty, analysis and measurement.

Neither Black conservative, nor Black liberal, nor Black radical intellectuals engage in this kind of micro-historical and social analysis because they do not plunge deep into Black history and life. Both Black conservative and Black radical intellectuals function from an ideological base and frequently substitute ideology for facts or reality. Manning Marable, for instance, in his biography of Du Bois: *W. E. B. Du Bois: Black Radical Democrat*[55] called Du Bois a radical, but not Marcus Garvey. But Garvey was a radical, one who spoke of Blacks being "beautiful" and equal to Whites, and one who engaged in activities that tried to free the Black or black image from White racist depictions, and free Black or black people from White racist domination. Garvey was as radical as radical gets in America—and only ideology, and rigid either-or thinking, and using the White left-right political continuum, with its left and right categories for analysis, prevents this from being seen.

Black conservatives and Black radicals have on more than one occasion talked about revolution, a Black "conservative revolution," a Black radical, or Marxist or socialist revolution. Manning Marable, Angela Davis, Barbara Ransby, Cedric Robinson, Robin Kelley, and Joy James are looking for the Marxist or socialist revolution or some kind of *radical* alteration of America that could be done with a Marxist or socialist solvent. Black people are not, and have not demonstrated in their history, that they are societal revolutionaries. Nor have they ever wished to be. This the socialists and the communists once found out in no uncertain terms. Blacks did not engage in a societal revolution in the 1950s and 1960s. They conducted a struggle for liberation to take White racism off and out of their lives and to establish themselves equally and fully into American society–the American welfare society that remained in tact throughout that lengthy struggle (although, it was changed by it at the same time). The Black Panthers, for instance, were not societal revolutionaries. They talked like that and tried to act that way, but more as posturing than anything else. All the years they existed, they existed and functioned in the Basin of American society. It is the same place that they ended their political existence in: the American welfare society remained in tact. They did little to change it.

A societal revolution is rarely pursued, and thus, rarely achieved. Some examples of success, such as the French, Russian, Chinese, and Cuban societal revolutions are a few that come to mind. Revolutions can only occur when the revolutionaries have possession of state power, that is, when they have political, military, police, ordinary and secret, judicial, and penal power, in short, great repressive power to hand. They need this power to carry out a societal revolution, which involves destroying a society and constructing another one. Those who possess state power can prevent this from happening–hence the revolutionary cry of "seize state power."

Black radicals are very naïve about a societal revolution. One such radical is Joy James. James thinks of herself as a revolutionary and is very critical of Black male or female intellectuals who are not revolutionaries. Her displeasure with them reaches the point where she denies that Black female academics are intellectuals. Her opinion is founded on that of the Black feminist and radical socialist bell hooks. In her book *Killing Rage*[56] hooks says that an intellectual is one who critically engages ideas. Black academics do that in the course of teaching and when they evaluate the ideas of the people they teach about. But James takes the notion of Black intellectual even further than hooks. For her, such a person has to be an activist as well, and preferably a revolutionary-like herself. She stated that "since many women in the academy are conservative

177

or liberal in their politics, tensions arise between those groups and individuals like myself, who advocate revolutionary politics."[57] James's "revolutionary politics" turn out to be radical public protest against state repression, injustice, economic exploitation, and the aggressive advocacy of certain ideas or policies, although, it is not always clear who is going to be the beneficiary of these actions. But this is hardly "revolutionary politics." They occur and can only occur during the process of a societal revolution itself. The four revolutions mentioned above amply demonstrate this.

Black conservative, Black liberal, and Black radical intellectuals all operate on the basis of an obscured or hidden premise. This would also draw in the Black Africancentrists, who also function from it. None of these intellectuals (with some individual exceptions in each group) focus on Black people as an ethnic group of the black race in America. None of these intellectual groups, as groups, are seeking to preserve and perpetuate Blacks in this country as a distinct people, a distinct historical, cultural, and social group of people. They are not like Du Bois, who remarked in a 1961 speech at the University of Wisconsin: "No! What I have been fighting for and am still fighting for is the possibility of black folk and their cultural patterns existing in America without discrimination; and on terms of equality. If we take this attitude we have got to do so consciously and deliberately."[58]

None of the four Black intellectual groups function on this conscious, deliberate premise. The Africancentrists want Blacks to be Africans and want their history, culture, and social life to be African. And, it was actually Black liberals who put the identity of African American in the public hopper for consumption and recognition. Jesse Jackson and some other Black liberal leaders and intellectuals led this campaign. Jackson publicly said, "it would not cost America anything to do that." But it costs Black people and is an effort to take their identity away from them, which they still resist.

Liberals and radicals have something else in common with conservatives: They seek to help Black people on an individual basis, although they differ in how they seek to do that. For Black conservatives, it's a matter of throwing the value of "individualism" at Blacks and other exhortatory phrases, while liberals and socialists seek to get the government to help Black individuals. Presently, there are some Black conservatives moving in that direction also, so a convergence between Black liberals and Black conservatives might be up ahead. Black socialists, too?

If Black socialists join the convergence, it would not only be a turn in their political thinking and action, but would take some time to occur. In June of 1998, Black socialists joined with what they called other "Black radicals," such as revolutionary nationalists, feminists, and other kinds of "leftist" activists, to establish the Black Radical Congress. The different kinds of Black radicals reflected how divided such people were; thus, presaging the great difficulty ahead for this new organization to adhere to its original plans and to be functional and productive. But there was agreement among the disparate groups that "now is the time for a revival of the militant spirit of resistance.... Now is the time to rebuild a strong uncompromising movement for human rights, full employment and self-determination."[59] Members of the new organization declared that "America's capitalist economy has completely failed us." The radical organization would seek to construct a "transformative politics that will focus on the conditions of Black working poor and poor people." Indeed, the eleventh point of the "Freedom Agenda" read: "Black radicals must build a national congress of radical forces in the Black community to strengthen radicalism as the legitimate voice of Black working and poor people, and to build organized resistance."[60]

The Black Radical Congress doubtlessly appeared radical to those who helped to construct it, but that is because they had a limited, and even romantic sense, of what radicalism was: namely, they believed it meant negative criticism, denunciation, belligerency, demonstrations, and boisterous criticism against the "oppressors," "the system," and "injustice." Anyone who analyzes Black life in America knows that the American "capitalist economy" has not failed all Black people, as one third of Black people, roughly ten million people, have succeeded rather well in this economy, but not without extensive government help. The Congress is an advocate of socialism, although it does not say which kind: utopian socialism, cooperative socialism, communal socialism, state socialism, or syndicalism. It could be a mixture of all these things.

But some problems arise. For instance, if Black radicals and their new organization are in favor of socialism and against capitalism, how will they fulfill their desire to help "poor Blacks" gain employment, because this would have to occur within the American capitalistic system. Poor Blacks and other Blacks can't wait for socialism to be established to obtain jobs. And if they get jobs in the capitalist economy, why would they seek to protest against it or try to tear it down? And what is meant by self-determination? What could this mean coming from socialists who are not clear about the kind of socialism they're interested in and wish to establish? What would self-determination mean for the revolutionary nationalists? Were they in favor of trying to establish a Black country in America and making it socialistic? Neither of these objectives was proposed or rationalized in the agenda.

If it were understood that "revolutionary nationalism" was "separatism," that was not declared as an objective in the "Freedom Agenda" either. Even if it were, it would be antithetical to the declared interest to construct a "transformative politics" in America. But it was not clear where that kind of politics would be established: within Black communities or within the larger American society? Nor was it clear what kind of transformation it would seek: transformation of the country or Black communities in the country? Which, of any of these things, would be the objectives of the new "resistance movement?" And in the first place, how does a resistance movement transform a society or community? Transformation takes construction, which is practical (also ideological). And if it is the transformation of a community, the Black ethnic community, nationally or in its local manifestations, then clearly more than some kind of resistance politics would have to be involved.

Finally, the Black Radical Congress seeks to be, along with the "new" Black radicalism, "the legitimate voice of Black working and poor people." As said earlier, Black upper-class and middle-class people work, too. Would Black radicals be seeking to make the "Black working people" and "Black poor people" part of the Black middle-class? That would not likely be their goal, because they see the middle-class as associated with capitalism, which they are against. And they certainly are against Black middle-class people. They wish to wrestle the leadership of Black communities from the Black middle-class because, they argue, it is not effectively leading these communities and not at all serving the interests of Black lower-class people.

Still, it is difficult to ascertain how Black radicals can serve working and poor Black people if they do not seek to help them attain employment in the American capitalist economy and lift them out of the Black lower-class and up into the Black middle-class. Black socialists and other Black radicals not only show great confusion in understanding their goal, they also show that they do not really come out of Black history and Black life to try to be political forces in America. Their thinking is White: absolutist, either-or, leftist, and singular. Their methodology is White as well, particularly when they equate radical activity exclusively with protest for rights and not with ethnic and community building. They're also exercising White thinking when they argue that social division among Blacks is necessary, radical, progressive, and helpful to Blacks, rather than being destructive to them. Of course, white racists would view this behavior with glee.

In the end, Black radicals are like Black conservatives and also like Black Africancentrists. All of these groups work on the peripheral borders of Black history and Black life; they try to influence it from the outside. Black radicals see Black people as a political entity shorn of their socio-cultural attributes and as a large chestnut, to try to pull the socialist chestnut out of racism and inertia and into serious political activity. In addition, white socialists are not solicitous of the help, and Black people, in general, show no interest in social democracy or democratic socialism.

This leaves Black Marxists or socialists chasing ideology, dreams, or visions. Black radicals could help to put more energy in the Black liberal posture, since they wish many of the same things for Blacks, specifically the same kind of government help, which also brings both close to some Black conservatives. Maybe there is the possibility of a coalition of Black intellectuals in the future that can presently be envisioned, or at the least slightly sensed.

One thing that would eliminate some of the tension and division between the three groups of intellectuals would be the three learning more about Booker T. Washington. The Tuskegean led Black people as the Grand Black Leader for twenty years, and these were years of Black material, social, and psychological progress during what historian Rayford Logan once called the "Nadir" period in Black history; when the "New Negro" was born. The latter was a concept that would become the metaphor and symbol of the Harlem Renaissance. There are things to learn from Washington and his years of ascendancy among Blacks during that period that would be beneficial to Black intellectuals, leaders, activists, and everyone in America.

Chapter Five
Goliath Holds Serve: Booker T. Washington and Black Intellectuals

Most Blacks have no knowledge, understanding, or memory of Booker T. Washington. This includes most Black or black intellectuals, leaders, and activists. The name still has prominence, but it usually leads to an emotional, rather than an intellectual, reaction. When it is an intellectual reaction, it is usually something brief, superficial, or inaccurate, with the prevailing feeling that everything relevant or important has been said. Among Black and black intellectuals (as well as other intellectuals and scholars) Washington's image and prestige was so low that those in possession of his vast papers could not sell them to a library or institute and they were subsequently given away to the Library of Congress. The present major biographer of Washington, Louis Harlan, and a team of scholars edited his vast papers and put them out in thirteen thick volumes. But, Black and black intellectuals overwhelmingly ignored them. The response of Black and black intellectuals to these volumes is reprehensible, utterly shameful, and irresponsible.

BLACK CONSERVATIVES AND WASHINGTON: FAVORING AND MISUNDERSTANDING

Black conservatives tend to show an appreciation of Booker T. Washington. One such conservative is Thomas Sowell. In a December 1994 issue of *Forbes* magazine,[1] Sowell wrote favorably and insightfully about Washington, paying particular attention to the leader's emphasis on "character" and its role in thought, social behavior, personal morality, and social morality. Black conservative Glenn Loury wrote the following about Washington in *One by One from the Inside Out:*

> Booker T. Washington's philosophy offers a...guide to the future for Blacks...the problem of underdevelopment–the "brains, property, and character" problem that Washington spent a lifetime trying to address–remains very much with us. Full equality of social standing in American society, the goal that Blacks now seek, can never be

attained until the fact of Black underdevelopment is squarely faced and reversed. As Washington grasped intuitively, equality of this sort rests more on the performance of blacks in the economic and social sphere than it does on the continued expansion of legal rights.[2]

As favorably as Loury depicts Washington there is an inaccurate image projected here. Washington did not place political, civil, or legal rights as a top priority in his efforts because he knew that Blacks would not be permitted full rights in the country. In trying to become a Black leader, Washington had to make a choice of what to emphasize. He chose Black modernization and development. This continued to be his basic choice and approach during and after he became the Grand Black Leader.

Washington's notion of the "social sphere" was different from what Loury suggested; namely, he thought of the "social sphere" as American society. For the Tuskegean, economic and social development had to occur within Black social life or the Black social world. Loury was inaccurate when he later said that "Washington was a conservative advocate of a philosophy of self-help." He also asserted that Washington believed:

> That progress...must be earned, not simply demanded...that true equality with the former oppressor...must ultimately derive from an elevation of their selves above the state of diminishment...justice is not the issue here. The issues are honor, dignity, respect, and self-respect, all of which are preconditions for true equality between any peoples. The classic interplay between the aggrieved black and guilty white, in which the former demands (and the latter conveys) a recognition of the historical injustice is, quite simply, not an exchange among equals.[3]

The first part of Loury's comments has validity. But, the latter part reflects misconceptions and even errors. Washington did not base his leadership or programs on any notion of White guilt. He based them on the great racism of white people and, in his mind, how that could be used to his advantage. The Tuskegean understood the great power that white people held then; it was power suffused with white supremacist/ebonicistic racism. It could snuff out the life of a Black person on the basis of a whim or "for fun." It was power that could crush not just Black efforts to progress, but Black progress once made. Therefore, Washington based his leadership and programs on White self-interest and the needs of Black people as they revealed them to him.

As such, the Tuskgean did something that Black conservatives as a rule do not do. He asked Black people what they wanted, which Black conservatives do not feel a need to do. This is also true of most Black liberals, radicals, and Africancentrists. Washington mainly looked upon "honor, dignity, respect, and self-respect" as psychological statuses and strengths to help Black people "up from slavery" and to modernize and develop their community. He looked at Black group strength (i.e., Black unity and Black economic, educational, social, and cultural development-in short, Black Power) as the key to Blacks achieving respect, rights, equality, justice, and freedom in America.

Most Black conservatives are against Black collective behavior, unless it is for something they call "self-help." However, their notion of "self help" is not in line with how Washington understood and employed the term. To Washington, "self help" was not a methodology for individual advancement. It was a methodology for group and individual advancement and individual and group transformation. Of course, Black conservatives stay leagues away from Black Power. But this is also true of most Black liberals and Black radicals, who invariably view Black empowerment in individual terms and at times in gender or coalition terms. As a rule, they do not view it as a methodology for independent Black group power as Washington did.

Black conservative intellectuals and Black conservatives tend to understand Washington superficially, because they do not do extensive research on him. In this way, they join other Black intellectuals who are just as remiss. If they did their research, they would be shocked and inclined not to lay claim to him, particularly if they were knowledgeable about his thinking, leadership, and programmatic efforts for Blacks.

Washington's name is called upon in the same grating manner that some white people in the South and North call upon Martin Luther King, Jr. King's words and phrases are used to oppose affirmative action, political appointments, or organizing Congressional or state legislative districts to give Blacks equitable representation. What's more, Black intellectuals abet this subtle racist behavior by putting the emphasis on race, rather than racism, as the primary argument between Whites and Blacks and as the primary cause of problems in Black life. In this manner, they are also supporting the American welfare society, which has not successfully guided Whites in understanding how to treat Black people with dignity, respect, and equality.

Whites will mouth that they favor these things or answer positively to them on survey questionnaires. They do this because it is easy to respond to America's abstract ideals, values, and morality, and because they understand that that is what researchers want to record. If, on the other hand, Whites are asked if they had any Black friends, if there were Blacks living in their neighborhoods, if there were Blacks in their country, social, or political clubs, if Black children attended schools with their children, the answers would be different. Invariably, there would be a lot of stammering, subterfuge, frustration, and even deviousness in trying to answer these questions.

When Whites use words like "character," "integrity," "morality," "responsibility," "righteousness" or "spirituality," they do not usually associate these words or their attributes with Black people. These are words that most Whites have always associated exclusively with white people. In short, for most Whites these words have always been racist code words. They still are and are still used in a perverted manner by most Whites to avoid, exclude, reject, and to discriminate against (partially or fully), or to suppress many Blacks. When Whites demand political candidates to show these desirable personality attributes, there is usually hidden in the demand the assumption and understanding that white candidates will do something for or on behalf of white people and will likewise take care of or do something to Black people and other people of dark hue.

In general, White people like the notion of being "taken at their word." They like for others to think that they mean what they say and that they are who they say they are. These notions are part of White racist folklore. In so many ways (and in so many instances), white people have functioned just the opposite of what they have said. Black people especially know this to be true. Intelligently and realistically, white people are to be judged on the basis of what they do, because they have vitiated, in relationship to Blacks, any notion that they are to be taken at their word. When Black conservatives take white people at their word, which many of them do, it not only shows naiveté, it shows an ignorance of or unwillingness to deal with the historical relationship between Whites and Blacks in America. This relationship is ongoing due to subtle verbal or concrete expressions of racism, which Black conservatives, acting as public surrogates, help to keep ongoing.

What is the following comment by Glenn Loury except a Black surrogate and abetting remark: "The essential truth, of which Shelby Steele reminds blacks, is that it is primarily the human condition, not our racial condition, that we must learn to cope with."[4] This is clearly coming out of White racist history. Many white intellectuals in America, Canada, and Europe like to talk about the metaphysical or general human condition. They like to regard this as the "universal" condition of humanity. But, there is no such thing as the "universal human condition." This is a metaphysical absolutist abstraction.

What exists are given human conditions that vary in their realities. Human beings all over the world are concerned about their specific national, group, or individual situations. These situations have been considerably shaped by America and other Western powers over a period of centuries, primarily shaped to the disadvantage of others and of victimized people. The latter have to look at their "condition," their "human condition," which includes all the manifestations of their victimization and the roles they play with respect to their specific human condition. What would thinking about some abstract, philosophical human condition do for them? How would it help them to throw off those still dominating them, in whatever way they're doing it, or to modernize and develop, or to move along a different individual, group, or historical course?

White racists, as Western history in general and American history specifically demonstrates, talk of universal or ideal values or conditions while engaging in dominating, oppressive, and exploitative behavior. They even use a universal language to rationalize doing so. Steele, Loury, and other Black conservatives who turn to philosophical abstractions, e.g. the "human condition, "individual equality," "group equality," or "justice," to depict the situation of Blacks in America can easily misrepresent it and prescribe inadequate responses.

If Washington were alive, he would completely reject conservative efforts to get Black people to look upon their situation in America in some abstract manner away from their existential reality. Conservative Glenn Loury remarked that "Black Americans must now bear up under the weight of a great trial. Our choice is to confront and dispel the difficulties, or to deny and avoid them. *The Content of Our Character* [Steele's book] is aptly titled, for the response that we choose to the current difficulties will reveal more about our own character than about the moral culpability of whites."[5] But, it is the "immoral culpability" of white people that Black people are concerned about.

Loury and Steele's thinking demonstrates the impact of racism on it. They come out of White racist history to analyze the Black situation in America and suggest that Black people, throughout their history, have had to deal with White morality or that, in general, white people today seek to relate to Blacks in moral terms. This certainly cannot be given credence, especially when Loury, Steele, and other Black conservatives talk about subtle White racism still being practiced in America. And how much character–or intelligence–would Black people be showing by thinking that their real concern was some esoteric, metaphysical, abstract "human condition" they had to deal with?

To add to this situation, Black conservatives often espouse a White racist notion of freedom. Individualism is not a concept of liberty or freedom. It is a concept of license. This is how white people have understood liberty or freedom throughout their history in America. Freedom means being able to do some things, but not others, because there is a boundary line around freedom to prevent crossing this line and infringing upon other people's freedom. Whites, functioning as racists, sought no limits to the way they could think or act: politically, economically, and socially toward Black people. This includes other dark-complected people in America. Whites wanted to act in a licentious manner, a whimsical manner, a manner devoid of care, concern, or responsibility, all of which are involved in a notion of liberty or freedom.

Booker T. Washington clearly understood how white people mistook license for liberty and how it often "ran down to murder." Black history, Black life in America—these existential realities—is where one would get a better view of what freedom meant, not from White racist history and life, which seems to fascinate and motivate so many Black conservatives. Regarding Booker T. Washington as simply a conservative shows how conservatives have a paucity of knowledge and understanding of him. Their identification with (and endorsement of) the Grand Black Leader constitutes the kiss of death for him with liberals and radicals. It also helps to keep his public image in a disparaged mold and helps to keep him as someone who Blacks should not think or learn about.

MISUNDERSTANDING AND MISREPRESENTATION PLAY ON

Marxist Manning Marable claims not to look at Washington as an "Uncle Tom," but he has said that "Du Bois was right: Washington's accommodationist approach toward white power was profoundly flawed, and at times even criminal, in that it gave legitimacy to the lynching and disfranchisement of black people. However, that doesn't make him an 'Uncle Tom.' Washington's primary role was to articulate the interests of the entrepreneurial, conservative wing of the emerging black middle class to the representatives of corporate and political power in the white world."[6] Despite Marable's initial disclaimer, it is hard not to see Washington as an "Uncle Tom," even a "betrayer" of Blacks, who abetted their lynching and disfranchisement according to Marable. These images are also intimated by Washington's concern with only a small group of

Black people (not the mass of them) and by his disposition as a leader who was in the hands of powerful (and other) white people.

Manning Marable was evaluating the Tuskegean in a Marxist ideological manner. This resulted in faulty comments about a man that he clearly has not done enough research on. Washington's primary interest was never the small group of "entrepreneurial, conservative" Black middle-class people, or even the Black middle-class itself. His primary concerns, from the time that he began constructing Tuskegee Institute until his death in 1915, were his youthful Black leaders and Black poor people in the rural villages of the South where most Black people lived then. Marable seems to believe that since Washington was a capitalist, he had to have been a conservative. But a capitalist is not necessarily a conservative. People like Andrew Carnegie, David Rockefeller, J. P. Morgan, Robert Ogden, William Baldwin, Cornelius Vanderbilt, and others like them, helped to transform America economically, politically, and socially in the late nineteenth and early twentieth centuries. Ideologically, Marable can only see capitalists as conservatives. And owing to the same ideology, he regards socialists as being progressive and radical, people on the left.

Marable is like most intellectuals in that they show that they don't truly understand conservatism in America. That understanding has been removed from them and is replaced with the racist absolutist, either-or, left-right political continuum and the fixed political categories and descriptions that are associated with it. Political conservatism in America has always meant two things: preserving *and* promoting the power, status, wealth, interests, and opportunities of white men; in short, it is white male racist affirmative action. And then there has been the general and larger expression of this political position: preserving *and* promoting the power, status, wealth, interests, and opportunities of white people in general.

When one looks clearly at the White conservative tradition in America, one sees that it has fundamentally always been a racist tradition. It can also be seen that white men have especially promoted it in a right and left manner, preserving features of this tradition and also progressively or radically promoting them. One would not be able to see Washington promoting conservatism (minus the racism) in this kind of manner–not if one held disparaging images of him, believed the pejorative myths about him, could only think of left being progressive, or believed that "self-help" was necessarily conservative action. This is also true if one believed every negative thing that W. E. B. Du Bois had to say about the Tuskegean.

Marable's dislike for Washington extends to his analysis of Henry Louis Gates, Jr., who is being dubbed by some as the new "Booker T." Marable writes that:

> The greatest degree of antagonism expressed today against any single liberal intellectual within the African-American community is probably reserved for Gates, who has been described publicly and privately as something of a "modern Booker T. Washington" in the realm of cultural studies and literary criticism over the past five years. Like the "Wizard of Tuskegee," Gates sees himself as something of an entrepreneur; he has extensive influence within foundational circles and inside the white media.[7]

Any comparison between Gates and Washington is shallow and superficial. Washington was a gargantuan leader, a "Goliath" among Blacks for nearly half his life. His "Goliath" status also existed among white people in America for twenty years. It was, after all, Du Bois who said that Washington was a leader of Black and white people in America. In *The Souls of Black Folk*, he remarked: "Booker T. Washington arose essentially the leader not only of one race but of two."[8] Kelly Miller, another contemporary of Washington's, said the following about the enormity of Washington and his leadership in toasting him at a banquet:

> Sir, you enjoy a degree of concrete achievement and personal distinction excelled by few men now living on this planet. You are not only the foremost man of the Negro race, but one of the foremost men of all the world. We did not give you that "glad eminence" and we cannot take it away, but we would utilize and appropriate it to the good of the race. You have the attention of the white world; you hold the passkey to the heart of the great white race. Your commanding position, your personal prestige, and the magic influence of your illustrious name entail upon you the responsibility to become the leader of the people, to stand as daysman between us and the great white God, and lay a propitiating hand upon us both.[9]

Is this the kind of public image, commanding public presence, great public prestige, and great power that Henry Louis Gates, Jr. or any other Black person in America has? Only Martin Luther King, Jr. ever came close to Washington's power, status, prestige, and possession of such a "propitiating hand" to lay on Black and white people. Miller's remarks counter the "Uncle Tom," "accommodationist," "sycophant" and "betrayer" imagery that has been heaped on Washington.

James Weldon Johnson was also of the times and his portrait of Washington equally noble when he said the following:

> The great body of Negroes, discouraged, bewildered and leaderless, hailed Mr. Washington as a Moses. This was, indeed, a remarkable feat-his holding the South in one hand, the North in the other, and at the same time carrying the major portion of his race along with him. The feat of uniting these three factions in the attempt to benefit the third has been tried before, but never achieved; and the founder of Tuskegee was the first to approach an accomplishment of it. The fact that he succeeded so far as he did, notwithstanding the popular conception of him as only a earnest educator and an energetic builder, stamps him as one of the world's greatest diplomats.[10]

Yet, Black historian Nell Painter's view of Washington was that he was nothing more than a Black educator,[11] which was also the understanding of James Anderson, as expressed in his book *The Education of Blacks in the South*.[12] Historian Nathan Huggins saw more to Washington than that and asserted that his leadership from 1895 on had a large dimension. He referred to Washington as an "emblematic leader," a kind of leader that was indicative of Blacks at the time, of which Washington was the foremost and best example. He said, "black leaders served as exemplars, presenting themselves as living proof that blacks could perform as citizens in ways that were above reproach. They could, thus, serve as agents of white society's philanthropy and good will, and they would serve Blacks as a symbol of racial pride and self-esteem. This exemplary characteristic of black leadership made for very limited possibilities."[13]

Up to a point, one could describe Washington's leadership this way. But it is not a full characterization. Huggins makes the mistake of putting Washington on the same plane with other Black leaders from 1895 on. Washington was Goliath compared to any Black leader during his ascendancy between 1895-1915. This is the image of Washington's leadership that comes from Du Bois, from Kelly Miller, and from James Weldon Johnson. They all saw the Tuskegean *leading* (not just exhibiting leadership qualities) Black and white people in the country.

Despite these highly credible testimonials, Louis Harlan found it difficult to swallow or to accept them. In his second volume about the Tuskegean, Harlan noted that "Washington never forgot, however, that it was the blacks whom he undertook to lead. He could not lead the whites; he could not even divide them. He could only exploit the class divisions the whites created among themselves, *working in the cracks* [italics mine] of their social structure.[14]   If Whites in the South were already divided, why would Washington seek to divide them? Washington was interested in upper-class and middle-class Whites in the South. He perceived them to be lesser enemies to Blacks than lower-class Whites. He was not interested in exploiting class divisions; instead, what he sought was upper-class and middle-class protection and help for Blacks.

Curiously, Harlan's comment was later contradicted by other comments he made in the second volume of his study of Washington. Harlan spoke of the Tuskegean leading Whites in the South and the North. After all, many whites were following his lead as to what to do with and for Blacks, what to do about relations between Blacks and Whites, and how to further the process of reuniting the two sections of the country and strengthening it. This was the image that Johnson projected of Washington and the gargantuan role he saw him playing in the country. The enormity of it was also due to the fact that the Alabamian was not a President, elected official, or one of the rich and powerful corporate economic elites, such as J.P. Morgan, Andrew Carnegie, or David Rockefeller.

Harlan further insulted Washington and desecrated his image by his comment that "psychoanalysis or role psychology would help us solve Booker T. Washington's behavioral riddle, if we could remove those layers of secrecy as one peels an onion, perhaps at the center of Washington's being would be revealed a person with a single-minded concern with power, a minotaur [half man and half bull], a lion, a fox, or Brer Rabbit, some frightened little man like the *Wizard of Oz*, or, as in the case of the onion, nothing."[15]

Notice the difficulty Harlan had calling Washington a human being! In typical racist fashion, he divested him of his humanity and human status. He invisibilized him and his humanity, referring to him as animal, half man, and as a vegetable. Black historians and other Black intellectuals did not comment on this racist assault. Nor did they raise any serious questions about Harlan's two-volume biography of Washington that was based on blaming him—the victim—for the woes of Black people (and not the white people who inflicted them) and referred to Washington's efforts to help the mass of Black people in the South modernize and develop as "wrong-headed." Indeed, the two-volume biography received lavish praise from Black historians and other intellectuals, with the first volume winning the Pulitzer Prize for its author. What were the chances of white people in the North and South (and by that I mean very powerful white people) and millions of Black people entrusting power and leadership for *twenty years* to a "frightened little man," and still less to an animal, vegetable, or insect?

Cornel West was critical of Washington because, as he asserted, he failed "to promote structural change in society."[16] But the years that Washington functioned as the Grand Black Leader were years when America was in the process of constructing its welfare politics and welfare society. Washington was in the very thick of these developments and significantly contributed to them as a new powerful Sub-Elite who also played a new powerful Grand-Elite role. These developments, and also the reuniting of the country, could not proceed, certainly not effectively, without cooperation between northern and southern Whites. In fact, the effort to cooperate could have been seriously impaired if northern and southern Whites found themselves fighting over the disposition of Blacks in the South, which could be triggered by Black and White conflict or battles in the area. This is where Washington came in.

THE ATLANTA ADDRESS:
THE WIZARDRY OF A FIVE-MINUTE SPEECH

Washington proffered a general plan to keep the South "racially quiet" or less racially confrontational in a public speech given in September of 1895. He believed this general plan would facilitate the process of re-cementing the country and would also remove or seriously reduce southern White opposition to the economic corporate elements, especially in connection with their efforts to transform the American economy and country. In return for this, Washington said he wanted the northern economic corporate elite to help the South and Blacks both economically and educationally. The Tuskegean presented northern Whites, southern Whites, and Black people with a deal, a deal that they all felt they could not refuse.

The importance of Washington's Atlanta Exposition Address continues to be misunderstood, misinterpreted, and usually disparaged by Black intellectuals. They usually make no effort to analyze it. Their standard approach is to respond to some aspects of the Address and then denounce and ridicule the whole thing. A favorite point of denouncement was Washington's pronouncement that Blacks would not agitate for the vote in the South, which he regarded as "extreme folly." Black liberal and Black radical intellectuals, with their either-or political thinking and their belief that having the vote would be the great guarantor of equality and panacea for freedom, were the ones to really go after Washington for what in their mind was his "betrayal" of Blacks. They would also be against what they called his "accommodationism" to Whites, because Washington did not agitate for political and civil rights and did not seek to promote social equality between the races, as reflected in his comment: "In all things that are purely social we can be as separate as the fingers."

Joy James referred to Washington's Atlanta speech as "infamous" in *Transcending the Talented Tenth*.[17] Du Bois had written to the *New York Age*, congratulating him on it, saying he had constructed a fit compromise, if only southern Whites would now follow through with it.[18] Manning Marable regarded the speech as a sell-out, and Washington as a "betrayer" of Blacks. He also argued that "Washington's public position of accommodation to racial inequality prepared the ideological ground for a series of repressive laws governing race relations."[19] This is patently false and shows Manning Marable following and accepting Du Bois's distortion of this situation, which he did repeatedly once he became Washington's adversary.

Historian Arnold Taylor showed in *Travail and Triumph* that repressive "Jim Crow" laws had been passed initially in the last years of the Reconstruction period, in the late 1870s. The laws were constructed to disfranchise Black voters,[20] as well as to discriminate against Black in public accommodations. The Supreme Court further facilitated such laws and actions in the early 1880s when it declared the Civil Rights Act unconstitutional and reinterpreted the Fourteenth Amendment that had protected the civil rights of Blacks by preventing state governments from violating them. It did this while permitting white individuals to do so and by taking the enforcement power from the Fifteenth Amendment that guaranteed Blacks the right to vote in the country.

In the early 1880s, Washington was just beginning to build his school. "Jim Crow" discrimination, exclusion, and disfranchising laws were passed in one state after another before he made his Atlanta speech. Other states would do these things after the Address. But Washington and his speech could hardly be blamed for the laws and political suppression, even less so for "laying the ideological ground" for Whites to do these things. They had their own ideological grounds, white supremacy/ebonicism, which they had planted in the late 1870s; in actuality, which they had resurrected after a temporary abatement during the Reconstruction period. A common racist practice is to blame the victim. This can also be done by inadvertent or surrogate behavior. Is it to be believed for one moment that white people needed Washington's authorization or sanctioning to disfranchise Black people? Is it to be believed that the United States government would have supported him and Blacks had they agitated for the vote, or even voiced moderate demands for the vote, especially when the government had abandoned recognizing and protecting the national citizenship and rights of Blacks, and had authorized and sanctioned southern state governments to take political and civil rights away from them?

The charge of being an "accommodationist" is the one that Black intellectuals vilify Washington with the most. This charge subsumes the others: "Uncle Tom," "sycophant," "betrayer," even "toady." David Levering Lewis called Washington the "Great Accommodator" in the Pulitzer Prize winning first volume of his biography of Du Bois and was generally disparaging of the Grand Black Leader in his book.[21] Black historian William Banks said Washington accommodated northern and southern Whites "rather than confronting their prejudices" because he thought it "would generate more opportunities for the students of Tuskegee–and for himself."[22] This is investing Washington with very selfish motivations. It also takes away the importance of Washington's Atlanta Address as a means to help Blacks generally in the South and as a means to help him get the endorsement to play the larger historical role that he sought that September.

The continuing common misunderstanding among Black intellectuals is that white people picked him to play the historical and leadership role he played for two decades in America. What powerful white people in the North and South did was to *endorse* his quest for the role. Washington knew that powerful northern and southern white people were going to hear his speech at the Exposition and that it would be reported in the newspapers around the country. He was initially hesitant about making this speech, but he concluded that it might have a big pay-off for himself, for his Tuskegee Institute, for the leadership and programmatic efforts he was already carrying out in the South (and had been since 1881), and for the economic development of the region that would help Blacks. In a five-minute speech that easily rivals and, in my view, far exceeds the importance of Lincoln's Gettysburg Address, Washington presented a proposal for promoting national reconciliation and national unity, for helping to consolidate the new national corporate economy, for helping a largely illiterate (and essentially unskilled) group of people to modernize and develop, and for helping the country to vigorously keep going through its economic, political, and societal transformation. Lincoln's address was a speech to chant the American ideal of equality and to commemorate some men who had fallen in battle.

Accommodating white people, their racism and their racist power and practices, was just something that Black people had to do in the late nineteenth and early twentieth centuries. This was something that Black people had done their entire history in America; Black slaves accommodated white masters and slavery, and nonslave Blacks accommodated White racists, White community racist power, and White racist segregation. In the late nineteenth century, northern Blacks saw that the national political parties no longer had an interest in them or southern Blacks. Eligible Black voters had lost, or were losing, the franchise in the South. In the North, the Black vote was bribed, taken for granted, or even ignored. In these circumstances, northern Blacks decided to turn inward and away from public agitation for rights, equality, and full integration into northern life. There were some Black women who sought to get the vote for Black women, but this effort did not meet with much success. Black women found white women suffragists universally racist and unwilling to work with them to obtain the franchise for all women in America.

The wall of racist segregation was up high. Blacks in the North, for the most part, decided to function on the other side of the wall, to build economic enterprises, to build and strengthen schools, churches, and families; in short, their collective racial existence depended upon soliciting White help, which was only available on the basis of accommodation. When white immigrants pushed Blacks out of jobs, residential areas, and businesses that served white people and out of remunerative sports, such as being jockeys and trainers in horse-racing events, this only accelerated accommodation and what has always been called "self-help." Historian August Meier said this very thing almost forty years ago in *Negro Thought in America 1880-1915*.[23]

When Washington stepped on the stage to address his audience (with the knowledge that he was going to have a national audience) and implicitly advocated accommodation, he fully understood what he was doing and made *instrumental* use of accommodation. Washington simply regarded accommodation as a foregone conclusion. White people had returned to their strong domination and suppression of Blacks that had been interrupted by the war and postwar political activities in the South. He knew that northern Blacks were accommodating. For more than ten years he had been making speeches in the North to white and Black audiences and he saw how Blacks in the region lived and were trying to live. Accommodating white people meant opening up space between themselves and Whites, which was achieved by putting or accepting the White racist wall between them. Washington knew that the last thing that southern Blacks wanted was to get socially involved with white people. If anything, they wanted to avoid them! So when he said that Whites and Blacks would maintain a social distance, the Whites, of course, cheered. Blacks wanted to cheer, too, but they knew it would not be prudent. They did clap like Whites when the Tuskegean made the remark, but for different reasons.

To Washington, the big thing about accommodation was that it was the key to getting help for Blacks in the South. At the time, the South was a poor region and it had a lot of poor, uneducated, and socially backward people. It needed outside help. It had to come from the North, from new corporate economic elements and their national government political allies. But the latter had to have some assurance that the South would remain politically quiet with respect to the way emerging northern political and economic Grand Elites were taking the country.

Washington stepped into the nexus knowing what was needed. He had been doing it for years, standing in the nexus between upper-class, middle-class, and lower-class Whites. In this instance, Washington worked to keep them separated and to get Blacks some protection and help. At Atlanta, he had to change strategy and did; he had to promote unity between Whites that were divided. He did that by stepping into the nexus with instrumental accommodation. But for Washington it was a quid pro quo: "I do something for you, you do something for me" and for Blacks in the South. Whites and Blacks, especially in the South, but also generally in the North, accepted the deal.

At the time, Blacks were not heavily involved in politics or seriously agitating for rights and political power, which Washington's present day critics do not know or callously ignore. Critics always point to the Tuskegean's opposition, which was mainly northern Blacks. They complained about the speech and had epithets for Washington. There were those who frowned upon Washington because he had not graduated from a northern college or university and was a principle of an industrial school. They just did not see what his credentials were. Yet, a lot of people, including Black people, North and South, did see them.

In *The Education of Blacks in the South*, James Anderson wrote, "Washington's training and essential character did not prepare him well for the struggle to gain the allegiance of black intellectuals and leaders. He was not an intellectual and was much more a man of action than an ideologue."[24] Washington was a man of action, but he was clearly an ideologue as well, espousing the "Tuskegee Idea," which was an ideology of racial consciousness, racial pride, racial unity, and racial strength. The Tuskegee Idea was part of Washington's general theory of modernization and development. Most northern and southern Black intellectuals were supportive of Washington, as August Meier has shown, but Du Bois and some of his northern opposition disparaged his intellectual capabilities, as did Louis Harlan in his two-volume biography.

In *The Black Response*, historian Robert Factor counters these accusations when he says that:

> It is one of the least appreciated facets of Washington's career and personality that he was highly theoretical insofar as a social theory may be regarded as a set of unproved assumptions which explain the isolated facts of social experience and relate them to each other. In the controversy with Du Bois it is Washington who emerges as the less pragmatic of the two and Du Bois who moves from one position to another in response to social trends.... Washington added to this delusion by denouncing abstract thought and thinkers and by emphasizing the practical and concrete. But as theory is a working hypothesis and guide to action, Washington was profoundly theoretical.[25]

The theory was a complex and elaborate one of modernization and development, which can be viewed whole by piecing it together from his speeches, writings, and correspondence. Washington was not just guided by theory, he implemented it through the concrete social and cultural construction that he had Blacks undergo under his leadership. Historian Robert Factor implied that pragmatism was confined to ideas when it could be ideas, strategies, procedures, or programs. In general, pragmatists do not change their ideas or methods, unless they feel compelled to give them up. Washington never changed the basic modernization position he initially created in the early 1880s. However, he did continuously modify it between that time and his death in 1915. For instance, in 1915, he publicly protested for Black rights and publicly advocated for higher education for Blacks. These were things he did very little of prior to 1915.

In his book *W. E. B. Du Bois and American Political Thought*, Adolph Reed, Jr. reiterated some of the usual erroneous views and images of Washington and said the following to explain why an opposition developed to challenge his leadership: "The urgency of critics' objections to the Tuskegean's stranglehold on black debate and access to support for uplift activity, in fact, derived principally from recognition that his machine's main function was to stifle challenges to the emerging Jim Crow order. They understood that disfranchisement and loss of civil rights would ultimately destroy black aspirations."[26] This is an image of

Washington as a "strawman" or a "boogey-man," coughed up out of radical ideological and either-or thinking. It pays too much homage to Du Bois's or Monroe Trotter's views of Washington's relationship to his essentially northern Black opposition and the purposes of the "Tuskegee Machine."

James Anderson expressed similar views when he described Washington's "Tuskegee Machine," saying it "was formidable because it consisted of wealthy white philanthropists, large amounts of capital, large sections of the black press, a cadre of black educators in small industrial schools, and powerful white politicians."[27] (There was more to the Tuskeegee Machine than this, which will be shown a little later in this chapter). In regard to Washington and his opposition, Anderson wrote:

> Some students of the Washington-DuBois controversy have concluded that the Trotter-Du Bois forces were "outgeneraled by that Machiavellian prince of Negroes, Booker T. Washington." Clearly, Washington continued to serve as the Negro power broker for northern philanthropists, but...Washington and the philanthropists, however, did not outmaneuver the Trotter-Du Bois forces on the ideological front. From 1902 to 1904, the philanthropists attempted to prevent a total break between the Washington and Du Bois camps. They failed, and out of their failure grew the radical Niagara Movement in 1905.[28]

Reed and Anderson have reduced Washington's leadership down to the simple matter of his work with philanthropists to squash Black radicals who publicly protested against "Jim Crow." This caricature of Washington's leadership entirely leaves out the national scope and purpose of it. Washington functioned as a national leader for the country and as a Grand Black Leader. He did not take his cues from white benefactors on how to lead Blacks, nor could he always get whites to do what he wanted them to do. At times he found stiff resistance and even refusal. Washington dealt with his Black opposition primarily on his own, and with respect to how he viewed the situation of Blacks in the country, and with respect to who was helpful or not helpful to them.

Contrary to Anderson's assertion that Washington's white benefactors sought to prevent a final break with his northern adversaries between 1902 and 1904, the Tuskegean had to persuade his benefactors to take an interest in his efforts to work out a compromise with them. A compromise was finally reached at the Carnegie Conference in New York City in 1904. Washington had to do a considerable amount of imploring to get some of his benefactors to attend the meeting, as they felt that this was a matter between him and his adversaries. But Washington wanted his benefactors present to remind his opposition of the extent of his power and because he wanted his benefactors to sign off on the compromise.

As for the Niagara Movement, it came into existence in 1905 and by 1907 it was a shell organization. In the following year, it was a paper organization that disappeared. The Niagara Movement was very elitist and never sought to build a mass following, not even a following among Black middle-class people. It was a movement that was continually riddled by jealousies and in-fighting and had too few victories–all of which made it vulnerable to Washington's actions against it.

The Tuskegean would not accept the idea of northern Black elites attempting to lead southern rural Blacks while living from such a great distance, and would not accept them trying to tell southern rural Blacks the best ideological approach on how to make continuous progress in their region or how to survive and develop. In order to lead rural and other Blacks, they would have to come live in the South before he would give them any credence. His northern opposition felt that their education and cultured status, and the fact that they lived in the politically progressive part of the United States, qualified them to lead Blacks anywhere in the country. Washington felt that southern rural Blacks, people "up from slavery," yet experiencing its continued effects, needed leaders out of that history and social environment.

Two years after the collapse of the Niagara Movement, the NAACP was established and the typical Black historian comment echoed by Black intellectuals is that this spelled the end of Washington's power, prestige, and leadership among Blacks. This, of course, is sheer fantasy. It is a fantasy recently perpetuated by David Levering Lewis during a discussion in his biography of Du Bois titled "Rise of the Crisis, Decline of the Wizard." The year the NAACP was functioning, Washington visited Europe where he was feted by royalty, peers, politicians, intellectuals, and journalists. He returned to America by way of New England, which he toured and was also feted. These events should not be passed over lightly. This was an area that had been hostile to Washington in 1905 when Monroe Trotter was arrested for heckling the Tuskegean as he gave a speech. Trotter continuously blasted Washington in his newspaper the *Guardian* that circulated throughout New England. And Boston, itself, had been a seat of Niagara support.

By 1910 Boston and New England were both seats of support in Washington's camp. These seats consisted of mostly Black middle-class people; especially those who would have been designated "Talented

Tenth" people. This changed circumstance and Washington's great power, prestige, and gargantuan leadership at this time were captured by this newspaper account:

> Returning to Boston Tuesday evening Dr. Washington found at the depot an automobile which had been provided by the United Committee of Colored Elks, which conveyed him to Paine Memorial Hall on Appleton Street, where a reception and band concert were being held at the Elks. Some seven or eight hundred ladies and gentlemen were present. They welcomed the Negro leader with cheers, hand-clapping, the waving of handkerchiefs, etc., and gave every evidence of a sincere pleasure in being able to entertain him as a guest of the occasion.... Negro Boston, as represented by these seven or eight hundred ladies and gentlemen, was certainly responsive to the occasion and drowned with applause again and again the eloquent words of appreciation which fell from the lips of the recently returned traveler.[29]

Manning Marable and other Black radicals would find this difficult to explain. The radicals would all agree with Marable's assessment that "Booker T. Washington called for 'separate, but equal' race relations throughout the South, justifying political disfranchisement and segregated public accommodations. Washington was intensely popular among northern capitalists and Republicans because he urged Blacks to work as strikebreakers, undermining labor unions, and he urged African-Americans not to agitate publicly for civil rights."[30]

Marable and others would have to explain why Washington was still the Grand Black Leader with a large Black middle-class following if that was how his actions were interpreted. Washington had that following in 1910 and years afterwards with a national rights organization, the NAACP, on the scene that carried out a public assault against legal segregation, coupled by a public demand for Black rights. The unions that Marable spoke of were racist to the core and excluded Black factory, mine, and dock workers. This forced Black laborers to establish their own separate unions. Perhaps northern Black middle-class people cheered Washington for sending Black strikebreakers from the South against racist enemies of Blacks. Marable seemed unable to fathom that white unions undermined themselves with their own racist practices. Blaming Washington and Black strikebreakers is like blaming Black victims, and in doing this, it inadvertently supports white racists who were excluding and oppressing Black laborers.

It was always to the South that Washington returned and where he mainly conducted his Grand leadership of Blacks. And it was in the South where he was literally worshipped by Black people, yet it is still thought that it was Marcus Garvey who established the first mass movement among Blacks in the United States. The black historian Hollis Lynch made that observation[31] and Cornel West made it in *Prophesy Deliverance* when he stated:

> Garveyism seized the moment primarily because of the cultural ambiguity contained in the two leading programs of the Afro-American petite bourgeoisie. Uprooted black rural folk in the hostile urban environment yearned for a new cultural self-identity and self-image. The NAACP and the NUL (National Urban League) lacked the imagination and resources to respond to such yearning; the so-called Harlem Renaissance certainly could not fulfill such existential longing. The Garvey movement filled this cultural vacuum, and it became the first mass movement among Afro-Americans.[32]

Washington had a hold on rural Blacks in the South and also had a hold over Blacks in the North. In both places, he always spoke to overflowing crowds with hundreds or thousands of people standing outside of buildings to see him when he came in and when he left. In the South, they flocked by the thousands to see him or to hear him speak, coming from miles around, leaving work and everything else behind to do so. Washington had a hold on rural Blacks, but also southern and northern urban Blacks, with the southern rural Blacks making up the mass movement he had initiated in the 1880s. This hold propelled him to Atlanta in 1895 and stayed with him (and under his general leadership) for the remainder of his life.

Washington's mass movement involved millions and reached a magnitude and quality of adulation, affection, loyalty, and devotion that Garvey could never have attained in America. This is revealed in a newspaper account of Washington's tour of Louisiana in April of 1915, the year he died. Washington was in very bad health and dying from a mixture of ailments. And it has to be remembered that this tour was five years after the NAACP had been established and was functioning as an organization, and when, as David Levering Lewis and other Black historians have said, Washington had been eclipsed by the new organization. The account read:

Meetings were held in New Orleans, St. Bernard Parish, New Iberia, Crowley, Lake Charles, Lafayette, Southern University, Baton Rouge, Alexandria, Gibsland, Shreveport, and Mansfield. Everywhere Mr. Washington and his party were met at railroad stations by crowds of black people; other crowds of white citizens gathered to see him and to hear him expound his gospel of industrial opportunity and racial goodwill.

Negroes came on mule back, in carriages, and in wagons, long distances–ten, twenty, thirty, and even forty miles. They gathered in the thousands at railroad stations to see the "wizard of Tuskegee." They stood for hours to get a chance to hear the most distinguished member of their race tell them of progress and opportunities in the Southland. There were literally miles of people and vehicles. Good-natured policemen were sometimes carried off their feet in the effort to keep a path open through the eager throngs, but there was no tare of disorder. Everyone was happy, sober, receptive.[33]

White people of power and distinction attended Washington's speeches throughout his tour of cities in Louisiana. Mayors and politicians introduced him. In Shreveport, he was introduced by N.C. Blanchard, the former governor of the state where he spoke to a crowd of 10,000 people. The Tuskegean's largest crowd in the state was 15,000 and it behaved as all the others. Under no circumstance could anyone attribute Washington's adulation among masses of Black people, and even masses of white people, solely to his northern white benefactors! It might be ventured that as bad as it was for Blacks in the South during Washington's ascendancy, it might have been worse, more suppressive and deadly, had he not been on the scene and doing what he was doing.

Black and other people of dark hue were being colonized, suppressed, and exterminated on the planet. Native Americans had recently been through a time of extermination and reservationizing. There had been talk in the early 1880s and 1890s of bringing people from India into the South to replace Black labor, following the practice of European countries drawing Indian and Islamic laborers to their African colonies.

What always worried Washington was white European immigrants flocking to the South. He feared that they would replace Blacks in the region as farmers and workers in factories and mines. He feared white unions coming south and pushing Blacks out of jobs and work—another reason he was so anti—union. This is another fact that Marable and other Black radicals do not mention. The Tuskegean spoke out against European immigrants being drawn south and said to his audience in

Atlanta (and to the South, in general) that they should "cast down their buckets" on those they knew and who were "loyal" to them and the South.

Washington was always concerned with something else that was just as important to him as Black modernization and development and the ultimate achievement of full freedom in the country: Black survival. He had taught Native Americans at his alma mater, Hampton Institute, and he knew something about how they lived and how they were treated in America. He used to say that Black people were the only people who had ever looked the "proud Anglo-Saxon" in the eye and lived. However, he did not see Anglo-Saxons as the greatest threat to Blacks.

That threat was the white immigrants coming into the country from eastern and southern Europe and Russia. Most were farmers and unskilled workers, and new economic corporations and their factories, mines, and docks were taking them in by the millions. Black chattel slavery had always had white immigrants remaining North or traveling west, rather than filing to the South to live and work. Washington feared masses of white farmers and unskilled workers moving south. He feared the displacement of Black farmers and Black industrial workers. Hundreds of thousands or millions of Blacks idle and not working would have white racists perceiving them as being useless. In a deeply racist regional-social context that meted out great public hatred, humiliation, and violence against Blacks as a matter of course, this could be a life-threatening situation for Blacks. They, themselves, did not have the power to stop this situation from evolving.

This thought had initially emerged in Washington's mind in the early 1880s when he and his colleagues, as well as his students, were building Tuskegee Institute. He hoped his school would help southern Blacks become skilled farmers and tradesmen, and would invest them with ideas, beliefs, and values that would make them think differently and better about themselves. He also felt that this education would be a form of self-protection and stimulant to action. These were survival mechanisms, which Washington wanted to spread, especially among rural Blacks throughout the South.

This was always an urgent matter with him. It was in working to establish these things, and to help rural Blacks to develop materially and as quickly as possible, that he developed his relentless approach to leadership. He seldom rested, constantly traveled to build constituencies, and constantly recruited, galvanized, and pushed people to act. In the process, he neglected his health. For fourteen years Washington led southern Blacks like this, through Tuskegee Institute and other agencies, always connected to the question and matter of survival, but also other critical things that were part of his "Tuskegee Idea," such as modernization and development and ultimate Black freedom in the country.

But incoming white immigrants were a potential serious threat to all this. He did not want Blacks competing against such people for work or space in the South. Blacks would lose the battle. He already knew how easily white people killed Black people and how easily they got away with it. And from his observation of incoming immigrants in the North, he knew how so many of them readily adapted to White racist thought, social behavior, and violence. Blacks in the South did not need to face another contingent of white people who did not value their lives.

Before a Boston audience in 1884, when European immigrant penetration into the South had become a big worry for him, Washington said: "since freedom there have been at least ten thousand colored men in the South murdered by white men and yet, with perhaps a single exception, the record at no court shows that a single white man has ever been hanged for these murders."[34] Washington had no way to stop white immigrants from coming south, but he knew southern Whites could. In his Atlanta Address he appealed to them to do so; asking them not "to look to the incoming of those of foreign birth and strange tongue and habits for the prosperity of the South."

Black historian Vernon Williams saw this statement as simply an example of Washington "revealing his nativist thought."[35] Williams showed disapproval of Washington's criticism of Blacks leaving the South or those wishing to leave the country to improve their situation. Washington felt that the South held the greatest opportunity for Blacks to develop as a people. However, it was never really an argument with him. Most Blacks lived in the South and would not be leaving it. Washington knew that they would have to make it in the region. But the South was underdeveloped economically and also poor. It had many poor white and poor Black people. It was a question, to a significant extent, of how poor people perceived and acted on the situation: i.e., developing leadership, inner strength to act and cope, devising programs, and marshaling and utilizing limited resources.

This is the kind of thing that Black conservatives like about Washington, his emphasis on individual effort. But this amounts to a superficial understanding of Washington. He was always concerned about Black people as a collective. Blacks, for him, were a racial group, the group and individuals in the group. Under no circumstance did he see *individual* effort as a panacea for Blacks. Thus, Washington, unlike Black conservatives, came out of Black history, emphasizing individual effort and success and the individual consciously contributing to the Black collective and helping it to be successful and vice versa. Washington frowned upon and condemned individuals seeking to advance themselves at the expense of Blacks, or seeking to advance themselves as a means of separating themselves from Blacks. Washington strongly felt that Blacks were in the struggle for survival, development, and freedom together.

One form of individual effort that Washington found hurtful to Blacks in the South were the individuals with education, technical, or economic skills, or financial resources that left the South. He also resented it because, in many instances, these individuals had been educated by poor Blacks, Blacks who had scraped together their meager resources to educate them and who had provided them with economic help and opportunities to be leaders, only to be abandoned when they, themselves, needed help. Today, capable Black people "migrate" to suburbs or isolate themselves in Black communities. In both cases, they leave needy Blacks behind. A favorite escaping place for a number of them is academia, where they spend a lot of time writing and talking about Black people in a generic sense, as if they and the needy Blacks were in the same psychological, educational, social, financial, political, and cultural place. Black middle-class people are in the process of seeking to take the lead in developing Black culture, to get away from having to rely upon what the needy Black people produce (those same needy Black people who have always been the creators and source of Black aesthetic culture).

A consequence of a *cultural dichotomy* is usually a social and political dichotomy. Many Black intellectuals—conservatives, liberals, and radicals—are promoting cultural dichotomy and promoting its negative consequences for the millions of Blacks who cannot follow Maya Angelou's poetic assertion: "And still I rise." At least, they can't do this alone. Washington was a promoter of Black aesthetic culture, music, humor, prose, and poetry. He saw Black aesthetic culture and Black religion as critical to the modernization and development process. They were requirements in helping to build racial consciousness, self-esteem, and to act as unifiers of Blacks in their individual and collective modernization and development efforts.

However, it should be said that when it came to religion, he was not interested in a religion for Blacks that was solely or even primarily other-worldly. And he was certainly less interested in a religion that was strictly scriptural. As he saw it, and constantly emphasized during his Grand Black leadership, Black Christianity had to always be related to Black modernization and development. This does not support the erroneous character of the remarks made by historian Vernon Williams that "by isolating the economy from other institutions and other social arrangements, Washington analyzed only one trait of a complex of characteristics."[36]

BLACK THEOLOGIANS AND ABANDONING THE BLACK NEEDY

The Blacks that the Alabamian was talking about were poor Blacks, people up from slavery. He knew that religion had to help them get far away from the crippling and restrictive effects of slavery. There are many Black people today who fall into the categories of poor and poverty. Large cities, north and south, are full of them. The same is true for many rural areas in the South. Black conservative Glenn Loury is right when he says that modernization and development are still a necessity for millions of Blacks.

This, however, does not seem to be a significant concern for the current Black intellectual clergy. Their primary concern over the past several decades has been how to develop a proper *Black* theology that would make it distinctive from White Christian theologies. In pursuit of this goal, they have discussed, and even battled over, the question of whether God is white or black, whether Jesus is white or black, how to devise a *radical* or *liberation* theology and what helps either to be such: Marxist doctrine, Black Power doctrine, Black cultural doctrine, Black nationalist doctrine?

One of the leading Black theologians in America, James Cone, remarked in an essay in *Black Theology*:

> Few outside persons realize how seriously and vigorously the various theological perspectives in the Black community have been debated, and the effect these debates have had in defining the issues to which Black theologians have addressed themselves in their writings. To be sure, there has been much discussion about the imperialistic and racist character of Euro-American theology and the need to develop an alternative Black liberation theology. But because we generally agree on that point, we have seldom debated it among ourselves. Our discussions have involved much more than simply reacting to the racism of White theologians and church people. More important has been our concern to develop a Black theological perspective that takes seriously the *total* needs of the Black community, here and abroad. Needless to say, we have not been in total agreement about our needs, and our differences are partly reflected in the published writings on Black Theology.[37]

It is difficult to talk about Black community in the United States, and yet, Black theologians in America are concerned about an international "Black community." This is fanciful theological thinking, reaching for a fanciful theological and religious utopia, which would have to be predicated on the fact of all or most black people in this broad region being substantially theologically alike in religious beliefs and in religious practices. Is this one of the *total* needs of Black people in the United States? Is it what theologian Charles Long says? That Black theology in America has to have a strong African orientation. This is Africancentrism at work, an expression of absolutist thinking that could crush Black theology in any form.

Black religious intellectuals are like most other Black intellectuals. The more significant ones are regarded as "public intellectuals" and have some part of the public ear; namely, academic intellectuals. Their primary concern is the same as that of most academic intellectuals, to show their intellectual abilities, their research and writing skills, their ability to speak publicly, and their ability to analyze each other's written or spoken discourse. This all takes place away from the Black people who have *total* needs. In the minds, perceptions, or interests of Black theologians are the Blacks in need Black middle-class people who are educated, prospering, and seeing themselves as having made it in the country? Or are they the Blacks still left behind? To be certain these people know nothing about the debates going on between Black theologians, and this would be true of most Black middle-class people. So it would seem, if this observation is correct, and I'm certain it is, that the *total* needs they address are the *total* needs of Black theologians!

There is no Black theology or Black religion that seeks to help emancipate the millions of Black people still in various degrees of misfortune in the country. These are people in need with no future except the kind of life they now live, that is, more of varying degrees of debilitation. Quinton Hosford Dixie and Cornel West edited a book of essays that carried the title *The Courage to Hope from Black Suffering to Human Redemption*. West closed out the essays with one entitled "Benediction," in which he referred to what always seems central to him, "the life of the mind" and also made the following comments:

> In our lunch "seminars" at Riverside Church [New York City] (often with James Forbes–now the distinguished Senior Minister), we [James, (Joseph) Washington, and West] intensely debated the

meaning of the Cross–the whence and wither of evil, the sources of struggle against suffering, and the mysterious grounds of hope. We favored those existential thinkers of lived experience–those who thought and lived with passion and concern about death, despair, and injustice without the crutches of dogma or doctrine (Kierkegaard, Nietzsche, Barth, Tillich, Thurman, and others). And we always rooted our fierce exchanges in the concrete realities of every day Black people dealing with the absurdities and indignities of American life.[38]

As one can see, Black esoteric intellectual discussions can take place other than in the academy or in writings. But one has to wonder how many of the Black people with *total* needs ever attended one of these "seminars" at Riverside Church. If needy people were in attendance at the session, how easy would the thoughts of the white philosophers and theologians (or the lone Black one–Howard Thurman) have been to understand? And how would what these men had to say–and they were *all* men–help any of the total needy people to obtain a job, or acquire daycare, or obtain transportation to work, or even make ends meet now that their public assistance has been seriously cut? Is a Black theology or Black religion incompatible with or incapable of addressing these "issues?"

There has been a questioning of the legitimacy of Black theology. One can see why. Black theologian Cheryl Townsend Gilkes offers this up as hope for the *total* needy:

At no time in their sojourn in the New World have black people been free from the constraints of economic exploitation, political exclusion.... To engage African American spirituality is to engage a system of conflict, fragmentation, reconnection, and reintegration— a system straining toward unity through dynamic interaction among multiple constituencies in a context of diversity and of varieties of religious experience, belief, action, and feeling within and beyond ritual settings.[39]

It is the opinion of Black theologian Walter E. Fluker that Cornel West has his attention focused on Black existence and that he has a remedial aid or solution, which comes out of his philosophical/religious thinking and which is his "politics of conversion," offered to help the *total* needy, Blacks that others seem incapable or unwilling to help. West is critical of the debate done by Black intellectuals and Black leaders about the situation of Blacks in America. Fluker writes that West

Argues that this debate conceals the most basic issue now facing black America: the *nihilistic threat to its very existence*...the threat of personal meaninglessness, despair, and unworthiness, brought about in large part by unbridled market forces and political chicanery, is the real challenge that confronts African Americans and the national community. West calls for a new kind of moral leadership, which moves beyond the "pitfalls of racial reasoning" and the lack of courage to address *"the market moralities of black life"*.... He recommends a *"politics of conversion"* fueled by a love ethic, which has historically sustained the African American community. Important for our purposes is his identification of memory and hope as key resources in the politics of conversion.[40]

For years, Jesse Jackson has been preaching hope for the people in *total* need in America through PUSH (People United to Save Humanity), his Rainbow Coalition, and his continuous efforts to get Blacks to become registered voters and/or participants in the American political process. Jackson has been extremely successful in doing this, even implementing his own chant: *keep hope alive!* For years Jackson promoted (and still does) his version of how Blacks in *total* need could convert themselves into stronger human beings, with better self-images. He still encourages them to say aloud in public: "I am somebody!" Trying to stimulate or inspire them, he still tells those in need that motivation is a "made-up mind." Jackson preaches self-love, love of Blacks and the Black community, and even love for other Americans. In that sense, he took over where Martin Luther King, Jr. left off, long before West and his chant.

King and Jackson were not just talkers and writers. They were politically-savvy action people; Jackson remains superb in his political skills. To carry their message, they both also went among and stayed among Black people. It is not by coincidence that King performed the way he did, and that Jackson performs the way he does. They were both out of the South and out of the Booker T. Washington legacy of how to help the downtrodden, the people "up from slavery." For Washington and King, these were the Black people in need; and for Jackson, these are the Black "boats" still "stuck on the bottom" who always need hands-on help.

Washington constructed his leadership and the Tuskegee Machine on the basis of the needs of Black people. He developed a needs theory of modernization and development. He argued for thirty-five years as a public intellectual and leader (and as a genuine organic intellectual and leader) that if you increase the needs and wants of Blacks, they will strive to fulfill them. Need and want of fulfillment, as Washington saw it, drove the modernization and development process. They were forces *pushing* against it, while leadership, culture, organization, serviceable institutions or agencies, and effective programs constituted the *pulling* part of the process.

IF THE TUSKEGEAN RETURNED TODAY

If Washington came back to America today the first stop on his national lecture tour would be to Black theologians and Black clergy. He would express favor in developing a distinctive Black theology and Black religion, but he would not put emphasis on a "suffering" Christ, or on the notion that Blacks have to engage in "redemptive suffering" to be linked to Jesus as a kind of basis for Blacks pursuing liberation, which is a preoccupation of Black theologians and Black clergy today. This has led to the argument of whether Christ was racially or symbolically black because his ministry focused on the oppressed.

Black theologian Cheryl Townsend Gilkes has implied that she accepts a black Christ,[41] while Black theologian Kelly Brown Douglas accepts the matter outright: "for the Black community," she says, "Christ is Black. That is to say, Christ has Black skin and features and is committed to the Black community's struggle for life and wholeness."[42] (Of course, Christ's racial features are more properly spelled black). Yet, it seems that there are more Black female theologians or clergy who accept or who would be amenable to a black Christ than their Black male counterparts–that is, a racially black Christ and not a "Black Christ" (a la James Jones) who stands as a symbol of oppressed people and redemptive suffering, with the latter as a prerequisite for liberation.

The last thing that Washington wanted Blacks to do was to concentrate on their miseries and suffering. He even put a positive face on slavery to give Blacks a "useable history" of that institution and past. For him, the latter included the moral achievement of Blacks coming out of chattel slavery with their humanity intact and reaching great heights in doing so. They did not come out of slavery hating white people and seeking revenge. Instead, they tried to find ways to achieve reconciliation with them, so that both could go forward from that generally horrendous, blighted institution and period.

In the first volume of his biography on Du Bois,[43] Black historian David Levering Lewis blasted Washington for "positive" thinking about Black chattel slavery and for proposing that there were "benefits" that

Blacks derived from it. But the two Black philosophers Howard McGary and Bill Lawson thought that Washington was making sense with respect to Blacks forgiving their oppressors, seeing reason and rationality in the behavior, in the same way that people have seen similar qualities in the efforts of Bishop Desmond Tutu and other black South Africans to bring reconciliation between oppressors and oppressed and as a means to advance the oppressed. They noted: "If forgiveness is compatible with self-respect then it is hard to understand how normal human beings could be forgiving given the brutalities of slavery. If, however, forgiveness involves acting in ways that promote one's rational self-interest, then we may be more inclined to understand the apparent forgiving attitude of black slaves. If we can show that there were good self-interested reasons for blacks to forgive their oppressors, then we may have good reason to think that this fourth type of explanation is viable."[44]

But slavery was not all there was to talk about with respect to Blacks having a "useable past." Washington was fully aware of how Blacks had contributed to the economic foundation and the economic and physical development of the United States, and especially the economic and physical features in the South. He knew that Blacks had participated in American wars to help defend and perpetuate the country. He knew that Blacks had largely contributed to America's distinctiveness as a country. He knew that Blacks had helped to contribute to–indirectly and effectively–White aspirations, motivations and determinations to succeed in this country, to avoid falling as low as Blacks. This was an indirect way for Blacks to help keep America's ideals alive, vibrant and useable, and enabled them to use these ideals as well.

Washington always held the view that Blacks had a greater love for America and cherished its ideals of liberty, equality, opportunity, justice, and freedom more than Whites. This was "the river" that many years later Vincent Harding saw running through Black people and Black history. The Tuskegean wrote and published a two-volume history of Blacks in America in which he talked of their multi-usable past. He also had a biography of Frederick Douglass written over his name, not only to lionize him, but to employ him as a symbol of how Blacks cherished American ideals and pursued them (this was prior to the establishment of the NAACP).

Washington wanted a Black theology and a Black religion that focused on the psychological, moral, and spiritual strengths of Black people, not their weaknesses and certainly less on the notion of redemptive suffering. One did not need to find a purpose in suffering, just the source of it so that one could act to mitigate and end it. That would take an inner strength, but not an inner strength alone, functioning as a panacea that so many Black intellectuals advocate today, as revealed in *How to Make Black America Better.*[45] This inner strength would work in conjunction with collective and constructive activities that would wipe away the conditions and practices that engendered suffering or group weaknesses. Washington felt that Blacks "up from slavery" had to have a religion that augmented their strengths and helped them undertake modernization and development and established a chapel at Tuskegee that taught that kind of Christianity.

The Tuskegean's second lecture tour stop would be among the Black conservatives where he would tell them that "individualism" was no panacea for Blacks in the country, because it would promote selfishness, would divide people, and would project the view that a Black identity and a Black group were not important. He argued that their focus should be on Blacks strengthening themselves individually and collectively in America and advancing in the country in both ways, with each helping the other to do that. He would be very critical of those Black conservatives (most of them) who are not interested in increasing the number, education, power, and wealth of the Black middle-class and showed no interest in that class functioning as the leadership class among Blacks.

Indeed, the Black middle-class, as Washington would argue and seek to get Black conservatives to understand, had to make a determined, even messianic, effort to help the neediest of Blacks. That help had to be in a hands-on manner. It would have to take place where Blacks lived and seek to address how they lived. Glenn Loury and Robert Woodson are among a small number of Black conservatives who can relate to this and who, Washington would argue, have the responsibility of taking this message to other Black conservatives.

The Tuskegean would tell Black conservatives that, while it was necessary for Blacks to take "White sensitivities" into account, this would not include taking their racist sensibilities into account as he had had to do. The burden is on white people to show and demonstrate by deeds that they are not racist in any form. This will not be easy for them because white people usually do not know how racist they might be. This is something they do not like to think about, hear about, or talk about and usually run away from learning about. Their first response is to immediately deny being racist. But what is the value of such a denial, as it denotes a refusal to engage in self-investigation. Calling Blacks "racists-in-reverse" for criticizing their racism and racist social behavior is understood for the defensive and self-serving reaction that it is.

Washington would say to Black conservatives that they have to encourage Whites to engage in self-investigation in order to learn what racism has done to them intellectually, psychologically, and morally and in order to learn about the kind of social behavior it compels or induces them to engage in. Black conservatives have to cease accepting White denials of their racism or their efforts to minimize it. White political and social thought and White behavior have been rooted in racism in this country, in racist foundationalism, which includes the intellectual afflictions and the racist psychology of white people. Subtle White racism keeps racist intellectual afflictions, racist psychology, and racist foundationalism alive and functional.

To the liberals, Washington would say that they have to have a program that combines external aid with internal group actions, organizations, and development, meaning that they should combine external political, economic, and other outside help for Blacks with internal Black community construction. Blacks have to be able to do things on their own to help themselves: to strengthen families, schools, and churches, and reconstruct neighborhoods. They have to build community modernization and development organizations or institutions. And they have to mobilize group or community financial and economic resources to help carry out these efforts. Group or community strength and community construction are the keys to attracting or getting help from government, economic, or other external sources.

Black conservatives continue to believe and espouse the idea that Washington was not in favor of government aid for Blacks. But they are wrong. He simply was not able to get much aid from that source, and, at the time, America had not yet significantly moved toward using the national, state, and city governments to provide social programs and aid to Americans. In Washington's day, America's welfare politics and welfare society were just emerging and beginning to function. What government aid or public assistance there was mainly went to white people. Even the American Socialist Party was not much interested in aiding Blacks, as it was essentially a racist "lily-white" party, beating the Republican Party of the 1920s to that reality. The only great potential source of help for Blacks was the then new corporate economic elites who had expressed an interest in national strength and unity by investing in the southern economy and even using cheap Black labor. There was also cheap white labor to draw on. Washington had to find a way to bend northern financial and economic power, as much as possible, to Blacks in the South, something that he had some success at.

The Tuskegean would say to Black liberals that Black group power,

Black community power, and Black internal development, combined with an aggressive and progressive politics, *vis-à-vis* American political institutions, would enable Blacks to get more assistance from outside sources. He would also say to them that they have to learn how to better exploit the strategic position of Blacks in the United States, their *strategic* and political societal position, as he had done in his day. He was also greatly concerned with getting financial and economic help for Blacks to finance educational development among them. He saw education as the great multiplier of educated, skilled people, and leaders, and thus, it was the centerpiece of modernization and development.

The Tuskegean presented financial, economic, and educational proposals to powerful, rich, northern and southern white men. This led to some of Washington's contemporaries accusing him of being a beggar. There are still Black intellectuals who cast this erroneous image of him. He was a fundraiser and sought financial aid from the rich in the way fundraisers of various kinds–political, educational, or religious–do in the country today. If the people he appealed to liked his proposals they gave him money to finance his projects. If they did not like them, they would turn him down, which happened a number of times. However, over the thirty-five years he received millions of dollars, "capital transfers" from economic corporate elites and many white middle-class donors, and he spread the overwhelming amount of this money among Blacks across the South.

His consistent White donors and his biggest contributors were part of his Tuskegee Machine as has been mentioned. There was also a Black side of the Machine, which included the centerpiece of Tuskegee Institute, the National Negro Business League, and ultimately the National Urban League, which was established at his suggestion to coordinate the efforts of northern agencies endeavoring to help Blacks who were migrating to the North from the South. There were also a number of Black newspaper editors and newspapers, as well as Black churches, Black lodges, and various women's groups that were part of the Machine. One of the women's groups was the "Mother's Conferences" established by Washington's wife, Margaret, first at Tuskegee Institute and then throughout the South. The aim of the conferences was to help Black women to become better wives, mothers, and homemakers.

MODERNIZATION AND DEVELOPMENT
AMONG BLACKS IN THE RURAL SOUTH

Washington considered the Tuskegee Machine, not conceptually, or ideologically, but in practical terms, as the "government" of Black people that had to act for Blacks in the face of American governments essentially turning their backs on them. Washington headed the Tuskegee Machine; and thus, he managed this "government" in a strong manner. At the same time, he encouraged manifestations of the Machine/government to act on the basis of their own initiative. Indeed, much of the activity of the Machine/government was carried out by one of its integral parts: the thousands of young Black teacher-leaders over the years, which scholars have yet to recognize. These were the people that Washington relied upon most to carry out modernization and development among Blacks in the rural South.

For years, modernization theorists and scholars focused their attention on urban modernization and development. Only in recent years have they acknowledged the importance of rural modernization and development for national development itself. Washington had an understanding of the importance of rural modernization and development many years before theorists and scholars arrived at an appreciation of it. He saw it as critical to the advancement of Blacks in America who were just "up from slavery" and who were overwhelmingly rural and agriculture at that time. He was able to persuade young Black men and women to go into these southern rural areas and lead Blacks in a process of cultural-social development and transformation.

The Tuskegean also relied heavily on the annual Farmer's and Worker's Conferences to help Blacks modernize and develop. These were initiated at Tuskegee Institute, but they were also held at institutes created by some of Washington's students, who patterned their schools after their mentor and leader's school in Tuskegee, Alabama. These institutes, and the annual conferences they sponsored, as well as other Farmer's and Worker's Conferences that Washington's young teacher-leaders established throughout the South, were all part of the Tuskegee Machine. The conferences were mass organizations that functioned as communication and transmission belts; they organized and mobilized rural Blacks. Washington led a mass movement of Blacks in the South. This has yet to be recognized by Black or white scholars who, when they are not disparaging him and his leadership of Blacks, are only able to see him as a Black educator, which usually is not free of disparaging remarks.

Washington held the first Farmer's Conference at Tuskegee Institute in the late 1880s and the first Worker's Conference in the early 1890s. One by one, farmers at the annual Conference stood up and told of their success at being farmers. A farmer would speak about the land he bought, about the building of a new house, or an extension on an old house, or about the church he had helped to build with others in his community. He would speak about building a new school or the way they had added to the physical construction of a school, the months in session, and the number of students enrolled and taught. Those who had saved money would talk about how they did so or even about how they had gotten out of debt.

The annual conferences at Tuskegee and other places across the South were mass institutions mobilizing and galvanizing Black people. They were communication channels and channels for spreading the "Tuskegee Idea." The farmers represented concrete Black modernization and development successes. They were models of it and agents to spread information to help others. At the Conference farmers explained the things they still needed or needed to do. In this manner, new ideas and ways often came from others at the Conferences who had already achieved that success.

The Worker's Conference met the day after the Farmer's Conference took place, when all the farmers had left Tuskegee. The Workers were usually local community leaders who attended the annual Farmer's Conferences at Tuskegee and other Farmer's Conferences throughout the South. The community leaders would meet and discuss what the farmers had said they had accomplished, what they needed, and what they were still trying to accomplish. By doing this, the leaders gathered ideas on how they could help farmers in the communities where they were leaders. They also helped each other draw up modernization and development plans that they hoped would be, and might be, applicable to their communities.

What Washington did with the two Conferences was to put leaders and led together, so that the leaders could learn what the led wanted and needed or that which they were aspiring to accomplish. This cut down tensions and anxieties between leaders and the led. It also cut down communication time and communication barriers between leaders and the led, and created a better foundation for them to bond together, to realize their interdependence and commonality and to understand the joint character and responsibility of leading and following.

The Mother's Conferences organized, mobilized, and galvanized Black women all over the South. The Southeastern Federation of Colored Women's Clubs, established in 1900 and led by prime mover and first president, Margaret Washington, also became part of the Tuskegee Machine. It organized, mobilized, and guided Blacks. The same could be said of the annual state and agricultural fairs, also established by the Machine and becoming part of it. From all of this, one can see that Washington does not have much in common with today's Black conservatives, who usually are not this collective-oriented and do not go near Blacks in need.

Thomas Sowell, the titular leader of Black conservatives, and a defender of the Tuskegean, would not find the latter very receptive toward him. Washington would object to Sowell's callous attitude toward Black people and his "white-washing" of American history and life. And he would also find Sowell's narrow stance—Blacks should try to make it through simple individual effort and just as simply work their way into the market—as very limiting approaches to helping them. Washington did not really use the market like Sowell and other Black conservatives say he did. He primarily used the people who owned the corporations and the market, or dominated both. Yet, very few Black conservatives seek direct aid from economic corporations to help Blacks. This is something that Black liberals like Jesse Jackson do, to which Washington would say "right on!"

There continues to be confusion about Washington's understanding of the relationship between White racism and Black economic progress. The Tuskegean was not confused about it, but Sowell remains confused about his position. For years, the economist has consistently argued that this racism does not impede the economic opportunities or development of Blacks and that this was Washington's position as well. This is simplifying and misrepresenting the Tuskegean's position. Washington lived at a time in the South when White racism, often-vicious White racism, was imposed on Blacks. This racism affected every major and minor area of their lives, even their economic actions or activities. Washington learned and knew that white people did not like competing with Black people and that Whites in the South, for the most part, viewed Black economic, educational, or social progress as a threat to their racist concepts of Blacks and the social order predicated on Black oppression and suppression. The racist notion of the "good Negra" or "good darkie," or the "Negra exception," could be windows of advancement and would produce individuals whom Whites would not likely retaliate against.

But more than one Black businessman found himself beaten up, closed down, or lynched because Whites could not abide Black competition or Blacks living better than they did. When a Black store-owning friend, and two other men, were lynched for these reasons, Ida B.

Wells-Barnett was inspired to conduct an individual crusade against lynching in the South that got her driven out of her hometown in Tennessee.

Du Bois made the following remarks to an audience of white economists in 1906:

> I know a Negro businessman worth $50,000 in a Southern city. He has a white clientele and he tells me that he dare not buy a horse and buggy lest the white people may think he's getting rich and boycott him; a barber in another city built a fine house on a corner lot and in a single year his white trade was gone. A black businessman in a country town of Alabama, where I made some studies preparatory to this paper, underbid his white fellow merchants in buying cotton seed and was shot down for his shrewdness.[46]

This was how racism affected Blacks in their effort to use the market and develop economically in the South, which Washington knew very well. This was Black integration in the South, and it was something that Washington encouraged from the time he began building Tuskegee Institute, when he had his students sell bricks and other items they made on campus to white and Black people in Tuskegee. Trading with Whites, however, could be risky, even life threatening. They always expected prices to be low, which could be risky and life threatening for Blacks, and a Black merchant was expected to extend credit, with no necessary promise of redeeming it. There were Blacks throughout the South (Washington knew of many) who had no serious hassles from Whites when trading with them and who achieved material success.

Racism was mainly connected to integration. Washington wanted Blacks to do most of their economic and social development behind the walls of racist segregation. There, White racism was not the big factor because Whites left Blacks considerably alone. Racism became a strong factor when Blacks engaged in integration with Whites. They had to do this to buy goods, services, or land. There was land for Blacks to buy in the South, and businesses and industries, small and mid-sized, could be established by Blacks. Yet, there was still a racist protocol that had to be observed when Blacks engaged in economic transactions with the Whites that facilitated them.

Thomas Sowell just does not seem to know or understand how Blacks have always used racism for economic and other advantages, including something simple like having a bus or train seat to oneself because Whites would not wish to sit next to you. It's strange that Sowell has this confusion. In his book *Civil Rights: Rhetoric and Reality*, he talked of how some Black men in the South had a monopoly in certain jobs. To him this showed the fairness and the advancement possibilities of the market and the absence of racism. The traditional "Black jobs" were not racist jobs to Sowell. In a recent book, *The Quest for Cosmic Justice*,[47] Sowell spoke of justice of this transcendental character and condemned those who demanded it. Actually "cosmic justice" was a "strawman" for Sowell, because people seeking jobs through affirmative action or through other government programs, all of which he detests, are looking for a more mundane, simple justice.

Sowell was right when he argued (as Booker T. Washington did) that "making" or "providing" "something the white man wants" or "something the society values" are two of the primary ways for Blacks to make economic and social advances. But black philosopher Bernard Boxill regards these as stupid and dangerous thoughts. He noted, "this really stupid and dangerous idea, which is of a piece with their [Washington's and other's] admonition to eschew politics, does not even state a necessary condition for getting ahead. If you have enough weapons, as kings and conquerors have proved throughout history, you do not need to have something the society values to get ahead."[48]

A society might value monarchy, as England does and has done, by providing great wealth for certain members of the English royal family, but clearly the analogy of "kings and conquerors" is hardly applicable to the people just "up from slavery" that Washington led and worked with, especially when these people were low on weapons. Either way, such people always have to prove themselves, show that they can do this or that, have something to offer. But isn't this how the American economic system works? If you have education, skills, and experience to *offer* employers, there's a chance you might attain employment. You would certainly have a better shot at attaining it than people who cannot offer these credentials.

Washington took his greatest pride in his young Black leaders. They were the critical part of the Tuskegee Machine, outside of Washington and Tuskegee Institute. Today, we are told repeatedly about the problems of many Black youth: their unruly character, their failure to succeed in school or stay in school, their low rate of high school graduation, their drug use, their violent behavior, their directionlessness, and their inevitable imprisonment. In Washington's day, there were millions of young Black people, children of parents "up from slavery." Many were illiterate and without economic skills or even significant social skills. These children did not have much hope or see much of a future for themselves in the South. In both periods there were Blacks who had some education or who were capable of acquiring it, who had some economic and social skills or who were developing them, and Blacks who had leadership ability or who could be educated and trained to be leaders. Washington saw the salvation of Blacks in the rural areas of the South and the key to their modernization and development to be Black youth: those who received significant education at or graduated from college or a training institute. Washington believed that if they could be persuaded to go into the rural areas, they could be leaders and teachers of other Black adults, youth, and children and could help them in undertaking modernization and development.

There have always been derogatory remarks made about the education that Tuskegee Institute offered. Washington's northern Black opposition made these remarks. It was, in their minds, and in the minds of many, just a technical or vocational school, mainly teaching economic skills. It was not a liberal arts school like Fisk University, Howard University, or Atlanta College. However, Tuskegee Institute did have some liberal arts instruction and some religious instruction. In regard to these matters, Wilson Jeremiah Moses wrote:

> Washington was contemptuous of education that was not aimed at the creation of material wealth and believed that persons of marginal ability who wasted their time studying Greek and Latin were assuring their own economic failure. Tuskegee, nonetheless, had a solid liberal arts curriculum, and students were provided the basic elements of cultural literacy, economics, history, and the arts of communication. The better graduates were encouraged to undertake advanced studies at such leading northern universities as Harvard and Cornell.[49]

Moses ignores how Washington was very concerned about character and character development. He was criticized by Du Bois and other Black contemporaries for emphasizing materiality, but Washington placed his own interpretation on this matter when he said, "let us see what is back of this material possession. In the first place the possession of property is evidence of mental discipline, mental grasp and control. It is an evidence of thrift and industry. It is an evidence of fixedness of character and purpose. It is an evidence of interest in pure and intelligent government."[50] He also remarked: "We may be inclined to exalt intellectual requirements over the material, but all will acknowledge that the possession of the material has an influence that is lasting and unmistakable."[51] Washington saw materiality leading to psychological, social, and even spiritual strengths and that was why teachers at Tuskegee taught materiality. This was the understanding he had imparted to his students, many of whom became his young teacher-leaders; and, this was the understanding he imparted to students at other institutes and colleges he had influence with or spoke at. Washington could not make any of these young people become leaders, and he could not make any go into the rural areas to lead Blacks.

At the time, the rural South was the most violent part of the United States. It was the place where lynching and burnings usually happened, where county sheriffs held great power and tended to view any educated or near-educated Black as "uppity" and dangerous. There were also Black leaders in rural areas—adults and clergy—who would resent these young people coming in, but Washington persuaded thousands of them to go. In *The Future of the American Negro*, published in 1900, five years after his Atlanta Address, Washington remarked: "What the race most needs now...is a whole army of men and women well trained to lead." He further said, "It is the work of Tuskegee, not to send into these places [southern rural areas] teachers who stand off and tell the people what to do, or what ought to be done, but to send those who can take hold and show the people *how* to do."[52]

Washington used to have "Sunday Evening Talks" with his students to prepare their minds and psychology for leadership. He spoke to them about character, integrity, morality, responsibility, courage, and dedication and always about the urgency of leading Blacks in rural areas and helping "their people" to modernize and to develop. Below are some of the things he said to his students and also to student leaders he spoke to at other institutes or colleges:

> When you go out to work, stop where the people need your help the most, where you can accomplish the most good, go not in the place where you are to be most pleasantly located, find the corner that is the darkest where the people have the least help and see how bright and cheerful you can make them.[53]

The Tuskegean also counseled them:

> Talk simply to them. Don't use any big words and high-flown sentences. Don't go out to show your education; talk to them in plain, simple words. Simply have the people sit down and talk to them in a plain commonsense way.[54]

He also said:

> If you have anything to write, write it in the plainest manner possible. Use just as few words as possible. If you get a word with one syllable that will express your meaning, use it in preference of two syllables...try to get one or two syllables instead of three or four.... There is great power in simplicity of speech.[55]

Washington fully understood the importance and power of speech and language in the process of modernization and development; he understood the power of effective communication. Communication was also related directly to the speed, timetable, or urgency of this activity, which the Tuskegean always regarded as being urgent. It was necessary for Blacks to show quick success because of the threat of European immigrants moving South, and because this would encourage white help. Washington also regarded effective communication between the leaders and the led to be critical for the modernization and development process.

The Tuskegean kept in contact with his young leaders. They would write to him, and he to them, and he would see them when he toured through Alabama and other Southern states promoting the "Tuskegee Idea," Tuskegee-type education, and development for southern Blacks. Here is what one teacher-leader wrote to him: "I am putting every effort to bring these people out of darkness into light. They say they are going to give me three months independent school after this term is out. So I will have a six-months [sic] school."[56] Another leader wrote: "I have an enrollment of 72 pupils. My work is hard yet I do not mind it. I believe I could go into any dark corner of the State and be satisfied, for I know and feel it to be my duty to help my race."[57] And another young leader wrote a letter to Washington that was reprinted in one of Tuskegee's newspapers (*Southern Letter*): "On the whole I can see a great improvement in the condition of the people since I have been teaching here. Not so many mortgage their crops...as had been the case before. They seem more saving and depend more on themselves. They take more interest in sending their children to school regularly every day."[58] Still another young leader said: "In this Conference we held I found that better homes, schools, and churches are being built by the race. Your school and conferences, I think, are the great cause of our people doing better here.... I know of fourteen persons that are saving for and buying homes."[59] And finally a leader remarked: "Our local conference is doing good work and these people are taking hold with a will.... Our Conference is trying to buy 355 acres of land situated around the church. It will cost $1,775. Many individuals are also buying land and building houses."[60]

Du Bois and other Black intellectuals used to write of the material development and progress of Black people, recording the amount of land purchased, the number of schools, churches, and homes purchased or constructed, the economic enterprises established, the number of workers and the kind of work they did. The written accounts would invariably praise the progress and even talk about its surprising quickness and its amount. However, if they were Washington's enemy, like Du Bois was, the Tuskegean and his leadership efforts would not be given credit for any of the development and progress. Du Bois was loath to augment Washington's public image. In keeping quiet about Washington's efforts and successes, Du Bois was protecting one of his own theories and chief arguments against Washington, namely that economic progress could not be achieved without politics or political power. Washington proved that to be an overblown contention.

Michael Dawson recently supported Du Bois's view in his book *Black Visions*. He had a brief discussion of Washington that essentially reflected no research on the Tuskegean and heavily relied upon what Black conservatives have said about Washington, which itself was based on meager research and further relied upon what the Tuskegean's enemies said about him (not drawing on any comments from some of Washington's contemporaries who were favorable to him). Dawson indicated that Du Bois, as well as others, held the theory of the one-to-one relationship between politics and economics and that this was a view that was passed on to others over several generations. He added, "thus Wells, Du Bois, and thousands of African Americans of this and succeeding generations argued that it was not possible for Blacks to separate political from economic development. One could not acquire property and wealth if the state and the leading forces of civil society denied you...property rights."[61] Not only did Washington deflate the political/economy theory, but he also would have pointed out to Dawson that some of "the leading forces of civil society" encouraged and aided Blacks in acquiring property. And what is one to make of the following comment by the political scientist: "In this context it is easier to understand both [sic] the bitterness which greeted Washington from the black community."[62] Dawson was really reflecting his own bitterness at Washington and equally reflecting his dearth of knowledge about him.

Washington would have liked to have had political help for Blacks where most Black people were, in the South. He tried from time to time to get such help from the national government and southern state governments, but he had only the meagerest successes. Washington knew that modernization and development, including economic development, depended on leadership, organization, encouragement, motivation, and mobilization of people and the resources they had or could obtain, and visible successes. Thomas Sowell, Glenn Loury, and economist Walter Williams, as well as other Black conservatives (and some white ones nowadays), talk of the value of "social capital:" education, economic skills, attitudes, relationships, values, beliefs, and so on and their relationship to modernization and development or economic and social development. Washington did not have that term, but it could have been one that he coined.

All Black people in the South mainly had was social capital, and not much of it. Washington focused his thirty-five year leadership of Blacks in the South on helping them to develop their social capital. To do this, he relied on his rural leaders and education, even more generally "school and community." Washington knew that Blacks, just "up from slavery" could not wait on politics or anything else outside of themselves to make efforts, to put a history of slavery behind them and to develop as a people. The vital needs were leadership, organization, mobilization, encouragement, motivation, and the proper programs with tangible successes. Washington dedicated his life to providing such things for Blacks in the South.

The Tuskegean looked upon modernization and development as something that should occur on a logical basis. It should occur in stages and as a process. Black sociologist John Brown Childs discerned Washington's theoretical orientation when he noted:

> It is characteristic of Washington's thought to emphasize laying a "firm foundation," meaning an economic one, and as the basis for all other political, social, and cultural development. His imagery throughout is materialistic and concrete. He emphasizes "substance" instead of "shadow," "reality" rather than "appearance." "Without a solid economic foundation," he wrote, "it is impossible for any race of people to make much enduring, much permanent progress." This economic foundation lay at the bottom of "religion, education, and politics." Washington's image of the solid economic foundation upon which society must be built parallels Marxist notions of economic base and ideological superstructure. Because of this focus on a solid base, which required both time and patience to construct, many have called Washington a "gradualist." But from Washington's point of view, the laying of an economic function was essential however long it took.

Washington's was not a simple deterministic view in which people are carried along by huge historic currents. He thought that people could play conscious, active roles in shaping history. Yet it was also possible, in his view, for history to pass people by. If people were not scientifically aware of the significance of the developing economic circumstances, they would not be able to benefit from those changes.[63]

A great fear that Washington had was that history would pass by Blacks in the South. He saw European immigrants possibly taking them out of the historical process. There were also the debilitating effects of slavery that were being passed onto the children and which alone could remove Blacks from the historical process. Washington often had the following anguished thought: "I confess that the thing that most concerns me is the real tangible, visible progress of the race.... I am most anxious that...the race...not become discouraged."[64] That was why Washington drove himself as Grand Black Leader in the South and why he drove the massive number of leaders he created or drew to his side.

There is a prevailing thought that Washington was the only leader that Black people had during the time of his ascendancy. But Washington worked with and through thousands of leaders and through the Tuskegee Machine with them. That was why he was so powerful among Blacks. Black intellectuals, especially Black radicals who think and write so ideologically, always want to say it was the power of Washington's white backers that drove him or that forced him to do things. They believe that he simply acted on their behalf. But Washington, first and foremost, always acted on behalf of rural Blacks in the South. He consciously and diligently protected his leadership and programmatic efforts to help them, even from overbearing white benefactors.

Enter Du Bois and the "Talented Tenth"

The Tuskegean's Black opponents were not much of a match for him. They liked to refer to themselves as the "Talented Tenth." But as an opposition that did not seek to establish a significant, let alone a mass, base they made a mistake taking on a person who understood and knew how to use power, and who had a massive support system across the North and the South and one that could be easily activated.

The opposition was very elitist. They were isolated from the mass of Blacks and liked it that way. They thought that intellect alone would overshadow Washington and win the day for Blacks. For them, this meant

Blacks attaining a recognition of their own human dignity and equality, acquiring the vote, and the doors of higher education opening to socially elevated Blacks.

The Talented Tenth looked primarily upon Du Bois as their leader. This was both a mistake and a reflection of how little they understood of how to function as a group among Blacks. Du Bois was no leader, which he knew and admitted of himself. But he still tried to be. Du Bois did not easily bend, was not very diplomatic, and had the failing of not remembering the names of people he had been introduced to, even people joining him and others in battle against Washington. But when Du Bois was not stimulating those doing battle with Washington by comments on his thinking and actions, his idea and his discussions of the Talented Tenth were stimulating them. This was an educated and culturally elitist group that, in every way, was equal to Whites in America and, in these ways, superior to most. Du Bois said of the Talented Tenth: "The Negro race, like all races, is going to be saved by its exceptional men. The problem of education, then, among Negroes must first of all deal with the Talented Tenth; it is the problem of developing the Best of this race that may guide the mass away from the contamination and death of the Worst, in their own and other races."[65]

Du Bois also said that the Talented Tenth must be "leaders of thought and missionaries of culture among their people." The Talented Tenth were to be intellectual and cultural leaders. Du Bois wanted them, men and women, to be educated in liberal arts colleges and universities where they would be educated in Western thought, culture, art, and in the physical and social sciences. The Talented Tenth would function in all major institutions of Black life and would always be a daily presence in that life. Thus, they would be role models for Blacks to see, hear, and emulate. And they were also to act as a public voice for Blacks, to represent them publicly to white people, in short, to be public intellectuals on behalf of Blacks.

At the time that Du Bois devised the Talented Tenth (actually took it over from others and made it his own), the Progressive Movement was in full swing and having a large impact on American politics using public protest methods, among other means, to do so. There were Black middle-class people like Monroe Trotter, Ida B. Wells-Barnett, Anna Cooper, Fannie Barrier Williams, Archibald and Francis Grimke, Mary Church Terrell, and Reverend Reverdy Ranson who were already protesting injustices committed against Blacks and demanding rights and other meliorations. Du Bois joined them in 1905 and that was when the concept of the Talented Tenth took on a radical dimension for him, i.e., aggressive public protest and vigorous public demand of rights and equality.

Joy James said that Du Bois "radicalize[d] the concept of black agency and leadership"[66] in 1940. But it had actually occurred thirty-five years earlier. Indeed, James made several misstatements in her discussion of Du Bois in her book *Transcending the Talented Tenth*. She erroneously reported that Du Bois was barred from teaching at Tuskegee, for instance. In fact, Du Bois refused employment there on a couple of occasions. He turned down a job offer at Tuskegee in order to work at Wilberforce University. Later, when Washington sought to lure him from Atlanta University, he rejected the offer saying, "I see many opportunities for usefulness and work at Tuskegee, but I have been unable to persuade myself that the opportunities there are enough [sic] larger than those here at Atlanta University to justify my changing at present."[67] James claimed that the bottom-line of the controversy between Washington and Du Bois was over what "qualifies a race leader and racial uplift in the early twentieth-century Afro-American leadership."[68]

Two years before he helped to form the Niagara Movement, Du Bois had acknowledged in *The Souls of Black Folk* that Washington was the gargantuan and accepted leader of Blacks. He did not disagree with Washington that industrial education was a good means to uplift the mass of Blacks. Du Bois's problem with the Tuskegean was the same for other Niagarites: They felt Washington was too powerful, that he rejected and even suppressed ideas not consistent with the "Tuskegee Idea," which to them was immediately gaining public dignity, political rights, civil rights, and higher education for some Blacks. They were also concerned about Washington's attractiveness to Black people in the North and the full spread of the "Tuskegee Idea" in the region. Many Black middle-class people in the North could accept Washington's programs for the mass of Blacks in the South, while still protesting against racism and for Black rights. Indeed, Washington worked out precisely this compromise with his northern opposition at the Carnegie Conference in 1904. But Du Bois and other members of the opposition rejected the compromise after making it. And Du Bois blasted people like Kelly Miller and Archibald and Francis Grimke for staying with the agreement. The following year the Niagara Movement was established. Its emphasis was on public rights and respect, voting, and higher education. Du Bois and other Black intellectuals were not going to let Washington intimidate them or censor them. Certainly, for Du Bois, it was Washington's great power that he strongly objected to and rebelled against.

James wrote that in later years–the 1930s and 1940s–Du Bois

employed a different conception of the Talented Tenth. Owing to his increasing radicalism derived from Marxist inspiration and observing Black "working class activists," Du Bois concluded that leftists and activists should be leading Blacks. Black historian Thomas Holt wrote about Du Bois's alteration of the Talented Tenth concept saying that, like James, Du Bois became disillusioned with the older view because of the way in which such people had been more interested in promoting their own interests. The way James erroneously saw this was that Du Bois essentially substituted Black "working class activists" and other Black activists for a Talented Tenth.

In actuality, Du Bois kept the Talented Tenth concept but converted it into a "planning group" for Blacks in order to plan the construction of a Black socialist cooperative commonwealth in the United States that an activist intellectual leadership would lead Blacks in carrying out. Thomas Holt, perceiving what Du Bois had done, wrote:

> Thus, the "talented tenth" of 1903 was reconstituted as the revolutionary vanguard for the 1930s, who would transform a disabling condition into a creative force. Booker T. Washington's philosophy had involved "the flight of class from mass" through material accumulation," Du Bois wrote in *Dusk of Dawn*, while his own program had involved a flight of class from mass through culture. It was now clear that class and mass must unite for the world's salvation. For Du Bois, therefore, race consciousness undertook the role of class consciousness in Marxian theory: the latter was the basis for Whites organizing their liberation; the former could serve as the resource for black liberation.[69]

The new plan was for a Talented Tenth that functioned as a "revolutionary vanguard," as a "planning group," as Du Bois actually said and from a racial consciousness. This meant that Du Bois was finally catching up with Washington's thinking about leading Black people. Holt had a strong loathing for Washington, saying that his leadership was "sterile and pusillanimous." This shows that Holt knew very little about Washington. The Tuskegean conducted his leadership in the heart of the racist South for thirty-five years, which could hardly be called cowardly. Washington could not get his northern Black opposition to come south to lead Blacks, like he and others were doing. They wanted to "lead" from New York, Chicago, Cleveland, Boston, Detroit, and other places. How heroic was that? Was this, in actuality, "pusillanimous" behavior? As seen, Washington did not take a "flight" from the mass. He sent Black leaders to the mass of Blacks to encourage economic and other kinds of materialistic development among them. And he made frequent trips into rural areas and small towns of the South to be among and to speak to Blacks precisely about materialistic development and its benefits.

A Talented Tenth Today? Yes and No

The concept of the Talented Tenth still hangs on with many, if not most, Black intellectuals. Nowadays, not many are likely to make a public identity with it because of its elitist and even aristocratic aura. Most Black intellectuals today like to think of themselves as democratic forces functioning in an elitist status. They like to think of themselves as intellectuals, not the common rung of Blacks or most Americans, especially when they function as academic intellectuals or academic public intellectuals. The doubts are brushed aside. Henry Louis Gates, Jr., for instance, has gotten around this troubling corner by claiming that people like himself are the "grandchildren" of the Talented Tenth, and as leaders in that line of succession, they have to go beyond the original group and think of themselves as elites who get closer to the mass of Blacks in order to lead them, in other words, a "democratic conception of elite leadership."

In Gate's book (co-authored with Cornel West) *The Future of the Race*, he writes: "It is only by confronting...white racism...and our own failures to...break the cycle of poverty...that we, the remnants of the Talented Tenth, will be able to assume...leadership...for, and within, the black community."[70] One has to ask the question: do the people of the Boston area consider Henry Louis Gates, Jr. and Cornel West, or even the entire group of Black Harvard intellectuals, their leaders, representatives, or spokespeople? And how would a "subtle defense" of affirmative action help the middle-class people in these areas. For that matter, how would statistics about aspects of Black life help or praising Black literary and artistic achievements help in these areas?

There is also West, the other author of *The Future of the Race*. He rejects the Talented Tenth concept, seeing it as elitist and as deprecating the ability of masses of Black people to think and act on their own. West simply believes the concept does not fit into the kind of global world that exists today. In his eyes, there is a need to make global responses and devise leaderships and coalitions that could effectively respond. These would be coalitions that protected, nourished, and enhanced the lives of not just Americans, but the world's people. West sees these leadership and political groupings as being able to deal with the "existential absurdities" of life in America, of a declining civilization, and of an essentially decadent world. In his book, the intellectual argues that Du Bois was unable to perceive and understand these things or get into a deep analysis of them, as other intellectuals had done, such as "Leo Tolstoy, Fyodor Dostoyevsky, Ivan Turgeniev, Alexander Herzen, Len Shestov, Anton Chekov...Franz Kafka, Max Brod, Kurt Tucholsky, Hermann Broch, Hugo Bergmann, or Karl Kraus. These omissions are glaring because the towering figures in both groups were struggling with political and existential issues similar to those facing black people in America."[71] This is something that West does regularly: drops names. Invariably, they are names of white male intellectuals, with West discernibly seeking to place himself in that august genealogy.

West is considered by Black and white intellectuals alike to be the most important Black intellectual in America. But West seems not to like what he sees as the restrictive identity of Black intellectual. He considers himself one of the foremost intellectuals in America, and he is. But not enough people apparently recognize this. West does identify with elements of Black culture: Black preaching styles, Black music, and Black literature. He doubtlessly wants the best for Blacks in America. However, West mainly comes from outside of Black people, even outside of Black history, or from a superficial penetration of both, to offer intellectual help for Blacks.

What is really striking about his section in *The Future of the Race* was his conscious demolition effort against Du Bois. He deprecated Du Bois's intellectual abilities and his intellectual assessments. According to West, Du Bois offered no significant intellectual help regarding the issues that really plague the world. He said, "my assessment of Du Bois primarily concerns his response to the problem of evil–to understand harm, unjustified suffering, and unmerited pain.... Does his work contain the necessary intellectual and existential resources to enable us to confront the indescribable agony and unnamable anguish likely to be unleashed in the twenty-first century."[72] He further stated that his, "fundamental problem with Du Bois is his inadequate grasp of the tragicomic sense of life...the sheer absurdity of the human condition. This [is a] tragicomic sense-tragicomic rather than simply 'tragic,' because even ultimate purpose and objective order are called into question."[73]

In showing that Du Bois, in mind and work, was not up to this task, one would have expected West to base his assessment on Du Bois's written work. But he didn't. He assigned weakness mainly to Du Bois's "Victorian" and "Enlightenment" intellectually-formed and culturally-formed backgrounds and to his use of the Talented Tenth concept. To

West, this prevented Du Bois from being able to deeply penetrate into Western history and life, more specifically, American history and life, and prevented him from being able to perceive, and then to explain, the existential, absurd, and tragicomic realities that had grossly assaulted the twentieth-century and that were ready for a new round of assault in the twenty-first century.

While Cornel West is touted as the most important Black intellectual, it is not a clear title for him, not as long as the image of Du Bois as an "intellectual giant" is still popularly held among Black, black, and a number of white intellectuals. Hence, the demolition effort in *The Future of the Race* is obviously an effort to defame and discredit Du Bois through a thin guise of simultaneous praise. West argues that Black people have never produced a really significant intellectual, although he does believe that Toni Morrison approaches that status. He also argues that the most profound Black expression of thought or sentiment about the "human condition" has come from Black preachers and musicians, and although he does not say it, also from a fully significant Black intellectual like himself! I want to quote West once more before addressing his conception of Du Bois's intellectual capabilities. He remarked in the book with Gates that similar to the Russian and Central European Jewish artists, Black artists dealt with:

> Madness and melancholia, doom and death, terror and horror, individuality and identity. Unlike [their counterparts]...black artists do so against a background of an African heritage that puts a premium on voice and body and sound and silence [leaving out rhythm and holistic thinking], and the foreground is occupied by an American tradition that highlights mobility and novelty, individuality and democracy [it was always individualism, not individuality, and can one have democracy with racism and slavery?]. The explosive products of this multilayered cultural hybridity...take us beyond Du Bois's enlightenment optimism.[74]

West obviously identified with the observations he made and just as obviously felt that Du Bois would have been unable to. As his work shows, West likes words like "dread," "absurdity," "tragic," "tragicomic," "nihilism," "commodification," "decadence," and "existential." He feels that these words point to the depths of human existence and that his discussions of them in his works reveal and explain these depths. But the truth is that West is not the equal of Du Bois as an intellectual because, as opposed to him, Du Bois was an original, innovative, profound, and courageous thinker. West's intellectual efforts consist mainly of reviewing and analyzing what other intellectuals have said and displaying his ability to analyze various areas of thought and culture, owing to the breadth and depth of knowledge he has. He seeks to show that he is not the typical intellectual who has limited intellectual and analytical interests.

Another characteristic of West is that he seeks to be all things to all people, which is what no intellectual can be. To add to West's intellectual woes (although he does not see them as that), he is a philosopher who defers to religion, but his religion and philosophy are without intellectual foundations. Both reflect a postmodern hostility to absolutist metaphysical foundationalism. But absolutist metaphysical philosophy is not the only way to do philosophy and is not even the only form of metaphysical philosophy. There is what I call *ordinary metaphysical philosophy*, which eschews absolutism, essentialism, and absolute foundationalism and which posits the concepts of *duration* and *durational*, *essential* and *essentiality* and/or *foundational* and *foundationality*. This philosophy makes and maintains a distinction between *essential* and *essence*, seeing one as necessary and the other as preference, wish, or hope, but not a concrete reality. A *priori* does not have to be conceived or employed in absolutist terms. A *priori* is an essential ingredient to thinking and speaking. Language is a priori, and has to be, otherwise thinking and speaking would be incomprehensible. Language is foundational, but it is something that changes and still remains foundational and a *priori*. West's intellectual oeuvre could benefit from ordinary metaphysical philosophy, which would enable him to put absolutist metaphysics and postmodern thought to the side, to let these two intellectual elements duke it out while he went an independent intellectual way.

This is what Du Bois did. He chartered his own intellectual course, actually courses, and established paths for others to follow. He learned the *Verein für Sozialpolitik*,* research methodology but he broke with this method and devised his own method of sociological research to study a concrete Black social community in Philadelphia.

* The Verein fur Sozialpolitik (Society of Social Policy) was a method of survey research practiced at the University of Berlin in the early 1890s and collected information from population groups in Germany that eventually led to state socialist programs.

Du Bois was one of the three progenitors of scientific sociology; the other two were Emile Durkheim of France and Max Weber of Germany. With his Atlanta University sociology studies that established the first school of sociology in the country, and his other sociological and historical writings, Du Bois was the progenitor of Black Studies in America.

With *The Negro* in 1915, Du Bois launched *Africanist* historical scholarship in America. With *Black Reconstruction*, twenty years later, he ultimately changed the way that American historians, Black, white, and otherwise wrote on the Civil War and Reconstruction in American history. Du Bois was the first significant scholar/intellectual of what is commonly referred to as the "African diaspora," which I refer to as the Western African Extensia. Du Bois inaugurated the study of the White racist world system and White racist world hegemony, which involved racism, colonialism, imperialism, and capitalism as interacting dynamics. This has yet to be discerned by Black and white scholars, or even Black or white socialists, like Cornel West. Thus, Du Bois anticipated by decades what they now call a "world system" involving capitalism. He was the foremost analyst of racism in his day. He discussed "authoritarian personality characteristics" (as part of his analysis of racism) long before European/American psychologists took up with the matter between the 1930s and 1950s. Du Bois was also one of the foremost journal editors in American history, editing *The Crisis* magazine as a national magazine for twenty-five years. He was also a life-long humanist and profound thinker of human freedom, which has only been faintly perceived by people who have recognized and commented on this or who have been inspired by Du Bois. And finally, Du Bois was the first "Third World" thinker, anticipating by decades individuals like Jawaharlal Nehru, Franz Fanon, and a host of "Third World" thinkers that immediately preceded and that were spawned by the Bandung Conference of 1955.

These accomplishments alone mark off Du Bois from Cornel West and many other intellectuals in America. But even where West thinks that Du Bois was behind "towering" thinkers on the subjects of "absurdity," "tragic," "tragicomic," "existential" ideas, and the like, the "towering" figures he referred to and that he used to belittle Du Bois would have a long way to go before they could catch up to some of the things he knew and some of the things he said.

BEYOND THE TALENTED TENTH:
DU BOIS'S PROPHETIC VISION

The genius of Du Bois was that he knew and also wrote about the *sources* of the "decadent," "absurd," "surreal," "tragic," "tragicomic," and "existential" malaise that characterized the twentieth century and that moved headlong into the twenty-first century. He knew what affected Blacks and functioned as the outside source of their inner turmoil and also paradoxically worked as a restraint on, as well as motivation for, their individual and group striving.

Du Bois began intellectually (but unfortunately, not with much formal conceptualization, which characterized his writing) dealing with these matters when he was a teenager attending Nashville, Tennessee's Fisk University in the 1880s. At Fisk and while living in the South, he found out what racism was, which he had not been able to do in his home village of Great Barrington, Massachusetts. In the South, racism clearly revealed itself as a belief system that declared some human beings to be not human or not fully human. They were declared to be "nonhumans," or "subhumans" or "Non-others." These conceptions spawned social practices that implemented such beliefs and that attempted to make victims of racism conform to the fanciful and malevolent images of them.

Du Bois saw this rather clearly as a teenager at Fisk and in the South, which was daily, visibly exhibited. This was none other than the *existential* and *absurd* depth of human irrational, pathological, immoral, and compulsive thinking; it was perverted, compulsive thinking that abstractly divested people of their human status, their humanity, their human rights, their human dignity, their human feelings, and the moral character of their human status and humanity. Such thoughts and commensurate social practices inevitably led to brutal, cruel, absurd, tragic, and tragicomic realities. As a teenager, and because of his focus on racism and the development of a racist analysis (the "social analysis" that West cast doubts upon Du Bois having), Du Bois's thought and analysis went beyond human existence to a greater depth where human existence was not only denied and rejected, but where they were considered by other human beings as unthinkable and illegitimate.

This thinking went beyond the usual existential analysis, which focused on human existence. Du Bois's existential thinking and analysis focused on human existence and non-existence simultaneously and interactively. It was a holistic matter for him. It included the role that history played in this existential situation, specifically, the role that Black history and White racist history played in this complex existential reality of Black people in the United States. It would be many decades after Du Bois had initiated and developed this kind of discussion that Jean Paul Sarte, Franz Fanon, Lewis Gordon, Charles Mills and others would take up the matter of the complex existential situation of human existence and non-human existence interacting with each other.

The early character of Du Bois's thinking on this complex subject was evidenced in his 1903 book *The Souls of Black Folk*. He referred to the "two-warring ideals" in the "double-consciousness" of Black people. One of these "warring ideals" was the racist notion that Blacks were not human, or were not fully so, and that they did not even exist. Blacks countered that perverse ideal with a healthy one of their own: in their own heads they were human, they existed, and they had human worth and dignity. As Du Bois said, it took "dogged strength" on Black people's part to keep this intellectual/psychological struggle from tearing their psyches asunder.

What Du Bois learned over the remainder of his life was an enlargement of what he had learned with respect to Blacks living in an imposed racist environment in the South in the late nineteenth and early twentieth centuries. In 1900, he gave this situation a name, the "color line," which he used off and on thereafter. But he always knew that this situation involved more than race and color and even human existence. It symbolized a racist "white world hegemony" and the White denial, rejection, debasement, suppression, exploitation, and destruction of much of the world's humanity. It symbolized Whites/Westerners's anti-human being and anti-humanity postures; it symbolized their conception of themselves as being "godly or "godlike." Was Du Bois not saying this with the following comments from *The Souls of Black Folk?*:

> Indeed, the characteristic of our age is the contact of European civilization with the world's undeveloped peoples. Whatever we may say of the results of such contact in the past, it certainly forms a chapter in human action not pleasant to look back upon. War, murder, slavery, extermination, and debauchery–this has again and again been the result of carrying civilization and the blessed gospel to the isles of the sea and the heathen without the law. Nor does it altogether satisfy the conscience of the modern world to be told complacently that all this has been right and proper, the fated triumph of strength over weakness, of righteousness over evil, of superiors over inferiors. It would certainly be soothing if one could readily believe all this; and yet there are too many ugly facts for everything to be thus easily explained away. We feel and know that

there are many delicate differences in race psychology, numberless changes that our crude social measurements are not yet able to follow minutely, which explain much of history and social development. At the same time, too, we know that these considerations have never adequately explained or excused the triumph of brute force and cunning over weakness and innocence.[75]

Compare Du Bois's comments with those of Franz Kafka that West quoted in *The Future of the Race*, and that he thought were so insightful: "What we need are books that hit us a most painful misfortune...that make us feel as though we had been banished to the woods, far from any human presence, like suicide. A book must be the ax for the frozen sea within us."[76]

Franz Kafka was a contemporary of Du Bois's until his death in 1924. His writings referred to the "menace" that was *implied* in the "modern world." His subjects in his fiction were threatened, up-tight, and anxiety-ridden individuals who functioned like x-ray machines to show society "terrifying truths" of Europe's bourgeois civilization and of its increasingly baneful bureaucratic character. The menace that Du Bois wrote about was not implied and Kafka never caught a glimpse of it.

The menace was the white racist, particularly the white male racist, who not only menaced Europe and European society, but the entire world, people from both white and dark races. The white male racists, especially of Europe, as Du Bois remarked many times, were willing to deceive, deprecate, kill, and trample over each other and other white people to gain control of the world's dark peoples and what they possessed. Du Bois saw this and said with his racist analysis that humanity did not have to be "banished to the woods, far from any human presence," as a "wake-up call" for human beings. As he indicated, white racists banished human status and humanity in thought and social practice as a matter of course. This was not exceptional behavior, but regular, common behavior. Saying to people that they were not people or full human beings and treating them that way was common behavior. Kafka saw it *becoming* the behavior of the European bureaucracy, but he could not fathom its deep source. What Du Bois saw as "the frozen sea" in Western white racists would, in his mind, take more than some profound philosophy, book, or body of "Great Books," or art, to thaw out and to free up, or to be a "wake-up" call to Whites.

In the 1890s, Du Bois had already concluded (with the use of his white supremacist/ebonicistic racist analysis and with his other racist analyses) that Whites/Westerners believed and felt that they owned the world and all therein: peoples, lands, resources. The dark races of people had no human rights or any kind of rights that Whites/Westerners had to accept or respect. They had no right to thought, belief, values, dignity, feelings, courtesy, respect, and decency. They had no right to land, resources, power, or even their lives. Only Whites/Westerners had these kinds of rights because they were, as their racist beliefs told them, "god-like" or "semi-divine." As Du Bois wrote:

> This theory of human culture and its aims has worked itself through warp and woof of our daily thought with a thoroughness that few realize. Everything great, good, efficient, fair, honorable is "white;" everything mean, bad, blundering, cheating, and dishonorable is "yellow;" a bad taste is "brown;" and the devil is "black." The changes of this theme are continually run in picture and story, in newspaper heading and moving-picture, in sermon and school book, until, of course, the King can do no wrong–a White Man is always right and a Black Man has no rights which a white man is bound to respect. There must come the necessary despisings and hatreds of these savage half-men, this unclean *canaille* of the world.[77]

Was Du Bois showing–contrary to West's assertion–that he understood "the problem of evil" in this world, how people could be victims of and have to endure "undeserved harm, unjustified suffering, and unmerited pain?" White racists, as Du Bois repeatedly said, believed and felt that they were "inherently" entitled to everybody and everything that existed on the planet. It was just a matter of taking everything and developing the capability to do so. Taking was done by *any means necessary*: war, extermination, segregation, banishment, defilement, public humiliation, deception, gross exploitation, by purchase, by treaty, or by cajoling–whatever practically or whimsically came to mind. Whites and Westerners did not have to feel pangs of conscience or guilt about any of this behavior. They were "godly" or "god-like," incapable of doing wrong, immoral, or evil things, and the "nonhumans" or "subhumans" were those against whom no wrong or evil could be done. In thought and social behavior, no matter how vile, Whites/Westerners were *always* "guiltless," "innocent" and "non-responsible." They were, in "essence," doing the "right,"and "good thing."

But Du Bois, employing his racist analysis, carried this understanding to an even greater existential, absurd depth. Racists were incapable of understanding evil, proven by the fact that they did not and could not regard their own evil behavior to be evil. So what they did, as Du Bois said, was to define groups of people as evil. That is, their victims possessed an evil nature. What's more, their very presence was evil incarnate. They could only think, speak, and act in an evil manner. Evil was ahistorically, permanently, and forever, transferred from behavior to people, rooted in them, in their alleged inferior nature. This was "cosmic" evil that could only be dealt with by "cosmic" good, meaning the white race, which was allegedly good in nature. Whites, in doing evil, did not do evil. Blacks and other people of dark hue were the only ones who could do evil. Was this existential, absurd, surreal, tragicomic?

In Du Bois's view, it was the great irrationality, pathology, immorality, and compulsive malevolence that Whites/Westerners produced, developed, and spread across the world. The process was initiated in the sixteenth century when white supremacy/ebonicism racism, the black African slave trade, and black African slavery were joined together. They were, indeed, fastened tightly together, as a tandem, by white supremacy/ebonicism, the racist metaphysic, that declared white people "divine" or "semi-divine," and black people "nonhumans" or "subhumans," on the same plane as apes or ape-like creatures. This white supremacist/ebonicistic racist metaphysics was put at the foundation of Western history, culture, and civilization.

Black chattel slavery in the Western Hemisphere ultimately came to an end, but the Western racist metaphysical foundation continued on and even deepened with the aid of "scientific racists," the spread of White racism, and the full establishment of the White racist hegemony (exercised through race). All of the major areas of Western civilization were interpenetrated by the racist foundationalism upon which they rested: its politics, economic institutions, bureaucracies, religion, philosophy, literature, art, science, technology, military forces, and colonial (global political) and imperialistic (global economic) practices. All of these features of Western civilization were perverted and corrupted by the interpenetration of White racist foundationalism.

Du Bois initially learned as a teenager, and even more so later in life, that racists invested their racist beliefs and the irrationality, pathology, and immorality (which produced a compulsive malevolence) associated with them in their non-racist beliefs. Their Christian, liberal, democratic, and their variety of humanistic beliefs, were all perverted and corrupted, turning all into their opposites. Whites did this without knowing, or clearly knowing, that they did, owing to their racist-produced inability to introspect, or significantly introspect, that they were engaged in such conversion and desecration.

Du Bois did not have concepts to assign to this behavior, but based on what I understood him to be saying I adduced them for him. The terms I came up with are *de-ethicalization* and *abnormalization*. Du Bois talked about these behaviors without conceptualization in a 1910 article titled "The Souls of White Folk." In this article, he said the following:

> American science...has made itself the handmaid of a miserable prejudice. In its attempt to justify the treatment of black folk it has repeatedly suppressed evidence, misquoted authority, distorted fact and deliberately lied.... Worse than this is our moral and religious plight. We profess a religion of high ethical advancement, a spiritual faith, of respect for truth, despising of personal riches, a reverence for humility, and not simply justice to our fellows, but personal sacrifice of our good for theirs. It is a high aim, so high that we ought not utterly to be condemned for not reaching it, so long as we strive bravely toward it. Do we, as a people? On the contrary, we have injected into our creed a gospel of human hatred and prejudice, a despising of our less fortunate fellows, not to speak of our reverence for wealth, which flatly contradicts the Christian ideal. Granting all that American Christianity has done to educate and uplift black men, it must be frankly admitted that there is absolutely no logical method by which the treatment of black folk by white folk in this land can be squared with any reasonable statement or practice of the Christian ideal.[78]

Racism injected into science converted it into a pseudo-science. Its injection into morality produced immorality and malevolence. White supremacist/ebonicistic racism injected in Christianity produced what Du Bois called an immoral "primitive paganism." The injection of racism into non-racist beliefs, which could also be injected into culture, institutions, and social relations, and which white racists in America did, was a two-step process. When the racist beliefs were injected into Christian beliefs (and practices), for instance, they were *de-ethicalized*, that is, divested of their morality, spirituality, and humaneness and were *abnormalized*, meaning, invested with racist irrationality, pathology, and immorality and compulsive malevolence. Where in Leo Tolstoy, Vladimir Solovyev, Fyodor Dostoevsky, Friedrich Nietzsche, Semyon Frank, Lev Shestov, Nicholas Berdyaev or Soren Kierkegaard would one read something like this—or in West's writings, for that matter?

This would not be something that West's surrealist thinkers would have understood. The surrealists, such as Andre Breton, Paul Eluard,

Louis Aragon and the psychoanalyst, Jacques Lacan accepted the view that rationality and intentionality equated with consciousness. They were interested in going beyond consciousness to understand human thought, motivation, and behavior, particularly the irrational dimensions of these things. They felt all of this could be understood by delving into the human unconscious. There they would find the "resources" of the unconscious: irrationality, chaos, "primitiveness," desire, childishness, whims, and so on. With these unconscious subterranean traits, along with the little bit of rationality they felt human beings possessed and exercised, they would seek to explain what they thought of as a "deeper" level of human thought and behavior. Jacques Lacan constructed a psychoanalytical theory and an approach to therapy on this basis. But Lacan and other surrealists would have been shocked to learn that the "unconscious subterranean" human traits could be found in the human consciousness where Du Bois found them. Sigmund Freud would have been shocked, too, as he looked to the unconscious for deterministic or compulsive irrational thought, desires, and social behavior, having an influence on the surrealists of the twentieth century who read his works.

West and his surrealist thinkers also wouldn't have been able to appreciate something else that Du Bois understood about racists injecting their racism into beliefs and social practices. This behavior produced a *racist instrumentality* (a concept of my own construction, based on Du Bois's writings). This meant that when Whites/Westerners injected racism into the major attributes of Western civilization, they also made them potentially and practically compulsive and pathological racist instrumentalities to do the work of racism. Could this, and the things said above, represent what West said Du Bois had not been able to provide because of his "Enlightenment" and "Victorian" backgrounds and restraints? Could Du Bois be showing some "psychological" and "existential" insights into the "human condition?" Could he have known something about "the truth of modern tragic experience?"

Du Bois concluded that the human reality, or the human condition, of Whites/Westerners, exhibited on a daily basis, was a reality and condition of considerable *abnormality*. Not just irrationality, but the gambit of racist afflictions that their racist beliefs and practices invested in them. The cultural anthropologist Ruth Benedict wrote: "We are handicapped in dealing with human society so long as we identify our social normalities with the inevitable necessities of existence."[79] Du Bois's observation was deeper and more profound. His argument, as his writings reveal, is that Whites/Westerners *made the abnormal, normal*, and that that abnormality was the "necessity of existence" for such people and their victims of dark hue.

Whites/Westerners were socialized in abnormality, which was taught, formally and informally, absurdly and tragically, to those socialized as being normal. To them, it seemed normal and natural to look upon themselves as "godly" or "god-like," and others, indeed, most of the population on the planet—especially black people, who were considered their direct antithesis—as not having human status and as being essentially outside of humanity and human morality. This, along with racist-inundated chattel slavery, was the beginning of the "tragic," "absurd," and often-surreal Black existence in America.

In the past, Blacks usually interacted with Whites when they were functioning as racists. Thus, Blacks have usually interacted with Whites as people engaging in compulsive, abnormal behavior. As Du Bois noted, Blacks were trapped in an absurd, contradictory, or paradoxical existence. They were human beings, but they always had to prove it, which they were not able to do to those constantly demanding proof. The greater absurdity was the contradicting reality of being humiliated, beaten down, or even killed for trying to demonstrate human status and humanity. Blacks were required to be moral and to demonstrate that they were and were not criminals when those demanding the demonstration believed that they were innately incapable of morality and were innately criminal.

These were things that Du Bois asserted. He also said that Blacks were presumed guilty and had to prove their innocence (the reverse of American legal thinking), which they were not able to do to those who suppressed them. Du Bois blared on one occasion: "The laws are made by men who as yet have little interest in him; they are executed by men who have absolutely no motive for treating the black people with courtesy or consideration; and finally the accused lawbreaker is tried not by his peers but too often by men who would rather punish ten innocent Negroes than let one guilty one escape."[80] Du Bois also wrote that Whites exhibited: "an absurd lack of logic, as for instance, accusing of bad manners those whom against every effort is made to give them no chance to see good manners."[81] And the following, Du Bois also penned: "But the major premise—the question as to treating black men like white men—never enters their heads, nor can they conceive it entering the black man's head."[82]

Whites could not imagine people of the dark races on the planet being any other way than the way they conceived them, as innately inferior and engaging in thought and social behavior that were inherently and permanently inferior. This fetid racist conception militated against the construction of a rational, objective, and just world or social order. It was incumbent upon Whites then, as they saw it (believing in their own innate superiority and the innate inferiority of all other people on the planet) to dominate the world and its lands, people, and resources and to try to advance the human species as best they could, given its massive innate cerebral, moral, and other deficiencies. Their believed and assumed nobility and humaneness, combined with their Christian beliefs, required that they shoulder this large responsibility, which they proudly called the "White Man's Burden." This was the "tragicomic" situation for Du Bois, not calling into question "ultimate purpose and objective order," which racism precluded in the first instance in America and around the world.

Of course, the real human burden was on the heads and backs of black people and other people of dark hue. Blacks in America had a microcosm of that worldwide burden placed on them, not only chattel slavery and racism, but a life of absurd and often painful, existential contradictions. These realities led Du Bois to talk about Blacks living "within the veil" and to speak of their need to develop intellectual and psychological attributes: "double-consciousness," "holistic thinking," "psychological resiliency" and "dogged inner strength" to cope, to endure, and to surmount imposed malignancy. Du Bois may not have liked the blues, but he knew from whence the music came, as he knew from whence came the "sorrow songs" before them, the Black "preaching style, and the Black religious sermons. About these sermons, he wrote the following in the posthumously published *Autobiography*:

> And so most striking to me, as I approached the village and the little plain church perched aloft, was the air of intense excitement that possessed that mass of black folk. A sort of suppressed terror hung in the air and seemed to seize them–a pythian madness, a demonic possession, that lent terrible reality to song and word. The black and massive form of the preacher swayed and quivered as the words crowded to his lips and flew at us in singular eloquence. The people moaned and fluttered, and then the gaunt-cheeked brown woman beside me suddenly leaped straight into the air and shrieked like a lost soul, while round about came wail and groan and outcry, and a scene of human passion such as I had never conceived before.[83]

As mentioned, when Du Bois talked about the "color line" that Whites/Westerners made a global reality, he was talking about something more than just race, prejudice, or racial discrimination. His view of racism, to use his own words, was that it was something "that logically ran down to murder!" He left far behind those contemporaries of his, Black, white, or other who talked about racism simply in terms of racial attitudes, prejudices, or discriminations. He invariably saw it in terms of human oppression and suppression, unceasing humiliation, and myriad forms of theft, exploitation, and human destruction. He summarized the consequences of conjoining racism and black African slavery in *The Negro* when he stated, "in the midst of this [human] advance and uplift this slave trade and slavery spread more human misery, inculcated more disrespect for and neglect of humanity, a greater callousness to suffering, and more petty, cruel, human hatred than can well be calculated."[84]

The de-ethicalized and abnormalized "White soul" was born! Du Bois said that it exhibited itself vividly in capitalism, making it a debased and inhumane economic system worldwide. It exhibited itself in the same manner in colonialism and imperialism. But Du Bois believed that its most vivid, vile expression was in war. For instance, in his response to the First World War in an essay in *Darkwater*, Du Bois wrote:

> This is not Europe gone mad; this is not an aberration, nor insanity; this is Europe; this seeming Terrible is the real soul of white culture–back of all culture,–stripped and visible today. This is where the world has arrived,–these dark and awful depths and not the shining and affable heights of which it boasted. Here is whither the might and energy of modern humanity has really gone.[85]

This was the Du Bois and his understandings and insights that West could not locate in his writings. West has said that Du Bois could never bring himself to identify with the harsh words of the great performing artist Josephine Baker: "The very idea of America makes me shake and tremble and gives me nightmares."[86] He said this as if Du Bois did not know the racist worst of Whites and America, as if he did not know that Blacks suffered from both. Du Bois lived in the South for many years, the years when racism was blatant and constant in its vilification of Blacks and brutal in the treatment of them.

In *The Crisis*, he wrote about and reported on Black "nightmares" and Black progress in America, even seeing some of the progress related to some of the "nightmares," such as the mistreatment of Black soldiers in America and Europe by white American soldiers, investing Black soldiers and other Blacks with defiance, courage, belligerency, and a greater determination that helped to elevate the image of the "New Negro" and that eventually helped to produce the artistic renaissance.

Du Bois was an unusual Black intellectual. He was not parochial like most Black intellectuals of his day, and which is the case today. He always had his eye on world movement and world history, particularly watching how Whites/Westerners were moving things. He saw them helping the world to make great material progress, but also at the great expense of humanity and human lives, which he did not feel evened out. He also thought Whites/Westerners, because of their great compulsive and pathological racism and de-ethicalized and abnormalized "White Soul," were suicidal. When the First World War was just a year old, Du Bois wrote an article entitled "The African Roots of War,"[87] in which he said that another war, such as the one raging then, was just around the corner. Eighteen years later, in 1933, he predicted in *The Crisis* that the second such war would break out in Europe in 1940, which eventually did occur in September of 1939.

During and after the First World War, Du Bois saw the West in the process of completing an epoch of history. The German philosopher Martin Heidegger spoke of the West completing its absolutist philosophical project. Du Bois saw the long White/Western racist history heading towards a climax. He predicted an even more horrendous war, which would produce a worldwide, post-war result of the dark peoples of the planet engaging in liberation actions to free themselves and their countries from White racist world hegemony.

Unlike many in his day and unlike many today, Du Bois did not see Hitler and the Nazis as aberrations in Western history and civilization. He saw them, as only a few have today, as *culminators* of that history and civilization, carrying their deep-seated, irrational, pathological, and immoral racist foundationalism to its logical conclusion: horrendous human humiliation, exploitation, suppression, and destruction. Hitler and the Nazis, to Du Bois, epitomized the de-ethicalized and abnormalized Western "White Soul." They were the ultimate expression of the White racist belief that malevolence, cruelty, deception, denigration, humiliation, and horrendous violence were normal and natural human responses. This went beyond the absurd or tragic; it reached the tragicomic level.

But what Du Bois regarded as the depth of the human tragicomic was when human beings–and he had southern white racists, Hitler, and Nazis in mind–thought that humiliation, the abuse, torment, and destruction of human beings were forms of "fun," "merriment," "recreation" or "sport." To him, this was what the lynching and burning of Blacks and the riddling of burning or dead bodies with bullets were to southern Whites and what the many forms of mephitic treatment of Jews in concentration camps were to their S.S. oppressors.

245

For eighty years, Du Bois talked and wrote about these kinds of miasmic things, seeing them as expressions of *racist alienation*. On this subject, he pushed beyond Karl Marx (who related alienation to labor commodification, appropriating the "fruits" of labor) and, like Hegel, to cultural reification. Du Bois indicated that racist alienation derived from human beings doing the simple, but hideous thing, of denying or deprecating the human status and moral status of human beings and acting against them on this basis. Thus, it was fundamentally racists themselves who were an alienated people, alienated from their own humanity and that of other human beings.

Racist beliefs, as Du Bois revealed in his writings, were instances of *cultural reification* that glorified abstract, fanciful expressions and that reflected no embodiment source; that did not represent any embodied or concrete reality. Racist alienation, which white racists exhibited, was about as alienated as a human being could become. This alienation process was not confined to, or determined by, any kind of economic system, or any type of society. Racist alienation, as Du Bois viewed it, ran logically to hating, humiliating, oppressing, exploiting, hurting, and killing people.

Referring to Hitler and the Nazis as the culmination of White/Western irrationality, inhumanity, and abnormality, Du Bois wrote in 1947's *The World and Africa* after learning about the holocaustic experience of the Jews that: "There was no Nazi atrocity—concentration camps, wholesale maiming and murder, defilement of women or ghastly blasphemy of childhood—which the Christian civilization of Europe had not long been practicing against colored folk in all parts of the world in the name of and for the defense of a Superior Race born to rule the world."[88] To Du Bois, it was the "civilized people" who were the great defilers and destroyers of human beings, not people casually regarded as "primitive" or "pagan." He did not use the word "holocaust" to refer to the defilement, instances of large-scale genocide, and cultural destruction that Whites/Westerners carried out for centuries against people of dark hue around the globe. His view of the Second World War was that it was, without using the word, a horrendous holocaust that reflected the irony of white people engaging in such brutal and destructive behavior against each other. This signaled to Du Bois how deep the racism and the racist afflictions went in white people, Western history, culture, and civilization and how they made all kinds of people sacrificial.

One could not get anything like I have just described across these pages, as being Du Bois's understandings and insights, in the course of Western history, human feelings, or the human condition in anything

West has written or that any Black preacher has sermonized about, or that some Black musician has conveyed, nor in the writings of West's genealogical "spiritual fathers." When Nietzsche spoke of the "death of God" and the death of absolutist, metaphysical philosophy (the latter of which was also described by William James and other American pragmatists), Du Bois, without formal conceptualization, was talking about and writing strongly about a racist metaphysics, racist foundationalism, and racist absolutism.* Further, he was referring to the racist "godly" or "god-like" "entity" of White racist thinking that still existed and that was wreaking oppression, destruction, and death all over the planet. Du Bois referred to this as the "white world hegemony."

When the German sociologist Max Weber was talking about the end of European "Medieval Enchantment" and mysticism, Du Bois was talking about White racist "Enchantment," its mysticism, and perverted romanticism, both of which were strongly functioning in America and Western Europe, and spreading across the globe like deadly infectious diseases. When Max Weber and some Western philosophers and literary writers were talking about the decline of rationality and bureaucracy taking an irrational turn, Du Bois said that the decline and turn could be traced back to the sixteenth century, when Western rationality became rooted in irrationality, pathology, immorality, and world inhumaneness (and not terminated in the insane asylum of the seventeenth century, as one of West's favorites, Michel Foucault, erroneously believed). In short, Western rationality was rooted in an irrational racist metaphysics that impacted Western thought and institutions, de-ethicalized and abnormalized them, as manifestations of *instrumental irrationality*, as opposed to the *instrumental rationality* of Weber, Theodor Adorno, and Jürgen Habermas of the Frankfurt School that even victimized white people in a racist manner. Needless to say, instrumental irrationality was not something ever conceived, even in a non-formal conceptual manner, by European or Western surrealists.

ACCOMMODATING GOLIATH

While Booker T. Washington did not know the full range and depth of Du Bois's intellectual capabilities or the extent or profundity of his thought and knowledge, he did regard him as the best person for talking

* Du Bois was a former student of William James and spoke of this in the year of Nietzsche's death, 1900.

about and against White racist beliefs, thoughts, and social actions. It was something that he himself could not often do publicly or with such openness. Du Bois did not like any kind of restrictions on his thought, except those he applied himself. The Tuskegean not only wanted Du Bois to keep up his running public intellectual assault against White racism, he, at times (and which is not known to present-day Black intellectuals) assisted Du Bois in doing so.

In 1911, for instance, Du Bois wanted to attend an international Congress on Race in London. His plan was to attack Washington there. When his intentions were made known to supporters of the Congress, they wished him to come, but asked him not to trash the Tuskegean because it might do damage to the proceedings. Du Bois had to be cajoled into attending the Congress knowing that he would not be able to attack Washington. The Tuskegean himself could have probably prevented Du Bois from attending the Congress and having anything to say there. He had great prestige and a substantial following in London and he was able to mobilize opposition against Du Bois. He also could have remonstrated with the white national leadership of the NAACP in America. But he didn't do any of these things. David Levering Lewis wrote in his biography of Du Bois that Washington ordered one of his major leaders, Robert Russa Moton, to go to London to counter the feisty intellectual. Lewis wrote: "Truly alarmed now, Booker Washington ordered Robert Moton to attend the Races Congress and do all he could to counter Du Bois."[89]

This was deliberate distortion. Lewis showed that he had read the correspondence between Washington and Moton about the London Congress. But the correspondence clearly shows that Moton had already made plans to attend the Race Congress and Washington did not know about it until his trusted leader informed him. Moton wrote: "I am planning to go to the Race Congress in London this summer. I thought it advisable for some one of us to be present.... I am convinced that Dr. Du Bois, [John] Milholland and Miss [Mary] Ovington will do everything they can in London this summer to undo the good that you did last year."[90] Washington replied in the following manner ten days later: "I am glad you are going to the Racial Congr[ess] in London. I think it well for some level headed people to be present."[91]

Why the deliberate distortion of the facts on Lewis's part? And Lewis distorted other facts. He presented the NAACP as a threat to Washington when, in fact, the organization came into existence because Washington decided not to oppose its establishment. The Grand Black Leader actually wanted someone or some institution to carry on the public fight for Black legal rights, which he had been attempting to do behind the scenes and at great expense. Mary White Ovington, one of the NAACP founders, made it clear that if the Tuskegean had opposed the organization, it would have been doomed:

> I think it's legitimate now [many years later] to raise the curtain a little. Our controversy was a part of the time in which we lived and was inevitable. It centered about Booker T. Washington. Was it possible to build up any organization, to get support for what we knew would become expensive work, without his sanction? Must we not at least ask him to be on our committee.... Could we ignore the man who was unquestionably the most influential and most famous Negro living?[92]

Lewis talked about the "twilight" of Booker T. Washington's prestige and leadership with the establishment of the NAACP. The facts show that Washington had the power (powerful and rich white men, Black newspaper editors, and other Black people) to prevent the organization from getting off the ground. He had the same power to crush it once it was functional, which was really the great fear of the white national leaders of the organization. They assured Washington that the new rights organization would not be publicly used against him. So, he gave it a green light for this reason and also for what he knew would be a forum for Du Bois to be a national leader with a national voice.

The Tuskegean even went one better with his voluble rival. He learned that the new organization had plans to establish a publicity and research department, and even a house organ and that thoughts of the white national leadership had turned to Du Bois, the only Black member of the national leadership, to head things up. Washington had initial reservations about Du Bois being in this particular position, and he made it clear to the white leadership of the body that if Du Bois's intention was to use publicity or a house organ to oppose him publicly, he was not in favor of having him in that position. Du Bois gained this position by *accommodating* Washington. Here is how Du Bois explained his acceptance of the position:

> With some hesitation I was asked to come as Director of Publications and Research, with the idea that my research work [at Atlanta University] was to go on and with the further idea that my activities would be so held in check that the Association would not develop as an organ of attack upon Tuskegee-a difficult order; because how, in 1910, could one discuss the Negro problem and not touch upon

Booker T. Washington and Tuskegee? But after all, as I interpreted the matter, it was a question of temperament and manner rather than of subject.[93]

In his new position, Du Bois established *The Crisis* as the house organ of the new NAACP, but used it as his own personal monthly magazine, much to the outrage of the white national leadership. He edited it for twenty-five years, making it one of the most popular monthlies in the country. It wasn't until 1934 that he lost control of *The Crisis* when he was forced to retire from the Association, and went back into teaching at Atlanta University. It was during these years that Du Bois began to follow in the footsteps of Washingtonian thought. He spoke of racial consciousness and using racism and segregation to the advantage of Blacks. He spoke of a leadership for the mass of Blacks and the need to combine public protest with cultural and social construction.

What he did not do, that Washington had done years earlier, was to have leaders rise from lowly and suppressed Blacks and let such Blacks have input into the agendas and leadership that affected them. He did not develop a full-blown ideology that was capable of extension or alteration to guide Blacks, nor did he establish mass institutions and a mass leadership to help Blacks. He also did not make an effort to train Black youth as leaders, and community builders, and builders of a Black future in America. Washington still holds rank on these matters.

It will be recalled that Adolph Reed, Jr. had a chapter in his book *Class Notes* titled: "What are the Drums Saying, Booker?" He, of course, was ridiculing Washington. But the truth is that Washington's drums—his efforts, words, and accomplishments—continue to say a lot, a lot that is meaningful to Black people, to the Black middle-class, and especially to those Blacks still trying to make it and to be fully free in the country. Black intellectuals and Black leaders have apparently lost the ability to hear the percussion sounds, especially those emanating from fully *Black* hands banging on the drums.

This has become a problem, specifically, of some Black women intellectuals and leaders, who no longer display a focus on the Black community, that has been the tradition of such people. The next chapter takes up the subject of Black women intellectuals in America.

═❨ Chapter Six ❩═
Why Black Female Intellectuals Tend to Shout

It was always clear, even if not crystal clear, that Black women would assert their public voices in American history and society. They would need strong voices; at times, voices that were on the shouting side because Black women had voices that not many people in America wanted to hear. Certainly, white men and white women did not want to hear them; and, for that matter, not many Black men wanted to hear them either. These groups had already attained public voices, although in regards to Black men and white women, their voices were heard, but not always listened to, or responded to, in positive ways by white men.

RACIST MIRROR AND DENIGRATING IMAGES

When Black women tried to exercise a public voice at the same time as the launching of the white female feminist movement in the early nineteenth century, they often found white women functioning as the strongest public castigators and silencers. White women felt that they had their own public image to protect, which had been kicked around enough by white men. To be regarded as close or similar to a Black woman in social status, and/or to be in any way treated like them, was just unthinkable cruelty and unfairness to these white women. Hence the white female feminist movement, as Robert and Pamela Allen said in *Reluctant Reformers*,[1] was saturated with racism that callously barred the entry of Black women and refused to accept allies of a kindred spirit, even in a struggle for emancipation and advancement. This was typical of all major white "progressive" movements in America.

In white women's racist minds, Black women simply were not kindred spirits. They were not even fully human. They were "animals," "beasts of burden," "masculine," rather than feminine. They were physically and facially ugly. White women, even feminist white women, joined white men in embedding these grotesque images of Black women in American culture, in White memory, in literature, and in anything that was a

251

conveyor belt of public images. This functioned as a way for white women to put restraints on the roaming eyes, hands, and sexual appetites of white men: their husbands, their lovers, and their betrothed—men whom Black women could not accuse of molestation or rape in any effective way. Black women were easy targets or objects of the indecent imagination, aggressive behavior, and sexual assault of these men. Thus, it was a protective shield for white women to publicly encourage images of Black women that represented them as sexually licentious or promiscuous, and also collectively as the national whore.

Between the latter eighteenth century and first half of the nineteenth century in America, white men and women imposed a physically grotesque and ugly image on Black women. This image was a *four-cornered mirror* that encircled them wherever they placed their bodies in the country. It was not a mirror that they could escape by living among Blacks, even if the mirror was not fully constituted there, although it was always fully constituted in the Black social world for the *black* Black girl or the *black* Black woman. It was impossible for anyone to know, and only a Black woman could, what it was like to wake up everyday to a four-cornered mirror that said you were physically grotesque, facially ugly, amoral, and a whore. Not only were you considered these things, but this was a mirror that you yourself had to drag around wherever you went and for all the days of your life.

The horror, gross inhumaneness, and injustice of it, combined with the agony of knowing your victimization acted as a channel for someone else's perverse thinking, beliefs, and values, was always a burden to Black women. The burden grew heavier when it was understood that the castigating racist mirror, and the humiliation and agonies associated with it, would be passed on to your daughter and become her loathsome millstone. There was the alternative of not having children, which ultimately compounded the unfairness and inhumaneness of the matter. Black womanist Karla Holloway wrote: "regardless of our station within our communities, our incomes, or our schooling, there comes some essential moment when black women must acknowledge the powerful imprint of our physical appearance."[2]

Even for the light-skinned Black woman, the racist mirror of grotesqueness and ugliness is her burden, as well, and can be just as wrenching. Patricia Williams remarked:

> There are moments in my life when I feel as though a part of me is missing. Those are the times when my skin becomes gummy as clay and my nose slides around my face and my eyes drip down to my

chin. I have to close my eyes at such times and remember myself....
When all else fails, I reach for a mirror and stare myself down until
the features reassemble themselves.[3]

Black women had not only the public image of being the national
whore to contend with, they also had to contend with this image padded
with the notion that Black women were sexually promiscuous, loose, and
uninhibited. This rendered Black women vulnerable to any man
(including Black men) who imbibed this baneful characterization. During
the days of slavery this image worked to perpetuate Black chattel slavery.
Such slaves took the status of the mother. And while most Black slave
children would be fathered by Black male slaves, white men (and any
other men) could father them, too, and any child born belonged to the
owner of the slave mother.

Of course, no Black slave woman (or nonslave Black woman, for that
matter) could claim being molested or raped, because such things were
not recognized by law. White women were vulnerable to sexual assault as
well, but not nearly to the same extent. However, they were forced into
the peculiar and perverted situation where they, as a way of putting it, had
to have a *right* to be raped to be able to charge a man with rape. But any
man could molest or rape a Black woman with impunity, that is, unless a
master wished to bring charges, which would likely be a charge of
trespassing or violation of property, which could draw a fine.

The only defense that a Black woman had against molestation or rape
was her ability to fend off her attacker. She might well be defensive and
cautious in the presence of Black men, as well, men who, like white men,
were encouraged by the culture and the social environment to take
advantage of her. A nonslave Black man might endeavor to defend a
nonslave Black woman from sexual molestation or assault. But this could
be dangerous and a life-threatening situation for a Black male slave to be
in. A Black slave woman was property. Only the owner of that property
had a legal right to protect it. As a rule, slave masters would not sanction
the role of a Black male slave protector of Black slave women. They would
not readily allow such slaves to have that kind of power, responsibility, or
moral stature. A Black male slave could well find himself in serious
physical trouble or physical danger if he endeavored to defend a Black
slave woman from physical or sexual assault, especially if the attacker was
a white man.

Black psychiatrist Gail Elizabeth Watt recently remarked: "Society's
message is that to be black and female is to be without sexual control, to
be irresponsible about our sexuality. Regardless of the circumstances, our

age or our appearance, someone may assume that we are sexually available or for sale at some price."[4] Dr. Watt was writing in the 1990s, which reveals how the noxious public image of Black women still pervaded American society and still functioned like a "cultural stalker" against them. Even at this late date, many Black women feel that any man, at any time, is capable of slipping into and wearing the cultural stalker suit. Kara Holloway wrote:

> African American women have learned well how and when to hide our bodies [or to be silent when the body itself, the ache of it, prompts verbal action]. Sometimes a lesson in public assault was an instructive moment. But at other times, the history of racist and sexist aesthetics has made us hate our hair and mask our bodies, and has encouraged the desperation of Kotex on our heads—or sedate teal blue dresses. At what cost this dissembling? When we mask in these ways, we actually, and perversely, privilege the gaze of others. The bodies that emerge when others control our images are disfigured and fragmented.[5]

A Fear of Intellectual/Analytical Independence?

It is the old story of how the oppressed or diminished abet their own condition in a myriad of ways. One of these ways is exhibited by a host of Black female feminists and womanists, specifically when they use the terms or concepts devised by white female feminists to evaluate and explain the historical and social experience of Black women, or their relationship with Black men, or the Black historical experience and Black life. The poet Audre Lorde remarked: "The master's concepts will never dismantle the master's house. They may enable us temporarily to best him at his own game, but they will never enable us to bring about genuine change."[6] Washington, and the Black Struggle for Liberation in the 1950s and 1960s, showed that this was not so. But Lorde's main point still carries validity: any oppressed or diminished people have to have their own intellectual capabilities, their own concepts, analytical frameworks, and interpretive capabilities, in order to present discourses on their own historical and social existence and that of others.

Du Bois once wrote, "instead of beginning with the exploitation of white labor as did most reformers of my day, it was the twist of my peculiar situation that made me begin with black skins, and the subjugation of the darker people."[7] Du Bois was a Blackcentric and

Africancentric. He focused on Blacks in America and looked outwardly. He also focused on black Africa and then looked back toward Blacks. His goal was to fully connect these two groups of people and these two perspectives, as much as evidence and logical analysis permitted. He insisted upon and reveled in intellectual independence, whether it was being independent of his instructors at Harvard, or at the University of Berlin, or even from Karl Marx, who he considered a great thinker. Du Bois always felt that a different story could be told, a better one, a truer one, and he was leery of formal concept and theories, as he felt that they could be limiting, even stifling. He liked to plunge into extant reality and analyze it, adducing what could be called non-formalized concepts and analytical categories or embedded concepts and categories.

One of the embedded concepts and analytical categories that he devised when analyzing Whites interacting with Blacks on a racist basis was that Whites constantly engaged in illogical behavior in a logical manner, carrying this illogical behavior to its logical conclusion. Du Bois presented an example of this kind of White racist behavior when he remarked: "The only logical folk in the South today are the Vardamans and Tillmans. They hold no illusions and know that you cannot treat a man as a man and as a beast at the same time.... Therefore, they argue, treat Negroes as beasts."[8]

On the surface this looks like a simple statement, but it is one of great profundity and reflects the embedded concepts in Du Bois's remark. He showed by the example that logic was not synonymous with reason or rationality and that illogical thinking could be done logically. To put it another way, reason could be used to promote irrationality. Thus, for Du Bois, reason and rationality were not only not synonymous, they were not even necessarily correlated. Race and racism were not the same things to him, and neither necessarily had anything to do with the other.

Du Bois did not employ the term gender much and did not have a formal gender analysis, but he analyzed the history and social situation of Black women in America and did not confuse this analysis with sex or sexuality, as so many Black women thinkers (as well as many white women thinkers) do. Black women thinkers presently show a reticence to engage in independent intellectual activity. This may seem like an arbitrary and un-called for statement. After all, today's Black women thinkers are focusing their intellectual efforts on Black women and showing how the experiences of Black women have been different from that of white women (and other women in the country, for that matter), even different from the experiences of Black men. But this amounts to something that is divisional or different, not necessarily independent. Independence would be in the way these various social realities would be interpreted. For instance, how do Black women thinkers interpret the relations between Black women and Black men? For the most part, the answer is that this is done on the basis of concepts and analytical techniques or categories borrowed from white feminist thinkers.

The concept of sexism is one of these borrowings. The term was devised by white feminist intellectuals in order to evaluate the experience of white women in America. Black feminists were initially reluctant to use the term to analyze the historical and social experience of Black women in the country. But Black female feminists like bell hooks, encouraged them to use it, saying in her work of 1981, *Ain't I a Woman*, that "consequently, when the women's movement raised the issue of sexist oppression, we argued that sexism was insignificant in the light of the harsher, more brutal reality of racism. We were afraid to acknowledge that sexism could be just as oppressive as racism."[9] hooks has since become a prominent Black female feminist and Black female feminist radical. She and other Black or black feminists (as well as Black or black womanists) continue to use the term sexism in their writings; this includes Karla Holloway, Joy James, Adrian Piper, and Black theologian Cheryl Sanders, whose book, *Living the Intersection*,[10] addresses sexism from a Black feminist standpoint. Similarly, black literary critic Hazel Carby works from this position, as evidenced in her book *Reconstructing Womanhood*.[11]

Because it is a form of racism, sexism can be just as oppressive as racism. Black or black women intellectuals (and, for that matter, other intellectuals in the country) have yet to attain this understanding. Black women in America have always had to face *four* forms of racism imposed upon them and executed in tandem clusters: white supremacy/ebonicism that denigrated their race and ethnicity and maleism/sexism (even from some Black men, though how extensive this has been has yet to be determined) that disparaged their gender and sexuality. White women are not without their share of the blame in this situation, as they have also imposed three of these forms of racism on Black women.

There are Black female intellectuals who use the words sex and sexuality interchangeably with each other, and each interchangeably with sexism, as do the Black female historians Darlene Clark Hine, Nell Painter, and Deborah Gray White. These historians also employ concepts of race, class, and gender in what they call an "intersectional analysis." As Black women intellectuals use it, this approach also came from white female feminist intellectuals. In turn, White feminist intellectuals, perhaps sensing or suspecting sexism's similarly to racism, and thus, putting themselves too close to Black women feminists and the white female historical experience too close to that of Black women, abandoned the concept, leaving Black feminists with it. In the minds of white female feminists, the white female experience in America was *universal*, the Black female experience was *particular* or *relative*. These concepts were suffused with a white supremacy/ebonicism/sexism that avowed the Black female experience to be of less standing and value.

But we do not have Black women intellectuals evaluating the Black female historical and social experiences on the basis of the four forms of racism. Indeed, it can be said that most Black female intellectuals are becoming, like their white female counterparts, taken with "intersectional analysis." This is particularly true of the intersectional analysis of race, gender, and social class. However, for their white counterparts, race does not usually translate into racism. Such people overwhelmingly stay as far away from racism as is possible. And even though race is a factor in Black female intellectuals intersectional analysis, in general, they do not evidence an understanding of the difference between racism and race. Most of the time they ignore a discussion of racism in favor of race, as if race has been independent of racism in American history and life.

ENTER PATRICIA HILL COLLINS

Like their Black male counterparts, Black female intellectuals do not have a racist analysis to work with, which stands to reason when they do not evidence knowing the difference between race and racism. But any analysis of Black women's history or life in America that ignores or plays down the many racisms impacting this history and life, or the Black experience in general, amounts to *flight analysis*. One of the outstanding Black female feminist theorists, Patricia Hill Collins, unwittingly engages in this flight analysis. This is reflected by her comments in *Fighting Words*:

> African-American women's positionality within both race-class collectivities and gender collectivities as two overlapping yet distinct forms of group organization, provides a potentially important lens for evaluating standpoint theory overall.... But standpoint theory seems less applicable to gender relations in the United States. Because women are separated from one another by race and class, they face different challenges both in conceptualizing themselves as a group at all and in seeing themselves as a group similar to race/class groups...despite my commitment to intersectionality as an important conceptual framework, continuing to leave intersectionality as an untheorized construct contributes to leaving

old hierarchies...being reformed under what I see as a new myth of equivalent oppressions.[12]

Collins obviously thinks that racism and race are the same thing, as she does not have racism as part of her intersectional analytical framework, which means that she is essentially in flight from that reality and that kind of analysis. Further, she doesn't seem to see how racism impacts and affects the functioning of all the social groups to which she has referred to: race, social class, and gender. Nor does she refer to ethnic groups (which does not seem to be part of her theoretical or analytical interest) or racism's relationship to ethnicity.

Women belong to racial groups, ethnic groups, social classes, and a gender group. Collins would add that they also belong to a sexual group and a country. Men have related to women in all of these categories in maleist/sexist terms, that is, in racist terms. This has seriously affected the way they function in all of these categories. Thus, racism cannot logically or analytically be removed from analyzing the life and history of women in America, or anywhere else in the world, for that matter, because maleism/sexism strongly exists all over the planet, in some places stronger than in other places.

Collins is rightly critical of those academics or social theorists who are sloppy in their discussions about oppression and give the impression that there are many oppressed groups in American society that are all oppressed equally. In her view, oppression was related to power possession and use. She notes:

> Within these politics, some groups benefit more from an assumed equivalence of oppression than others. Although this approach is valid as a heuristic device, treating race, class and gender as if their intersection produces equivalent results for all oppressed groups obscures differences in how race, class and gender are hierarchically organized, as well as the differential effects of intersecting systems of power on diverse groups of people.[13]

To talk about power, power distribution, social relations, and oppression, it is necessary to do so within the framework of America's welfare society, which was not a framework that Collins perceived or employed. In fact, her analysis of Black and other women was in flight from this, which meant that it was also in flight from the racism of the welfare society, i.e., white supremacy/ebonicism, maleism/sexism and other forms of racism. This racist interiority runs through the society's hierarchical social classes and societal sections and down into the Basin of the society where the worst form of racist expression occurs. Racial groups, ethnic groups, social classes, gender groups, and sexual groups all adhere to and are interpenetrated to some extent by this racist inner lining.

With respect to Black women, Black feminists like Collins have extracted Black women from the racist inner lining of America to analyze their social situation with a race/class/gender intersectional analysis. This amounts to flight analysis and results in consequence social analysis. With her broad analytical framework, Collins cannot explain or account for why, historically or socially, so many Black women feel the continuous pressure of the grotesque images that remain draped over them and their lives. Nor can she explain their constant internal battles with them. These images do not have their source in race, class, or gender, but in the three separate and simultaneously conjoined forms of racism: white supremacy/ebonicism/sexism.

Black women of all racial complexions, educational attainments, and social classes are chastised, diminished, or distressed by these racist afflictions. But Black female intellectuals do little to examine how racism and its racist afflictions have affected Black women with respect to race, gender, social class, and ethnicity. Black women intellectuals who talk of class elevation and improvement for Black women, or who talk about how the class factor is overwhelmingly the crucial factor for determining social qualifications and social advances, have trouble explaining the four-cornered mirror of grotesqueness and ugliness for Black women of all classes. Of course, the Black male intellectuals who talk about the great determinant capacity of social class obviously focus this argument on Black men more than they do Black women, even though they do not usually specify any gender in these discussions.

Thus, borrowing ideas and analytical tools from white female feminists can distort and obscure the realities of Black women's history and social life in America and can even lead to some erroneous conclusions and presentations. When Collins and other Black female intellectuals accept that white female feminists keep racism off their intersectional analyses, they sanction white female feminists's analyses of Black and white female relationships, their own relationship with white men, and the relationship of white women to American history, culture, and society, as if racism has never existed in the country, and as if they, themselves, have no racist thoughts or motivations. The racist image of white women as the universal standard of beauty, femininity, eloquence, and grace still hangs on in America. Meanwhile, Black women have had to constantly deal with those images on the opposite side of the four-cornered mirror. Their origins are not in race, gender, or social class, but in the four forms of White racism (with the addition of White maleism).

THE PATRIARCHY FALLACY

Another problematic concept for Black female intellectuals is the use of the white feminist concept of *patriarchy*. It is clearly an erroneous major analytical tool for such intellectuals to use. Black feminist religious scholar Katie Geneva Cannon wrote in *Katie's Canon*: "Black women are the most vulnerable and the most exploited members of American society. The structure of the capitalist political economy in which Black people are commodities, combined with patriarchal contempt for women, has caused the Black woman to experience oppression that knows no ethical or physical bounds."[14] It cannot be convincingly argued that all Black women in America are oppressed. There are a number of Black women who live very well in this country; and there are those who do not seem to be particularly affected or disturbed by the grotesque public images. For instance, there are some Black women whose beauty has been deemed commercially viable, and some are getting very rich from this. But obviously this is not the mass of Black women. The mass of Black women still have grotesque images and other afflictions to deal with.

Exaggerations have to be corrected, however, and this one seems to have been significantly produced by employment of the patriarchy concept. Black womanist religious scholar Marcia Riggs wrote in *Awake Arise & Act: A Womanist Call for Black Liberation* that one of the calls of Black womanists was the "debunking [of] social myths so as to undermine the black woman's acceptance of sexist oppression [and] the black man's acceptance of patriarchal privilege."[15] Black feminists have written of Black women being abused by Black men with patriarchy and sexism. But when one looks historically at the abuse of Black women in America, one notes that it has come mainly from the hands of white men and white women. In either case, it had to do with *ownership*: Black women were owned as slaves, and white people felt that they owned Black women or had the right to own the consequences of ownership of Black women.

The major reason why white female feminists jettisoned sexism was because they sensed or suspected that it was a form of racism involving the notion of ownership; White men owning them as lovers, wives, and friends. This is one of the fundamental things about racism. Racism is about ownership and the domination of people on the basis of owning them. White women who lived in America during the centuries of slavery saw how white men not only owned Black people, but also how they owned white women. This ownership was not just the legal ownership of Blacks as slaves, it was also mixed with the racist notion of ownership, i.e., with the concept of the racist's victim being thought of as a thing, object, or possession that could be owned.

White female feminists do not want many common images or symbols between themselves and Black women, even Black female feminists. Sexism was one of those words that linked them in terms of ownership. That connection was slashed with the word patriarchy. But now Black female intellectuals use the concept of patriarchy, not realizing the racist motivation and purpose of its initial employment, and certainly not thinking from the framework of the Black historical experience in using it.

Something they would have to explain is how Black slave men could act in a patriarchal manner toward Black slave women or even Black slave children. The Black historical experience makes it very clear that both Black men and Black women experienced a long period of being owned and dominated and that Black children went from ownership and domination as child slaves to adult slaves. This represents a period of two hundred and thirty years of being owned and dominated. Millions of Blacks also endured a second form of servitude that lasted from the 1880s to the 1940s. This took place only sixty years ago. So the question remains: where is the tradition of Black men acting in patriarchal ways or the tradition of Black men as patriarchs? Certainly patriarchs existed in black Africa–from whence came the black slaves–but this was not a cultural ideal and behavioral practice that black Africans could plant and secure in North America. Black chattel slavery, racism, and racist practices prevented this.

There is also the other matter that most Black female intellectuals have yet to discern: white feminists had to pervert the word patriarchy to be able to make use of it the way they have. Historically, the concept meant the practice of powerful men dominating other men and, through them, their families. In each household, husbands related to wives, children, and other household women in maleist/sexist terms. Thus, they dominated, controlled, and even exploited them on the basis of racism and on the assumption that they were "nonhuman" or "subhuman" things, objects, and property, thus, theirs to own. These men wanted to own women so that they could own and control their bodies, more specifically, their wombs. This, they believed, guaranteed the supply of human labor, the most efficient and productive labor there was. Marriage was originally an institution that men established to legally enable them to control women so that they could control their wombs and the human labor that flowed from them. The earliest laws against adultery were laws to prevent the theft of human labor and potential wealth and power.

Clearly, Black history in the United States does not show a significant manifestation of patriarchy. Black men in America have not been powerful enough to dominate and control other Black men and, through them, Black families and households. This was clearly impossible during the centuries of Black chattel slavery. But it was also impossible among nonslave Blacks during these centuries, because no nonslave Black community, North or South, was ever that free of White racism and White racist power and intrusion. In short, White racists would have been totally against a small group of Black men having more power with respect to the Black community than they had. They would have been equally against an effective organization of Black men in a Black community, which patriarchy would have promoted. Black power, in any form, was anathema to White racists. That was true in the seventeenth, eighteenth, and nineteenth centuries, as well as the twentieth century.

There were some Black men who owned Black women because there were some Black slaveholders during the first phase of Black slavery in America. But in general, Black men were not permitted to hold Black people in bondage during the second phase of Black slavery in America. However, during the two phases of Black slavery there were nonslave Blacks and there were Black men who did domestically dominate Black women and even Black families. This did not grow out of, or reflect, patriarchal beliefs, tradition, or practices. And it should be noted that one could also find women playing dominant and/or predominantly strong roles in Black families during this time. A number of things could account for Black male dominance in a Black family during this period: the father/husband had the economic means to be dominant; the father/husband had the physical and emotional power to be dominant; the father/husband had more education, was more cultured, and had an elevated social status in the Black community; or, perhaps, the father/husband was publicly respected and treated decently by white people, which added to his prestige and augmented his dominance in the family.

Traditionally, Black men have dominated Black churches. This was not done as a manifestation of patriarchy, but was related to two other things: a reaction to racism and an expression of racism. Black men found the church to be a place where they could exercise leadership and power that was denied them in the larger society. Black women fully recognized this racist exclusionary reality, and they essentially acquiesced to Black men being the dominant element in the most important Black institution. Many Black male ministers and other Black male church officials also sought to dominate Black churches on the basis of maleist/sexist beliefs and power. When Black women rebelled within Black churches, it was usually against this double expression of racism.

Black male violence against a Black woman in a Black family should not be interpreted in some automatic manner as an expression of patriarchy. It could be a manifestation of displaced aggression, violence, thought, and social behavior that was meant to be directed toward white people, but instead was executed against Black women or others in a Black family or household. Much of "Black-on-Black crime" could be explained in this manner. The Black male or Black father/husband in a Black family or Black household might be motivated by maleism/sexism and would seek domination on this basis. On this basis, he might even engage in violence in order to establish the idea that he owned the wife or other females in the family or household. Alice Walker wrote about such maleism/sexism in her novels *The Third Life of Grange Copeland* and *The Color Purple*, but she located this thought and social behavior not in maleism/sexism, that is, in racism, but in patriarchy. Walker specifically located it in what she believed to be America's patriarchal society, which she saw as the source of racism. However, racism and patriarchy are not synonymous. They exist quite independently of each other and do not have to have any relationship at all, as when men dominate men on the basis of age or by possessing what other men regard as superior wisdom, experience, strength, or courage, or on the basis of an hereditary principle, or by a tradition and practice of patriarchy.

Historically, Black men have held the leadership positions in Black confrontations with, and struggles against, white people. Both Black female feminists and womanists mistakenly note that this historical behavior and its continuation are an expression of patriarchy. Michele Wallace did this in her book *Black Macho*,[16] and bell hooks did this, too, in her book *Yearning*. In particular, hooks noted that "insistence on patriarchal values, on equating black liberation with black men gaining access to male privilege that would enable them to assert power over women, was one of the most significant forces undermining radical struggle."[17] If this were a reference to the struggle of the 1950s and the 1960s, which was a successful struggle, it is hard to see where the internal undermining took place. hooks ignores the fact that many Black women did not consciously seek to challenge Black men for leadership, because they did not want that leadership disorganized, fragmented, and vitiated, and they thought it best at the time—in the throes of intense battle—to keep leadership ranks and Black ranks closed and unified. hooks's comments reflect a leftist and radical fetish, as well as either-or, absolutist thinking. Her comments also reflect her use of a white female feminist intellectual frame to understand a Black situation.

In the past, what were the chances that white men would relate to Black people in confrontations and struggles if Black women led them? The answer is obvious, and Black male patriarchy is not even a consideration; but white male white supremacy/ebonicism/sexism racism is. In recent years, Black women have been exercising a collective public voice. White men and white women are still not readily interested in listening to any Black female public political voice, no matter how loudly it shouts. Black women are now in a position to be public political leaders of Black people and are engaging in this behavior, something that is likely to continue with great vigor and that can be very good for Black people. But they did not always have this option.

SOCIAL CLASS AND GENDER EMPHASIS

But the matter of Black male patriarchy is not something that holds the attention of most Black women, nor even the attention of most Black female intellectuals. Of more concern to these intellectuals is the conceptual and analytical category of social class. This is another leftist and radical fetish that has gained adherents among many Black liberal intellectuals, male and female, and increasingly among Black feminist and Black womanist intellectuals. This is all occurring not just because there are now noticeable social classes among Blacks, but mainly because Black male and female intellectuals of all stripes are seeking to avoid dealing with racism in their historical and social analyses. A very negative consequence of this is that they do not develop an extensive knowledge of racism and do not develop an extensive and effective racist analysis to investigate and analyze Black historical and social realities, and the specific historical and social relationships between Blacks and Whites in this country. This also results in the obscuring and suppressing of these realities.

When gender is employed in a singular or over-emphasized manner this also happens. Black women intellectuals of all kinds are also turning towards gender as concept, subject, and category of analysis and as an analytical device. This growing emphasis can be traced to White feminist thinkers who use the term legitimately, but who also employ a gender analysis to avoid dealing with racism in their various historical and social analyses. Black women intellectuals are employing it this way, too, taking their lead from their white female intellectual counterparts.

Leftist, radical, philosopher, and political activist Angela Davis falls into this category of Black women intellectuals putting an emphasis on social class and gender in their analyses. In an interview with Black philosopher George Yancy, she remarked, "Within the Communist Party U.S.A....there was a continuous struggle to legitimize the leadership of women and to find ways to integrate a gender approach into the class analysis of the party."[18] It has already been shown how the left-right political thinking and continuum are predicated upon maleism/sexism and white supremacy/ebonicism, or a racist metaphysic, that interpenetrated left and right political discussions. Because Davis did not have an effective racist analysis, she didn't realize that the Communist Party U.S.A. had already factored in a "gender approach" that was covered up by the concept of social class and the emphasis on a class analysis.

Men dominated the Communist Party, as Davis noted. But men constitute a gender group, which means that the Party was dominated by men–not by class, which would mean women, too. But, the domination went beyond gender. The male domination of the Party was predicated on maleism/sexism, the basic reason for women being excluded from leadership positions, and the basic reason why Angela Davis could not see the racist character of the domination of the Communist Party: owing to the fact that maleist/sexist racism acted through male gender, invisibilizing it and simultaneously obscuring it by an emphasis on class analysis, which was itself interpenetrated and used by racism to obscure its presence.

When white male Marxists talk of gender relations, they invariably extract them from the social class in which the genders are found and talk about male-female relations as if they have no class context or basis (similar extractions occur in regards to race, ethnic group, or community). This kind of thinking and analysis can be traced to Frederick Engels, specifically to his books *The Condition of the Working Class in England* and *Origin of the Family, Private Property and the State*. In these works, Engels argued that gender was historically and socially conditioned, rather than biologically conditioned. There have been white female Marxist feminists who have applauded him for this observation. But Engels's reference in his books was mainly to female gender, even when he talked about men dominating women and forcing them into a gendered status and into playing a gender role or roles.

Like other philosophers of his time, Engels equated men with social class, and he viewed the class struggle as though only men constituted the social class and were the only people involved in that kind of struggle. His thinking and books did not conceptually and ideologically focus on the "gender struggle" within the class struggle, or on how it affected the class struggle, or on the way European men were endeavoring to make history. White female Marxist feminists do not say that Engels *did not* engage in a class analysis, just that he erroneously equated class with men. And they express objection to his (and other male Marxists's) efforts to make social class the only social division that counts, when there is gender that is also argued to be important. But which gender? Male? Female? Or both? Is a social class made up of only one gender? And if it is, is one still talking about social class? White female Marxists (and other kinds of white female feminist thinkers) seem to think so, the way they write on these matters.

White female feminists have their counterparts among Black female Marxist feminists and other Black female feminists for the simple reason that the latter two groups take their intellectual cues on class and gender from the former two groups. As seen above, Angela Davis wanted to factor in a "gender approach," namely, a female gender approach. Many Black female intellectuals talk about a singular Black female gender approach and analysis. However, there are two genders that appear in all races, ethnic groups, social classes, and other human groupings. American and Western social analysis lacks a significant or sophisticated two-fold gender analysis because such holistic thinking and analysis is generally lacking in both places. Black intellectuals are brought up in a group culture where holistic thinking is historical and is the cultural reality and preference. But a number of Black intellectuals abandon that inculcation, or severely play it down, when they come under White tutelage, seek to get in with white thinkers, or seek to win their favor. These responses are reflected in the Black intellectuals who seek to be classified as "left" or "right," or "radical" or "conservative," which are one-dimensional intellectual/political postures that result, in each instance, in one-dimensional social analysis or analyses. It also results in the singular female gender analysis of social class that Angela Davis wanted done with respect to the Communist Party U.S.A.

BLACK CULTURE AND BLACK GENDERS

One of the main themes of Black women-created dramas and fiction is Black male oppression of Black women. The writing mainly attributes this less to patriarchal beliefs and values (despite what is claimed), than to simple Black male immorality or degeneracy. Portraying Black men in a very negative manner is a staple of Black female drama and fiction. One can find it in Lorraine Hansberry's *A Raisin in the Sun*, Ntozake Shange's *For Colored Girls Who Have Considered Suicide...*, Toni Morrison's *Song of Solomon, Sula,* and *Beloved,* Alice Walker's *The Color Purple*, Gloria Naylor's *The Women of Brewster Place* and Terry McMillan's *Waiting to Exhale*. These negative images are not bound by the social class of the men, as they spread across Black male class statuses. In reference to Black female dramatists and fiction writers projecting negative images of Black men, Michele Wallace wrote in *Invisibility Blues*: "Although it is possible to be critical of the failure of such work to challenge fundamentally mainstream or racist conceptions of black humanity or agency, it is important to observe that so-called 'negative images' will probably be necessary to any kind of reformulation or restructuring of prevailing conceptions of 'race' and 'ethnicity.' They seem particularly necessary to the inauguration of a public black female subjectivity."[19]

This is a faulty argument that is constructed of other faulty arguments Wallace makes in her book. Wallace has stated that presenting "positive" images of Blacks does not "reverse" racism. That may be, but they do not feed it like negative images do. However, Wallace feels that, "not only does reversal, or the notion that Blacks are more likable, more compassionate, smarter, or even 'superior,' not substantially alter racist preconceptions, it also ties Afro-American cultural production to racist ideology in a way that makes the failure to alter it inevitable."[20] Negative images of Black men and women clearly tie Black cultural production to "racist ideology," and will not alter White racist perceptions of Blacks at all. Nor will fanciful, idealistic, or wild depictions of Black men and women.

But the real issue, Wallace argued, had to do with Black cultural production itself, not the "positive" or "negative" images of Black characters or situations. She remarked:

> Who produces Afro-American mass culture, how and for what audience? Can this information be used to distinguish Afro-American popular culture from mass culture? Is the distinction viable? Moreover, how does black audience reception affect the production of mass culture, and is it possible to differentiate black audience reception from a mainstream audience? What relationship do questions of consumption and commodification have to the validity of an Afro-American oppositional avant-garde or the potential for continuing or amplifying Afro-American practices of cultural resistance? How does Afro-American cultural practice incorporate or fail to incorporate feminism, anti-racism, gay

267

liberation and other contemporary critiques and issues such as homelessness and Rainbow Coalition politics?[21]

So in the end Wallace is not really concerned with the images of Black men, or Black women, or Black culture, per se. For someone who does not feel that "positive" images of Black people can alter racism she seems unperturbed by the very political character she invests in Black culture and the very large role she assigns it. Wallace seems to believe that these images of Black people will transform American society. But in what way will negative images of Black women or men aid these projects? How would a "public black female subjectivity" based on negative imagery do this? Can this be achieved by the traditionally grotesque ugly and whore-like images of Black women?

And why is it necessary to present the matter in the first place as one of projecting "positive" or "negative" images of Black people? Why not *realistic* images of Black men, Black women, and Black people in drama, fiction, and in other artistic forms? Black women and men did some realistic things to survive slavery, racism, racist segregation, political and social denial, violence, and constant public humiliation. Is there not something to be said about this? Is there not, in all of this, a great feeling of self and group worth, a great feeling and zest for life and the purpose or purposes of life, and of the redemptive character of life that is viewed from the point of view of individual and group worth, purpose, dedication, sacrifice, struggle, creative or strategic cooperation, and the great determination to be a free people in this country? Why can't Black literary and artistic people tell this story (as a historical and social reality) of real people dealing with their real lives and their *realistic* ways of living them and responding to them?

That kind of realism requires looking at white people and America in realistic ways. It has to be considered simply amazing that Black intellectuals of all kinds, including literary and artistic people, talk and write about Black people as if white people do not exist in America and have nothing to do with their lives. Nobody invisibilizes white people in America more than Black intellectuals do. They also constantly invisibilize America itself. Neither is done on a racist basis, but rather as reactions to White racism. It also represents an unwillingness to, or an inadequate ability to, or a fear of dealing with these matters.

THE INADEQUACY OF CLASS ANALYSIS

Cornel West wrote the following in *Race Matters*: "The fundamental crisis in black America is twofold: too much poverty and too little self-love. The urgent problem of black poverty is primarily due to the distribution of wealth, power, and income-distribution influenced by the racial caste system that denied opportunities to most 'qualified' black people until two decades ago."[22] Nowhere in these comments did he mention white people, especially white men. Who but white men have the combination of great power and great wealth in America? And who primarily determines distribution of these things that affect Black people in all social classes, and thus, the lives and lifestyles of all Black people? Cornel West, bell hooks, Robin Kelley, Joy James, Katie Geneva Cannon and Michele Wallace talk about "commodification," which they all say affects Black people and Black life in America in a crippling manner. But they do not talk about the people primarily responsible for this "commodification" and its effects.

Instead, they place blame on the capitalistic economy or the capitalistic system. But what is that saying? They speak about these things as if they were not made up of people, as if they were *peopleless*, taking their cues, as it were, from Karl Marx (who, not so coincidentally, fashioned the concept of commodification and wrote about the capitalistic system as if it were peopleless, constantly failing to point out and emphasize that the capitalists—certainly the ones he wrote about—were men). Capitalists owned and/or managed the new economic corporations and the new corporate economy that Marx saw emerging in Europe and America. Capitalists did the commodifying. In America, owners and/or managers of these oligopolistic economic corporations and the corporate economy were, and overwhelmingly still are, white men. Thus, it is white men who are primarily responsible for the "market commodification." But why is it that Black intellectuals seldom, if ever, mention this? Commodification is seen as consumption, not as production and distribution. Indeed, it is seen as not having any producers and distributors! Thus, as consumption it lies with the victims of commodification, who then are responsible for it by using it or being slavish toward it. Thus, it is the victim who is to be blamed.

West argues that Blacks (and he usually does not qualify the depiction) are susceptible to their victimization by commodification because of their "nihilistic" predisposition: their lack of self-love, self-esteem, and self-worth and their feelings of self-hatred. If commodification were related to the production and distribution of it, and it was argued that it had deleterious effects upon Blacks, then the "nihilism" could be related to the economic corporate owners and/or managers, who would be overwhelmingly white men. But if commodification is isolated from production and producers and distribution and distributors, then the negative affects of commodification are self-imposed. Thus, Blacks impose this upon themselves because of their alleged "nihilistic" psychological, moral, and spiritual weaknesses, which consumption commodification reinforces in something of a vicious cycle.

West does not seem to realize how much his concept of Black "nihilism" resembles the racist concept of the "mark of oppression" that white racist psychologists made popular decades ago. Many white psychologists are still strongly influenced by this concept, especially when they analyze Black psychological attributes and behavior. Black psychologist Adelbert Jenkins has chastised this racist behavior with criticisms that would apply to Cornel West's conceptualization. He wrote: "The second distortion...is the tendency to describe the psychological functioning of the black American in negative terms. This stems in part from the almost complete lack of interest in studying the effective and constructive aspects of the psychological functioning of black Americans.... Even where the data suggests strengths and capabilities, these traits are often interpreted as defenses to cover up the deficiencies and insecurities that are 'really there underneath.'"[23]

There is also a basic fact about human beings that West ignores too often: human beings do not exist or live outside of culture. That is, human beings always live with ideals, beliefs, and values. They may not be the ideals, beliefs, and values that one likes or would like people to have, but it is the nature of human beings to live by these ideal constructions. In the midst of the hardest "street culture," one would always find people living by ideals, beliefs, values, and certain traditions and customs that give stability and coherence to their inner existences and social lives. Blacks who have not made it in America are not as self-loathsome, despondent, hopeless, directionless, belief-less and value-less as West suggests. As Jesse Jackson says, a large part of the Black poor "work every day," reflecting their self-esteem, self-respect, dedication, and sense of value and purpose in life.

Hence, we are back to the basic point of Black intellectuals not probing deeply into Black history and life to be intellectuals or creative artists. Black history and Black life are very complex, incapable of being adequately or truthfully revealed by absolutist either-or thinking or representations, and still less by single "positive" or "negative" images.

One has to look at Black history, and Black life, and relations among Black people in America in holistic terms. That is the basis for looking at these things in realistic terms and in depicting, or evaluating, Black realistic responses.

Realism, as said, has to take White racists and their afflicted behavior into account, as well, because it has had and still has a direct and indirect impact on Black history and on Black life in the country. Can West's "nihilism" really be explained without associating it with White racists and their own afflictions? He seems to think so, not understanding that the racism, white supremacy/ebonicism, would live on in the "nihilism," as its effects or consequences (i.e., the psychological "condition" of Blacks it had strongly helped to produce and would continue to help perpetuate as long as the "nihilism" lasted). With this in mind, a question emerges: does West's "nihilism" concept make him a Black radical or a Black conservative?

Another manifestation of faulty thinking about social class made by many Black male and female intellectuals is the way they relate social class only to economic matters, that is, to economic skills, opportunities, income, or wealth and all the social benefits that derive from these things. They see the future of Blacks related to social class and social-class determinants, and they see the problems of Blacks in the future related to social class. Black conservatives, as well as many Black liberals, are strong adherents of this view. And of course, Black Marxists think social class is the be-all-and-end-all of social and analytical categories.

The black conservative Orlando Patterson proclaimed in Henry Louis Gates's documentary, "Two Nations of Black America," that America's economic problems were class-based, not racially-based. He then said that these problems affected all Americans, cutting across race, class, and ethnicity and concluded by saying that it was actually "an American problem." This made the matter, then, a national, not a class, problem. For Patterson to say that it was something that cut across race, class, and ethnicity was minimizing the class factor and also vitiating his single-class argument.

However, there are Black feminists who are making the matter a gender, rather than a class, matter for Blacks. If one argues that it is a class matter, then two genders have to be of concern (admittedly, this has not been the concern of Black male analysts of social class who ignore or obscure the Black female gender). Black women intellectuals want to emphasize female gender, but at the expense of Black male gender, and thus, they diminish a class analysis. But this argument always ignores the

271

actual history and social life of America and shows the faulty character of the argument.

Economic benefits in America have always been tied to racism, as the white male racist affirmative action program amply demonstrates. It simultaneously demonstrates the racist-inundated gender equation in regards to economics and its benefits. Would Orlando Patterson, or any other black or Black intellectual, be willing to deny that the white race is wealthier than the black race, or the red race, or the bronze race in America? And if the white race owned all the private property and the black race owned none, would this still be considered *class division* based on ownership of private property, or would it be considered *racial division* based on such ownership? The white race might well own or monopolize public property and the black race might be kept from this kind of ownership, or monopoly, or permitted to have only small amounts of each. Would this be a manifestation of a class division based on the monopoly, or ownership, of public property; or would this be a racial division based on these realities?

Mentioning private or public property is not a necessary reference to social class. A race, a gender group, an age group, or foreigners in a country, and people who are not even part of the local stratification system, could own such property. Automatically and exclusively associating either form of property with social class is absolutist, ahistorical, and absolutist a *priori* thinking. It is also absolutist, ahistorical and ideological to argue that only class struggle occurs in history and society. There is also ethnic group and gender group struggle. Moreover, people also cooperate with each other–individuals, social groups, social institutions, and even social classes–in communities and societies.

From the days of Black chattel slavery Black history shows Black people cooperating and conflicting with white people to resist or to mitigate oppression and to advance themselves. This means that Black people have cooperated with slavery, racism, and racist segregation to do both of these things in their history. These are the kinds of responses that oppressed people are forced to make to oppressors and oppression.

THE DIALECTIC FLOUNDERS

Black womanist and professor of Christian ethics Marcia Riggs exhibits impatience with the entire race-class debate conducted between Black intellectuals. She notes, "to argue whether race or class is more determinative of black life chances today is to engage in a misleading debate." Riggs then insists that;

If one argues that race and class are dialectical factors that have created a complex situation of black oppression, then the following two interrelated (yet distinguishable) issues come to the fore. First, maintaining a race-class dialectic of black oppression presses one to evaluate public policy designed to alleviate the oppression of Blacks.... Second, positing a race-class dialectic exposes the need to examine the meaning and/or role of class within the black community.[24]

Here Riggs is showing an ahistorical and ideological preoccupation with oppression with respect to Blacks. All Blacks in America today are not oppressed, as millions live very well in the country and live in a considerably free manner. Riggs's comments are like the kind made by some Black nationalists, Black liberals, and Black radicals who argue that Blacks have made no progress in America, when nothing could be further from the truth. Riggs also shows a failure to understand how the *dialectic* works. In America, it doesn't work in any significant intellectual or practical manner.

This is precisely the misunderstanding that plagues Black Marxists, with Manning Marable leading the way. An important aspect of Du Bois's socialist analysis was his analysis, using his racist analytical device, to show how white supremacy/ebonicism affected white socialists in their thinking and functioning in America. Du Bois did not regard the Socialist Party as a very progressive party because its racism prevented it from being so. He was convinced that the Socialist Party was essentially a *suppressive* party—especially where Black people were concerned. Thus, when Du Bois began taking up with Lenin's thinking in the 1920s, and in a direct fashion with Karl Marx's thinking in the early 1930s, he was prepared to see that Marx's dialectic and his dialectical concept of history were up against, and were being thwarted by, racism.

In actuality, Du Bois did not like the dialectic. It had philosophical limitations, and long before the 1930s, he had given up on the idea of the inexorable laws of history or historical and social development. He accepted human agency in these processes, albeit with the masses led by an elite. But the inexorable dialectical movement of history—Du Bois thought it too mechanical, deterministic, and inadequate. He wrote to George Streator, a Black Marxist labor leader, that "I am not interested in working out a perfect dogmatic system on the basis of the Marxist brand of Hegelianism."[25] Du Bois believed the dialectic suppressed subjectivity and subjective agency. But he also believed that racism suppressed the historical functioning of the dialectic.

Marxist doctrine projected the proletariat or factory workers as the progressive and even redemptive forces of history. White socialists, white communists, and white factory workers, as Du Bois observed, were all generally saturated with white supremacy/ebonicism, which prevented the functioning of the dialectic. It did so by investing all of these elements with a compulsive racist subjectivity that mitigated, and even blocked, the dialectical, i.e., the "objective" movement of history they were trying to promote in America. Du Bois used the concept "working class," but he usually equated this term with white industrial workers and, owing to what he perceived as its racism, regarded it as a suppressive and even reactionary social class. He saw Western white factory workers joining with the Western big capitalists to promote racism, colonialism, and imperialism around the world, reflecting his insight into the absurd and tragic in human existence. He stated:

> The new colonial theory transferred the reign of commercial privilege and extraordinary profit from the exploitation of the European working class to the exploitation of the backward races under the political domination of Europe. For the purpose of carrying out this idea the European and white American working class was practically invited to share in this new exploitation, and particularly were flattered by popular appeals to their inherent superiority to "Dagoes," "Chinks," "Japs," and "Niggers."[26]

Yet despite such insights, Manning Marable argued that Du Bois wasn't much of a political and social thinker. This had also been the view of Herbert Aptheker, the curator of Du Bois's papers, who felt that Du Bois's idealism prevented him from being a significant thinker or theorist. Aptheker failed to perceive that Du Bois was an idealist and materialist in thought and in interaction. In short, Du Bois was a holistic thinker. This is especially true when compared to Aptheker's own absolutist either-or materialistic thinking. Manning Marable, as indicated in his book *W. E. B. Du Bois*, believed that Marx and Engels were better thinkers than Du Bois was. He argued in his work that Du Bois was getting better as he continued to evolve as a Marxist-Leninist. The irony is that Du Bois was never a Marxist-Leninist at any time. Nor was he even a Marxist, as he was always a *Du Boisian* in his thinking and analyses. Even Aptheker acknowledged this, although he failed to perceive Du Bois's comprehensive thinking and analysis.

Du Bois was a better sociologist than Karl Marx was. He dealt extensively with racism, something Marx knew little about. Marx's economic substructure and his cultural-social superstructure, his broad analytical device, would fit inside of Du Bois's broad analytical device–his White over Black hierarchical social structure and social system–through which he analyzed American history and society.* Du Bois also had a complex intersectional analysis for history and society, which Marx did not have. He used that intersectional analysis, involving a racist, a racial, a social class, and a white male gender analysis in a modular way in writing *Black Reconstruction.* Du Bois's historical sociological study still baffles scholars because of its complex analytical exposition, making it a Du Boisian analysis rather than a Marxist one, as so many individuals have claimed.

Du Bois's Analytical Legacy Ignored

There are Black intellectuals who call upon Du Bois's name and associate themselves with him and his thinking. But the truth is that they don't know much about his thinking and do very little research into his eighty years of writing. (Likewise, they do virtually nothing with Washington's extant record). Most seem not to go beyond the essays "Conservation of the Races," and "The Talented Tenth" and his book, *The Souls of Black Folk.* A few look into his autobiographies, *Dusk of Dawn* and *Autobiography.* However, the intersectional analysis that both Black female and Black male intellectuals follow does not come from Du Bois. Instead, they primarily take it from white female feminist analysts, with the Black male intellectuals usually getting their analysis indirectly through the written and spoken words of Black female intellectuals whom they do not want rebuking them for leaving off a gender analysis. But, as is common place now, they both leave off a racist analysis and racism in their intersectional analyzing, or they minimize their utilization and end up, unlike Du Bois, in doing what is also now common, consequence social analysis.

When racism is ignored, and when a racist analysis is not employed against American history and social life, then the racist interiority of the history and life is made invisible. It is erased from analytical consideration.

---

* This appears in the diagram of the American welfare society on page 124, which was constructed on the basis of Du Bois's explicit and embedded conceptualizations.

And something else is erased and ignored: there is a big difference between a racial, social class, and gender analysis, and a racist analysis. The first three analyses are all predicated on the assumption that the analysis is about human beings. This is not the assumption of the racist analysis, which operates on the basis that racists regard people as being "nonhumans," "subhumans," or "Non-Others" and endeavor to analyze them that way. Thus, this analysis takes history and social life down to the basic or primordial irrationality, pathology, and immorality, i.e., deep abnormality of that life. These are realities that a racial analysis, a social class analysis, or a gender analysis cannot get to, and thus ignores, which results in superficial, ahistorical, unbalanced, and even fanciful, social analyses.

A racist analysis can also be employed to evaluate a racial, social class, gender, or even an ethnic group analysis to see if any or all of them are functioning from racist premises. The other analyses mentioned cannot reach these premises or disclose their own racist orientation because they focus on human beings, not "nonhumans" or "subhumans." In America, a racial, social class, gender, and an ethnic group analysis have all been used and continue to be used consciously and unconsciously to ignore or to erase racism. This results in America's idealism and exalted self-image being emphasized, as if they constituted America's reality.

A white supremacist/ebonicistic racist analysis shows that America has never had a "moral dilemma," as has often been said and as had been proclaimed by sociologist Gunnar Myrdal in his massive book, *The American Dilemma*. A "moral dilemma" requires knowing the difference between good and bad, good and evil, or justice and injustice. It requires the ability to feel guilt, and remorse for negative thoughts and social behavior. As a people, whites have never demonstrated this kind of discernment, guilt, or remorse when interacting with Blacks. In their minds, they were always "guiltless," "innocent," and "non-responsible." And they invariably blamed Black victims. A "moral dilemma" was simply not possible. In addition, because white racists in this country invested their racist beliefs into America's non-racist beliefs, turning them into racist beliefs and further inverting things, immorality became morality, abnormality became normality, pathology became banality, and evil became good. Only a racist analysis can disclose this kind of intertwined and twisted intellectual/psychological/social reality.

WHAT TO DO ABOUT POLITICS?

It might have been hoped that the Black feminists and Black womanists coming onto the scene, in their collective realities, would have come up with something very new for Black intellectuals and Black leaders and other Blacks to think about, which would have been possible for them to do, given the thoughts they were generating. I have in mind the concept of *Black Politics* (and I do not mean *Black American Politics*, as the two are not the same). All Black intellectuals and leaders know about Black American Politics. They all, along with many others (such as Black elected officials, lawyers, church officials, doctors, club women, community activists, labor leaders, cab drivers, local and national Black organizations and institutions), participate in, and contribute to, Black Politics. Yet, none, or not many, have a conscious conceptualization or understanding of this reality. And Black female intellectuals are not helping out in this matter, not even those who call themselves leftists, progressives, and activists.

Black Politics should not be confused with Black political parties. In the late nineteenth and early twentieth centuries there were efforts made to establish formal Black political parties, all of which failed. The same can be said for the 1970s. Independent political parties always have a tough time in America. They are up against two entrenched, powerful, and rich national parties that have massive local, state, and national constituencies, making it extremely difficult to compete with them. A formal Black political party would have an even harder time competing and succeeding. One would think that third parties would have a great appeal for Blacks. But third parties in America have overwhelmingly been white parties with racist orientations. Traditionally, third parties have not sought Black membership; indeed, in many cases they were formed to oppose Blacks through the political system. With respect to political party affiliation and support, Blacks have been left with two choices: the Republican and the Democratic parties.

If one were to look at the historical record, one would see that Black people have tended to be a one-party people. For decades they were members of, or supported, the Republican Party, especially when it was for them, or as Frederick Douglass once said, when it was "the ship and all else the sea." However, the Republican Party became "lily-white" in the early twentieth century, aligning itself with the new and very powerful economic corporate elites and their powerful production and commercial institutions. The Democratic Party had these allies too and picked up more when the depression hit the country and the general economy went down, and still more when state socialism and welfare politics were utilized to resurrect the economy and American life.

Indeed, welfare politics and state socialism became principal ways to finance the American economy by creating aggregate demand. It not only restored American corporations, it gave them permanent government and consumer financial help, both of which could be expanded or contracted, as needed, by government fiscal and spending policies and practices, and by Federal Reserve Bank actions, even by large-scale financial institutions. The Democratic Party hit upon a method of serving the rich by putting large amounts of public money–through fiscal policies and public assistance–into the hands of the American people, who then spent a great deal of it with economic corporations, and the corporate economy (and with mid-sized businesses and industries, and a myriad of professional people in America). This made the rich richer and the middle class affluent.

The Republican Party favored giving large amounts of money directly to the rich and the powerful corporate economic institutions they owned and/or managed. They did this through public assistance and fiscal programs and, when possible, by shifting money from cut or diminished social programs to them. The Democratic Party not only offered Blacks the best deal, but also the only deal. Hence, beginning in 1928, Blacks began to move in numbers to the Democratic Party, making it their sole party by 1936. Since that time, as a people, they have been nailed to this party and engaged in one-party politics.

Today there are Black upper-class and Black middle-class people moving into the Republican Party again, but not many, and not enough so that the white Republican leadership can publicly say that it is no longer exclusive and is becoming diversified. There are white Republicans who are seeking more diversification in the party, but it is a diversification of people who feel and politically think individualistically and who have substantial bank accounts. A number of these Black Republicans benefited from affirmative action, and then subsequently turned against it and this type of aid for Blacks, condemning it right along with white Republicans (who, incidentally, are the greatest promoters of white male racist affirmative action). When Black Republicans condemn affirmative action for Blacks they especially hurt other Black middle-class people, aspiring Black middle-class people, and the Black middle-class itself. Black liberal and Black radical intellectuals and leaders have often roundly chastised Black Republicans for this practice.

Black Politics does not need formal Black political parties, because such parties would not be necessary. Black Politics is politically *internal politics*, the politics that occurs within the Black community, or in general, within the Black social world of America. The people who participate in these politics are Black people only. They are the kind of people referred to earlier in this section, along with the people who are members of and who represent the national Black institutions that function in local Black communities. These would be the elements that would define Black Politics, establish the procedures and the institutions to engage in it, and devise a local community Black Political Agenda (BPA). Various Black communities in a state could collectively gather into a state-wide Black community organization that would define state Black Politics, establish the procedures and institutions to engage in them, and devise a state Black Political Agenda, which could be changed as needed and which would be carried out by united Black communities in each state.

At local and state levels, the Black Political Agenda, or BPA, would have two parts: the politics and the programs that would augment and transform Black communities. Each part would be carried out by Black people and Black American Politics, the politics that would guide the way local Blacks and state-wide Blacks related to the state Democratic and Republican parties (or any party in a state) and to local and county governments, and the state government, to get help in implementing local and state Black Political Agendas. The state BPA would also include the political, economic, educational, and other programs that the Black communities of a state would beseech the national Democratic and Republican parties and the national government to implement on behalf of Blacks in the state to help transform the Black communities therein.

As argued previously, Blacks have to learn to relate to the Democratic and Republican parties more intelligently and flexibly. It is suggested that they learn to swing a community or state-wide vote to candidates of either party (and possibly a third party at the local or state level) that offers them the most for what they seek. Ideally, this would mean voting for local, county, and state officials of either party that seemed the most supportive and helpful towards Black communities. Blacks in a state would vote for the Presidential candidate, or the U.S. Senatorial candidate, or the House of Representative candidate who was perceived to be the most supportive or helpful. Blacks, *remaining in the Democratic Party*, would carry out this new political behavior. They would have a political base, and would also be able to function politically as independent voters.

One thing is clear, the BPA, whether local, state, or national, cannot be the agenda of the Congressional Black Caucus, the NAACP, the Urban League, the Southern Christian Leadership Conference, the National Council of Negro Women, the National Political Congress of Black

Women, or the National Black Feminist Organization. It cannot be the agenda of any current national Black organization. The NAACP and the Urban League are venerable organizations and have been very helpful to Blacks in their existence in this country. They have been on the frontlines in seeking full rights, equality, and freedom for Black people. But these organizations are bi-racial, rather than Black organizations, even if Black people make up most of their leadership and membership. These two organizations continue to issue annual reports on the state of Blacks in America and offer up agendas for action, but neither could be regarded as the BPA.

This Agenda has to be put together by Black people in local communities and states. There certainly could be a national BPA, but that would require the existence of a national Black organization and leadership. There are numerous Black organizations that are national, or purport to be, and that obviously is the problem. What national Black political leadership there is is fragmented, duplicative, and divisive. Thus, they are not conducive to dealing with the larger problem at hand: helping Black people in need, and augmenting and transforming Black communities. A national Black leadership is needed. It would have two sources. Individuals from national Black organizations could be part of it, based on an agreed upon selection process. Other leaders would come from the state community organizations, also based upon an agreed upon selection process. The national organization could then be called the National Black Leadership Council (NBLC), and would draw up a national BPA that would be based on submitted state Black Political Agendas, and that would be implemented by local and state community organizations that would allow for some flexibility in implementation at these levels, and that would also allow for the possibility of modifying, or changing, a national program or prescription as dictated by local or state need.*

* More of this proposed new political program can be found in Appendix II.

It is going to take more than individual initiative and action, and even more than community activities and volunteerism, to help the mass of Black people to transform their lives and communities in this country. There is not likely to be a struggle of the kind experienced in the 1950s and 1960s, unless white people slip back into mephitic public racism and attempt to take the country with them. But with or without a big struggle, there is a great need for national leadership to return to Black life, a national leadership that can work effectively with local and state leaders and organizations to help Blacks in need and Black communities in need.

Black intellectuals like to think of themselves as national leaders. But they are individualistic, atomistically fragmented, and resistant to any kind of political consensus or collective political organizations; and they usually have difficulty maintaining collective intellectual or academic organizations. But even if Black intellectuals were to acquire the consensual political thinking, leadership skills, and organizational unity and strength that is necessary, they would not be very helpful to Black individuals and communities in need of help. At best they would be spokespeople or representatives in this new situation, but not leaders, and certainly not the kind of leaders required for two basic reasons: they would not likely be amenable to letting Blacks in need draw up or help to draw up the Agenda they would want to see implemented, nor would they provide the daily hands-on leadership that Blacks in need and Black communities in need require. Even with a changed posture, Black intellectuals would not be able to significantly get beyond being leaders of Blacks in need from an intellectual and social distance.

FRAGMENTATION OF BLACK WOMEN INTELLECTUALS

Alone, Black women intellectuals or Black women leaders would not be able to provide the local, state, or national leadership suggested. A single gender leadership is neither appropriate, nor workable. The general leadership would have to be double-gendered. But at the moment, Black women intellectuals and Black women leaders provide the same kinds of impediments to this project as their male counterparts do: they are fragmented in both instances, with additional fragmentations occurring between Black activist intellectuals and "traditional" intellectuals, and Black activist leaders and "traditional" Black women leaders.

The main split between Black women intellectuals is the split between those calling themselves *feminists* and those calling themselves *womanists*. The largest category, feminists, emerged from the ranks of what they hoped would be a general feminist movement in America, but which was, in fact, a white supremacist/ebonicistic/sexist-inundated and middle-class white woman's political-social movement. Most Black female feminists separated out of the movement and formed their own feminist groups and national feminist organizations. bell hooks, who attained and still holds an important position among Black feminists, also helped to produce some ambiguities into the very concept of feminism. Black feminist Beverly Guy-Sheftall explained this occurrence when she stated:

> hooks would also help to redefine feminism as a broad political movement to end all forms of domination: "Feminism is not simply a struggle to end male chauvinism or a movement to ensure that women have equal rights with men," hooks wrote, "It is a commitment to eradicating the ideology of domination that permeates Western culture on various levels—sex, race, and class, to name a few—and a commitment to reorganizing U.S. society so that the self-development of people can take precedence over imperialism, economic expansion, and material desires.[27]

Booker T. Washington argued that Blacks on the bottom should have strong materialistic values and desires because they could be motivational and inspirational. Clearly, economic expansion would be of help to such Blacks. And it must be asked: since when are Black people, or any other people in America, subjected to imperialism? What does this amount to? And who constitutes the victims? What can be seen from the comments above, and even more so from her own numerous writings, is that hooks has abandoned a strict feminist posture and has added her socialistic thinking to her feminist thinking to broaden it. However, she doesn't do this to promote feminist objectives. She does this to promote socialist objectives.

Strictly speaking, feminists would be seeking to end male domination, control, and exploitation of their lives. They seek equality with men in American society and a fundamental change in that society that could make all of this possible. But this is not hooks's focus, although it was at one time. hooks, along with some other Black feminists, white feminists, and Black and white male socialists, is trying to keep the democratic socialist ideal alive and to construct a politics around this ideal. hooks and other feminists (Black and white) are seeking to use the Black feminist and the white feminist movements for their socialistic purposes, just as some socialists and other kinds of radicals sought to use the Rainbow Coalition to advance their political ideals and agendas. bell hooks's main interest is not Black women. She is more interested in something called "woman," something abstract, absolute, ahistorical, and transcendental. Her approach is like that of a white female feminist. In general, Black women are not critical to this concept, at least no more critical than white women, Mexican women, African women, or Asian women are. Black feminists like bell hooks could not fit into a Black Politics unless they focused their feminism directly on Black women and on ways to aid and develop their advancement in America.

When Black female feminists join white or other feminists in coalitions to promote a general feminism and seek to represent the interests of Black women (as well as the generality of women in America), they are engaging in an expression of Black American Politics. Black female feminists would not go into the coalition and the Politics as individuals with individualistic motivations or with an individualistically constructed agenda. They would be taking the Black feminist agenda into general feminist organizations and meetings, as defined by Black feminists, and representing and speaking from that stance.

There are Black female feminists who want a sharp line drawn between themselves and white female feminists, and also want that line drawn between themselves and Black female feminists who they regard as being similar to, or replicas of, white female feminists, and those Black female intellectuals who function on an at-large basis, i.e., "radical" Black female intellectuals. These Black female feminists now call themselves *womanists*. Writer, editor and novelist Alice Walker coined the term. In her acclaimed work *In Search of Our Mothers' Gardens*, she noted that the term derives from the oft-heard southern Black woman's refrain to a young black girl: "You acting womanish child." Walker refers to the term as a tool to give Black feminists and other Black women a title that would embrace the historical, cultural, and social experience of Black women, one that was independent of white women and even independent from their similar experiences in this country.

However, the term remains largely underdeveloped, particularly when it comes to the analytical side of a womanist stance. It is Patricia Hill Collins's view that Walker's womanist concept has "two seemingly contradictory meanings." On the one hand, she noted that

> Walker suggests that Black women's concrete history fosters a womanist worldview accessible primarily and perhaps exclusively to African American women. Womanish girls acted in outrageous, courageous, and willful ways, using attributes that freed them from

the conventions long limiting white women. Womanish girls wanted to know more.... They were responsible, in charge, and serious.

On the other hand, Walker aspires to a universal meaning of womanist that transcends particular histories, including that of African-American women. Walker sees womanists as being "traditionally universalist," a philosophy invoked by her metaphor of the garden, where room exists for all flowers to bloom equally and differently.[28]

It seems to me that Walker is not thinking and writing in a contradictory or illogical fashion, but in a holistic manner typical of Black thinking. And it also seems clear that this is what her metaphor of the garden of different flowers, each flowering abundantly, stands for. Moreover, there is a certain amount of generalizing about women and the experience of women that can be done from a particular group experience. This is quite legitimate, including the legitimacy of making recommendations to other women about what they can do to change, improve, or enhance their lives, with the right of other women to refuse those proffers. What makes something universal is not simply its abstract formulation, but its wide acceptance and implementation.

What white female feminists still do, even though they have been criticized for it, is to regard the historical and social experience of white women as the paradigm of the female experience and continually suggest that this is the female experience, the model for it, and the sole explanation for it. This is not what Walker does. But generalizing that is not done carefully can lead to extremism in thought, even sexist thinking. Indeed, Walker trudges close to this boundary line and threatens to cross over it when she talks about Black women being "superior" to white women. She means it, in some ways, culturally, and as attributes that Black women have attained from experience, and not as an inherent superiority. But there is considerable romanticism involved in this womanist conception and standpoint, one that counsels caution and vigilance in construction and use.

For Walker, another function of the womanist concept was to give Black female intellectuals and other Black women a voice within Black nationalist rhetoric, which was previously dominated by Black men and which, more often than not, focused on the historical and social experiences of Black men and Black male literary figures and artists. As said before, Black nationalism was primarily racial thought, not nationalist thought. If and when womanists come to this realization, they will be facing another one: they have to conclude whether or not Blacks are a racial or an ethnic group in the United States.

The Blackcentric view is that they are an ethnic group of the black race. And if Black Womanists accept that perspective, they then have to arrive at the understanding that Black women are not the only ones who can speak to the experience of Black women in America, even if they can do it better than anyone else. Black men can speak to that experience, as well, just as Black women can speak to the Black male socio-historical experience. In short, Black womanists cannot genderize Black history in a singular manner, nor can Black female feminists–the way they both argue Black men have done. Alice Walker and other Black womanists claim that they seek reconciliation between Black men and women of different sexual preferences.

Geneva Smitherman agrees. She sees womanists concerning themselves with helping Blacks as a collectivity. She writes that the term womanist refers to an "African-American woman who is rooted in the Black community and committed to the development of herself and the entire community."[29] Like many have argued, and continue to argue, Black womanist Shirley Williams adds that Black female feminists, like their white counterparts, are considerably anti-male. If this is the case, this would be an instance of single genderizing with respect to Black history and Black life and it could only provoke hostility and a serious division between Black men and Black women, and thus, Black people.

WHAT IS THE BLACK COMMUNITY?

Hostility and division between Black men and Black women and rips in the Black community can be aggravated or encouraged by the way Black men and Black women write Black history. Historical knowledge is critical to the functioning of historical groups like Black Americans. Where they have been, what they are doing, or where they might be heading is fundamentally a historical question that requires an historical answer. What Black history is becomes a crucial question. The historical answer to it is that Black history is not the history of the black race in America, which would *include* Blacks, *but also* black West Indians, black Hispanics, and nowadays (in a more limited manner) the various black Africans who live in this country. This would raise the next historical question: what is the Black community, as opposed to the black community?

Is there such a thing as a black community? Has there ever been one in America? The answer to that is, yes! Early in Black history members of the black race were posited here as black slaves, which produced a black slave community in the English colonies. By the eighteenth century, these first black people were evolving into an *ethnic* community that could trace its lineage from the black African slaves and their Black progeny. Other arriving black people had to make history with these Black people, because white people lumped all black people together on the basis of a racist view of the black race and also by a myriad of racist practices.* So we are back to those germane questions posed previously: who are Black people? What is Black history? What or who is the Black community?

Marcia Riggs has provided an answer to the latter, which, when examined, is more problematic than she might have thought. She stated:

> What do I mean by the term "black community?" From a sociological perspective, there are two general definitions of community: a "territorial" or "ecological" usage and a "relational" or "socio-psychological" one. Although case studies of particular territorial (geographical) black communities will provide significant empirical evidence for this analysis, the primary meaning of black community in this discussion is relational or socio-psychological. This definition holds that blacks as a group in the United States share a common identity and have "special claims on each other."[30]

As can be seen, Riggs used the word black and Black interchangeably, not recognizing that one was a reference to race and the other to ethnicity. Indeed, she evidenced no recognition of, or reference to, the category of ethnicity, or ethnic group, or ethnic community at all. She regarded Black people to be just a racial group and lumped them in with all black people in America. But can it be said, as Riggs does, that all black people in America share only a common racial identity, particularly when there is a plethora of black ethnic groups in the country, including the largest among them, the Black people? Do Black people, black Jamaicans, black Trinidadians, or black Nigerians have "special claims on each other?"

---

* For instance, the Marcus Garvey movement showed the reality of Black people and their relation to various black people in the country. The hostility that existed between the different black people then still exists today and, indeed, it is sharper.

Riggs failed to see that race, ethnicity, and community are all historical categories. But this is a common failure among Black intellectuals, male or female, feminists or womanists. Black history shows that Black people evolved from a racial group to an ethnic group, a racial community to an ethnic community. A careful study of history shows that Black people are different from other black people in this country and that those differences were multiplied over the twentieth century when a myriad of black people took up residence in the United States. What's more, these differences continued intact into the twenty-first century.

Like Riggs, Black feminist historian Evelyn Brooks Higginbotham evidences no understanding of this concept. Or perhaps her viewpoint is fueled by simple indifference to these historical and sociological realities. In an article published in a Black woman's reader titled, *We Specialize in the Wholly Impossible*, she wrote: "We should challenge both the overdeterminancy of race *vis-à-vis* social relations among blacks themselves and conceptions of the black community as harmonious and monolithic. The historic reality of racial conflict in America has tended to devalue and discourage attention to gender conflict within black communities and to tensions of class or sexuality among black women."[31]

As seen, Higginbotham does not deal with the Black community as being something distinctive in American history and life, and thus, she does not see how Black people and the myriad of black ethnic groups in the country relate to the question of the "harmonious and monolithic character" of the black community. She seems to be primarily concerned with "gender relations" and "gender conflicts" in the Black community. She wants to focus more attention on the conflict between Black men and women in Black history, than upon the cooperation between them in that history. This cooperation was a major reason why Blacks in America survived, developed, and made progress as a people. It is the reason why they were able to struggle as successfully for freedom as they have in this country. Deep and widespread conflict between Black men and women, over the history of Black people in this country, would have made all of the above things "wholly impossible!"

THE ROLE OF BLACK WOMEN'S HISTORY

Like so many Black feminist historians, Evelyn Higginbotham wants to project the role of Black women into Black history. She, like other such historians, has argued that Black male historians have suppressed this knowledge and understanding. This is also the view of Darlene Clark

Hine, Nell Painter, Deborah Gray White, Bettye Gardner, and others. And it is the stated purpose of these Black feminist historians to, as they see it, "correct" the writing of Black history and to talk clearly and at length about the role that Black women have played in Black history (as I understand that history). This is, of course, a legitimate and necessary thing to do. But the interest and effort to do so should be based on the most accurate understanding of Black history and Black historical writing.

Black feminist historians have exaggerated and continue to exaggerate the way Black men have written exclusionary history, leaving Black women out of their historical accounts. Much of the historical writing by Black male historians was writing done that did not make distinctions between Black men and Black women. Until recent times, discussions of slavery were usually about Black slaves in general; they were discussions on how both male and female slaves were subject to slave law, slave punishment, slave diet, denial of education, and other slave conditions. This kind of discussion has also characterized much of the writing on Blacks as nonslaves in America.

What did occur in a pronounced manner was that when there was a reference to gender in Black historical writing, it was usually a reference to the Black male gender, and biographies were usually of Black men. If there was any singling out of a stellar performance or significant contribution, it would be those of Black men, although individual Black women like Phyllis Wheatley, Sojourner Truth, Harriet Tubman, Ida B. Wells-Barnett, Mary Church Terrell, and Mary McLeod Bethune, and their individual achievements, were written on by Black male historians as well.

It simply cannot be said, as many Black feminist historians and other kinds of Black and black female intellectuals have said, mainly by implication, rather than explicit argument, that Black male historians wrote only male genderized history. That is, what I would call *Black malestory*. On the other hand, there are Black women historians, feminists and others, who are consciously writing Black female genderized history, which has been described as *Black herstory*. Darlene Clark Hine, a prominent Black female historian, does this. Indeed, she is a leader in the field of Black herstory. She once wrote: "Black women's history is just beginning to emerge as a vital area within women's and Afro-American history, and much work remains to be done."[32] She is doing her part, and she is encouraging other Black female historians to do the same.

Yet, Black herstory has caused some hostility among Black male historians and other Black male intellectuals. Nell Painter has referred to this situation, while also expressing her regret for its occurrence. She has stated:

The indisposition to see black women's history as a legitimate field is weakening considerably, and today black women's history is seldom seen as undermining essential black unity. Yet some recent writing includes passages that seem to pit black women against black men in a contest for the claim of the most oppressed. Even now, concentration on the history of black women is sometimes seen as a veiled attack on black men, or on "the black man." This is regrettable, because men and women are neither at war nor identical entities.[33]

Black men and Black women have had similar and different histories in America, within Black history itself, and within the larger American history. This is the holistic view, requiring holistic historiography. Learning more about the way Black women have made history in this country will advance the holistic perspective and historiography. And integrative Black historical writing can also augment this knowledge. Bettye Gardner, for instance, is an advocate of Black herstory and also favors Black integrative history. She has said: "There are presently a number of black women working in the area of black women's history who can be contacted to serve as consultants and resource persons in regard to the teaching of black women's history as well as the integration of that history into Afro-American history courses."[34] Integrative Black histories would be holistic and could then be called *Black ourstory*. But I would regard *Black ourstory* to refer to Black people only, which does not preclude discussing how people outside of that group and that history related to it or even how they made contributions to it.

Now *Black ourstory* obviously has more good portent for the matter of political and social unity among Black men and Black women and the Black community. Single-gender Black historical writing can be very divisive. Its divisive character can be minimized if there is an understanding by those engaged in it that they are seeking to contribute to the larger Black history in America, or Black ourstory, as described. It is presently easier for Black male historians to write an integrative Black history, which is occurring, although there are Black female historians also doing this, too.

There is also the urge to "center" Black female history in Black history. The process of centering is not about being integrative, or about how both Black men and Black women have made and contributed to Black history. Rather, it is about showing how only or mainly Black women have contributed to and have made Black history. There are those Black female historians who talk about "centering" Black women's history in the larger American history and talk of Black woman's involvement in that history and their contribution to it as a means of reinterpreting that larger history. Darlene Clark Hine has expressed this interest, seeing her specialized work in Black female history leading up to that effort, and has noted that this is: "the building, excavating, and boundary-crossing essential to centering Black women in American history."[35]

Thirty-seven years before Hine made this remark, John Hope Franklin had argued that Black history could be centered in American history, so that the role that Blacks had played in it would be made clear and it would provide a basis for profoundly reinterpreting American history. From 1947 onwards, there have been Black male historians who have repeated that view, such as Benjamin Quarles, Vincent Harding, Nathan Huggins, and Thomas Holt. Yet no Black historian, male or female, has even undertaken this kind of historical scholarship, save for the small expression of it in writing about Blacks during the Reconstruction period after the mid-nineteenth century war, and the effort made by Nell Painter with her book *Standing at Armageddon*, which focused on American history between the late nineteenth and early twentieth centuries. But Painter made no effort to employ Black history as a basis for interpreting or reinterpreting this larger history which, in any case, would have required the inclusion of more Black history than she provided in her book.

Black historians usually shun writing on the larger American history, leaving it to white male historians. This illustrates that the interest to use Black history as a basis for reinterpreting or reconstructing American history continues to remain as essentially talk. Yet it has to be observed that when projecting this interest Black male historians do not phrase the matter in terms of centering Black male history and using that as the basis for reinterpretation. Darlene Clark Hine's interest, however, was to center what she considered the restricted Black women's history and employ it for reinterpretive purposes. She did not qualify this interest by saying that Black men were also at the center of American history, which they were, but that she was just going to focus on Black women. This conveys the impression that Hine feels that the history of Black women is more critical to understanding American history than the history of Black men is. It also suggests that Black women contributed more, sacrificed more, or suffered more throughout it. If that were not the impression that Hine was trying to provide, it was one that she nevertheless did. And it is the type of thing that provokes hostility between Black male and female historians and other kinds of Black male and female intellectuals.

Black women historians also have another matter that they have to attend to with respect to writing Black history, and in regard to its impact on Black male-female relations and their stability, and the unity or disunity of the Black community. Black womanists, including Black womanist historians, seem more interested in the Black community and wish to look at Black male-female relationships in this larger contextual framework. They see this framework as affecting or impacting these relationships. The division between Black feminists and Black womanists presages different ways of looking at Black history. When looking at Black history and Black life in America, Black feminists, including Black feminist historians, seem to be mainly interested in the relationship between Black men and women, particularly the power dimensions of this relationship. This means they look upon Black history and Black life in a dichotomous manner, seeing Black men and Black women as competitors for space and activity in Black history and the larger American history.

The Black feminists, including Black feminist historians, are showing the impact of white female feminist thinkers on their own thoughts and interests when they concentrate their analysis on this dichotomy. Writing Black history from the perspective of white female feminists can only amount to a serious distortion of Black history and Black male and Black female relationships. This would essentially be the case even if they modified some of the white feminists concepts and analytical categories, such as the concepts of "patriarchy," "working class," "male dominance" and "female dependency."

On the other hand, Black womanist historians are attached to a crippling Black nationalist ideology and also do not have a consistent or developed view of Black community, which they say they wish to make the focus of their historical writing. They show confusion about whether the Black community is a reality, inasmuch as they consistently confuse it with the black community, and show an even greater confusion when they speak of the "Afro-American" or the "African American" community. But this is also confusion presented by Black feminist historians and a host of Black male historians as well. These are matters that all have to be dealt with and cleared up, along with the difficulties that currently prevail around the subject of Black men and Black women in Black history and American history.

WOMANISTS AND THE AFRICANCENTRISTS

There are Black womanists who flirt with fostering these kinds of divisions in another way without realizing it and, in fact, seem to believe that they are promoting Black female-Black male unity and the unity of what I call the Black ethnic group and Black ethnic community. These are Black womanists seeking to work out a reconciled relationship between the Black womanist viewpoint and the Africancentrist viewpoint. They see this as difficult to do because they believe that Africancentrism is considerably, if not fundamentally, maleist/sexist.

It is interesting that womanist theologians are the ones mainly seeking this rapprochement. Delores Williams, for instance, is part of this group. She asserted that "serious problems plague Asante's Afrocentric vision of male-female relationships. First, it is thoroughly sexist. He apparently adheres to white Western patriarchy's ways of depicting women as either queens, goddesses, or temptresses."[36] Williams was also critical of his wife, Kariamu Welsh Asante, for accepting this sexism.

Theologian Cheryl Sanders argued that some Africancentrists would reject the womanist concept entirely. She said: "one would expect some Afrocentrists to dismiss the womanist concept and to devalue the history of African American female leadership, as having only marginal significance as witness to the spirit, history, and transformative power of Afrocentrism."[37] Womanist theologian Lorraine Cummings said, "The Afrocentrists present the African American male perspective, which too often defines African American women in traditional roles." But on the other hand, she insisted that "womanism and Afrocentrism" were compatible, because both "focus on our heritage, legacy, and cultural richness."[38] This was also the view of theologian Cheryl Townsend Gilkes, who said "the term *Afrocentric*...signifie[d] a commitment to standing in the middle of the black experience, either in the United States or in Africa or worldwide, and starting one's thinking there,"[39] which is her concept of the womanist viewpoint.

But Gilkes also shows confusion in her understanding of the differences between Africancentrism and what I call Blackcentricity. She would regard them to be one and the same. Indeed, she insisted that all Black thought in America was "Africancentric," going back to its earliest expressions in the country and up to the present day when a name appeared for it. She remarked: "And so Afrocentricity becomes, as we name it now, part of a large idea and strategy which is actually old in our community. I think one can say the Afrocentric idea existed among those slaves who told missionaries and others who wanted to know about black folks, to talk to the folks who have lived it."[40]

Black slaves were hardly Afrocentric, Africancentrist, or Africancentric, but they, as they evolved, were the ones who devised Blackcentricity in thinking, culture, and social life, as incoming black African slaves found out. Womanist thought shows a strong Black nationalist orientation, and it shows that most of them view Black nationalism and Afrocentrism or Africancentrism as equivalents, which seems to be an unconscious way to hold onto romantic Black nationalist thought. And womanist theologians show a lack of critical thinking when they see the compatibility of the womanist and Africancentrist viewpoint simply because both focus on the black African cultural legacy and richness. Womanist theologians, for instance, seem not to realize that the Africancentrists and the Kemetologists are very critical of Black and white Christians, because neither wishes to deal with the ancient Kemetic religion's impact on the development of Christianity. That impact, as well as something of the impact of Kemetic religion on Judaism, is discussed further in Appendix I.

Womanist theologians and other womanists who seek to link with Africancentrists have not only to consider specific links, but they should also question the relationship of Africancentrism to the Black experience in America. Africancentrism, as it is presently conceived, structured, and implemented by most of its advocates, is an absolutist, all-embracing philosophical and analytical perspective that could function to crush, suppress, or obscure the Black experience in America.

In general, Black women live very differently from black African women, and there are ways that black African men relate to black African women that would never be accepted by Black women in this country, which neither religious beliefs, moral chants, or traditional chants would induce them to accept. Womanists, theological or secular, are concerned about the kinds of education that Black children receive in schools, while Africancentrists wish to duplicate black African life in the United States. But typically African life favors men and deprecates and subordinates women (notwithstanding African Queens, women of royalty, matrilineal descent–which, incidentally, leads to men ascending the throne, not women–or the few female African warriors). European countries had queens and women of royalty and women were still dominated, controlled, and exploited in Europe. Some Russian women fought in uniformed military units during the First World War and some Soviet women did so during the Second World War, yet they still did not have full rights in these two countries.

What Black children learn about Africa, about Black history and life, about their own life and relationships in the Black social world in America, and in the rest of the Western world is critical. Black education that is Blackcentric, that reaches out to Africancentricity and Africa, and America and Western history and life—a Black-centered, holistic approach—will provide them with this critical education and will keep them centered, balanced, and directional. To have a sense of where one is going is also the function of Black Politics. Black female intellectuals are part of Black Politics and are presently contributing to it by trying to help recast Black male and Black female relationships, by raising broad issues for the Black community to consider, and by trying to use well-researched and well-written history to give the community the reality and wisdom of Black history as a guide to political behavior. This is Blackcentricity at work. Conscious and diligent efforts to develop this intellectual/analytical perspective must be endorsed by both male and female intellectuals. A deeper examination of the Black experience in America–including Blacks's interaction with Whites–is critical to forming and implementing Black Politics and to helping Blacks engage imaginatively and resourcefully in Black American Politics and in their pursuit of full freedom within this country.

Chapter Seven

Conclusion

Admittedly, this book was hard-hitting. This was one of the criticisms leveled against Harold Cruse and his book, *The Crisis of the Negro Intellectual.* He and his work were also accused of being divisive, of being "unfair" to Black intellectuals, Black leaders, and Black activists, and of "betrayal"—of "airing Black linen" for Whites to see. This was an inappropriate complaint because Cruse was more concerned with "airing Black Linen" for Black intellectuals and other Blacks to see. He intended his book to be hard-hitting because he sought to jerk Black intellectuals, leaders, and others from what he regarded as their wrong-headed thinking and political behavior; namely, Cruse felt that they weren't trying to develop Black people as a people in America, especially along ethnic, community, aesthetic cultural, and economic lines. He felt that there was an alternative to merely asking Black people to focus only on integration and on being "Americans" with rights.

I was not interested in putting Cruse's book and thoughts under evaluation as a kind of review. As this book has shown, I was more concerned with what Black intellectuals were thinking and doing now: how they were thinking about Black people, Black life, about Blacks in need in America, about Black history, American history, life, and politics, and about what Black intellectuals were saying about Black people and their relationship to black Africa, and other black people. For the same reason that Cruse was, I was hard-hitting on these matters in an attempt to snap Black and black intellectuals out of certain intellectual and political modes—out of what I regard as their "comfort grooves" in functioning as intellectuals in America that led to inadequate thinking and analyses. Cruse could have used this term himself because the idea of the intellectual "comfort groove" was something he was also talking about. To Cruse, Black intellectuals, politicians, and others were in the comfort groove of integration, which had been made possible by essentially avoiding the discomforting realities of Black history and Black life and by not being very critical of white people in the way they made history and functioned in America. More pejoratively for Cruse, they let white intellectuals and other whites lead them in their intellectual and political behavior. To him, this assured a less critical exegesis or more belligerent political behavior. In Cruse's time, many Black intellectuals and leaders were against Black Power; it made them uncomfortable and made Whites even more uncomfortable.

THE "CULTURAL WARS"

Encouraged to some extent by Cruse's book, and the White racist reaction that obstructed and retarded integration and its benefits, and the White racist effort made to take away Black gains and the development of Black life over the past three decades, today's Black intellectuals spend a great deal of time writing and talking about Black history, Black culture (especially Black aesthetic culture), and Black social life. They also spend time writing and talking about the relationship of Black people to black Africa and other black people, especially about the relationship of Black people to what is called the "Black" or "African Diaspora:" the area from West Africa, to England, to the Western Hemisphere and that is also often referred to as the "Black Atlantic" or the "Black World." This is similar to what former black African, black West Indian, and Asian colonized people did. As they fought against their colonizers and the culture they had imposed on them, they turned to their past and their traditions, their colonial pre-history and lives. They began focusing great attention on them to get their historical and cultural bearings, to strengthen historical/traditional identities, to have stability in transition from colonialism to independence, and for the purpose of trying to use the past and traditional life as bases for constructing societies in newly independent countries. This would give rise to what is now called post-colonial thought and studies and also to "cultural studies."

Black Studies occurred among Blacks when Blacks discovered the limitations to integration, namely the continuing White racist resistance against it and the subtle ways in which this resistance was expressed. This subtle racism weakened or destroyed some Black institutions. Hence, Black intellectuals began to focus on Black history and Black life in America. This resulted in Blacks taking their liberation struggle to college and university campuses and launching what would later be called "the cultural wars." In time the cultural wars would take on other forms and involve other people. But in those days (the late 1960s and throughout the

1970s), Black intellectuals and other Blacks were interested in *Black Power* and were attempting to make it a theoretical and practical force in America.

A combination of White racist reaction and the fear that some Black leaders and Black intellectuals had of Black Power, and the cultural and social gains of a number of Blacks, brought an end to Black Power theorizing and political application, although Black Studies or African Studies programs on college and university campuses were manifestations of Black Power, an institutionalized power. This power solidified when a program was converted into a department with curriculum development and staff-hiring capabilities. In either form, this was Black Power within the context of institutionalized White racist power. In its functioning, this broader context would squeeze from or severely pare down the power orientation of the Black Studies and African Studies programs and departments and would force them into an essentially academic mold, where they presently exist.

However, this proved a boost to these programs and departments, because they had to develop a stronger academic orientation, which had to be their chief justification for being on college and university campuses. This restored the power dimension of the studies programs or departments to some extent. But the academic success and orientations of the programs and departments, and also the "cultural wars," contributed to the production of the comfort grooves of Black scholars and other Black intellectuals. Numerous Black scholars and other kinds of Black intellectuals were now able to talk in an "expert" manner about Black history, culture, and social life. There was also a concomitant growth of interest on the part of Whites to learn more about these things. White intellectuals even created a category of "organic intellectuals" to give special status to some of these Black intellectuals, those who they regarded as being particularly knowledgeable about Black history and life, who were also content to stay confined to those areas and who would not employ this knowledge as a means to provide a critical evaluation of white people: their history and social life in the country; particularly how their centuries-old perpetration of racism had affected them and the country. The "organic" label was mainly penned on Black male intellectuals, but some Black women intellectuals received the label as well.

There are Black intellectuals who would reject the organic intellectual label, but who believe that they are such intellectuals anyway. These are the Africancentrists who show variation within, but who all think that they speak as the most authentic and representative voice of Black people. This is the comfort groove of such intellectuals, but it is at the same time, a false viewpoint. Africancentrists are essentially in flight from Black people. They look upon Black people in America to be black Africans, that is, Africans in a different time and space. They argue that Black history, culture, and social life are black African history, culture, and social life in a different time and space. This pits the Africancentrists against other Black intellectuals and produces a mini "culture war" among them, which is currently taking place, to some extent, on college and university campuses, but mainly takes place in scholarly or political publications that rock the comfort groove of both groups.

SKIMMING THE BLACK EXPERIENCE

My book is decidedly against the Black intellectual comfort groove. In my view, it makes such intellectuals intellectually complacent and parochial and keeps them from becoming the critical intellectuals they are capable of becoming and ones that Blacks and America currently need. This includes both Black male and Black female intellectuals. Given the history of Black people in America, they have a human experience that cries out for an illustrious critical excavation. It is an experience that provides the opportunity to develop profound thought: political and social philosophies, political theories, moral theories, profound sociological and psychological analyses, and profound discussions about oppression and the human responses to it. It is the experience that provides the possibility to present a deep historical analysis of America and of white people and the history they have made in this country, and specifically the relationship they have had with Blacks in this country, which has always been predicated on their racist afflictions.

The Black experience has the legitimate capacity to be the great or ultimate judge of the validity of all the sublime images that white historians, and other white intellectuals and other white people throw out about America: about it being liberal, democratic, Christian, progressive, open, a just society, and free society. The Black experience needs profound translation by Black intellectuals. But Black intellectuals, for the most part, have fled a deep intellectual penetration into the Black experience. Most do no more than skim it, which inevitably leads to inadequate analyses and presentations. Indeed, there is a good deal of romanticizing about Black history and Black life in America done by Black historians and other Black intellectuals that distorts, suppresses, or obscures knowledge about that history and life.

THE NATIONALIST CONFUSION

Black nationalism continues to be misunderstood by most Black intellectuals who employ that phrase or engage in that kind of discussion. Invariably, their discussion is about the black race and the black racial community in America as they live and function in America. These are not discussions about Blacks seeking to build a separate country on the American continent, and they are certainly not about Blacks migrating from the country to go to black countries, to live and to try to build up such countries. These are expressions of Black nationalism and the two forms it has taken in Black history, but mainly as intellectual or ideological expressions and not as practical activities. Simple discussions about Black people or the Black community–about Black culture, institutions, social life, or social relations–are not discussions about, or even relate to, nationalism or nation-state building. Many Black intellectuals are in the grip of the Black nationalist rhetoric and ideology. They are thus in the grip of romanticism and have a semi-critical presentation at best, which is their comfort groove, and which I critiqued extensively in this book.

DETACHING BLACKS FROM WHITE RACISM

The comfort groove of most Black intellectuals in America is to avoid dealing with white people, except in the most peripheral manner. This also leads to not dealing extensively with American history and American society, and thus, gaining a more critical perspective on Black history and life. The result is that Whites and America go essentially unevaluated by Black intellectuals who have the basis–the Black experience and even the personal involvement necessary–to provide the best of these evaluations. In turn, they essentially detach Black people from American history, from American society, and from Whites functioning as racists, including the way Whites's racist beliefs and social practices have impacted them in America. These impairments are the basis on which they relate to Blacks. Thus, Black intellectuals consistently write about Black people as if they lived in a vacuum in America, which leads to the inevitable conclusions that white racists certainly draw: Black people are solely responsible for their own situation in this country. White people have nothing to do with it. White people are "guiltless," "innocent," and "non-responsible." These are long-standing White racist delusional self-images in America. And Black writing that abstracts Blacks from American history, society, and White racist behavior feeds these images and the deluded and fanciful thinking of whites.

Inadequate Racist Analysis

The Black intellectuals who epitomize this kind of abstracted thinking and abstracted writing are the Black conservative intellectuals. Indeed, most of them function as surrogate intellectuals for the subtle white racists of America. In general, these intellectuals consciously and deliberately ignore, or severely play down, the racist history and racism of white people. They not only do this, but they also seemingly have no knowledge of the long-standing white male racist affirmative action program in America. The only affirmative action program they know about, write about, and always condemn is the one in the white racists's minds (and in their own minds) and the one that has been "established" for Black people and that allegedly "privileges" them. Ignoring white people, or ignoring or playing down White racism, and pouncing hard and negatively on Black intellectuals, Black leaders, and masses of Black people is the comfort groove of Black conservative intellectuals. Black liberals and Black radicals contest them, but this is mainly for show, because intellectuals among these two groups are similar to the Black conservative intellectuals in various ways.

Like Black conservative intellectuals, Black radical and Black liberal intellectuals show a confused understanding of race and racism. Like their conservative adversaries, they do not have much of a racist analysis, and thus, they do not (and, indeed, cannot) extensively engage in this kind of analysis. Therefore they do not evaluate the impact of racism on the racist perpetrators, without which there can be no significant evaluation of White-Black relations in this country. Black conservative, liberal, and radical intellectuals are all mainly concerned about aiding the Black *individual* in America, but not the Black *community*. The only difference is that they disagree on how that should be done.

Black female intellectuals exhibit the same kind of intellectual inhibitions and practices as the other groups. They too lack a significant racist analysis. Further still, they have joined with their white female counterparts to propose a broad intersectional analysis, a line of thinking actually taken from these counterparts. Consequently, they have not made an effort to develop a racist analysis and do not have one, or a significant one, as part of their intersectional analysis. They usually combine gender and social class. This means that they join most Black intellectuals, and white intellectuals, who write about Black history, culture, or social life and Black-White relations without a racist analysis, or at least without a significant one. Again, this results in writing about Black people as if they live in a vacuum in America and as if their existence in this country can be explained by just their own thoughts and social behavior. Black women intellectuals, and this includes Black womanists, are like the general run of Black male intellectuals who avoid plunging into the depths of Black history and the Black experience to be intellectuals in America. Inadequate thinking and analyses result.

THE DU BOISIAN IN ME

Harold Cruse's writing style in *The Crisis of the Negro Intellectual* was crisp, direct, and tonal. This alone turned a number of Black and white readers off; his writing style became a way to criticize him and his book without dealing with what he had to say and why he did so. My style in this book generally fell in this area, but it also included a person's thoughts in a full enough manner to disclose and critique them. This meant that I gave some positions a sharp reading. But this is what critical thinking and critical analysis is about. I have no interest in criticism-for-criticism's sake, or knowledge-for-knowledge's sake, or even truth-for-truth's sake, for that matter. I am a Du Boisian scholar, specifically a historical sociologist, which Du Bois also was. Du Bois was also a socialist, which I am not. He became, at the very close of his life, a card-carrying communist, but no more than that, and mainly to defy the United States Government by suiting up and also to get back at Black middle-class people who were not supportive of him in the last years of his life—when he had been supportive of such people for decades—and when he was doing battle with the U.S. government. While Du Bois is touted by Black intellectuals, not many have made a thorough effort to work over his vast corpus of writings to explain him as a Black and American—or as a Western—intellectual, even though this corpus has been collected and is in print. Du Bois was the best analyst of racism in his day. But today's Black intellectuals virtually ignore what he had to say about racism, which he saw in a more complicated manner than most Black intellectuals today have understood it to be.

301

WASHINGTON AND DU BOIS AGAIN

I also took Black intellectuals to task about their treatment of Booker T. Washington. The neglect of the Tuskegean by such people has not only been awesome, but in my view, reprehensible. Washington was a gargantuan leader and was widely and deeply loved and respected by Black people. He was also one of the early modernization leaders that would become commonplace toward the middle of the twentieth century and afterwards. He produced a comprehensive theory of modernization and development, which still remains unknown to most Black intellectuals. Yet, they invariably project an image of him as being a non-intellectual. Reading the vast corpus of his correspondence and writings that have been published could easily disprove this.

It should also be noted that Du Bois had a lot to do with Washington's image as a non-intellectual. In fact, he helped to project it. He argued that Washington was unrelentingly practical, while he, on the other hand, was the person of imagination and ideas. These negative images of Washington carried on long after his death. Today's Black intellectuals are smitten by them and function from them, which has helped to turn them away from researching the thought, leadership, and programmatic efforts of the Tuskegean, and away from the great appreciation that Blacks of his time had of him and his efforts.

It must also be remembered that Du Bois thought of himself as a member of the "Talented Tenth," mainly those northern Blacks who were educated and cultured and who opposed Washington. They lost dismally in their contest with him, but mostly due to their own flawed and self-defeating behavior, such as not seeking to build up a broad Black constituency in the North. There are not many Black intellectuals today who would think of or describe themselves as being of the Talented Tenth. But when they accept the description of the "organic intellectual," they are pretty much trudging down that lane. Du Bois saw himself and other Talented Tenth people providing Black people with intellectual guidance and functioning as cultivated people for them to emulate.

BETTER INTELLECTUAL GUIDANCE FOR BLACKS

Black organic intellectuals subscribe to this first role of the Talented Tenth, seeking to give Blacks intellectual guidance. But I have raised questions in this book about the kind of intellectual guidance they have been providing Blacks. My concern is that they generally function from various comfort grooves, and in doing so, they are not thoroughly examining Black history and the Black experience to devise their thoughts; still less do they use Black history or the Black experience to critique the history of white people and White behavior in America, and American history, and American society, or the *racist interiority* of them. That *interiority* involves white supremacist/ebonicistic racism and the intellectual, psychological, moral, and even spiritual, afflictions of racism on white people, which they have, in turn, invested as the deep and extensive inner lining of American history and society, giving each its fetid racist interiority. The racist analysis I used in this book, and that I partly used to expose and discuss what I regarded as some of the limitations of Black intellectual offerings, I initially took from Du Bois and developed over the years.

Any discussion of America as a liberal society, a democratic society, or a liberal democratic society, when, in fact, it is structurally and functionally a *welfare society* and has been since the 1930s–and that presently exists widely in Europe–only shows the comfort groove from which many kinds of intellectuals like to write. It also demonstrates how inadequate thought and analysis can be, even when presented in elaborate ways. The comfort groove becomes more graphically apparent when intellectuals, Black, white, and other, seek to remove White racism from American society and from historical and social analysis, that is, removing America's White racist interiority from analysis; this is also why a Marxist analysis has always been inadequate in explaining American history and life. Non-Marxists, eliminating the racist interiority from analysis, along with its impact on history, culture, social life and people, are providing similar inadequate evaluations and presentations.

Racism, not race, has always been the big historical and social determinant factor and problem in America. Race has to do with biology and refers to people. Racism is a cluster of abstract, fanciful, and miasmic beliefs that refer to nothing extant or concrete; that is to say, it refers to nothing that exists. But people have used these irrational and perverted concoctions, which have induced them to engage in irrational and malignant historical and social behavior. This particular irrationality and malevolence cannot be captured or explained by a racial, social class, gender, or ethnic group analysis, nor by combining them all together, as in an intersectional analysis. These four analyses are about people. Racism is not about people; it is not even about human existence. Only a racist analysis can capture the reality and workings of racism. This same analysis can also indicate when a racial, social class, gender, or ethnic group analysis is predicated on racist beliefs and assumptions, and thus, are false or perverted analyses.

As I said earlier, I wrote this book to jar Black intellectuals from complacency and inadequacy and from their comfort grooves when functioning as intellectuals in America. Postmodern thought and analyses that puts a premium on language and discourse and that erases or downplays reality, which a number of Black intellectuals have accepted, also restrains and even cripples their ability to function as intellectuals in America, especially as critical intellectuals. If Black intellectuals (male and female) could function in a more critical manner, neither would have to shout to be heard and listened to in the country.

Ancient Kemet and Judaism and Christianity

Ancient Kemetic religion was over fifteen hundred years old before the appearance of the Jews in history. The Christians date the early first century, B.C.E., which means that Christianity appeared three thousand years after Kemetic religion had been firmly established in the Kemetic civilization. The Kemetic religion, had wide influence all across the Mediterranean and into the Near East (as the Middle East was called at one time). Indeed, at one point in its history, Kemet conquered parts of the Near East and spread its religion and culture there.

The Kemets had lived for a lengthy period of time in the Israel that Exodus Jews went to, but it also has to be remembered that Jews lived in Kemet for centuries before fleeing to Israel, and thus, came under the influence of Kemetic language, religion, and culture while in the county as slaves, in the same way that Blacks came under the influence of the English language, the Christian religion, and European and American culture as slaves.

The triangle was an important symbol for the ancient Kemets. It had mathematical, religious, and philosophical significance for them. They had two interlocked triangles, one representing male energy, the other representing female energy. They called the interlocked triangle the "star of creation,"[1] which would in time become the "Star of David" for the Jews. Circumcision had its origins among the Kemets, and this practice was eventually passed on to the Jews and other people in ancient Africa and the Near East. Moses forbade images of the Jewish God Yahweh, which Donald MacKenzie said the Kemetic pharaoh Akhenaten had earlier forbade with respect to the god Aton.[2] Henri Daniel-Roper wrote that the ancient Jews did not have a priesthood and took that idea and practice from the Kemetic priesthood.[3] The Kemets had "42 Negative Confessions," which included: "I never cursed the Netcher (God), "I have not stolen," "I have done no murder" and "I have not defiled the wife of any man." These confessions and others would be worked into the "Ten Commandments." The Kemetic supreme god, and supreme god of the universe, known by Amen-Ra, Ptah, the All, and also by other names, was unknowable by humans, but could fathom its own nature, existence, and being, which would become a Jewish and Christian religious belief.

Kemetic scholars point out that Black and white Christians end the Lord's Prayer with the word Amen, which is none other than the name of the Kemetic Creator-God Amen-Ra, with the word "Amen" meaning: "that which is not known." And the Kemetic concept of God clearly had an impact on the Jewish, Christian and Islamic conception of the Creator-God, which can be discerned in the following passage:

> God is One and only, and none other existeth with Him-God is the One, the One who hath made all things.... God is from the beginning, and He hath been from the beginning. He hath existed from of old when nothing else existed, and what existed He created after He came into being.... God is hidden and no man knoweth His form. No man hath been able to seek out His likeness; He is hidden to...men, and He is a mystery unto His creatures.... God is Truth, He liveth by Truth, he feedeth thereon, He is the King of Truth, and He hath established the earth thereupon. God is life, and through Him only man liveth.... God begetteth, but was never begotten; he produceth, but was never produced.... He createth, but was never created.... God Himself is existence.... God hath made the universe and He hath created all that therein is.... He is the creator of the heavens, and the earth, and of the deep, and of the water, and of the mountains.... God is merciful unto those who reverence Him, and He heareth him that calleth upon Him. God knoweth him that acknowledgeth Him. He rewardeth him that serveth Him, and He protecteth him that followeth Him.[4]

Eminent Egyptologist James Breasted, of the University of Chicago's Oriental Institute, argued that the religious and moral heritage that ancient Kemet left in the world had been preserved and transmitted by Jews and Judaism. It could also be said that it was preserved and transmitted by Christianity by way of Judaism and by what Christians took directly from Kemetic religion. In *Dawn of Conscience*, Breasted wrote:

> The fundamental conclusions that form the basis of moral convictions, and continue to do so in civilized life at the present day, had already been reached in Egyptian life long before the Hebrews began their social experience in Palestine, and those Egyptian moral convictions had been available in written form in Palestine for centuries when the Hebrews settled there.... The sources of our heritage of moral tradition are therefore far from having been

confined to Palestine, but must be regarded as including also Egyptian civilization. The channel by which this inheritance has reached the Western world has chiefly been the surviving Hebrew literature preserved in the Old Testament.[5]

Black and white Christians in America today, as well as other Christians in the country (and elsewhere in the world, for that matter) close the Lord's Prayer with "Amen." The Kemetic Creator-God, or the "Great Soul," (or Amen-Ra, Ptah, or All), created the god Osiris. Osiris was called "Lord" and was regarded as "The Word"–the Word that called everything to life. Osiris became the god of resurrection in Kemetic religion and the final judge of the human soul and its disposition—to heaven or hell–which were originally Kemetic words and designations.

Osiris and his wife, Isis, who were also brother and sister, had a son, Horus. But this was done not through sexual intercourse. Instead, as one version of this belief has it, Amen-Ra sent the god Netch Kneph and the goddess Netcher Het-Heru to impregnate Isis, which they each did by placing an ankh to her nostrils. The ankh, itself, was the Kemetic cross, which was also regarded as the "life force." Horus was born on December 25 by "immaculate conception." At his birth, he was visited by Three Wise Men (which is depicted in a mural) who brought him gifts. Hence, Isis and Horus were the first "Madonna and Child," as can be seen in many paintings and statues from Kemetic culture. Isis would be converted into Mary by the Christians, while Osiris and Horus would be fused together by Christians to help create Jesus and to aid in the construction of the Christian story of the birth of Jesus.

The Kemetic word karast would later be interpreted by ancient Greeks as *Christos* and as *Christ* for later Christians (and *Krishna* for the Indians of the sub-continent). The Kemetic word, set, meant evil. When "an" was added to the word it became set'an, meaning great evil, and would later become the Jewish and Christian word Satan. Baptism originated with the ancient Kemets, as all pharaohs had to be baptized, i.e., cleansed of all impurities before ascending to the throne. According to the New Testament, Jesus resurrected Lazarus from the dead. Osiris was resurrected, or "called forth" from the dead every year, which shows a relationship to that biblical story.

Kemetic religion was an ethical religion, the concept of which was inherited by Jews and Christians. Its ethical nature was owing to the ethics of the goddess Maat, who was created by the Creator-God and sent to the Kemets as a beacon of light, a moral force, and as a "messiah" or "savior." Indeed, the "42 Negative Confessions" that were used to make the final

307

judgment of the human soul were also known as the "42 Admonitions of Maat." Maat, Osiris and Horus were all combined by the Christians to produce the concept of the "Messiah" or "Savior," and also the "Holy Trinity." The first written holy scripture was the *Egyptian Book of the Dead*, or as it was also called *The Book of the Coming Forth by Day*. Along with the *Pyramid Texts* and the *Book of Thoth*, the Book of the Dead would have an important impact on the construction of the Old Testament. From these and other religious and/or moral sources, the Kemets developed and practiced the "Maatian Way." It involved morality and virtues, and, indeed, the "Seven Cardinal Virtues of Maat" that were connected to the good life, the moral life, and salvation. At a much later time, the "Maatian Way" and the "Seven Cardinal Virtues" of Maat would find their way into the construction of the "Christian Way" and "Christian Virtues."

Most Black theologians have been running as fast and as far away as they can from ancient Kemetic religion and its impact on Judaism, Christianity, and Islam and even on their own versions of Christianity, i.e. versions of Black Christianity. It has always been said that white people gave black African slaves and their descendants in America the Bible and the Christian religion. But both of these religions have their deep roots in the ancient black people of ancient Egypt and ancient Egyptian civilization. In a significant way, this represents Blacks returning to, or linking up with, through the medium of Whites, their own millennial religious heritage.

A thing that stands strongly in the way of seeing this restoration is the Black adherence to the Biblical "Exodus" story. Black religious historian Albert Raboteau has discussed the impact of this story on Black religion and Black people, showing how it helped to invest them with a sense of being special or "chosen" and of having liberation as a supreme goal in America.[6] Clearly, this was helpful to Black people in dealing with slavery and their generally oppressed condition in America. But this positive use of the "Exodus" story and the "plight of the Israelites" also had a negative dimension. Strong adherence to these stories has made it impossible for Black theologians, clergy, and many other Black people to see ancient Kemet for what it was: the great black civilization.

The Old Testament excoriates the Kemets and suppresses knowledge of the glories of that civilization and even the knowledge of what the ancient Hebrews took from it. Black people since Black chattel slavery have identified with slaves of ancient Egypt, but not ancient Egypt itself.

On the other hand, the slave history of Blacks in America has not prevented them from identifying with America, a country where Blacks were enslaved and in other ways oppressed. Blacks have to advance beyond the traditional "Exodus" and "Israelite" preoccupations of the Bible. At the least, they should put them in a proper perspective that makes it possible to focus on the glories of ancient Kemet, and specifically the religious links with it.

Thinking this way and elaborating on it would be radical thought for Black theologians. But this is something they ignore. In their efforts to make Black theology radical, they have invested it with Marxist thought, Black nationalist thought, and various other kinds of liberation thought borrowed from various sources. They have also tried to make Black Christianity theologically and practically different from White Christianity. What all this does, however, is to maintain a barrier that was long ago erected between Blacks and their religious heritage from ancient Egypt.

Black male theologians have maintained that erected barrier. Will Black female theologians seek to remove the barrier and plunge into the ancient Kemetic source? These theologians show no signs of doing this, even though some say they are seeking to reconcile Africancentrism with womanist theology. Africancentrists are mining the ancient Kemetic religious past (including resurrecting the goddesses of Maat and Isis) and are making the connections between it and Christianity, as revealed in issues of *The Journal of African Civilizations, in John Jackson's Christianity Before* Christ[7], Dr. Charles Finch's *Echoes of the Old Darkland*[8], and Anthony Browder's *Nile Valley Contribution to Civilization.*[9]

There are other similarities between Kemetic religion, Judaism, and Christianity. The Kemets certainly did not develop their religion to pass on to anyone, but this did occur, and both Christianity and Judaism became its transmission belts in Africa, the Near East (Middle East), Europe, North America and other parts of the Western Hemisphere. It was through these channels that Black people and black people of the Western Hemisphere were reconnected to the ancient Kemets and to the religion that the Kemets practiced and that constituted part of their religious heritage.

APPENDIX II:
Prolegomenon

Today, there is no general Black leadership, and the Black political body is fragmented, isolated, individualistic, fanciful, delusional, susceptible to posturing and has no real sense of engaging with *Black Politics* that are designed to help Black people in America, specifically those millions still "stuck at the bottom." What could interrupt this situation and force Blacks back to a general leadership and to a consciousness of *Black Politics* would be the emergence of *new* and differently oriented local Black leaders. This would include some individuals drawn from those "stuck at the bottom." There are enough Black local leaders, community organizers, and activists who could initiate this new and different leadership across the country and who could consciously and actively seek to recruit and train individuals *"up from varied misery"* for local leadership.

I suggest that those new leaders, along with Black middle-class elements in Black communities who wish to join in the effort, help Blacks in these communities to organize what I call a *community corporate organization*. This organization would be located in cities with sizable to large Black populations. In many cities, there would be just one organization, but in very large cities with very large Black populations, there might have to be two or more.

This organization would embrace the entire local Black community. It would be composed of political, financial and economic development, educational, religious, family, health, youth, cultural, publicity, and treasury divisions. Each division would be led by an elected chair with the requisite knowledge, leadership ability, and organization skills necessary to organize community efforts. Initially, that person would likely be one of the local leaders, organizers, or activists or a Black middle-class individual who wishes to be a part of this new leadership, organizational, and programmatic effort. But each elected division leader would be obligated to recruit individuals as assistants and staff from those "up from varied misery" and to train some of them as leaders within the divisions and as the liaison with people "up from varied misery" in the community. These assistants would eventually help to identify potential new leaders for the community.

There is likely to be more than one Black community in a state. In many states, there will be several of them. In this case, the several local corporate community organizations could establish a joint leadership that would be comprised of local division heads. This joint leadership could be called The State Black Leadership Council. Its goal would be to seek to coordinate Black modernization and development in Black communities in the state. This would be done by drawing up a general Black modernization and development agenda (State Black Agenda) that would be based on local community Black Political Agendas that, like the local agenda, would be revised and updated periodically. This method would allow for continuous adjustment between local Black community and statewide Black community needs and objectives.

Each local community organization would have as part of its membership, or it would work closely with, local elected or appointed politicians to carry out its modernization and development efforts. The State Black Leadership Council would have as part of its membership, or it would work closely with, all elected and appointed state officials to coordinate and direct Black local and state political activity. It would do this based on the principle of flexible voting for Democratic and Republican party candidates at the local, state, and national levels and on the basis of how candidates and elected officials related to the devised State Black Political Agenda and its periodic alterations.

State Black Leadership Councils would elect individuals from their bodies who would be representatives of their Councils and also representatives of the Black people from their respective states on the National Black Leadership Council. The elected representatives would have a voice in determining the criteria for selecting and would also participate in the selection of members to the National Black Leadership Council. The latter would be presented with state Black Political Agendas that would be the basis for constructing the National Black Political Agenda. This Agenda would stand as the Black Platform for the presidential and congressional elections, i.e., the programmatic basis on which the National Black Leadership Council, the State Black Leadership Councils, and Black people across the country would relate to and vote for presidential and other national political candidates during a presidential election year. In off-election years, State Black Leadership Councils would lead Black people in relating to and voting for gubernatorial and national congressional candidates. These actions would be based on the State Black Political Agenda and the flexible voting principle.

It would be wise for Blacks to remain members of the Democratic Party. White Democrats have been voting Republican in gubernatorial, congressional, and presidential elections for years. It is time for Blacks to be that flexible, which will put more than a little bit of pressure on the Democratic Party to do better by Black people and will put pressure on the Republican Party to want to do more. When both political parties realize how organized and determined this new Black political body is, and when they see that they will have to continue to deal with it, they will be moved to some new thinking.

The role that Black intellectuals would play in this new Black political and public effort-this execution of welfare politics-would be simple: they would cease thinking of themselves as spokespeople, representatives, or leaders of Black people. The leaders of Black people would automatically have these designations. Black intellectuals could provide various forms of help to Black people, such as analyzing White racism, analyzing and providing knowledge about Black history, functioning as consultants to local community organizations or to individual divisions, by evaluating local Black leaders, organizations, and programs, and by conducting surveys of community members with respect to what was occurring in their communities and in their lives. Black intellectuals could also offer special courses or help to establish institutes, conferences, or workshops at their institutions to aid local community leaders and organizations; and they could also help by contributing money to local organizations.

Local leaders and organizations should also be willing to solicit help from local area Whites, not as local leaders, but as consultants and as people willing to provide hands-on training. These Whites could then serve as spokespeople to other Whites in the area in order to help them to be clear about what Black people were locally doing. There are many white people who would also like to see America's racist malaise end, and their help should be encouraged and sought.

What is being proposed here has to be ongoing for many years as there are millions of Black people who need to undergo modernization and development and need to advance in the United States. This proposal does not dissolve into an advocacy of a sustained confrontation with white people in the country. Struggling people always reserve the right to confront opposition—and doubtless there will be some confrontation in this new effort because there will be some racist resistance to it. But the main goal is for Black leadership to emerge at the local, state, and national levels that interact with each other and who are dedicated to helping Blacks "up from varied misery" develop and advance in the country and that is dedicated to building strong and viable local Black communities.

This is a proposal for a new Black Politics that would also be the foundation on which Blacks participated in Black American Politics. Thus, it would be the foundation on which they participated in welfare politics in an effort to get their Black Political Agendas implemented through various channels: local, state, and national political parties, local, state, and national governments, economic corporations, collegiate educational institutions, and various other institutions.

Clearly this program of modernization and development is going to cost a great deal of money over a lengthy period of time. At a minimum, it will cost hundreds of billions of dollars over a lengthy period of time. Black people themselves have a great deal of money to put into this ongoing program. The new Black leadership would have the responsibility of finding ways to secure this money from Blacks and making use of it to help finance modernization and development and to finance building strong and viable Black communities. Both Black Politics and Black American Politics have to be built on strong Black communities and Black financial and economic power.

As a major way for Blacks to acquire money to help Blacks in need and for a sustained cultural and social construction to occur, I propose that local Black communities across the country convert a portion of their consumer spending, what I call *consu-dollars*, into financial and investment dollars. It is estimated that Black people annually spend 500 to 600 billion dollars in America. Most of this money is spent outside of Black communities and contributes to what Black conservative Tony Brown calls, "exporting Black capital." This conversion of *consu-dollars* into *financial* and *investment* dollars would be under the general supervision and guidance of the State Black Leadership Council, but it would be carried out operationally by local leaders and local organizations. American Blacks should withhold 10 percent of their annual consumer spending and convert that spending into annual financial and investment dollars. This would amount to withholding, let's say, approximately 50 billion dollars annually, with an annual conversion and creation of 50 billion financial and investment dollars. In twenty years, this would amount to a trillion dollars. In thirty years, it would amount to a trillion and a half dollars, all of which could be spent on developing Black people and Black life.

Critical to this particular project would be Black women. Black female feminists and Black womanists write and talk about the relationship of Black women to the American economy: the kind of work they do, the remuneration they receive (or do not receive), their contributions to family income, and their relationship to the global economy. But neither writes or talks very much about Black women as agents of financial and economic transformation among Blacks and Black communities.

White slaveholders used Black women's bodies for creating labor that they continuously grossly exploited. And they also used Black slaves as collateral to create great financial wealth and economic power for themselves, their families, and for the country. Today, Black women can help to produce great financial and economic power for Black people in America. And in an ironic twist, they can use the rich and powerful white males and the economic corporations that they own and/or manage to do so. Black women do most of the annual Black consumer spending. Thus, they would be the logical ones to call upon to lead Blacks nationally in *withholding ten percent* of that consumer spending and in helping Blacks at the local level to withhold such spending to achieve the annual national percentage and the commensurate objective of annually converting consu-dollars into financial and investment capital.

The American economy and other economies of the Western world are marked by a great amount of financial capital and the ability of those who possess it to move it easily across national boundaries and, indeed, across all areas of the globe. National governments are reluctant to tax financial capital because of their fear that it will take flight. But the American people spend hundreds of billions of dollars annually in the domestic corporate economy, which helps to provide, as well as replenish, the large amounts of financial capital that possessors export and globally invest.

American consumers do not have to be so reluctant. Indeed, American consumers are the other big factor in the American economy. The public emphasis has always been on the owners and/or managers of the economic corporations, government fiscal policies, Federal Reserve Bank actions and labor unions. But consumer spending is also critical to the American economy, as well as to foreign trade. This makes consumers a big financial and economic factor that is often overlooked. Organized labor has been essentially eclipsed and/or throttled in the American economy. But consumers have yet to realize the great power they have and that they can wield in this economy, specifically with respect to foreign trade, foreign imports, job out-sizing, and even halting and reversing the flow of illegal immigrants into the country. American consumer spending directly and significantly affects domestic capital accumulation, domestic economic production, domestic sales, foreign imports, foreign trade, foreign investment, and national employment. Consumer spending can also directly relate to the development and viability of ethnic (and other) communities.

315

Consumer spending should become a consciously organized expression of welfare politics in America. It certainly could become so for Black people, something the new Black leadership can help Black people and Black communities carry out. W.E.B Du Bois was an advocate of Blacks using their consumer spending as the basis for exercising political, financial, and economic power in America and as a means to develop Black communities. His proposal was chiefly criticized because it was argued that Black people were too poor to do this. Booker T. Washington heard those same criticisms, but he ignored them. Yet, the criticisms prevented Du Bois's proposal from going anywhere. However, an argument that today's Blacks do not have the money or effective consumer power to affect politics or the economy in this country, or to augment their lives and give themselves considerable autonomy in directing their lives and their communities, would be naïve or disingenuous. What is required is the leadership, the organization, the will, the interest, and the determination of Black people.

By annually withholding ten percent of their consumer spending from the corporate and small capitalistic economies, Blacks would reduce the amount of financial capital annually exported from the country and would simultaneously provide themselves with billions of dollars annually for group financial and investment activities. A portion of the withheld consu-dollars could also be converted into production capital for Black economic enterprises. The large economic corporations in America give little to no thought to financial investment and economic development in Black communities. Their interest is primarily to financially exploit Black communities by sucking capital from them. They achieve this by encouraging and conditioning Black spending habits that send Black consu-dollars racing off to them. What's more, these economic elements have had some Blacks to help them by working out ways to target Black consumers. The interest being expressed here is not to stop Black consumer spending in the corporate or small capitalistic economy, but to substantially reduce the annual amount of spending in each and in using the withheld funds for local, state, and national Black community modernization and development.

Black people have to have and have to control financial capital. This is one of the great motor powers of the American domestic economy (and any domestic economy); and, financial capital begets financial capital and attracts such capital like a magnet that helps to augment its amount. Thus, the annual construction of financial capital would be a basis for augmenting financial and production capital by using the financial capital as collateral for borrowing money. The guarantee of the collateral and the ability to borrow would be the proven ability to annually collect a large amount of capital from local Black communities and to convert it into a large amount of financial capital. This is clearly within the ability of Black people to do, and it is something that they cannot be kept from doing. This program does not reject individual Blacks saving and accumulating individual financial wealth. But this is mainly a middle-class approach to acquiring financial wealth. Blacks in need are not in the middle-class. That would be their destination. This requires collective saving and acquisition of financial wealth, i.e., local community wealth that would be shared by all member of the community.

Let's look at a hypothetical example of how local Black communities, as well as state-wide Black communities, can withhold (and save) Black consu-dollars and convert them into financial capital so that we can get a better sense of the great potential for Blacks to become a big financial and economic factor in America, and to make better use of their financial wealth for themselves and the country. Let's say there were 30,000 people in a local Black community and that each was asked to withhold $100 from their annual spending and deposit it with the their local community organization, that, in turn, would deposit it in a financial institution used by the organization and the community. This would amount to withholding $3,000,000, which could then be converted into financial capital. We shall call this group, group A.

Let's also say that there were five Black communities in the same state with the same size population, totaling 150,000 Black people in that state. If each person withheld $100 from their annual spending, then that would amount to $15,000,000 in financial capital. We shall call this group, group B.

In group A, three million dollars would be annually spent on the Black community, money that had not been there before, with a borrowing capability to augment that annual figure. In group B, Black people in the state would be annually spending fifteen million dollars (plus borrowed money) on themselves to augment their communities and their own lives. Over a ten-year period, Group A would be spending at least 30 million on itself, and Group B would be spending at least 150 million on itself. Of course, all the money would not have to be annually spent. This would be something determined by authorized local and statewide authorities. But collecting and converting capital would annually occur. And it would have to take place annually for years to come in order to be able to help millions of Black people and Black communities to modernize and develop. Black women would be key to seeing that each member of a Black family withheld and saved $100 from their spending, or that a family of five withheld and saved $500.00 each year. Even poor Black people would be able to afford this proposal, as reflected in the amount of money (thousands annually) that individual poor Blacks extravagantly spend on designer clothing and footwear, alcohol, junk food, entertainment, gambling on state and national lotteries, and so on.

Booker T. Washington was not daunted by people who told him that poor Blacks were too poor to engage in the kind of economic activities and cultural and social construction he wanted them to. He discarded that kind of skepticism and defeatism and sent young Black leaders into the rural areas of the South, the poorest places in the region, to get Blacks to save and utilize their meager amounts of money to improve their lives and their futures in the country. They eagerly took up the great task and sacrifice. They did so because they had the leadership and programmatic thrust that helped them and that inspired them to do it.

The proposed local Black leadership and organization could do this today. The financial and economic development division, the family division, and the religious division could all work with Black women to be withholders and collectors of consu-dollars. These consu-dollars would then be annually converted into the financial and investment dollars by the leadership of the community organization. There could be investment in local existing Black businesses and in the creation of new Black businesses. The local organization could also buy stock in national corporations and develop an investment portfolio for the local organization and community. The financial and economic development division could also solicit outside investment in the Black community, in Black businesses, or small-sized industries. Local communities could jointly buy stock in national or local corporations, even significant ownership in such corporations.

Much of the financial capital would go into helping Blacks buy or improve their homes. Claiming and renovating vacant buildings or houses should occur. Neighborhood beautification programs should be established and maintained, and parks should be constructed where possible. The youth division could be drawn upon to recruit and pay neighborhood youth to help beautify the neighborhoods and maintain beautification of neighborhoods. The Black community should be divided into neighborhoods and a plan should be made to simultaneously improve each neighborhood with the others. For example, five families in each neighborhood should be assisted in improving their homes simultaneously, or five vacant houses should be renovated in each neighborhood simultaneously, so that neighborhood modernization and development occurs in a coordinated and integrated manner and so that no neighborhood is left feeling slighted or left behind.

The cultural division could be directly and continuously brought in to engage in neighborhood transformation, beautification, and the promotion of community events as well. The latter could be street fairs, Black history celebrations, or entertainment activities, such as musical events and establishing community musical groups, including a swing band. It could also establish a community Black choir that would put on annual Easter and Christmas concerts as paying events for the larger public. There could be annual art shows and the establishment of a community theater and nightclubs, just as there once existed in Black neighborhoods, that would be open to the public.

In each neighborhood, there should also be the establishment of community health, nutrition, and exercise facilities. If this cannot be done, then such facilities should be established on a centralized basis and should be made accessible to all Blacks in the community. Blacks are the recipients of very poor health care in America. They do not receive adequate information, education, counseling, or guidance on matters of health, such as dieting, exercise, or the general maintenance of their physical condition. Obesity, for instance, is a massive problem among Black men and women in this country and produces a catalog of health problems. And many Blacks do not have a doctor or even know how to use a doctor's services.

The community health division would have the responsibility of intervening in this health and medical crises and would lead the local Black community in making drastic changes and improvements to this situation. This division could also join with the family and religious divisions, as well as the publicity division, to carry out this activity, which should be done on the basis of an ongoing campaign. Indeed, there should be two campaigns: one directed at Black adults and that might be carried out in conjunction with the education division, which would conduct an adult education campaign in schools and churches with respect to health and medical instruction and care, and one that would be directed at youth, with the youth division working with other divisions to carry out a similar campaign for young people in the community.

There would be a great amount of investment in Black education in local Black communities. This would be beyond what was attained from state and national government sources and, at the same time, would supplement what was attained. A special project I would like to see all Black communities engage in is providing money for annual educational scholarships. But I would like to see this directly done with the purpose

319

of transforming Black schools, or schools where most of the student body is Black, into substantial academic institutions.

There are numerous ways to raise scholarship money for Black schools. I propose a method that would be carried out jointly by the education, culture, and financial and economic development division, with the aid of the publicity division. I propose that rich or wealthy Black individuals or groups adopt a local Black organization and a local Black community and the Black or predominantly Black schools that the children of the community attend. The individuals or groups would offer a contribution, whether or not it can be classified as charity, of two million dollars to improve the education of the community and schools adopted. This would be done on the basis that the local Black community match half of this amount. The two million dollars would be placed in a bank with which the local organization and community did business where it would collect interest. Local Blacks would then be given a certain amount of time to raise their million-dollar match to the donated contribution. None of the money in the bank (or perhaps some other kind of financial institution) could be used until then. When the money is matched, the contributors would be publicly honored and thanked by the local Black community and the community's matching success would be celebrated.

When the three million mark has been achieved, the entire amount would remain in the bank or financial institution and the annual interest on the money would be used to provide scholarships for Black students to go to colleges, universities, or technical schools, with an encouragement, but not a requirement, for them to attend Black or predominantly Black colleges, universities, and technical schools. Over the years, Blacks in the local community could add to this scholarship fund and augment the amount of interest money for annual scholarships. Scholarships should be substantial and as numerous as possible so that many Black youngsters would have a chance to be recipients.

There would also be special requirements associated with the scholarships. Recipients would be required to sign an agreement to pay back half of the scholarship at some future date when the individual was earning an income. This money would be put back into the general fund. The scholarship would represent not only an individual achievement, but the local Black community's commitment to advancing the education of Black children. Paying back half of a scholarship award would also represent a personal thanks for that commitment and the individual recipient's own commitment to helping advance the education of his or her original community. The scholarships would also become incentives for young Blacks to become better students and would also become a stimulus to change the academic atmosphere and performance of Black or predominantly Black schools, whether they be elementary, middle, or high schools.

There should also be people in each of these schools to help the schools in their transformation and to help in perpetuating good academic performances and results from students. The people to do this would have the responsibility of identifying Black children who showed intellectual ability, a desire to learn, and a desire to be academic achievers. They would also have the responsibility of identifying those students who could be potential scholarship recipients. In addition, they would also be part of the committee established by the local education division that determined who should receive scholarships. These individuals would not be teachers (although, they may have previously been teachers). Instead, they would be special advisors to the students and would work with school officials and parents to bring them all in on helping the students achieve academic success.

The education division of the local Black community organization would work with the public school superintendent, or some other public school official, and the local school board to establish and maintain (that is, to pay the salaries of) these Special Academic Advisors or Coordinators. These Special Academic Advisors or Coordinators would be the ones to hand out the scholarships to graduating high school seniors, which would be done with much fanfare at annual awards dinners. It would also probably be wise to offer some kind of recognition or award to high achievers who finish elementary and middle schools, which would take place at the schools. This could function to keep young academic achievers on that stellar road, and thus, aid the Special Advisors or Coordinators in their efforts. In addition, handing out awards in school could prove inspirational and motivational to other students.

Black students would be encouraged to pursue academic excellence and scholarships if there were a strong appreciation of education in the Black community. This could be promoted by the education, family, religious, and youth divisions all working together to get Black families to accept and observe an agreement to significantly reduce the number of hours that Black children and youth watch television. Encouragement could come from these same divisions working to assure that the hours between six and eight in the evening would be set aside for Black children and youth to study. All Black families would know of this practice and this would be an encouragement for them to observe it.

A third thing that could provide encouragement would be an adult education program that could take place in schools, churches, or homes. This program could lead to a high school diploma for adults and could even lead to eligibility for advanced educational scholarships. Indeed, it might even be worthwhile to establish a Parent Education Award that would offer a financial incentive to parents who succeeded in completing their high school education. This award would also be presented with great fanfare at a public ceremony.

The next thirty or forty years are crucial years for the Black people who have not made it in America and for transforming Black communities and elevating Blacks in need into the American middle-class. This would mean lifting most Blacks, and hopefully all, from the Basin of America's welfare society. This is not something that Black intellectuals could do. But they can be partners with Black leaders and local Black community organizations in helping to pursue and accomplish these great goals. There was never a more propitious time for Black intellectuals and other Blacks in America to "seize the time." But this "time" calls for big vision and big and bold efforts. Du Bois held the belief that what benefited Black people also benefited America. It would make America right with itself, which could then help it be right with the world.

References

CHAPTER ONE: REVISITATION AND BEYOND

1. Harold Cruse, *The Crisis of the Negro Intellectual* (New York: Morrow, 1967).
2. William M. Banks, *Black Intellectuals: Race and Responsibility in American Life* (New York: Norton, 1996) 233.
3. James Baldwin, *The Fire Next Time* (New York: Dial P, 1963) 108-109.
4. E. Franklin Frazier, *Black Bourgeoisie* (Glencoe, Illinois: Free P, 1957).
5. ——, "Failure of the Negro Intellectual," *E. Franklin Frazier on Race Relations, Selected Writings*, ed. G. Franklin Edwards (Chicago: U of Chicago P, 1968) 274.
6. Frazier, "Failure," 274.
7. Nathan Hare, *The Black Anglo Saxons* (New York: Marzani and Munsell, 1965).
8. Frederick Douglass, *My Bondage and My Freedom* (Chicago: Johnson, 1970) 309.
9. Booker T. Washington To Emmett Jay Scott 16 January, 1914, *The Booker T. Washington Papers,* Volume 12: 1912-14, ed. Louis R. Harlan and Raymond Smock (Urbana: U of Illinois P, 1982) 417.
10. Booker T. Washington To Timothy Thomas Fortune 28 January, 1912-1914, *The Booker T. Washington Papers*, Volume 12: 1912-1914, ed. Louis R. Harlan and Raymond Smock (Urbana: U of Illinois P, 1982) 420.
11. Harold Cruse, *Black Rebellion or Revolution* (New York: Morrow, 1968).
12. Cruse, *Black Rebellion*, 201.
13. Jerry Gafio Watts, *Heroism and the Black Intellectual Ralph Ellison, Politics, and Afro-American Intellectual Life* (Chapel Hill: U of North Carolina P, 1994) 8.
14. Watts, *Heroism*, 8-9.
15. Adolph Reed, Jr., *Class Notes: Posing as Politics and Other Thoughts on the American Scene* (New York: New P, 2000) 84.
16. Reed, *Class Notes*, 79.
17. William M. Banks, *Black Intellectuals: Race and Responsibility in American Life* (New York: Norton, 1996) 245-246.
18. W. D. Wright, *Black Intellectuals, Black Cognition, and a Black Aesthetic* (Westport, Connecticut: Praeger, 1997).

CHAPTER TWO: RACISM AND RACE: LOLLING AND LUMBERING IN AN INTELLECTUAL WASTELAND

1. Roy L. Brooks, *Rethinking the American Race Problem* (Berkeley: U of California P, 1990).
2. William Julius Wilson, *The Declining Significance of Race: Blacks and Changing American Institutions* (Chicago: U of Chicago P, 1977).
3. Roy L. Brooks, *Rethinking the American Race Problem* (Berkeley: U of California P, 1990) xiii.
4. Cornel West, *Race Matters* (Boston: Beacon P, 1993).
5. West, *Race Matters*, 32.
6. Cornel West, "Afterword," *The House that Race Built: Black Americans, U.S. Terrain*, ed. Wahneema Lubiano (New York: Pantheon, 1997) 301.
7. *Keeping Faith: Philosophy and Race* (New York: Vintage, 1996).
8. Henry Louis Gates, Jr., and Cornel West, *The Future of the Race* (New York: Vintage, 1996).
9. Frederick Douglass, "Prejudice Against Color," *The Life and Writings of Frederick Douglass, Volume II: Pre-Civil War Decade 1850-1860*, ed. Philip S. Foner (New York: International, 1950) 129.
10. Douglass, "Prejudice," 129.
11. Charles W. Mills, *Blackness Visible: Essays on Philosophy and Race* (Ithaca: Cornell UP, 1998).
12. W. E. Burghardt Du Bois, *The Suppression of the African Slave Trade to the United States of America, 1638-1870* (Baton Rouge: Louisiana State UP, 1969) 198-199.
13. Nathan Irvin Huggins, *Black Odyssey: The African-American Ordeal in Slavery* (New York: Random, 1990) xvi.
14. Lerone Bennett, Jr., *Forced Into Glory: Abraham Lincoln's White Dream* (Chicago: Johnson, 2000).
15. Shelby Steele, *The Content of Our Character: A New Vision of Race in America* (New York: St. Martin's, 1990).
16. *A Dream Deferred: The Second Betrayal of Black Freedom in America* (New York: Harper, 1998).
17. Shelby Steele, *The Content of Our Character: A New Vision of Race in America* (New York: St. Martin's, 1990) 175.
18. Glenn C. Loury, *One by One from the Inside Out: Essays and Reviews on Race and Responsibility in America* (New York: Free P, 1995) Ch. 15.
19. W. E. B. Du Bois, "Disfranchisement," *W. E. B. Du Bois Speaks: Speeches and Addresses, 1890-1919*, ed. Philip S. Foner (New York: Pathfinder P, 1970) 235.

20. "The Negro and the Warsaw Ghetto," *W. E. B. Du Bois Speaks: Speeches and Addresses, 1920-1963*, ed. Philip S. Foner (New York: Pathfinder P, 1970) 253.

21. Gordon W. Allport, *The Nature of Prejudice* (Garden City, New York: Doubleday, 1954).

22. Kate Millett, *Sexual Politics* (New York: Avon, 1971) 86.

23. Qtd. in W. D. Wright, "The Faces of Racism," *The Western Journal of Black Studies*, 11.4 (1987): 173.

24. Floya Anthias, "Race and Class Revisited-Conceptualization of Race and Racisms," *The Sociological Review*, 38 (1990): 38.

25. Naomi Zack, ed., *Race/Sex: Their Sameness, Differences, and Interplay* (New York: Routledge, 1997)

26. Qtd. in Theodore Isaac Rubin, M.D., *Anti-Semitism: A Disease of the Mind-A Psychiatrist Explores the Psycho-dynamics of a Symbol Sickness* (New York: Continuum, 1990) 105.

27. William J. Wilson, *Power, Race, and Privilege: Race Relations in Theoretical and Sociohistorical Perspectives* (New York: Macmillan, 1973).

28. Paul Gilroy, "One Nation Under a Groove: The Cultural Politics of Race and Racism in Britain," *Anatomy of Racism*, ed. David Theo Goldberg (Minneapolis: U of Minnesota P, 1990) 265-266.

29. *Against Race* (Cambridge: Harvard UP, 2000).

30. Patricia Hill Collins, *Fighting Words: Black Women and the Search for Justice* (Minneapolis: U of Minnesota P, 1998) 280.

31. Alazar Barkan, *The Retreat of Scientific Racism* (New York: Cambridge UP, 1992) 1.

32. Qtd. in Arnold H. Taylor, *Travail and Triumph: Black Life and Culture in the South since the Civil War* (Westport, Connecticut: Greenwood P, 1976) 42.

33. Qtd. in Arnold H. Taylor, *Travail and Triumph: Black Life and Culture in the South since the Civil War* (Westport, Connecticut: Greenwood P, 1976) 42-43.

34. Barbara J. Fields, "Ideology and Race in American History," *Region, Race, and Reconstruction: Essays in Honor of C. Vann Woodward*, ed. J. Morgan Kousser and James M. McPherson (New York: Oxford UP, 1982) 144.

35. Henry Louis Gates, Jr., ed., *Black Letters in the Enlightenment: Race and Difference* (New York: Oxford UP, 1990) 5.

36. Qtd. in J. L. A. Garcia, "Racism as a Model for Understanding Sexism," *Race/Sex: Their Sameness, Difference, and Interplay*, ed. Naomi Zack (New York: Routledge, 1997) 48.

37. T. W. Adorno, E. Frenkel-Brunswick, D. J. Levinson, and R. N. Sanford, *The Authoritarian Personality* (New York: Harper, 1950).

38. Kwame Anthony Appiah and Amy Gutmann, *Color Consciousness: The Political Morality of Race* (Princeton: Princeton UP, 1996) 38.

39. Charles W. Mills, *Blackness Visible: Essays on Philosophy and Race* (Ithaca: Cornell UP, 1998) xiv.

40. Ronald L. Taylor, "On Race and Society," *Race & Society*, 1.1 (1998): 1-2.

41. James P. Comer, *Beyond Black and White* (New York: Quandrangle/New York Times, 1972) 118.

42. Matthew Frye Jacobson, "Becoming Caucasian: Vicissitudes of Whiteness in American Politics and Culture," *Identities*, 8.1 (2001): 99.

43. Lewis R. Gordon, *Bad Faith and Antiblack Racism* (Atlantic Highlands, New Jersey: Humanities P, 1995) 6.

44. Charles W. Mills, *Blackness Visible: Essays on Philosophy and Race* (Ithaca: Cornell UP, 1998) 6.

45. Lucius T. Outlaw, Jr., *On Race and Philosophy* (New York: Routledge, 1996) 11.

46. Qtd. in George Yancy, ed., *African-American Philosophers: 17 Conversations* (New York: Routledge, 1998) 236.

47. David Lionel Smith, "What is Black Culture?" *The House that Race Built*, ed. Wahneema Lubiano (New York: Pantheon, 1997) 180.

48. W. E. Burghardt Du Bois, *The Negro* (New York: Oxford UP, 1970) 9.

49. Richard A. Goldsby, *Race and Races* (New York: Macmillan, 1971) 5.

50. Richard Osborne, "The History and Nature of Race Classification," *The Biological and Social Meaning of Race*, ed. Richard Osborne (San Francisco: W. H. Freeman, 1971) 165.

51. L. C. Dunn, "Race and Biology," *Race, Science and Society*, ed. Leo Kuper (New York: Columbia UP, 1975) 40.

52. James C. King, *The Biology of Race*, rev. ed., (Berkeley: U of California P, 1981) ix.

53. Qtd. in Suzanne Fleming, "All About Eve," *Michigan Today*, 22 (1990): 2.

54. Michael J. Bamsha and Steve E. Wilson, "Does Race Exist?" *Scientific American* 289.6 (2003): 80.

55. Vincent Sarich and Frank Miele, Race: *The Reality of Human Differences* (Boulder, CO: Westview P, 2004)

56. Adolph Reed, Jr., *Class Notes: Posing as Politics and Other Thoughts on the American Scene* (New York: New P, 2000) 144.

57. Richard Delgado, and Jean Stefancic, *Critical Race Theory: An Introduction* (New York: New York UP, 2001) 7-8.

58. Kwame Anthony Appiah, *In My Father's House: Africa in the Philosophy of Culture* (New York: Oxford UP, 1992).

59. Tommy L. Lott, *The Invention of Race: Black Culture and the Politics of Representation* (Malden, Massachusetts: Blackwell, 1999) 50.

60. Lott, *Invention*, 52.

61. Lott, *Invention*, 56.

62. Manning Marable, *Beyond Black and White: Transforming African American Politics* (New York: Verso, 1995) 186.

CHAPTER THREE:
ROMANCING THE BLACK NATIONALIST STONE

1. Sterling Stuckey, *Slave Culture: Nationalist Theory and the Foundation of Black America* (New York: Oxford UP, 1987).

2. Stuckey, *Slave Culture*, viii-ix.

3. Stuckey, *Slave Culture*, 3.

4. Qtd. in Julius Lester, ed., *To Be A Slave* (New York: Dell, 1968) 8.

5. Qtd. in Norman P. Yetman, ed., *Life Under the "Peculiar Institution:" Selections from the Slave Narrative Collection* (New York: Holt, 1940) 45.

6. Qtd. in Yetman, *Life Under,* 217.

7. Qtd. in Yetman, *Life Under,* 63.

8. Qtd. in Yetman, *Life Under,* 95.

9. Sterling Stuckey, *Slave Culture: Nationalist Theory and the Foundation of Black America* (New York: Oxford UP, 1987) 3.

10. John W. Blassingame, *The Slave Community: Plantation Life in the Antebellum South* (New York: Oxford UP, 1972).

11. George P. Rawick, *From Sundown to Sunup: The Making of the Black Community* (Westport, Connecticut: Greenwood, 1972).

12. Eugene Genovese, *Roll, Jordan, Roll: The World the Slaves Made* (New York: Pantheon, 1974).

13. W. D. Wright, *Historians and Slavery: A Critical Analysis of Perspectives and Irony in American Slavery and Other Recent Works* (D. C.: UP of America, 1978).

14. Larry Neal, *Visions of a Liberated Future: Black Arts Movement Writings* (New York: Thunder Mouth P, 1989) 137.

15. V. P. Franklin, *Black Self-Determination: A Cultural History of the Faith of the Fathers* (Westport, Connecticut: Lawrence Hill, 1984) viii.

16. Franklin, *Black Self-Determination,* viii.

17. Franklin, *Black Self-Determination,* x.

18. ——, *Living Our Stories, Telling Our Truths. Autobiography and the Making of the African American Intellectual Tradition* (New York: Scribner, 1995).

19. ——, *Black Self-Determination,* 191.

20. Franklin, *Black Self-Determination,* 203.

21. Booker T. Washington, "A Speech Before the New York Congregational Club," *The Booker T. Washington Papers*, Volume 3: 1889-95, ed. Louis R. Harlan, Stuart B. Kaufman, and Raymond W. Smock. (Urbana: U of Illinois P, 1974) 283-284.

22. V. P. Franklin, *Black Self-Determination*, 195.

23. Toni Morrison, "The Site of Memory," *Inventing the Truth, The Art, and Craft of Memoir*, ed. William K. Zinser (New York: Book-Of-The-Month Club, 1987) 110-111.

24. Qtd. in Genevieve Fabre and Robert O'Meally, ed. *History and Memory in African-American Culture* (New York: Oxford UP, 1994) 4-5.

25. Brenda Dixon Gottschild, *Digging the Africanist Presence in American Performance: Dance and Other Contexts* (Westport, Connecticut: Greenwood P, 1996) 4.

26. Gottschild, *Digging*, 67.

27. Ralph Ellison, *Invisible Man* (New York: Random, 1952).

28. James Baldwin, *Nobody Knows My Name: More Notes of a Native Son* (New York: Dell, 1954).

29. Bernard R. Boxill, *Blacks and Social Justice*, rev. ed. (Lanham, Maryland: Rowman and Littlefield, 1992) 173.

30. W. E. Burghardt Du Bois, *The Souls of Black Folk* (Greenwich: Fawcett, 1961) 17.

31. Qtd. in *New Dimensions in African History: The London Lectures of Dr. Yosef ben-Jochanan and Dr. John Henrik Clarke*, ed. Dr. John Henrik Clarke (Trenton: Africa World P, 1991) 76-77.

32. Ali Mazrui, "On the Concept of 'We are All Africans,'" *American Political Science Review*, 58.1 (1963): 88-97.

33. Bernard Lewis, *Cultures in Conflict: Christians, Muslims, and Jews in the Age of Discovery* (New York: Oxford UP, 1995) 64-65.

34. Colin Palmer, "The African Diaspora," *Black Scholar*, 30.3-4 (2000): 57.

35. Elliott P. Skinner, "Transcending Traditions: African, African-American and African Diaspora Studies in the 21st Century-the Past Must be the Prologue," *Black Scholar*, 30.3-4 (2000): 6.

36. Molefi Kete Asante, *The Afrocentric Idea* (Philadelphia: Temple UP, 1987) 9.

37. Brenda Dixon Gottschild, *Digging the Africanist Presence in American Performance: Dance and other Contexts* (Westport: Connecticut: Greenwood P, 1996) xiv.

38. ABC News and *Washington Post Poll* in Lee Sigelman and Susan Welch, *Black Americans's Views of Racial Inequality: The Dream Deferred* (New York: Cambridge UP, 1991) xi; "Poll Says Blacks Prefer to Be Called Black," *The Joint Center for Political and Economic Studies Poll of 1990*, Jet, 79.17 (1991): 8; *Jet*, 85.4 (1994): 37; *Jet*, 86.17 (1994): 46.

39. Joseph E. Holloway, ed. *Africanisms in American Culture* (Bloomington: Indiana UP, 1990).

40. Marimba Ani, *Yurugu: An African-Centered Critique of European Cultural Thought and Behavior* (Trenton: Africa World P, 1994).

41. Erriel D. Roberson, *Reality Revolution Return to the Way* (Columbia, Maryland: Kujichagulia P, 1996).

42. Wilson Jeremiah Moses, *The Golden Age of Black Nationalism, 1850-1925* (New York: Oxford UP, 1978) 40.

43. Wahneema Lubiano, "Black Nationalism and Black Common Sense: Policing Ourselves," *The House that Race Built: Black Americans, U.S. Terrain*, ed. Wahneema Lubiano (New York: Pantheon, 1997) 233-234.

44. Cornel West, *Prophetic Thought in Postmodern Times: Beyond Eurocentrism and Multiculturalism*, Volume I (Monroe, Maine: Common Courage P, 1993) 164.

45. *Race Matters* (Boston: Beacon P, 1993) 104.

46. Qtd. in "Does Academic Correctness Repress Separatism of Afrocentrist Scholarship?" *The Journal of Blacks in Higher Education 2* (1993-1994): 42.

47. Qtd. in "Does Correctness," 45.

48. Qtd. in "Does Correctness," 42.

49. Arthur M. Schlesinger, Jr., "Nationalism and History," *The Journal of Negro History*, 29.1 (1969): 29.

50. *The Disuniting of America* (New York: Norton, 1992) 94.

51. Jacob H. Carruthers, *Intellectual Warfare* (Chicago: Third World P, 1999) 139.

52. Arthur M. Schlesinger, Jr., *The Disuniting of America*, rev. ed. (New York: Norton, 1998) 171.

53. Schlesinger, *The Disuniting*, 100.

54. Mary Lefkowitz, *Not Out of Africa: How Africancentrism Became an Excuse to Teach Myth as History* (New York: Harper, 1996).

55. Arthur M. Schlesinger, *The Disuniting of America*, rev. ed., 83.

56. Clarence E. Walker, *We Can't Go Home: An Argument About Afrocentrism* (New York: Oxford UP, 2001) 47.

57. Walker, *We Can't Go Home*, 48.

58. James Breasted, *The Dawn of Conscience* (New York: Scribner's, 1947) 384-385.

59. Joseph Kaster, "What was Ancient Egypt? Egypt's Place in the History of Civilization," *The Wisdom of Ancient Egypt*, trans. and ed. Joseph Kaster (New York: Barnes & Noble, 1968) 10.

60. Kaster, "What was Ancient Egypt?" 10.

61. P. E. Peet, "Writing and Literature," *The Legacy of Egypt*, ed. S. R. K. Granville (Oxford: Clarendon P, 1942) 71-72.

62. Erik Hornung, *Idea Into Image: Essays on Ancient Egyptian Thought* (New York: Timken, 1992) 13.

63. Jay Lampert, "Hegel and Ancient Egypt: History and Becoming," *International Philosophical Quarterly*, 35.1 (1995): 45.

64. Dan Flory, "Racism, Black Athena and the Historiography of Ancient Philosophy," *The Philosophical Forum*, 38.3 (1997): 196.

65. Clarence E. Walker, *We Can't Go Home: An Argument About Afrocentrism* (New York: Oxford UP, 2001) 132.

66. Molefei Kete Asante, *The Afrocentric Idea* (Philadelphia: Temple UP, 1987) 9.

67. —, *Kemet, Afrocentricity and Knowledge* (Trenton: Africa World P, 1990) 6.

68. Paul Gilroy, *The Black Atlantic Modernity and Double Consciousness* (Cambridge: Harvard UP, 1993).

69. Joyce Ann Joyce, "African-Centered Womanism: Connecting Africa to the Diaspora," *The African Diaspora: African Origins and New World Identities*, ed. Isidore Okpewho, Carole Boyce Davies, and Ali A. Mazrui (Bloomington: Indiana UP, 1999) 539.

70. Robin D. G. Kelley, "But a Local Phase of a World Problem:" Black History's Global Vision," *The Journal of American History*, 86.3 (1999): 1045-1077.

71. Laura Chrisman, Jasmine Griffin, and Tukufu Zuberi, "Introduction to Transcending Traditions," *Black Scholar* 30.3-4 (2000): 3.

CHAPTER FOUR: THREE OF A KIND: BLACK CONSERVATIVES, BLACK LIBERALS, AND BLACK RADICALS

1. Kelly Miller, *Radicals and Conservatives and Other Essays on the Negro in America* (New York: Schocken, 1968) 25.

2. William Henry Ferris To Booker T. Washington 26 November, 1907, *The Booker T. Washington Papers*, Volume 9: 1906-08, ed. Louis R. Harlan, Raymond W. Smock, and Nan E. Woodruff (Urbana: U of Illinois P, 1980) 410.

3. Kelly Miller, *Radicals and Conservatives*, 26.

4. August Meier, *Negro Thought in America, 1880-1915: Racial Ideologies in the Age of Booker T. Washington* (Ann Arbor: U of Michigan P, 1963) 245.

5. Orlando Patterson, *The Ordeal of Integration Progress and Resentment in America's "Racial" Crisis* (D.C.: Civitas/Counterpoint, 1997) 22.

6. Patterson, *Ordeal*, 22.

7. Richard L. Zweigenhaft and G. William Domhoff, *Diversity in the Power Elite: Have Women and Minorities Reached the Top?* (New Haven: Yale UP, 1998) 194.

8. Jonnella E. Butler, "Democracy, Diversity, and Civic Engagement," *Academe*, 86.4 (2000): 53.

9. Paul N. Goldstene, *The Collapse of Liberal Empire Science and Revolution in the Twentieth Century* (New Haven: Yale UP, 1977).

10. M. Morton Auerbach, *The Conservative Illusion* (New York: Columbia UP, 1959).

11. Barry Goldwater, *The Conscience of a Conservative* (New York: Hillman, 1960).

12. —, *The Conscience of a Majority* (Englewood Cliffs, New Jersey: Prentice-Hall, 1970).

13. Edward N. Wolff, *Top Heavy* (New York: New P, 1996) 67.

14. John H. McWhorter, *Losing the Race: Self-Sabotage in Black America* (New York: Free P, 2000) xi.

15. McWhorter, *Losing the Race*, xiii.

16. McWhorter, *Losing the Race*, 162.

17. Alexander Thomas, M. D., and Samuel Sillen, Ph.D., *Racism and Psychiatry* (New York: Brunner/Mazel, 1972) 51.

18. McWhorter, *Losing the Race*, 212.

19. McWhorter, *Losing the Race,* 2.

20. Richard Hofstadter, *Anti-Intellectualism in American Life* (New York: Knopf, 1963).

21. Qtd. in Sandra Van Dyk, "Toward an Afrocentric Perspective: The Significance of Afrocentricity," *Molefi Kete Asante and Afrocentricity: In Praise and in Criticism*, ed. Dhyana Ziegler (Nashville: Winston, 1995) 2.

22. Lerone Bennett, Jr., "The Status of Race in American Culture," *The Declining Significance of Race? A Dialogue Among Black and White Social Scientists*, ed. Joseph R. Washington, Jr. (Philadelphia: U of Pennsylvania, 1979) 84.

23. Joseph White, Jr., "Guidelines for Black Psychologists," *Black Scholar*, 1.5 (1970): 57.

24. Qtd. in *Black Women Writers at Work*, ed. Claudia Tate (Harpenden Herts, England: Oldcastle, 1983) 122.

25. Cornel West, "The Dilemma of the Black Intellectual," *The Journal of Blacks in Higher Education*, 2 (1993/1994): 66.

26. Qtd. in Stan Faryna, Brad Stegson, and Joseph G. Conti, ed. *Black and Right: The Bold New Voice of Black Conservatives in America* (Westport, Connecticut: Praeger, 1997) 146.

27. Thomas Sowell, *Civil Rights: Rhetoric or Reality?* (New York: Morrow, 1984).

28. Brian W. Jones, "Two Visions of Black Leadership," *Black and Right: The Bold New Voice of Black Conservatives in America*, ed. Stan Faryna, Brad Stegson, and Joseph G. Conti (Westport, Connecticut: Praeger, 1997) 36.

29. Thomas Sowell, "Whither Western Civilization?" *Western Civilization, Volume II: Early Modern Through the Twentieth Century*, ed. William Hughes (Sluice Dock, Guilford, Connecticut: Duskin, 1995) 236.

30. Telly Lovelace, "No Need for a Government Handout," *Black and Right: The Bold New Voice of Black Conservatives in America*, ed. Stan Faryna, Brad Stegson, and Joseph G. Conti (Westport, Connecticut: Praeger, 1997) 46.

31. Jesse Lee Peterson with Brad Stetson, *Rage to Responsibility: Black Conservative Jesse Lee Peterson* (St. Paul: Paragon House, 2000).

32. Lawrence E. Harrison and Samuel P. Huntington, ed. *Culture Matters: How Values Shape Human Progress* (New York: Basic Books, 2000).

33. Richard J. Herrnstein and Charles Murray, *The Bell Curve: Intelligence and Class Structure in American Life* (New York: Free P, 1994).

34. Gary Franks, "The Role of Black Conservative Leaders in the 1990s," *Black and Right: The Bold New Voice of Black Conservatives in America,* ed. Stan Faryna, Brad Stegson, and Joseph G. Conti (Westport, Connecticut: Praeger, 1997) 60-61.

35. Robert L. Woodson, Sr., *The Triumphs of Joseph: How Today's Community Healers are Reviving Our Streets and Neighborhoods* (New York: Free P, 1998) 121.

36. Greg Robinson, "Ralph Ellison, Albert Murray, Stanley Crouch, and Modern Black Cultural Conservatism," *Black Conservatism: Essays in Intellectual and Political History,* ed. Peter Eisenstadt (New York: Garland, 1999) 164.

37. Roy L. Brooks, *Rethinking the American Race Problem*, (Berkeley: U of California P, 1990) xii.

38. Derrick Bell, *And We Are Not Saved: The Elusive Quest for Racial Justice* (New York: Basic Books, 1987).

39. Charshee C. L. McIntyre, *Criminalizing a Race Free Blacks During Slavery* (Queens: Kayode, 1993).

40. Adolph Reed, Jr., *Class Notes: Posing as Politics and Other Thoughts on the American Scene* (New York: New P, 2000) 101-108.

41. Joseph G. Conti and Brad Stetson, "Are You Really A Racist? A Common-Sense Quiz," *Black and Right: The Bold New Voice of Black Conservatives in America*, ed. Stan Faryna, Brad Stegson, and Joseph G. Conti (Westport, Connecticut: Praeger, 1997) 70.

42. Qtd. in John White, *Black Leadership in America: From Booker T. Washington to Jesse Jackson,* 2nd ed. (New York: Longman Group U.K., 1990) 186.

43. Stanley Crouch, *Notes from a Hanging Judge: Essays and Reviews,* 1979-1989 (New York: Oxford UP, 1990) 4.

44. Reverend Jesse L. Jackson, *Straight from the Heart,* ed. Roger D. Hatch and Frank E. Watkins (Philadelphia: Fortress P, 1987) ix.

45. Manning Marable, *Beyond Black and White: Transforming African American Politics* (New York: Verso, 1995) 61.

46. —, *Speaking Truth to Power: Essays on Race, Resistance, and Radicalism* (Boulder: Westview P, 1996) 22.

47. Marable, *Beyond Black,* 275.

48. W. E. B. Du Bois, "Socialism and the Negro Problem," *W. E. B. Du Bois Speaks: Speeches and Addresses, 1890-1919,* ed. Philip S. Foner (New York: Pathfinder P, 1970) 240-241.

49. Robin D. G. Kelley, *Race Rebels: Culture, Politics, and the Black Working Class* (New York: Free P, 1996) 4.

50. Cedric J. Robinson, *Black Movements in America* (New York, Routledge, 1997) 153.

51. Adolph Reed, Jr., *Stirrings in the Jug: Black Politics in the Post-Segregation Era* (Minneapolis: U of Minnesota P, 1999) 190.

52. Reed, *Stirrings in the Jug,* 188.

53. Sharon M. Collins, "The Making of the Black Middle Class," *Social Problems,* 30.4 (1983): 369-380.

54. Martin Kilson, "Critique of Orlando Patterson's 'Blaming-the-Victim Rituals,'" *Souls,* 3.1 (2001): 82.

55. Manning Marable, *W. E. B. Du Bois: Black Radical Democrat* (Boston: Twayne, 1986).

56. bell hooks, *Killing Rage: Ending Racism* (New York: Holt, 1995).

57. Joy James, *Transcending the Talented Tenth: Black Leaders and American Intellectuals* (New York: Routledge, 1997) 139.

58. W. E. B. Du Bois, "Whither Now and Why," *The Education of Black People: Ten Critiques 1906-1960 by W. E. B. Du Bois,* ed. Herbert Aptheker (Amherst: U of Massachusetts P, 1973) 150.

59. "Black Radical Congress, 1998," *Let Nobody Turn Us Around: Voices of Resistance, Reform, and Renewal-An African-American Anthology,* ed. Manning Marable and Leith Mullings (New York: Rowman & Littlefield, 2000) 627.

60. "Black Radical Congress, 1998," 626.

CHAPTER FIVE: GOLIATH HOLDS SERVE: BOOKER T. WASHINGTON AND BLACK INTELLECTUALS

1. Thomas Sowell, "Up From Slavery," *Forbes,* (1994): 84-89, 92-93.
2. Glenn C. Loury, *One By One From the Inside Out: Essays and Reviews on Race and Responsibility in America* (New York: Free P, 1995) 68-69.
3. Loury, *One by One*, 73.
4. Loury, *One by One*, 251.
5. Loury, *One by One*, 251.
6. Manning Marable, *Beyond Black and White: Transforming African American Politics* (New York: Verso, 1995) 171.
7. Marable, *Beyond Black and White*, 169.
8. W. E. Burghardt Du Bois, *The Souls of Black Folk* (Greenwich, Connecticut: Fawcett, 1961) 47.
9. Kelly Miller, *Radicals and Conservatives and Other Essays on the Negro in America* (New York: Schocken, 1968) 40.
10. James Weldon Johnson, *Black Manhattan* (New York: Atheneum, 1969) 131-132.
11. Nell Irvin Painter, *Standing at Armageddon: The United States*, 1877-1919 (New York: Norton, 1987) 94.
12. James D. Anderson, *The Education of Blacks in the South*, 1860-1935 (Chapel Hill: U of North Carolina P, 1988).
13. Nathan Irvin Huggins, *Revelations: American History, American Myths* (New York: Oxford UP, 1995) 213.
14. Louis R. Harlan, *Booker T. Washington: The Wizard of Tuskegee Institute 1901-1915* (New York: Oxford UP, 1983) ix.
15. —-, *Booker T. Washington: The Making of a Black Leader* (New York: Oxford UP, 1972) ix.
16. Cornel West, *Prophesy Deliverance! An Afro-American Revolutionary Christianity* (Philadelphia: Westminster P, 1982) 166.
17. Joy James, *Transcending the Talented Tenth: Black Leaders and American Intellectuals* (New York: Routledge, 1997) 17.
18. W. E. B. Du Bois, *The Autobiography of W. E. B. Du Bois: A Soliloquy on Viewing My Life from the Last Decade of Its First Century,* ed. Herbert Aptheker (New York: International, 1968) 209.
19. Manning Marable, "Booker T. Washington and the Political Economy of Black Education in the United States 1860-1915," *A Different Vision: African American Economic Thought*, Volume I, ed. Thomas D. Boston (New York: Routledge, 1997) 169.

20. Arnold H. Taylor, *Travail and Triumph: Black Life and Culture in the South since the Civil War* (Westport, Connecticut: Greenwood P, 1976) Ch. 2.
21. David Levering Lewis, *W. E. B. Du Bois: Biography of A Race, 1869-1919* (New York: Holt, 1993) 429.
22. William M. Banks, *Black Intellectuals: Race and Responsibility in American Life* (New York: Norton, 1996) 40.
23. August Meier, *Negro Thought in America, 1880-1915: Racial Ideologies in the Age of Booker T. Washington* (Ann Arbor: U of Michigan P, 1963) Chs. 2-3,6.
24. James D. Anderson, *The Education of Blacks in the South*, 1880-1915, (Chapel Hill: U of North Carolina P, 1988) 104.
25. Robert L. Factor, *The Black Response to American Men, Ideals, and Organization from Frederick Douglass to the NAACP* (Reading, Massachusetts: Addison-Wesley, 1970) 187.
26. Adolph Reed, Jr., *W. E. B. Du Bois and American Political Thought: Fabianism and the Color Line* (New York: Oxford UP, 1997) 61.
27. Anderson, *The Education of Blacks in the South*, 1880-1915, 106.
28. Anderson, *The Education of Blacks*, 107-108.
29. "An Account of Washington's Reception in New England," *The Booker T. Washington Papers, Volume 10: 1909-11*, ed. Louis R. Harlan, Raymond W. S. Smock, Geraldine McTigue, and Nan E. Woodruff (Urbana: Illinois UP, 1984) 322-232.
30. Manning Marable, *Speaking Truth to Power: Essays on Race, Resistance, and Radicalism* (Boulder: Westview P, 1996) 62.
31. In his introduction to *Philosophy & Opinions of Marcus Garvey*, ed. Amy Jacques-Garvey (New York: Atheneum, 1969) i.
32. Cornel West, *Prophecy Deliverance! An Afro-American Revolutionary Christianity* (Philadelphia: Westminster P, 1982) 141.
33. William Anthony Avery, "An Account of Washington's Louisiana Tour," rpt. in *The Booker T. Washington Papers, Volume 13*: 1914-15, ed. Louis R. Harlan, Raymond W. Smock, Susan Valenza, and Sade M. Harlan (Urbana: U of Illinois P, 1984) 322-323.
34. Booker T. Washington, "A Speech Delivered Before the Women's New England Club, *The Booker T. Washington Papers, Volume 3*: 1901-1902 (Urbana: U of Illinois P, 1977) 29.
35. Vernon J. Williams, Jr., "Booker T. Washington, Myth Maker," *A Different Vision: African American Economic Thought, Volume I*, ed. Thomas D. Boston (New York: Routledge, 1997) 194.

36. Williams, "Booker T. Washington" 194.

37. James H. Cone, "Epilogue: An Interpretation of the Debate Among Black Theologians," *Black Theology: A Documentary History, Volume One 1966-1979*, 2nd rev. ed., ed. James H. Cone and Gayroud S. Wilmore (Maryknoll, New York: Orbis, 1993) 425.

38. Cornel West, "Benediction," *The Courage to Hope: From Black Suffering to Human Redemption*, ed. Quinton Hosford Dixie and Cornel West (Boston: Beacon P, 1999) 225.

39. Cheryl Townsend Gilkes, "Some Folks Get Happy and Some Folks Don't: Diversity, Community, and African American Christian Spirituality," *The Courage to Hope: From Black Suffering to Human Redemption*, ed. Quinton Hosford Dixie and Cornel West (Boston: Beacon P, 1999) 211-212.

40. Walter E. Fluker, "The Politics of Conversion and the Civilization of Friday," *The Courage to Hope: From Black Suffering to Human Redemption*, ed. Quinton Hosford Dixie and Cornel West (Boston: Beacon P, 1999) 105-106.

41. Cheryl Townsend Gilkes, "We Have a Beautiful Mother: Womanist Musings on the Afrocentric Idea," *Living the Intersection: Womanism and Afrocentrism and Theology*, ed. Cheryl J. Sanders (Minneapolis: Fortress P, 1995) 33.

42. Kelly Brown Douglas, *The Black Christ* (Maryknoll, New York: Orbis, 1994) 106-107.

43. David Levering Lewis, *W. E. B. Du Bois: Biography of A Race, 1869-1919* (New York: Holt, 1993) 169.

44. Howard McGary and Bill E. Lawson, *Between Slavery and Freedom: Philosophy and American Slavery* (Bloomington: Indiana UP, 1992) 92.

45. Tavis Smiley, ed., *How to Make Black America Better* (New York: Doubleday, 2001).

46. W. E. B. Du Bois, "The Economic Future of the Negro," *W. E. B. Du Bois Speaks: Speeches and Addresses, 1890-1919*, ed. Philip S. Foner (New York: Pathfinder P, 1970) 159.

47. Thomas Sowell, *The Quest for Cosmic Justice* (New York: Free P, 1999).

48. Bernard R. Boxill, *Blacks and Social Justice*, rev. ed. (Lantham, Maryland: Rowan and Littlefied, 1992) 49.

49. Wilson Jeremiah Moses, "From Booker T. to Malcolm X: Black Political Thought from 1895-1965," *Upon These Shores: Themes in the African-American Experience 1600 to the Present*, ed. William R. Scott and William G. Slade (New York: Routledge, 2000) 200-201.

50. Booker T. Washington, "The Negro and the Signs of Civilization," *The Booker T. Washington Papers, Volume 6: 1901-02*, ed. Louis R. Harlan, Raymond W. Smock, and Barbara S. Kraft (Urbana: U of Illinois P, 1977) 300.

51. Washington, "The Negro," 299.

52. Booker T. Washington, *The Future of the American Negro* (New York: New American Library, 1969) 228.

53. "A Sunday Evening Talk: Self-Denial," *The Booker T. Washington Papers, Volume 3: 1889-95*, ed. Louis R. Harlan, Stuart B. Kaufman, and Raymond W. Smock (Urbana: U of Illinois P, 1974) 131.

54. "A Sunday Evening Talk: The Work To Be Done," *The Booker T. Washington Papers, Volume 3*, 551.

55. *Character Building* (New York: Doubleday, 1902) 40-41.

56. Qtd. in *The Southern Letter*, 4.9 (1888): 1.

57. Qtd. in *The Southern Letter*, 4.9 (1888): 3.

58. Qtd. in *The Southern Letter*, 7.10 (1890): 3.

59. Qtd. in *The Southern Letter*, 13.11 (1886): 3.

60. Qtd. in *The Southern Letter*, 17.4 (1901): 3.

61. Michael C. Dawson, *Black Visions: The Roots of Contemporary African-American Political Ideologies* (Chicago: U of Chicago P, 2001) 285.

62. Dawson, *Black Visions*, 285.

63. John Brown Childs, *Leadership, Conflict, and Cooperation in Afro-American Social Thought* (Philadelphia: Temple UP, 1989) 16.

64. Booker T. Washington, "Some Charges Against the Race," *The Southern Workman*, 32.11 (1903): 496.

65. W. E. Burghardt Du Bois, "The Talented Tenth," *The Negro Problem* (New York: Arno/New York Times, 1969) 33.

66. Joy James, *Transcending the Talented Tenth: Black Leaders and American Intellectuals* (New York: Routledge, 1997) 24.

67. William Edward Burghardt Du Bois To Booker T. Washington 10 April, 1900, *The Booker T. Washington Papers, Volume 5: 1899-1900*, ed. Louis R. Harlan, Raymond W. Smock, and Barbara S. Kraft (Urbana: U of Illinois P, 1976) 480.

68. Joy James, *Transcending the Talented Tenth*, 22.

69. Thomas C. Holt, "The Political Uses of Alienation: W. E. B. Du Bois on Politics, Race, and Culture, 1903-1940," *American Quarterly*, 42.2 (1990): 315.

70. Henry Louis Gates, Jr., and Cornel West, *The Future of the Race*, (New York: Vintage, 1996) xv.

71. Cornel West, "Black Strivings in a Twilight Civilization," *The Future of the Race*, 76.

72. West, "Black Strivings," 56-57.

73. West, "Black Strivings," 57.

74. West, "Black Strivings," 78.

75. W. E. Burghardt Du Bois, *The Souls of Black Folk* (Greenwich, Connecticut: Fawcett, 1961) 123.

76. Qtd. in Henry Louis Gates, Jr. and Cornet West, *The Future of the Race* (New York: Vintage, 1996) 54.

77. W. E. B. Du Bois, *Darkwater: Voices from Within the Veil* (New York: Schocken Books, 1969) 44.

78. —, "The Souls of White Folks," *W. E. B. Du Bois: A Reader*, ed. Meyer Weinberg (New York: Harper, 1970) 303-304.

79. Qtd. in Clinton M. Jean, *Behind the Eurocentric Veils: The Search for African Realities* (Amherst: U of Massachusetts P, 1991) 13.

80. W. E. B. Du Bois, "The Relations of the Negroes to the Whites in the South," *W. E. B. Du Bois on Black Sociology and Black Community*, ed. Dan S. Green and Edwin D. Driver (Chicago: U of Chicago P, 1978) 262.

81. *The Crisis*, 2.4 (1911): 155.

82. W. E. B. Du Bois, "Ashamed," *W. E. B. Du Bois: The Crisis Writings*, ed. Daniel Walden (Greenwich, Connecticut: Fawcett, 1972) 89.

83. —, *The Autobiography of W. E. B. Du Bois: A Soliloquy on Viewing My Life from the Last Decade of Its First Century*, ed. Herbert Aptheker (New York: International, 1968) 120.

84. —, *The Negro* (New York: Oxford UP, 1970) 90.

85. —, *Darkwater: Voices from Within the Veil* (New York: Schocken Books, 1969) 39.

86. Qtd. in West, "Black Strivings in a Twilight Civilization," *The Future of the Race* (New York: Vintage, 1996) 72.

87. W. E. Burghardt Du Bois, "The African Roots of War," *W. E. B. Du Bois Speaks: Speeches and Addresses*, 1890-1919, ed. Philip S. Foner (New York: Pathfinder, 1970) 255.

88. —, *The World and Africa: An Inquiry into the Part which Africa has Played in World History* (New York: International, 1947) 23.

89. David Levering Lewis, *W. E. B. Du Bois: Biography of a Race, 1869-1919* (New York: Holt, 1993) 439.

90. Robert Russa Moton To Booker T. Washington 13 May, 1911 *The Booker T. Washington Papers, Volume 11: 1911-12*, ed. Louis R. Harlan, Raymond W. Smock, and Geraldine McTigue (Urbana: U of Illinois P, 1981) 155.

91. Booker T. Washington To Robert Russa Moton 23 May, 1911, *The Booker T. Washington Papers, Volume 11*, 166-167.

92. Mary White Ovington, *Black and White Sat Down Together: The Reminiscences of an NAACP Founder,* ed. Ralph E. Luker (New York: Feminist P, 1995) 58.
93. W. E. B. Du Bois, *Dusk at Dawn: An Essay toward an Autobiography of a Race Concept* (New York: Schocken, 1968) 72.

Chapter Six: Why Black Female Intellectuals Tend to Shout

1. Robert L. Allen, and Pamela P. Allen, *Reluctant Reformers: Racism and Social Movements in the United States* (Garden City, New York: Doubleday, 1975).
2. Karla F. C. Holloway, *Codes of Conduct: Race Ethics and the Color of Our Character* (New Brunswick: Rutgers UP, 1995). 36.
3. Qtd. in Holloway, *Codes of Conduct,* 40.
4. Dr. Gail Elizabeth Wyatt, *Stolen Women Reclaiming Our Sexuality: Taking Back Our Lives* (New York: Wiley, 1997) xvii.
5. Karla F. C. Holloway, *Codes of Conflict,* 66.
6. Qtd. in Patricia Hill Collins, *Fighting Words: Black Women and the Search for Justice* (Minneapolis: U of Minnesota P, 1998) 123.
7. Qtd. in William D. Wright, "The Socialist Analysis of W. E. B. Du Bois," diss., U of Microfilms International, 1985) 331.
8. Qtd. in Wright, "The Socialist Analysis," 309.
9. bell hooks, *Ain't I a Woman?: Black Women and Feminism* (Boston: South End P, 1981) 1.
10. Cheryl J. Sanders, "Black Women in Biblical Perspective: Resistance, Affirmation, and Empowerment," *Living the Intersection: Womanism and Afrocentrism and Theology,* ed. Cheryl J. Sanders (Minneapolis: Fortress P, 1995) 126.
11. Hazel V. Carby, *Reconstructing Womanhood: The Emergence of the Afro-American Woman Novelist* (New York: Oxford UP, 1987).
12. Patricia Hill Collins, *Fighting Words: Black Women and the Search for Justice* (Minneapolis: U of Minnesota P, 1998) 210-211.
13. Collins, *Fighting Words,* 211.
14. Katie Geneva Cannon, *Katie's Canon: Womanism and the Soul of the Black Community* (New York: Continuum, 1995) 60.
15. Marcia Y. Riggs, *Awake, Arise & Act: A Womanist Call for Black Liberation* (Cleveland: Pilgrim P, 1994) 2.
16. Michele Wallace, *Black Macho and the Myth of the Superwoman* (New York: Warner, 1979).

17. bell hooks, *Yearning: Race, Gender, and Cultural Politics* (Boston: South End P, 1990) 16.

18. Qtd. in George Yancy, ed., *African-American Philosophers: 17 Conversations* (New York: Routledge, 1998) 25.

19. Michele Wallace, *Invisibility: Blues From Pop to Theory* (New York: Verso, 1990) 4.

20. Wallace, *Invisibility*, 1.

21. Wallace, *Invisibility*, 3-4.

22. Cornel West, *Race Matters* (Boston: Beacon P, 1993) 63.

23. Adelbert H. Jenkins, *The Psychology of the Afro-American: A Humanist Approach* (New York: Pergamon P, 1982) 85.

24. Marcia Y. Riggs, *Awake, Arise & Act: A Womanist Call for Black Liberation* (Cleveland: Pilgrim P, 1994) 15.

25. W. E. B. Du Bois To George Streator Atlanta, Georgia, 21 March, 1938, *The Correspondence of W. E. B. Du Bois, Volume II Selections 1934-1944,* ed. Herbert Aptheker (Amherst: U of Massachusetts P, 1976) 92.

26. Qtd. William D. Wright, "The Socialist Analysis of W. E. B. Du Bois," diss., U of Microfilms International, 1985, 334.

27. Beverly Guy-Sheftall, "Black Feminism in the United States," *Upon These Shores: Themes in the African-American Experience 1600 to the Present,* ed. William R. Scott and William G. Slade (New York: Routledge, 2000) 362.

28. Patricia Hill Collins, *Fighting Words: Black Women and the Search for Justice* (Minneapolis: U of Minnesota P, 1998) 61-62.

29. Geneva Smitherman, "A Womanist Looks at the Million Man March," *Million Man March/Day of Absence*, ed. Haki R. Madhubuti and Maulana Karenga (Chicago: Third World P, 1996) 104.

30. Marcia Y. Riggs, *Awake, Arise & Act: A Womanist Call for Black Liberation* (Cleveland: Pilgrim P, 1994) 9-10.

31. Evelyn Brooks Higginbotham, "African-American Women's History and the Metalanguage of Race," *"We Specialize in the Wholly Impossible," A Reader in Black Women's History,* ed. Darlene Clark Hine, Wilma King, and Linda Reed (Brooklyn: Carlson) 17.

32. Darlene Clark Hine, "Lifting the Veil, Shattering the Silence: Black Women's History in Slavery and Freedom," *The State of Afro-American History Past, Present, and Future*, ed. Darlene Clark Hine (Baton Rouge: Louisiana State UP, 1986) 223.

33. Nell Irvin Painter, "Comment," *The State of Afro-American History*, 81-82.

34. Bettye J. Gardner, "The Teaching of Afro-American History in Schools and Colleges," *The State of Afro-American History*, 174.

35. Darlene Clarke Hine, *HineSight: Black Women and the Reconstruction of American History* (Brooklyn: Carlson, 1994) xviii.

36. Delores S. Williams, "Afrocentrism and Male-Female Relations in Church and Society," *Living the Intersection: Womanism and Afrocentrism and Theology,* ed. Cheryl J. Sanders (Minneapolis: Fortress P, 1995) 50.

37. Cheryl J. Sanders, "Afrocentric and Womanist Approaches to Theological Education," *Living the Intersection,* 162.

38. Lorine L. Cummings, "A Womanist Response to the Afrocentric Idea: Jarena Lee, Womanist Preacher," *Living the Intersection,* 59.

39. Cheryl Townsend Gilkes, "We Have a Beautiful Mother: Womanist Musings on the Afrocentric Idea," *Living the Intersection: Womanism and Afrocentrism and Theology,* ed. Cheryl J. Sanders (Minneapolis: Fortress P, 1995) 26.

40. Gilkes, *Living the Intersection,* 27.

APPENDIX I: ANCIENT KEMET AND JUDAISM AND CHRISTIANITY

1. Wayne B. Chandler, *Ancient Future: The Teachings and Prophetic Wisdom of the Seven Hermetic Laws of Ancient Egypt* (Baltimore: Black Classic P, 1999) 70.

2. Donald Mackenzie, *Egyptian Myths and Legends* (New York: Gramercy Books, 1994) 330.

3. Henri Daniel-Roper, *Israel and the Ancient World: A History of the Israelites from the Time of Abraham to the Birth of Christ* (London: Eyre & Spittiswoode, 1949) 80.

4. Qtd. in *The Book of the Dead: The Hieroglyphic Transcript and Translation Into English of the Papyrus of Ani,* ed. E. A. Wallis Budge (New York: Gramercy Books, 1960) 106-107.

5. James Breasted, *The Dawn of Conscience* (New York: Scribner's, 1947) 384-385.

6. Albert J. Raboteau, "African-Americans, Exodus, and the American Israel," *Strangers & Neighbors: Relations between Blacks & Jews in the United States,* ed. Maurianne Adams and John Bracey (Amherst: U of Massachusetts P, 1999) 57-63.

7. John G. Jackson, *Christianity before Christ* (Austin: American Atheist P, 1985).

8. Charles S. Finch III, M.D., *Echoes of the Old Darkland Themes from the African Eden* (Decatur: Khenti, 1991).

9. Browder, Anthony T. *Nile Valley Contributions to Civilization: Exploding the Myths, Volume 1* (D.C.: The Institute of Karmic Guidance, 1992).

Selected Bibliography

Allen, Robert L., and Pamela P. Allen. *Reluctant Reformers: Racism and Social Movements in the United States*. Garden City, New York: Anchor, 1975.

Allport, Gordon W. *The Nature of Prejudice*. Garden City, New York: Doubleday, 1964.

Anderson, James, D. *The Education of Blacks in the South*, 1860-1935. Chapel Hill: U of North Carolina P, 1988.

Ani, Marimbe. *Yurugu: An African-Centered Critique of European Cultural Thought and Behavior*. Trenton: Africa World P, 1994.

Appiah, Kwame Anthony. *In My Father's House: Africa in the Philosophy of Culture*. New York: Oxford UP, 1992.

Appiah, Kwame Anthony and Amy Gutmann. *Color Consciousness: The Political Morality of Race*. Princeton: Princeton UP, 1996.

Asante, Molefi, Kete. *The Afrocentric Idea*. Philadelphia: Temple UP, 1987.

Kemet, Afrocentricity and Knowledge. Trenton: Africa World P, 1990.

Auerbach, M. Morton. *The Conservative Illusion*. New York: Columbia UP, 1959.

Baldwin, James. *The Fire Next Time*. New York: Dial P, 1963.

Nobody Knows My Name. More Notes of a Native Son. New York: Dell, 1954.

Banks, William M. *Black Intellectuals: Race and Responsibility in American Life*. New York: Norton, 1996.

Barkan, Alazar. *The Retreat of Scientific Racism*. New York: Cambridge UP, 1992.

Bennett, Lerone, Jr. *Forced into Glory: Abraham Lincoln's White Dream.* Chicago: Johnson, 2000.

—. "The Status of Race in American Culture," *The Declining Significance of Race? A Dialogue among Black and White Social Scientists.* ed. Joseph R. Washington Jr. Philadelphia: U of Pennsylvania, 1979.

Blassingame, John W. *The Slave Community: Plantation Life in the Antebellum South.* New York: Oxford UP, 1972.

Boxill, Bernard R. *Blacks and Social Justice.* Rev. ed. Lanham, Maryland: Rowman & Littlefield, 1992.

Breasted, James. *The Dawn of Conscience.* New York: Scribner's, 1947.

Brooks, Roy L. *Rethinking the American Race Problem.* Berkeley: U of California P, 1990.

Browder, Anthony T. *Nile Valley Contributions to Civilization: Exploding the Myths Volume I.* Washington D.C.: The Institute of Karmic Guidance, 1992.

Cannon, Katie Geneva. *Katie's Canon: Womanism and the Soul of the Black Community.* New York: Continuum, 1995.

Carby, Hazel. *Reconstructing Womanhood: The Emergence of the Afro-American Woman Novelist.* New York: Oxford UP, 1987.

Carruthers, Jacob H. *Intellectual Warfare.* Chicago: Third World P, 1999.

Childs, John Brown. *Leadership, Conflict, and Cooperation in Afro-American Social Thought.* Philadelphia: Temple UP, 1993.

Clarke, John Henrik, ed. *New Dimensions in African History: The London Lectures of Dr. Yosef ben-Jochanan and Dr. John Henrik Clarke.* Trenton: Africa World P, 1991.

Collins, Patricia Hill. *Fighting Words: Black Women and The Search for Justice.* Minneapolis: U of Minnesota P, 1998.

Collins, Sharon M. "The Making of the Black Middle Class," *Social Problems* 30.4 (1983): 369-380.

Comer, James P. *Beyond Black and White*. New York: New York Times, 1972.

Cone, James H. "Epilogue: An Interpretation of the Debate among Black Theologians." *Black Theology: A Documentary History. Volume One 1966-1979*. Rev 2nd ed. ed. James H. Cone and Gayraud S. Wilmore. Maryknoll, New York: Orbis, 1993.

Crouch, Stanley. *Notes from a Hanging Judge. Essays and Reviews,* 1979-1989. New York: Oxford UP, 1990.

Cruse, Harold. *The Crisis of the Negro Intellectual*. New York: Morrow, 1967.

—. *Rebellion or Revolution?* New York: Morrow, 1968.

Dawson, Michael C. *Black Visions: The Roots of Contemporary African-American Political Ideologies*. Chicago: U of Chicago P, 2001.

Douglass, Frederick. *My Bondage and My Freedom*. Chicago: Johnson, 1970.

Douglas, Kelly Brown. *The Black Christ*. Maryknoll, New York: Orbis, 1995.

Du Bois, W. E. B. *The Autobiography of W. E. B. Du Bois: A Soliloquy on Viewing My Life from the Last Decade of Its First Century*. ed. Herbert Aptheker. New York: International, 1968.

—. *Darkwater Voices from Within the Veil*. New York: Schocken, 1969.

—. *Dusk at Dawn: An Essay toward an Autobiography of a Race Concept*. New York: Schocken, 1968.

—. *The Negro*. New York: Oxford UP, 1970.

—. *The Souls of Black Folk*. Greenwich, Connecticut: Fawcett, 1961.

—. *The World and Africa: An Inquiry into the Part Which Africa has Played in World History*. New York: International, 1947.

Ellison, Ralph. *Invisible Man*. New York: Random House, 1952.

Fabre, Genevieve and Robert O'Meally, ed. *History and Memory in African-American Culture*. New York: Oxford UP, 1994.

Factor, Robert L. *The Black Response to America: Men, Ideals, and Organization from Frederick Douglass to the NAACP*. Reading, Massachusetts: Addison-Wesley, 1970.

Faryna, Stan, Brad Stetson, and Joseph G. Conti, ed. *Black and Right: The Bold New Voice of Black Conservatives in America*. Westport, Connecticut: Praeger, 1997.

Finch, Charles S. III, M.D. *Echoes of the Old Darkland Themes from the African Eden*. Decatur: Khenti, 1991.

Foner, Philip S., ed. *W. E. B. Du Bois Speaks: Speeches and Addresses, 1890-1919*. New York: Pathfinder P, 1970.

—, ed. *W. E. B. Du Bois Speaks: Speeches and Addresses, 1920-1963*. New York: Pathfinder P, 1970.

Franklin, V. P. *Black Self-Determination: A Cultural History of the Faith of the Fathers*. Westport, Connecticut: Lawrence Hill, 1984.

—. *Living Our Stories, Telling Our Truths. Autobiography and the Making of the African American Intellectual Tradition*. New York: Scribner, 1995.

Gardner, Bettye J. "The Teaching of Afro-American History in Schools and Colleges." *The State of Afro-American History Past, Present, and Future*. ed. Darlene Clarke Hine. Baton Rouge: Louisiana State UP, 1986.

Gates, Henry Louis, Jr., ed. *Black Letters in the Enlightenment: Race and Difference*. New York: Oxford UP, 1990.

Gates, Henry Louis, Jr., and Cornel West. *The Future of the Race*. New York: Vintage, 1996.

Gilkes, Cheryl Townsend. "We Have a Beautiful Mother: Womanist Musings on the Afrocentric Idea." *Living the Intersection: Womanism and Afrocentrism and Theology*. ed. Cheryl J. Sanders. Minneapolis: Fortress P, 1995.

Gilroy, Paul. *The Black Atlantic Modernity and Double Consciousness.* Cambridge: Harvard UP, 1993.

Goldsby, Richard A. *Race and Races.* New York: Macmillan, 1971.

Goldstene, Paul N. *The Collapse of Liberal Empire Science and Revolution in the Twentieth Century.* New Haven: Yale UP, 1977.

Goldwater, Barry. *The Conscience of a Conservative.* New York: Hillman, 1960.

—. *The Conscience of a Majority.* Englewood Cliffs, New Jersey: Prentice-Hall, 1970.

Gordon, Lewis R. *Bad Faith and Antiblack Racism.* Atlantic Highlands, New Jersey: Humanities P, 1995.

Gottschild, Brenda Dixon. *Digging the Africanist Presence in American Performance Dance and Other Contexts.* Westport, Connecticut: Greenwood P, 1996.

Harlan, Louis R. *Booker T. Washington: The Making of a Black Leader.* New York: Oxford UP, 1972.

—. *Booker T. Washington: The Wizard of Tuskegee Institute,* 1901-1915. New York: Oxford UP, 1983.

Harlan, Louis R., Stuart B. Kaufman, and Raymond Smock, ed. *The Booker T. Washington Papers, Volume 3: 1889-95.* Urbana: U of Illinois P, 1974.

Harlan, Louis R., Raymond Smock, and Nan E. Woodruff, ed. *The Booker T. Washington Papers, Volume 9:* 1906-08. Urbana: U of Illinois P, 1980.

Harlan, Louis R., Raymond W. Smock, and Geraldine McTigue, ed. *The Booker T. Washington Papers, Volume 11: 1911-12.* Urbana: U of Illinois P, 1981.

Harlan, Louis R. and Raymond Smock, ed. *The Booker T. Washington Papers, Volume 12: 1912-14.* Urbana: U of Illinois P, 1982.

Harlan, Louis R., Raymond W. Smock, Susan Valenze, and Sade M. Harlan, ed. *The Booker T. Washington Papers, Volume 13: 1914-15*. Urbana: U of Illinois P, 1984.

Higginbotham, Evelyn Brooks. "African-American Women's History and the Metalanguage of Race." *"We specialize in the Wholly Impossible": A Reader in Black Women's History*. Ed. Darlene Clarke Hine, Wilma King, and Linda Reed. Brooklyn: Carlson, 1995.

Hine, Darlene Clarke. *HineSight: Black Women and the Reconstruction of American History*. Brooklyn: Carlson, 1994.

Hofstadter, Richard. *Anti-Intellectualism in American Life*. New York: Knopf, 1963.

Holloway, Joseph E., ed. *Africanisms in American Culture*. Bloomington: Indiana UP, 1990.

Holloway, Karla F. C. *Codes of Conduct: Race Ethics and the Color of Our Character*. New Brunswick: Rutgers UP, 1995.

hooks, bell. *Ain't I A Woman?: Black Women and Feminism*. Boston: South End P, 1981.

—. *Killing Rage: Ending Racism*. New York: Holt, 1995.

—. *Yearning: Race, Gender, and Cultural Politics*. Boston: South End P, 1990.

Hornung, Erik. *Idea into Image: Essays on Ancient Egyptian Thought*. New York: Timken, 1992.

Huggins, Nathan Irvin. *Black odyssey: The African-American Ordeal in Slavery*. New York: Random House, 1990.

—. *Revelations: American History, American Myth*. New York: Oxford UP, 1995.

Jackson, John G. *Christianity before Christ*. Austin: American Atheist P, 1985.

Jackson, Reverend Jesse L. *Straight from the Heart*. ed. Roger D. Hatch and Frank E. Watkins. Philadelphia: Fortress P, 1987.

Jacques-Garvey, Amy, ed. *Philosophy and Opinions of Marcus Garvey*. New York: Atheneum, 1969.

James, Joy. *Transcending the Talented Tenth: Black Leaders and American Intellectuals*. New York: Routledge, 1997.

Jean, Clinton M. *Behind the Eurocentric Veils: The Search for African Realities*. Amherst: U of Massachusetts P, 1991.

Jenkins, Adelbert H. *The Psychology of the Afro-American: A Humanist Approach*. New York: Pergamon P, 1982.

Kaster, Joseph. "What was Ancient Egypt? Egypt's Place in the History of Civilization." *The Wisdom of Ancient Egypt*. Trans. and ed. Joseph Kaster. New York: Barnes and Noble, 1968.

Kelley, Robin D. G. *Race Rebels: Culture, Politics, and the Black Working Class*. New York: Free P, 1996.

King, James C. *The Biology of Race*. Rev. ed. Berkeley: U of California P, 1981.

Lefkowitz, Mary. *Not Out of Africa: How Africancentrism Became an Excuse to Teach Myth as History*. New York: Harper, 1996.

Lester, Julius, ed. *To Be A Slave*. New York: Dell, 1968.

Lewis, Bernard. *Cultures in Conflict: Christians, Muslims, and Jews in the Age of Discovery*. New York: Oxford UP, 1995.

Lewis, David Levering. *W. E. B. Du Bois: Biography of A Race 1869-1919*. New York: Holt, 1993.

Lott, Tommy L. *The Invention of Race: Black Culture and the Politics of Representation*. Malden, Massachusetts: Blackwell, 1999.

Loury, Glenn C. *One by One From the Inside Out: Essays and Reviews on Race and Responsibility in America*. New York: Free P, 1995.

Lubiano, Wahneema. "Black Nationalism and Black Common Sense: Policing Ourselves." *The House that Race Built*. ed. Wahneema Lubiano. New York: Pantheon, 1997.

Marable, Manning. *Beyond Black and White: Transforming African American Politics*. New York: Verso, 1995.

—. *Speaking Truth to Power. Essays on Race, Resistance, and Radicalism*. Boulder: Westview P, 1969.

—. *W. E. B. Du Bois: Black Radical Democrat*. Boston: Twayne, 1986.

Mazrui, Ali. "On the Concept of 'We are All Africans.'" *American Political Science Review*, 58.1 (1963): 88-97.

McGary, Howard and Bill E. Lawson. *Between Slavery and Freedom: Philosophy and American Slavery*. Bloomington: Indiana UP, 1992.

McIntyre, Charshee C. L. *Criminalizing A Race: Free Blacks During Slavery*. Queens: Kayode, 1993.

McWhorter, John H. *Losing the Race: Self-Sabotage in Black America*. New York: Free P, 2000.

Meier, August. *Negro Thought in America, 1880-1915: Racial Ideologies in the Age of Booker T. Washington*. Ann Arbor: U of Michigan P, 1963.

Miller, Kelly. *Radicals and Conservatives and Other Essays on the Negro in America*. New York: Schocken, 1968.

Mills, Charles W. *Blackness Visible: Essays on Philosophy and Race*. Ithaca: Cornell UP, 1998.

Morrison, Toni. "The Site of Memory." *Inventing the Truth: The Art and Craft of Memoir*. ed. William K. Zinser. New York: Book-of-the-Month-Club, 1987.

Moses, Wilson Jeremiah. "From Booker T. to Malcolm X: Black Political Thought from 1895-1965." *Upon These Shores: Themes in the African-American Experience, 1600 to the Present*. ed. William R. Scott and William G. Slade. New York: Routledge, 2000.

—. *The Golden Age of Black Nationalism, 1850-1925*. New York: Oxford UP, 1978.

Neal, Larry. *Visions of a Liberated Future: Black Arts Movement Writings*. New York: Thunder Mouth P, 1989.

Outlaw, Lucius T. *On Race and Philosophy*. New York: Routledge, 1996.

Ovington, Mary White. *Black and White Sat Down Together: The Reminiscences of an NAACP Founder*. ed. Ralph E. Luker. New York: Feminist P, 1995.

Painter, Nell Irvin. *Standing at Armageddon: The United States 1877-1919*. New York: Norton, 1987.

Palmer, Colin. "The African Diaspora," *Black Scholar,* 30.3-4, (2000): 56-59.

Patterson, Orlando. *The Ordeal of Integration Progress and Resentment in America's "Racial" Crisis*. D.C.: Civitas/Counterpoint, 1997.

Peterson, Jesse Lee with Brad Stetson. *Rage to Responsibility: Black Conservative Jesse Lee Peterson*. St. Paul: Paragon House, 2000.

Rawick, George P. *From Sundown to Sunup: The Making of the Black Community*. Westport, Connecticut: Greenwood, 1972.

Reed, Adolph, Jr. *Class Notes: Posing as Politics and Other Thoughts on the American Scene*. New York: New P, 2000.

—. *Stirrings in the Jug: Black Politics in the Post-Segregation Era*. Minneapolis: U of Minnesota P, 1999.

—. *W. E. B. Du Bois and American Political Thought: Fabianism and the Color Line*. New York: Oxford UP, 1997.

Riggs, Marcia Y. *Awake, Arise & Act: A Womanist Call for Black Liberation*. Cleveland: Pilgrim P, 1994.

Robinson, Cedric J. *Black Movements in America*. New York: Routledge, 1997.

Schlesinger, Arthur M., Jr. *The Disuniting of America*. Rev. ed. New York: Norton, 1998.

Skinner, Elliott P. "Transcending Traditions: African, African-American and African Diaspora Studies in the 21st Century-the Past Must Be the Prologue." *Black Scholar*, 30.3-4 (2000): 4-12.

Smiley, Tavis, ed. *How to Make Black America Better*. New York: Doubleday, 2001.

Sowell, Thomas. *Civil Rights: Rhetoric or Reality?* New York: Morrow, 1984.

—. *The Quest for Cosmic Justice*. New York: Free P, 1999.

Steele, Shelby. *The Content of Our Character: A New Vision of Race in America*. New York: St. Martin's, 1990.

Stuckey, Sterling. *Slave Culture: Nationalist Theory and the Foundation of Black America*. New York: Oxford UP, 1987.

Tate, Claudia, ed. *Black Women Writers at Work*. Harpenden Herts, England: Oldcastle, 1983.

Taylor, Arnold H. *Travail and Triumph: Black Life and Culture in the South since the Civil War*. Westport, Connecticut: Greenwood P, 1976.

Thomas, Alexander, M.D. and Samuel Sillen, Ph.D. *Racism and Psychiatry*. New York: Brunner/Mazel, 1972.

Walker, Clarence E. *We Can't Go Home: An Argument About Afrocentrism*. New York: Oxford UP, 2001.

Wallace, Michele. *Black Macho and the Myth of the Superwoman*. New York: Warner, 1979.

—. *Invisibility Blues: From Pop to Theory*. New York: Verso, 1990.

Washington, Booker T. *Character Building*. New York: Doubleday, 1902.

—. *The Future of the American Negro*. New York: New American Library, 1969.

Watts, Jerry Gafio. *Heroism and the Black Intellectual: Ralph Ellison, Politics, and Afro-American Intellectual Life*. Chapel Hill: U of North Carolina P, 1994.

West, Cornel. "Benediction." *The Courage to Hope: From Black Suffering to Human Redemption*. ed. Quinton Hosford Dixie and Cornel West. Boston: Beacon P, 1999.

——. *Keeping the Faith: Philosophy and Race*. New York: Routledge, 1993.

——. *Prophesy Deliverance! An Afro-American Revolutionary Christianity*. Philadelphia: Westminster P, 1982.

——. *Prophetic Thought in Postmodern Times: Beyond Eurocentrism and Multiculturalism, Volume I*. Monroe, Maine: Common Courage P, 1993.

White, John. *Black Leadership in America: From Booker T. Washington to Jesse Jackson*. 2nd ed. New York: Longman Group, 1990.

Williams, Delores S. "Afrocentrism and Male-Female Relations in Church and Society." *Living the Intersection: Womanism and Afrocentrism and Theology*. ed. Cheryl J. Sanders. Minneapolis: Fortress P, 1995.

Wilson, William Julius. *The Declining Significance of Race: Blacks and Changing American Institutions*. Chicago: U of Chicago P, 1977.

——. *Power, Race, and Privilege: Race Relations in Theoretical and Sociohistorical Perspectives*. New York: Macmillan, 1973.

Wolff, Eduard N. *Top Heavy*. New York: New Press, 1996.

Woodson, Robert L. Sr. *The Triumphs of Joseph: How Today's Community Healers are Reviving Our Streets and Neighborhoods*. New York: Free P, 1998.

Wright, W. D. *Black Intellectuals, Black Cognition, and a Black Aesthetic*. Westport, Connecticut: Praeger, 1997.

——. *Historians and Slavery: A Critical Analysis of Perspectives and Irony in American Slavery and Other Recent Works*. D.C.: UP of America, 1978.

——. *The Socialist Analysis of W. E. B. Du Bois* Diss. U Microfilms International, 1985.

Wyatt, Gail Elizabeth, M.D. *Stolen Women: Reclaiming Our Sexuality, Taking Back Our Lives*. New York: Wiley, 1997.

Yancy, George, ed. *African-American Philosophers: 17 Conversations.* New York: Routledge, 1998.

Yetman, Norman P., ed. *"Life Under the "Peculiar Institution": Selections from the Slave Narrative Collection.* New York: Holt, 1940.

Zack, Naomi, ed. *Race/Sex: Their Sameness, Differences, and Interplay.* New York: Routledge, 1997.

Zweigenhaft, Richard L. and G. William Dormhoff. *Diversity in the Power Elite: Have Women and Minorities Reached the Top?* New Haven: Yale UP.

Index

Villiard, Francis Oswald, 7

Walker, Alice, 263, 267; coined term "womanists", 283–285
Walker, Clarence, 38, 98–100, 102
Wallace, Michele, 263, 267–268, 269
Walters, Alexander, Bishop, 7
Washington, Booker T., 113, 153, 166, 183, 254, 302, 316; advice to present
    Black clergy, Black conservatives, and Black liberals, 211–215; advocate of
    Black Power, 9, 184–185; assisted W. E. B. Du Bois, 248–250; Atlanta
    Address, 193–194, 195, 196, 205; challenged White leadership of Blacks,
    6–7; conflict with Francis Oswald Viliard, 7; conservative, moderate, and
    radical, 19; criticism, 198–199; criticism by Adolph Reed, 16–17; criticism
    by Louis Harlan, 192–193; criticism by Manning Marable, 188–190, 194;
    critique of being accommodationist, 194–195; exalted material values and
    material construction, 221–222, 282; fear of European immigrants moving
    South, 203–204, 205, 226; fundraiser, 79, 215; Grand Black Leader, 6, 7,
    17, 114, 181, 184, 188, 190–193, 199, 201–203, 226; great concern was
    Black survival, 204–205; his reality distorted by Black nationalists, 81;
    instrumental use of accommodation, 196–197; leadership of southern and
    northern Blacks, 17, 161, 229–230; modernization and development
    program, 184, 206, 210–211, 215, 216–218, 225–226, 302; not Black
    nationalist, 79; opponents, 226–228, 302; promotion of education for
    Blacks, 136, 198, 215, 221; rejection of individual panacea for Blacks,
    205–206, 213; reliance upon youthful leaders, 220–221, 222–224; role in
    developing Black's savings, 318; suggested creation of Urban League, 7;
    support of most Black intellectuals, 114; understanding of White racism's
    relation with Black economic progress, 218–219, 220; understood how
    Whites favored license, 188; used "Tuskegee Machine" as a Black
    "government", 216–218; viewed White liberals as helpers, 7; views on
    religion, 206–207; V. P. Franklin's animosity towards, 79–80;
Washington, Margaret Murray, 215, 217–218
Watt, Gail Elizabeth, 253–254
Watts, Jerry, 13, 14
Welfare ideology: mixture of liberalism and state socialism, 122, 123, 142
Welfare society, 147–149, 162–163, 214, 303; Basin, 125, 126-127, 149, 156,
    157, 162, 164; benefits to economic corporations, 157, 158, 278; emergence,
    120–124; Grand Elites, 125, 126-127, 197; hierarchical stratification of
    societal elites, 127; Middle Elites, 125, 126, 163;
Middle Section, 125, 126, 127; Power Cap, 125, 126, 127, 148, 157–158, 164;
    racist interiority of, 133–135, 146–147, 157–158; Sub-Elites, 125, 126;
    welfare politics, 125–126, 147–148, 158–159, 214, 278, 313

About the Author

W.D. Wright is Emeritus Professor of History at Southern Connecticut State University. He holds a Ph.D. from the State University of New York at Buffalo. Dr. Wright, a scholar, intellectual, and historical sociologist, is the author of five books on Black history and life. He has taught Black history for sixteen years and has taught American history for over thirty years. With the writing of *Crisis of the Black Intellectual*, Dr. Wright continues to carry on the double legacy of W.E.B. Du Bois: that of employing critical thought and analysis to help Black people have a better understanding of themselves.